VEGETABLE OF THE DAY

KATE McMILLAN

PHOTOGRAPHY BY ERIN KUNKEL

weldon**owen**

CONTENTS

A VEGETABLE FOR EVERY DAY

Roots, shoots, tubers, bulbs, pods, gourds, leafy greens, and more—vegetables come in all sizes, shapes, colors, and seasons. They can launch a meal, ride alongside a main course, or sit in the center of a dinner plate. They are also rich sources of vitamins, minerals, fiber, and phytochemicals, which means that everyone should be eating more of them.

This book encourages you to do just that. It guides you on how to select vegetables with the season in mind and how to cook them in new and more interesting ways. In spring, you'll know to reach for a bunch of asparagus and pair it with the season's iconic morels and a heady shallot butter. In summer, you'll turn to shiny purple eggplants for the grill or sauté pan, and to tomatoes for salads, gazpacho, and bruschetta. Come fall and winter, you'll fashion soups, gratins, and braises out of hard-skinned squashes, knobby roots, dark leafy greens, and hearty tubers.

In the following pages, you'll find 365 seasonal recipes divided by months of the year. Each chapter opens with a monthly calendar page, and each day is inscribed with a different recipe title. But this is not a hard-and-fast kitchen diary. Instead, it is a flexible road map designed to help you to cook a wider variety of vegetables in a greater number of ways according to what's fresh in the market or the backyard garden. That means that while you should strive to cook seasonally, you should also feel free to meander through the weeks to find dishes that appeal.

Each recipe is flexible as well. You can often trade out one herb or spice for another, one root vegetable or leafy green for another, or one garnish for another. You can lighten the calorie load by substituting milk for cream, or you can dress up a dish by adding a salsa, a dollop of crème fraîche, or a scattering of grated cheese or chopped nuts. Dozens of color photographs are included to both inspire and guide you.

With this savvy compendium of daily culinary ideas on hand, you'll find that it is both easy and satisfying to bring new flavors and aromas to your table and more healthful, seasonal vegetables to your daily diet.

Start a new chapter in the New Year by making one resolution that's easy to keep: put vegetables at the center of the plate as often as possible. Stock up on the stars of the season: sturdy roots, dense-fleshed winter squashes, crunchy crucifers, and fiber-rich greens. Deep in the heart of winter, prepare vegetable dishes that offer plenty of comfort, such as a bubbling kale gratin, a hearty seven-vegetable tagine, a white bean soup with ribbons of chard, or a platter of roasted cauliflower.

1
SPICY SAUTÉED KALE & CHICKPEAS
page 12

2
CHOPPED CHARD WITH LEMON & ANCHOVY
page 12

3
WINTER SQUASH SALAD WITH MINT
page 14

8
FARRO WITH CARAMELIZED ROOT VEGETABLES
page 17

9
BRUSSELS SPROUTS & POTATO HASH WITH FRIED EGGS
page 18

10
BROCCOLI WITH SPICY CHEDDAR SAUCE
page 18

15
ROASTED BEETS WITH BABY ARUGULA & RICOTTA SALATA
page 23

16
CREAMED SPINACH
page 23

17
SAUTÉED BROCCOLI RABE WITH PICKLED ONION
page 24

22
SEVEN-VEGETABLE TAGINE
page 26

23
KALE CHIPS
page 28

24
FILO ROLLS WITH SPINACH, ARUGULA & FETA
page 28

29
POLENTA WITH WILD MUSHROOMS, CHARD & CHEDDAR CHEESE
page 32

30
SAUTÉED ASIAN GREENS
page 32

31
SAUTÉED BRUSSELS SPROUTS WITH OLIVE OIL & LEMON ZEST
page 32

january

1

SPICY SAUTÉED KALE & CHICKPEAS

serves 4

3 large cloves garlic, very thinly sliced

¼ cup (2 fl oz/60 ml) olive oil

1 lb (500 g) dinosaur kale, tough stems removed, leaves and tender stems coarsely shredded

1 can (15 oz/470 g) chickpeas, rinsed and drained

1 small fresh hot chile, seeded and minced, or generous pinch of red pepper flakes

Salt

Dinosaur kale, also known as cavolo nero or Lacinato kale, has slender, blue-green crimped leaves and a mild cabbagelike taste. Here, it is sautéed with chickpeas to make a hearty side dish, with just a touch of chile heat.

In a large frying pan, warm the garlic in the oil over medium-low heat, stirring often, until softened but not browned, about 7 minutes. Place about half of the kale in the pan. Cover and let wilt for about 2 minutes, and then uncover and add the remaining kale. Using tongs, turn the greens to coat with the oil and garlic. Cover the pan and cook until the kale is tender, 15–20 minutes.

Uncover and stir in the chickpeas, the chile, and 1 tsp salt. Raise the heat to medium and sauté until the chickpeas are heated through, about 5 minutes. Remove from the heat and serve.

2

CHOPPED CHARD WITH LEMON & ANCHOVY

serves 4

1 large bunch chard, 12–14 oz (375–440 g)

3 Tbsp olive oil

¾ cup (6 fl oz/180 ml) vegetable or chicken broth

2 or 3 olive oil–packed anchovy fillets, rinsed

2 Tbsp fresh lemon juice

Freshly ground pepper

½ cup (2 oz/60 g) chopped yellow onion

½ cup (3 oz/90 g) canned diced tomatoes

A heady mix of lemon juice and briny, salty anchovy enhances chard in this flavorful braise. The leaves and stems of chard should be separated for this recipe, as the stems require longer cooking, almost as if they are a different vegetable. They're well worth the extra step, adding sweet flavor and celery-like texture.

Separate the stems from the chard leaves by cutting along both sides of the center vein. Stack the leaves, roll up lengthwise, and cut crosswise into strips ¾ inch (2 cm) wide. Trim off the tough ends from the stems and discard. Cut the stems crosswise into ½-inch (12-mm) pieces.

In a frying pan, heat 1 Tbsp of the oil over medium-high heat. Add the chard stems and sauté for 5 minutes. Add ¼ cup (2 fl oz/60 ml) of the broth and cook until the stems are tender and the pan is almost dry, about 4 minutes. Remove the pan from the heat and push the stems to one side. Add the anchovies to the pan, and use the back of a spoon to mash them until they are creamy. Stir in the sautéed stems, add the lemon juice, and season with pepper. Transfer the cooked stems to one side of a platter; keep warm.

In a clean frying pan, heat the remaining 2 Tbsp oil over medium-high heat. Add the onion and sauté until golden, 6–7 minutes. Stir in the sliced chard leaves in 3 or 4 batches and cook each batch until wilted before adding more leaves. Add the tomatoes and the remaining ½ cup (4 fl oz/120 ml) broth, and cook, stirring occasionally, until the chard is tender, about 10 minutes. Spoon the leaves next to the stems and serve.

3

WARM SQUASH SALAD WITH MINT

serves 8

2 small butternut squashes, about 2½ lb (1.25 kg) each

½ cup (4 fl oz/125 ml) olive oil

Salt and freshly ground pepper

¼ cup (2 fl oz/60 ml) red wine vinegar

1 small red onion, very thinly sliced

1 tsp minced fresh oregano

1 clove garlic, thinly sliced

½ tsp red pepper flakes

¼ cup (½ oz/15 g) fresh mint leaves

Butternut squash tastes sweet and nutty and is rich in fiber and nutrients, especially vitamin A. In this fall salad, it's dressed with a bright-flavored vinaigrette and garnished with fresh mint. To turn the salad into a vegetarian main course, cut the squash into cubes instead of rings before roasting, then toss the salad with 4 cups (20–24 oz/ 625–750 g) cooked couscous or quinoa just before serving.

Preheat the oven to 400°F (200°C).

Peel each squash and cut crosswise into slices 1 inch (2.5 cm) thick. Using a spoon, scrape out the seeds and discard.

Lightly oil 2 baking sheets. Arrange the squash slices in a single layer on the sheets and brush on both sides with ¼ cup (2 fl oz/ 60 ml) of the oil. Season with salt and pepper. Roast, turning once, until just tender, about 30 minutes.

Meanwhile, in a small bowl, whisk together the remaining ¼ cup oil, the vinegar, onion, oregano, garlic, and red pepper flakes. Season with salt and pepper.

Transfer the squash to a platter. Pour the dressing over the top and let stand until the flavors have blended, about 20 minutes. Garnish with the mint and serve.

4

VINEGAR-GLAZED BRUSSELS SPROUTS WITH CHESTNUTS & WALNUT OIL

serves 4

1 Tbsp olive oil

1 lb (500 g) Brussels sprouts, trimmed

Salt and freshly ground pepper

1 Tbsp unsalted butter

1 cup (8 fl oz/250 ml) chicken broth

3 oz (90 g) vacuum-packed chestnuts, coarsely chopped

1 Tbsp firmly packed golden brown sugar

2 Tbsp red wine vinegar

2 tsp roasted walnut oil

In this dish, the rich walnut oil, sweet brown sugar, and tart wine vinegar work together to temper the cabbagey taste of Brussels sprouts, while the chestnuts add texture and flavor. Look for vacuum-packed roasted and peeled chestnuts in gourmet shops and well-stocked supermarkets.

In a large frying pan, warm the oil over medium heat. Add the Brussels sprouts in a single layer and sprinkle lightly with salt. Cook, stirring once or twice, until the sprouts are golden brown and caramelized on all sides, about 4 minutes.

Raise the heat to medium-high and add the butter, broth, and chestnuts. Bring the broth to a boil and stir to scrape up any browned bits on the bottom of the pan. Reduce the heat to medium-low, cover partially, and simmer until the sprouts are just tender when pierced with a knife and most of the liquid has evaporated, 20–22 minutes.

Add ¼ cup (2 fl oz/60 ml) water to the pan, stir in the sugar and vinegar, and raise the heat to medium-high. Cook, stirring occasionally, until the liquid reduces to a glaze, 2–3 minutes. Remove the pan from the heat and stir in the walnut oil. Season with salt and pepper. Transfer to a bowl and serve.

5

Woodsy thyme pairs beautifully with the hearty flavors of wintry ingredients. Here, it seasons brown lentils, which star in a salad that is rich in texture and color; chopped bacon crowns kale-laced lentils, roasted carrots, and sautéed onions.

WARM LENTIL & KALE SALAD WITH BACON

serves 6

6 small carrots, finely chopped

4 Tbsp (2 fl oz/60 ml) olive oil

Salt and freshly ground pepper

1 large red onion, thinly sliced

1 large bunch kale, ribs removed, leaves thinly sliced

4 large cloves garlic

10 fresh thyme sprigs

1 cup (7 oz/220 g) brown lentils, picked over and rinsed

4 cups (32 fl oz/1l) chicken broth

6 slices bacon

1 tsp sherry vinegar

Preheat the oven to 400°F (200°C). Line a baking sheet with foil. Place the carrots on the prepared sheet, drizzle with 2 Tbsp of the oil, sprinkle with ¾ tsp salt and ¼ tsp pepper, and toss to coat. Spread the carrots out evenly. Roast, stirring once or twice, until tender, about 15 minutes. Let cool to room temperature.

Meanwhile, in a frying pan, warm the remaining 2 Tbsp oil over medium heat. Add the onion, ¼ tsp salt, and several grinds of pepper and sauté until the onion is soft and lightly caramelized, about 15 minutes.

Bring a saucepan of water to a boil. Add 1 Tbsp salt and the kale and cook until tender, about 6 minutes. Drain.

Place the garlic and thyme on a square of cheesecloth, bring the corners together, and secure with kitchen string. In the same saucepan used to cook the kale, combine the lentils, broth, ½ tsp salt, ¼ tsp pepper, and the cheesecloth bundle. Bring to a boil, reduce the heat to medium, and simmer, uncovered, until the lentils are tender but not mushy, 15–20 minutes. In a frying pan, cook the bacon over medium heat, turning once, until crisp and browned, about 7 minutes. Transfer to paper towels to drain. Let cool and then coarsely chop.

Drain the lentils and discard the cheesecloth bundle. Transfer to a bowl. Stir in the cooked kale, the vinegar, and ½ tsp salt. Top with the carrots, onion, and bacon, and serve.

6

These tartlets are as pretty as they are satisfying, with thinly sliced potatoes and onion, and a generous sprinkling of cheese cradled in puff pastry. Accompany them with a simply prepared green vegetable, such as broccoli or green beans steamed until tender-crisp.

POTATO & GRUYÈRE TARTLETS

serves 4

2 Tbsp olive oil

1 Tbsp finely chopped fresh rosemary

Salt and freshly ground pepper

1 russet potato, peeled, halved lengthwise, and thinly sliced

1 small yellow onion, halved and thinly sliced

1 sheet frozen puff pastry, about ½ lb (250 g), thawed and cut into four 5-inch (13-cm) squares

1 cup (4 oz/125 g) shredded Gruyère cheese

Preheat the oven to 400°F (200°C). In a bowl, stir together the oil, rosemary, ½ tsp salt, and ⅛ tsp pepper. Add the potato and onion slices and toss to coat.

Lay the pastry squares on a baking sheet. Using a sharp paring knife, cut a ½-inch (12-mm) border along the edge of the pastry, being careful not to cut more than halfway through. Inside the border, prick the pastry all over with a fork.

Sprinkle 2 Tbsp of the cheese inside the border of each tartlet. Divide the filling among the tartlets. Sprinkle the remaining cheese over the filling.

Bake until the edges are puffed and brown and the cheese is golden, about 20 minutes. Let the tartlets stand for 10 minutes. Serve warm or at room temperature.

JANUARY 8

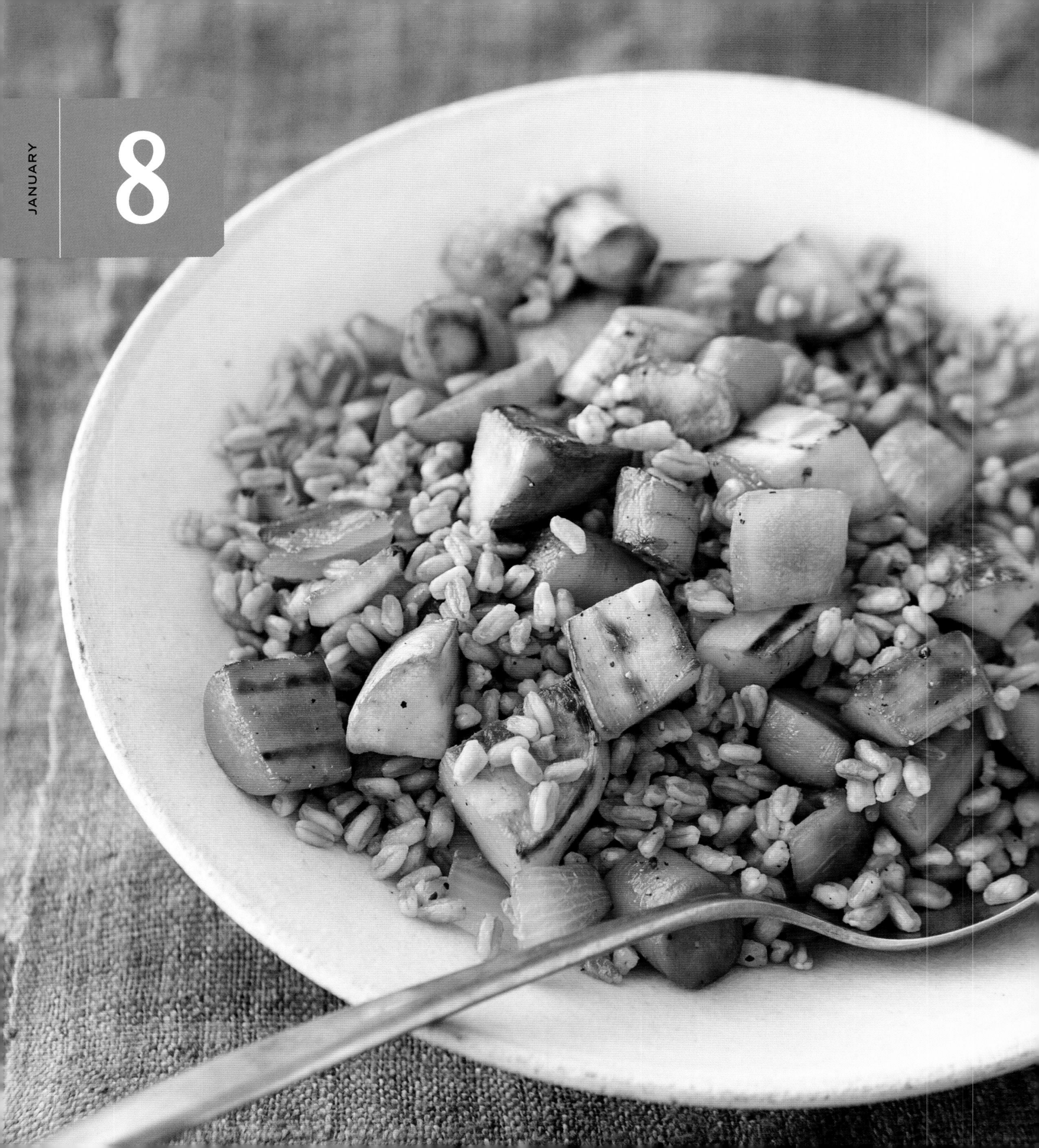

7

Dark, vitamin-rich kale flourishes in the heart of winter. Skip the cream for this no-guilt gratin, which calls for sautéing the greens before topping with golden bread crumbs. To make fresh bread crumbs, use any leftover good-quality bread: slice it, toast it, and then whirl it in a food processor until coarse crumbs form. You can also bake the gratin in ramekins to make individual servings.

KALE GRATIN WITH PARMESAN BREAD CRUMBS

serves 6

1½ cups (3 oz/90 g) fresh whole-wheat sourdough bread crumbs

½ cup (2 oz/60 g) grated Parmesan cheese

3 Tbsp olive oil

2 cloves garlic, minced

2 lb (1 kg) kale, tough stems removed, leaves chopped

Salt

Preheat the oven to 375°F (190°C).

In a bowl, stir together the bread crumbs, cheese, and 1 Tbsp of the oil until well blended.

In a large frying pan, warm the remaining 2 Tbsp oil over medium heat. Add the garlic and cook, stirring constantly, until fragrant but not browned, about 1 minute. Add the kale and sprinkle with ¼ tsp salt. Stir until the kale is wilted and coated with the oil. Add ¼ cup (2 fl oz/60 ml) water, cover, and steam until the kale is tender, 6–10 minutes. Transfer to a shallow gratin dish and smooth the top. Sprinkle with the bread crumb mixture.

Bake until the bread crumbs are golden brown, about 15 minutes. Let cool slightly and serve.

8

Farro, a hearty, healthful, and highly prized Italian grain, fits comfortably into menus year-round. In winter, toss it with roasted root vegetables such as turnips, parsnips, and carrots, as it is here. This dish is sweet and savory and loses nothing when served at room temperature, making it a great option for both the lunch box and the salad plate.

FARRO WITH CARAMELIZED ROOT VEGETABLES

serves 4–6

1⅓ cups (8 oz/250 g) farro

1¾ cups (14 fl oz/430 ml) vegetable or chicken broth

Salt and freshly ground pepper

2 Tbsp olive oil

1 small yellow onion, cut into ¼-inch (6-mm) pieces

1 turnip, peeled and cut into ¼-inch (6-mm) pieces

2 parsnips, peeled and cut into ¼-inch (6-mm) pieces

2 carrots, cut into ¼-inch (6-mm) pieces

1 Tbsp honey

In a heavy-bottomed saucepan, heat the farro over medium-high heat, stirring often, until lightly toasted and aromatic, about 3 minutes. Add the broth and 2 tsp salt and bring to a boil. Reduce the heat to low, cover, and simmer until all the liquid is absorbed and the farro is tender but with a bit of a bite remaining at the center, 12–15 minutes. Transfer to a large bowl and slightly cool.

In a large frying pan, heat the oil over medium-low heat. Add the onion, turnip, parsnips, and carrots, and toss to coat with the oil. Sauté the vegetables until they start to release their liquid, about 5 minutes. Raise the heat to medium-high and cook until they are golden and have begun to caramelize, 10–15 minutes. Stir in the honey and season with salt and pepper.

Add the vegetables to the bowl with the farro and toss to combine. Adjust the seasoning if necessary. Serve warm or at room temperature.

9

BRUSSELS SPROUTS & POTATO HASH WITH FRIED EGGS

serves 4

4 Tbsp (2 oz/60 g) unsalted butter, plus more for frying

3 Tbsp olive oil

1 yellow onion, chopped

1 lb (500 g) Brussels sprouts, trimmed and thinly sliced

¾ lb (375 g) Yukon gold potatoes, diced

2 tsp fresh thyme leaves

Salt and freshly ground pepper

1 cup (8 fl oz/250 ml) chicken or vegetable broth

4 eggs

An unexpected twist on a classic, Brussels sprouts add a delicious crunch to traditional hash. This is wonderful served with a warm baguette for any meal. If you have leftover Brussels sprouts or potatoes, this recipe is a great way to use them up. Just adjust the cooking times and use less broth.

In a large frying pan, melt 3 Tbsp of the butter with the oil over medium-high heat. Add the onion and cook, stirring occasionally, until soft, about 5 minutes. Add the Brussels sprouts, potatoes, and thyme. Season generously with salt and pepper and cook, stirring often, until the vegetables caramelize, about 15 minutes. Add the broth and cook until the liquid is absorbed and the vegetables are fork-tender, about 5 minutes. Adjust the seasoning.

In another frying pan, melt the remaining 1 Tbsp butter over medium heat. Crack the eggs into the pan and fry until the whites are set and the yolks have begun to thicken but are still soft, about 4 minutes. Season with salt and pepper.

Spoon the hash onto plates, top with the fried eggs, and serve.

10

BROCCOLI WITH SPICY CHEDDAR SAUCE

serves 4–6

2 or 3 large heads broccoli

3 Tbsp unsalted butter

3 Tbsp all-purpose flour

2 cups (16 fl oz/500 ml) whole milk, warmed

Salt and freshly ground black pepper

⅛ tsp cayenne pepper

3 oz (90 g) sharp Cheddar cheese, grated

Crunchy green crucifers, such as broccoli or Brussels sprouts, boast a natural affinity for sharp cheeses. Even suspicious young appetites will dig into florets doused in a gooey cheese sauce. You can vary the flavor with Swiss or fontina, but aged Cheddar is a crowd favorite.

Trim the thick stalks from the broccoli heads. Cut the heads lengthwise into halves or thirds, depending on the size. Bring water to a boil in a steamer pan. Arrange the broccoli on the steamer rack, cover, and steam until easily pierced with a fork, 5–7 minutes. Drain and cover to keep warm.

Meanwhile, in a saucepan, melt the butter over medium-high heat. When it foams, remove the pan from the heat and whisk in the flour to make a thick paste. Return the pan to medium-high heat, and cook, stirring, for 2–3 minutes. Slowly whisk in the milk. Bring to a boil, continuing to whisk. Reduce the heat to low and simmer, stirring occasionally, until the sauce is slightly thickened, 7–10 minutes. Stir in ½ tsp salt, ⅛ tsp black pepper, and the cayenne and continue to simmer, stirring occasionally, until the sauce is thick enough to coat the back of a spoon, about 10 minutes. Add the cheese and stir just until melted, about 2 minutes. Remove from the heat.

Arrange the broccoli in a bowl, top with the hot sauce, and serve.

11

WARM ROASTED BEETS WITH CURRY SPICES

serves 4

1 tsp ground cumin

1 tsp ground coriander

½ tsp ground turmeric

½ tsp ground cloves

Salt and freshly ground pepper

6 beets

2 Tbsp olive oil

Frost-tinged harvests concentrate the flavor of beets, bringing their flavor close to candy this time of year. Make them extra tantalizing with warm spices, such as an Indian-inspired combination of cumin, coriander, turmeric, and cloves. This would be a good companion to yogurt-marinated chicken or fish.

Preheat the oven to 350°F (180°C).

In a small bowl, combine the cumin, coriander, turmeric, and cloves. Add 1 tsp salt and 1 tsp pepper and mix well.

If the greens are still attached to the beets, remove them, leaving 1 inch (2.5 cm) of the stem intact. Place the beets in a small roasting pan and rub them with the oil and then with the spice mixture, coating them evenly. Roast the beets, turning them once or twice, until tender when pierced with a fork 1–1¼ hours. Let cool just until they can be handled, then cut off the stems and peel the beets.

Cut the beets lengthwise into wedges and serve warm or at room temperature.

12

EDAMAME HUMMUS WITH GRILLED NAAN

serves 4–6

FOR THE HUMMUS

1 bag (10 oz/315 g) frozen shelled edamame, cooked according to package instructions

2 cloves garlic

2 Tbsp tahini

Grated zest and juice of 1 lemon

¼ cup (2 fl oz/60 ml) extra-virgin olive oil

½ tsp ground cumin

Salt and freshly ground pepper

6 pieces naan

Olive oil for brushing

Sea salt

2 Tbsp chopped fresh flat-leaf parsley

Edamame adds a nutty flavor and a beautiful green color to an already delicious dip. Any leftover hummus will keep in the refrigerator for up to 5 days and can also be used as a spread on sandwiches and wraps. Look for naan bread in a specialty food store or Indian market.

To make the hummus, in a blender or food processor, combine the edamame, garlic, tahini, lemon zest and juice, oil, and cumin. Add 1 tsp salt, ¼ tsp pepper, and 2 Tbsp water, and purée. Adjust the seasoning if necessary. Transfer to a bowl.

Heat a ridged grill pan over high heat. Brush both sides of each piece of naan with oil. Grill, turning once, until toasted, 2–3 minutes per side. Transfer the hot naan to a cutting board and immediately sprinkle with sea salt and the parsley. It is important to do this while the naan is hot so the salt and parsley will adhere to the oil. Cut the bread into slices and serve with the hummus for dipping.

13

Pomegranate molasses, a Middle Eastern product, has hints of fruitiness and a concentrated sweet-sour taste. Here, its intensity combines with lemon juice and olive oil to create a dressing with a full range of flavors. Toasted pistachios heighten the nuttiness of the bulgur, and roasted peppers and dried cranberries add bursts of color.

BULGUR SALAD WITH ROASTED PEPPERS, CHICKPEAS & PISTACHIOS

serves 6

1½ cups (9 oz/280 g) bulgur

2¼ cups (18 fl oz/560 ml) chicken broth

¼ cup (2 fl oz/60 ml) fresh lemon juice

¼ cup (3 oz/90 g) pomegranate molasses

2 tsp sugar

Salt and freshly ground pepper

6 Tbsp (3 fl oz/90 ml) extra-virgin olive oil

1 can (15 oz/470 g) chickpeas, drained and rinsed

¾ cup (3 oz/90 g) pistachio nuts, toasted

2 jarred roasted red peppers, finely diced

½ cup (½ oz/15 g) chopped fresh flat-leaf parsley, cilantro, or mint

1 cup (4 oz/125 g) sweetened dried cranberries or dried sweet cherries

2 cups (1 lb/500 g) plain yogurt (optional)

Place the bulgur in a heatproof bowl. In a small saucepan, bring the broth to a boil. Pour the broth over the bulgur, cover, and let stand until the liquid has been absorbed, about 30 minutes.

Meanwhile, in a bowl, whisk together the lemon juice, molasses, sugar, 1½ tsp salt, and several grinds of pepper until the sugar dissolves. Slowly whisk in the oil until well blended.

In a small bowl, stir together the chickpeas and ½ tsp salt. Whisk the dressing and then add it, along with the chickpeas, to the bowl with the bulgur and stir to mix well. Cover and refrigerate for 2 hours.

In a bowl, stir together the pistachios and a pinch of salt. Add the pistachios, diced peppers, parsley, and cranberries to the bulgur and toss well. Adjust the seasoning. Serve with the yogurt, if desired.

14

Humble potatoes are enlivened with a wine reduction, bright parsley, and dry-cured Spanish chorizo. To peel the chorizo, lightly run a sharp knife down its length. With your fingers, peel the skin away from the sausage, as if unwrapping it.

SAUTÉED POTATOES WITH CHORIZO & PARSLEY

serves 4

1½ lb (750 g) large waxy potatoes, quartered

½ cup (2 oz/60 g) peeled, thinly sliced mild or hot dry-cured chorizo

¼ cup (1½ oz/45 g) finely chopped red onion

¼ cup (2 fl oz/60 ml) dry white wine

2 Tbsp chopped fresh flat-leaf parsley

In a saucepan, combine the potatoes with water to cover and bring to a boil. Reduce the heat to medium and cook until the potatoes are fork-tender, about 20 minutes. Drain and keep warm.

Heat a frying pan over medium-high heat. Add the chorizo and sauté until most of the fat is rendered, about 2 minutes. Pour off the fat and continue cooking the chorizo until lightly browned, 1–2 minutes. Add the onion and sauté for 1 minute. Add the potatoes and wine and cook until most of the liquid evaporates, about 1 minute.

Transfer to a bowl, toss with the parsley, and serve.

15

A mix of colorful beets, deep green arugula, and snowy white cheese can brighten the usually cool, gray days of January. Be careful when working with red beets, as their juice can stain your fingers, countertop, and cutting board. Rinse fingers or work surfaces immediately with water, and use lemon juice to remove persistent stains.

ROASTED BEETS WITH BABY ARUGULA & RICOTTA SALATA

serves 4

3 beets of any color, about 1 lb (500 g) total

4 Tbsp (2 fl oz/60 ml) olive oil

2 Tbsp fresh orange juice

1 Tbsp fresh lemon juice

¼ tsp Dijon mustard

Salt and freshly ground pepper

2 cups (2 oz/60 g) wild or baby arugula, tough stems removed

4–5 oz (125–155 g) ricotta salata cheese, crumbled

Preheat the oven to 350°F (180°C).

If the greens are still attached to the beets, remove them, leaving 1 inch (2.5 cm) of the stem intact. Place the beets in a small roasting pan and rub with 1½ Tbsp of the oil. Roast the beets, turning once or twice, until tender when pierced with a fork, 1–1¼ hours. Let cool. Peel the beets and cut into thin wedges.

In a bowl, using a fork, mix together the orange and lemon juices, the remaining 2½ Tbsp oil, the mustard, ½ tsp salt, and ¼ tsp pepper. Add the sliced beets to the bowl and turn gently to coat with the dressing. Add the arugula and toss until well mixed. Top with the ricotta salata and serve.

16

This classic side dish teases out the underlying sweetness of spinach with a touch of aromatic nutmeg. The rich sauce, which calls for half-and-half and milk, and is flavored with sautéed shallots and garlic, gives this favorite accompaniment to grilled steak a new profile.

CREAMED SPINACH

serves 6

3½ lb (1.75 k) spinach, tough stems removed, leaves coarsely chopped

1 cup (8 fl oz/250 ml) half-and-half

1 cup (8 fl oz/250 ml) whole milk

3 Tbsp unsalted butter

¼ cup (1½ oz/45 g) minced shallots

1 clove garlic, minced

3 Tbsp all-purpose flour

½ cup (2 oz/60 g) grated Parmesan cheese

Salt and freshly ground pepper

Freshly grated nutmeg

In a large saucepan, bring ½ cup (4 fl oz/ 125 ml) water to a boil. Working in batches, add the spinach to the pan and cover, letting each batch wilt before adding the next one. Cook until the spinach is tender, about 5 minutes. Drain the spinach and rinse briefly under cold running water. Squeeze handfuls of the spinach to remove any excess water and place in a bowl. Reserve the pan.

In a small saucepan, bring the half-and-half and milk to a simmer over medium heat. Remove from the heat. In the large saucepan used for the spinach, melt the butter over medium heat. Add the shallots and garlic and cook, stirring frequently, until the shallots soften, about 2 minutes. Whisk in the flour. Reduce the heat to medium-low and let bubble for 1 minute. Gradually whisk in the hot milk mixture, raise the heat to medium, and bring to a boil, whisking frequently. Reduce the heat to medium-low and simmer until lightly thickened, about 5 minutes. Stir in the spinach and cook until heated through, about 5 minutes more.

Whisk in the Parmesan, and season with salt, pepper, and nutmeg. Transfer to a bowl and serve.

17

SAUTÉED BROCCOLI RABE WITH PICKLED ONION

serves 8

1 small red onion, thinly sliced

¼ cup (2 fl oz/60 ml) Champagne vinegar

1 tsp sugar

2 bunches broccoli rabe, about 4 lb (2 kg) total

2 Tbsp extra-virgin olive oil

Salt and freshly ground pepper

Broccoli rabe is an intriguing alternative to everyday broccoli, with pleasantly bitter, mustardy tones. Onion slices briefly immersed in a simple hot pickling solution of vinegar and sugar provide a crunchy, piquant garnish.

Put the onion in a small heatproof bowl. In a small saucepan, combine the vinegar and sugar and bring to a boil over medium heat. Remove from the heat, pour over the onion, and let marinate for 15 minutes. Drain the onion and rinse briefly with cold running water.

Trim away the tough ends of the broccoli rabe. Chop the broccoli rabe into 3-inch (7.5-cm) pieces.

In a large frying pan, warm the oil over medium-high heat. Add the broccoli rabe and 1 tsp salt and cook, stirring occasionally, until tender to the bite, about 5 minutes. Add the onion, season with pepper, and stir to combine. Transfer to a platter and serve.

18

SPANISH TORTILLA WITH LEEKS

serves 6

7 Tbsp (3½ fl oz/105 ml) olive oil

1½ lb (750 g) Yukon gold potatoes, peeled and cut into slices ⅛ inch (3 mm) thick

1 leek, white and pale green part, thinly sliced

3 eggs, plus 3 egg whites

Salt

Spain's iconic egg-and-potato omelet can be served at room temperature on summer days, or directly from a hot frying pan on winter nights. The tricky part of preparing this dish is flipping the omelet. Iberian cooks typically use a special hinged pan that simplifies the flip. But any large, flat plate or lid, handled carefully, will get the job done.

In a frying pan, warm 5 Tbsp of the oil over medium-high heat. Add the potatoes and leeks and cook, stirring occasionally, until tender, about 20 minutes. Transfer the potato and leek mixture to a colander to drain. Wipe out the pan.

In a large bowl, beat together the eggs, egg whites, and 1 tsp salt. Gently stir in the potatoes and leeks.

In the frying pan, warm the remaining 2 Tbsp oil over medium-high heat. Add the potato-egg mixture, press it into a thick cake with a spatula, and cook until set, about 5 minutes, adjusting the heat to prevent scorching. Loosen the tortilla by working the spatula under it, then continue to cook, shaking the pan occasionally, until the bottom is well browned, about 5 minutes more.

Slide the tortilla onto a large, flat plate. Invert the pan over it and carefully turn the pan and plate together. Return the pan to the stove top and continue to cook the tortilla until the second side is browned, about 5 minutes.

Slide the tortilla onto a platter and let stand for at least 10 minutes. Cut into wedges and serve.

19

This recipe makes a decadent main course. It's a great family meal, and it's also good party fare because you can assemble the dish a day in advance and then slip it into the oven just before serving to heat through and brown the mashed potatoes. For a special occasion, make the shepherd's pie in individual ramekins and cut the baking time to about 10 minutes. Serve with a crisp green salad.

VEGETABLE SHEPHERD'S PIE

serves 6

3 russet potatoes, peeled and cut into 1-inch (2.5-cm) pieces

Salt and freshly ground pepper

¾ cup (6 fl oz/180 ml) whole milk, plus 1 cup (8 oz/250 ml), warmed

5 Tbsp (2½ oz/75 g) unsalted butter, at room temperature

⅛ tsp freshly grated nutmeg

2 sweet potatoes, peeled and cut into 1-inch (2.5-cm) pieces

3 parsnips, peeled and cut into 1-inch (2.5-cm) pieces

5 Tbsp (3 fl oz/80 ml) olive oil

1 yellow onion, chopped

2 cloves garlic, minced

3 portobello mushrooms, stems removed, caps cut into 1-inch (2.5-cm) pieces

1 can (14½ oz/455 g) diced tomatoes, with juice

1 tsp dried thyme

1 Tbsp all-purpose flour

Preheat the oven to 450°F (230°C). Line a baking sheet with parchment paper.

In a large saucepan, combine the potatoes, 1 tsp salt, and water to cover by 1 inch (2.5 cm). Bring to a boil over medium-high heat, reduce the heat to medium-low, and cook, uncovered, until tender when pierced with a knife, about 15 minutes. Drain the potatoes, return to the pan, and mash until smooth. Add the ¾ cup milk and 4 Tbsp (2 oz/60 g) of the butter and stir to combine. Stir in the nutmeg and season with salt and pepper.

In a bowl, toss the sweet potatoes and parsnips with 3 Tbsp of the oil and season well with salt and pepper. Transfer to the prepared sheet, spread in an even layer, and roast, stirring once, until caramelized, about 25 minutes.

Reduce the oven temperature to 375°F (190°C) and place a rack in the upper third of the oven.

In a frying pan, warm the remaining 2 Tbsp oil over medium-high heat. Add the onion, garlic, and mushrooms and cook, stirring frequently, until the onions are soft and the mushrooms begin to brown, about 8 minutes. Transfer to a large bowl. Stir in the sweet potatoes, parsnips, tomatoes, and thyme. ⟫→

In a small saucepan, melt the remaining 1 Tbsp butter over medium-high heat. Add the flour and cook, whisking constantly, for 2 minutes. Whisking constantly, slowly add the 1 cup hot milk, and continue to cook, stirring frequently, until the sauce thickens, about 3 minutes. Add the sauce to the bowl with the vegetables and stir to combine.

Transfer the vegetable mixture to a 9-by-13 (23-by-33-cm) baking dish and spread evenly. Top with heaping mounds of the mashed potatoes. Bake until the pie is bubbly and the mashed potatoes are golden brown, 15–20 minutes. Serve hot.

20

Nearly all of the winter squashes have beautiful sunny yellow to orange flesh that turns sweet in a hot oven. The advantage of delicata squash is that its cream-colored, green-striped skin is thin enough to eat—a time-saver for the cook because you can skip the usual peeling step.

ROASTED DELICATA SQUASH WITH SAGE

serves 4

2 Tbsp finely chopped fresh sage, plus 1 or 2 sprigs for garnish

¼ cup (2 fl oz/60 ml) olive oil

1 delicata squash, about 1½ lb (750 g)

Salt and freshly ground pepper

Preheat the oven to 400°F (200°C).

In a small bowl, stir together the chopped sage and oil and let stand while you prepare the squash.

Cut the squash in half lengthwise and scoop out the seeds. Cut each half crosswise into 4 equal pieces. Place the pieces on a baking sheet and drizzle with the sage oil. Using your fingers, spread and rub the oil to coat the squash thoroughly. Season with salt and pepper.

Roast the squash, uncovered, until tender and browned in spots, 35–40 minutes. Transfer to a platter, garnish with the sage sprigs, and serve.

21

In this recipe, mild cauliflower is the perfect foil for savory olives and tangy lemon zest. You can substitute romanesco cauliflower, often called romanesco broccoli, for the white cauliflower. Bright chartreuse with cone-shaped florets, this botanical mutation of cauliflower is slightly sweeter and more tender than its better-known kin.

ROASTED CAULIFLOWER WITH LEMON & OLIVES

serves 4

1 head cauliflower, about 1½ lb (750 g)

⅓ cup (3 fl oz/80 ml) olive oil

Grated zest from 1 lemon, plus 2 lemons, thinly sliced

½ cup (75 g) pitted green olives, coarsely chopped

Salt and freshly ground pepper

Preheat the oven to 400°F (200°C).

Trim the cauliflower and cut into 2-inch (5-cm) florets. In a roasting pan large enough to hold the cauliflower pieces in a single layer, combine the cauliflower, oil, lemon zest, lemon slices, and olives. Season with salt and pepper and toss to mix well. Spread in a single layer.

Roast, stirring occasionally, until the cauliflower is browned and tender when pierced with a fork and the lemons have caramelized, about 20 minutes. Remove from the oven and serve.

22

Seven is a lucky number in Morocco, and one of the country's most popular dishes is couscous with seven vegetables, the ingredients for which vary with the region and the season. This is a winter version and includes zucchini and green beans, which are typically available in markets year-round. Traditionally, the stew is cooked in a couscoussière, a special two-tiered pot, with the couscous on the bottom and the stew on top, or in a conical earthenware tagine. But a large, heavy pot works fine, too. Ladle the piping-hot vegetables over the couscous.

SEVEN-VEGETABLE TAGINE

serves 6

2 turnips, peeled and quartered

1 carrot, cut into cubes

1 celery rib, sliced crosswise

1 yellow onion, finely chopped

1 tsp ground cumin

1 tsp ground ginger

½ tsp sweet paprika

½ tsp ground turmeric

Pinch of cayenne pepper

1 delicata or butternut squash, about 1 lb (500 g), halved, seeded, peeled if using butternut squash, and cubed

1 zucchini, cubed

¼ lb (125 g) green beans, trimmed and cut into 1½-inch (4-cm) lengths

1 can (15 oz/470 g) chickpeas, drained and rinsed

Salt and freshly ground black pepper

2 or 3 canned tomatoes, quartered

¼ cup (⅓ oz/10 g) chopped fresh cilantro

¼ cup (⅓ oz/10 g) chopped fresh flat-leaf parsley

In a large, heavy pot, combine the turnips, carrot, celery, onion, cumin, ginger, paprika, turmeric, and cayenne. Pour in 1 cup (8 fl oz/250 ml) water and bring to a boil over medium-high heat. Reduce the heat to medium, cover, and simmer for 10 minutes.

Add the squash, zucchini, green beans, and chickpeas. Season with salt and black pepper. Cover and cook, stirring occasionally, until the vegetables are tender, about 20 minutes. Lay the tomato quarters on top of the vegetables, cover, and cook until the tomatoes are heated through, about 5 minutes.

Sprinkle the cilantro and parsley over the top and remove from the heat. Let stand, covered, for 10 minutes to allow the flavors to blend, then serve.

23

KALE CHIPS

serves 4

1 bunch kale

1 Tbsp olive oil

Few drops of Asian sesame oil (optional)

Salt and freshly ground pepper

Superfast to make, this healthful, tasty snack is guaranteed to be a hit in even the pickiest kid's lunch box. Once you have rinsed the kale, make sure it is completely dry before you add the oil and seasonings, or it will steam in the oven, turning out soggy rather than crisp. You can experiment with different flavorings, such as garlic salt, paprika, and flavored oils.

Preheat the oven to 350°F (180°C). Line a rimmed baking sheet with parchment paper.

Trim away and discard the ribs from the kale leaves, then tear the leaves into 2-inch (5-cm) pieces. Put the torn leaves in a bowl, add the olive oil, the sesame oil (if using), ½ tsp salt, and ¼ tsp pepper, and toss to coat the leaves evenly with the oil and seasonings. Transfer the kale to the prepared baking sheet, spreading the pieces in a single layer.

Bake the kale pieces until crispy and browned on the edges, about 15 minutes. Transfer to a bowl and serve. Or, let cool completely and store in an airtight container at room temperature for up to 3 days.

24

FILO ROLLS WITH SPINACH, ARUGULA & FETA

serves 6–8

2 bunches arugula, about ½ lb (250 g) each, stems removed

1 small bunch spinach, about ½ lb (250 g), stems removed

½ lb (250 g) feta cheese

¾ cup (6 oz/185 g) unsalted butter

14 sheets filo dough, each about 13 by 17 inches (33 by 43 cm), thawed if frozen

Earthy spinach and salty feta cheese are traditional partners in Greek cuisine. Here, they are pumped up with peppery arugula in crunchy, butter-rich small pastries that are a variation on the traditional spanakopita. Use an aromatic, tangy authentic Greek feta, if possible. Failing that, look for a good sheep's and/or goat's milk feta. Serve these rolls as an appetizer, accompanied with a high-quality retsina or a crisp, grassy Sauvignon Blanc.

Preheat the oven to 350°F (180°C). Line a rimmed baking sheet with parchment paper. Rinse the arugula and spinach thoroughly and place in a large, heavy saucepan with the rinsing water still clinging to the leaves. Place over medium-high heat, cover, and cook, stirring occasionally, until wilted, 3–5 minutes. Drain into a sieve, then press against the greens with the bottom of a spoon to force out as much moisture as possible.

Finely chop the greens and place in a bowl. Crumble the cheese into the greens and mix gently. In a small saucepan, melt the butter over low heat, then pour it into a small bowl. Place the stack of filo sheets near your work surface, and keep the sheets covered with a barely damp kitchen towel to prevent them from drying out.

Remove 1 filo sheet from the stack, lay it on the work surface and brush lightly with some of the melted butter. Top with a second sheet and brush lightly with butter. Cut the stacked sheets lengthwise into 6 equal strips. Spoon a scant 1 tsp of the filling on a strip, positioning it in the center near the end closest to you. Fold the bottom edge of the strip over the filling, fold in both sides of the strip over the filling, and then roll up into a tight cylinder. Place on the prepared baking sheet and brush lightly with butter. Repeat with the remaining strips and then the remaining filo sheets until all of the filling and sheets have been used. You should have 42 rolls.

Bake the rolls until golden brown, about 25 minutes. Transfer the pan to a wire rack and let the rolls cool slightly on the pan. Arrange the rolls on 1 or 2 platters and serve.

25

These bites make excellent party fare, or lend a festive touch to a Sunday roast dinner. Any small round potato will do for this recipe. A pastry bag fitted with a star tip is the key to making the little packages pretty. Chilling the filling briefly will make piping easier and help the peaks maintain their fluted pattern.

MINI TWICE-BAKED POTATOES

serves 4–6

Canola oil for greasing

24 small Yukon gold potatoes, about 1 inch (2.5 cm) in diameter

1/2 cup (4 oz/125 g) sour cream

1/4 cup (2 fl oz/60 ml) whole milk

1/4 cup (1/3 oz/10 g) minced fresh chives, plus 1-inch (2.5-cm) pieces for garnish

Salt and freshly ground pepper

Preheat the oven to 450°F (230°C). Lightly brush a baking sheet with oil.

Arrange the potatoes in a single layer on the prepared sheet. Bake until the potatoes are tender when pierced with a fork and the skin has begun to wrinkle and pull away from the flesh, 15–20 minutes. Let stand until cool enough to handle.

Cut 12 of the potatoes in half lengthwise. Using a melon baller, cut out a scoop of flesh from the center of each half, leaving a wall of flesh about 1/4 inch (6 mm) thick. Transfer the scooped flesh to a food mill or ricer. Return the hollowed-out potato halves, hollow side up, to the baking sheet. Pass the potato flesh through the mill or ricer into a large bowl.

Peel the remaining 12 potatoes, and then pass the flesh through the mill or ricer into the bowl. Add the sour cream, milk, minced chives, 2 tsp salt, and 1 tsp pepper and stir to make a smooth filling. Refrigerate the filling for 5–10 minutes. Transfer the filling to a pastry bag fitted with a large star tip. Pipe the filling into the hollowed-out potato halves, mounding it about 1 inch (2.5 cm) high. The filling will shrink as it bakes.

Bake the filled potatoes until the tops are lightly browned, 5–7 minutes. Remove from the oven and let cool slightly. Garnish with the chive pieces and serve.

26

This winter salad doubles the crunch with peppery broccoli and mildly bitter radicchio. If the flavor of raw broccoli is too strong for you, blanch the florets for a few minutes, then put them in ice water to halt the cooking. The hard-boiled eggs add protein and heft.

CHOPPED SALAD WITH BROCCOLI, RADICCHIO & EGG

serves 4

1/4 cup (2 fl oz/60 ml) extra-virgin olive oil

3 Tbsp fresh lemon juice

1 1/2 Tbsp whole-grain Dijon mustard

Salt

1 lb (500 g) broccoli

1 head radicchio, about 1/2 lb (250 g), cored and chopped

2 oz (60 g) smoked or regular mozzarella cheese, cut into 1/4-inch (6-mm) cubes

1/4 cup (1 1/2 oz/45 g) slivered or chopped almonds

2 eggs, hard-boiled and grated or finely chopped

In a large bowl, whisk together the oil, the lemon juice, mustard, and 1/4 tsp salt.

Remove the tough stems from the broccoli. Finely chop the tender stems and the florets. Transfer to the bowl and add the radicchio, cheese, and almonds. Stir gently to mix well and coat all the ingredients with the dressing. Add the eggs, fold in gently just until combined, and serve.

27

WHITE BEAN SOUP WITH RED CHARD

serves 6

2 Tbsp olive oil

2 large sweet onions, about 1 lb (500 g) total, finely chopped

2 bunches red chard, about 1 lb (500 g) total, leaves torn into bite-sized pieces, ribs and stems chopped

Salt

2 cloves garlic, minced

¼ tsp dried thyme

6 cups (48 fl oz/1.5 l) chicken or vegetable broth

2 cans (15 oz/470 g each) cannellini or white kidney beans, drained and rinsed

¼ cup (1 oz/30 g) grated Parmesan cheese

This is classic wintertime comfort food. Take the time to braise the chard and onions properly. Cooked over low heat until tender and mellow, they yield a sweet, caramelized flavor. For extra richness, add a piece of Parmesan cheese rind to the broth as it simmers.

In a large pot, heat the oil over medium-high heat. Add the onions and chard ribs and stems, and stir to coat well with oil. Season with ⅛ tsp salt, reduce the heat to medium, and sauté until the vegetables soften, 10–15 minutes.

Add the garlic and thyme and cook, stirring constantly, until the garlic is fragrant but not browned, 1–2 minutes.

Add the broth and bring to a simmer. Add the beans and chard leaves, return to a simmer, and cook, stirring occasionally, until the chard is wilted, 5–7 minutes. Ladle the soup into bowls, garnish with the Parmesan, and serve.

28

WOK-SEARED BABY BOK CHOY WITH CHILE OIL & GARLIC

serves 4

4 heads baby bok choy, about 1 lb (500 g) total

1½ Tbsp canola oil

3 cloves garlic, thinly sliced

½ tsp red pepper flakes

Salt

¼ cup (2 fl oz/60 ml) chicken broth

2 tsp Asian chile oil

1 Tbsp sesame seeds, toasted

A trio of bold ingredients—red chile oil, garlic, and red pepper flakes—deliver potent flavor to this quick and easy stir-fry, a side dish guaranteed to perk up midwinter meals. The addition of nutty sesame seeds just before serving tempers the heat.

Cut the tough base from each head of bok choy. Separate the heads into individual stalks by snapping them away from the cores.

In a wok or a large frying pan, heat the canola oil over medium-high heat. Add the garlic and red pepper flakes and cook, tossing and stirring, until fragrant but not browned, 20–30 seconds. Add the bok choy and a pinch of salt and cook, tossing and stirring, until the bok choy just begins to wilt, 1–2 minutes. Add the broth and cook, stirring occasionally, until the bok choy is just tender and the broth evaporates, 1–2 minutes. Add the chile oil, stir well to coat the bok choy, and remove from the heat.

Stir in the sesame seeds, transfer to a bowl, and serve.

29

POLENTA WITH WILD MUSHROOMS, CHARD & CHEDDAR CHEESE

serves 6–8

This vegetarian dish makes a warming meal on a cool winter or fall evening. You can use any mushrooms in the mix and substitute spinach or kale for the chard. The cheese infuses the polenta with a nutty flavor; Parmesan or fontina work well, too.

Sea salt and freshly ground pepper

1½ cups (10½ oz/330 g) polenta

2 bunches chard, tough stems removed

1 fresh rosemary sprig, about 6 inches (15 cm) long

1 Tbsp extra-virgin olive oil

4 Tbsp (2 oz/60 g) unsalted butter

1 Tbsp minced shallots

1 lb (500 g) assorted wild mushrooms such as chanterelles, porcini, morels, or lobster mushrooms, coarsely cut or left whole depending on size

1 cup (4 oz/125 g) shredded or crumbled white Cheddar cheese

In a saucepan over high heat, bring 8 cups (64 fl oz/2 l) water and 1½ tsp salt to a boil. Slowly add the polenta, stirring constantly. Reduce the heat to low and cook, stirring often, until the polenta pulls away from the sides of the pan, about 40 minutes.

Meanwhile, bring a large pot of water to a boil over high heat. Add the chard leaves and rosemary sprig. Reduce the heat to medium and cook until the chard ribs are easily pierced with a fork, about 15 minutes. Drain well. Chop coarsely and squeeze dry. Set aside.

In a frying pan over medium-high heat, warm the oil with 1 Tbsp of the butter. Add the shallots and mushrooms and cook until the mushrooms are tender, 8–10 minutes. Using a slotted spoon, transfer to a bowl. Reserve the juices.

When the polenta is ready, stir in the remaining 3 Tbsp butter, all but ¼ cup (1 oz/ 30 g) of the cheese, 1 tsp salt, and 1 tsp pepper and cook until the butter and cheese have melted, 3–4 minutes longer. Return the frying pan used for the mushrooms to medium-high heat. Warm the reserved juices, then add the chard and mushrooms and cook, stirring, until hot and well coated. Season with salt and pepper.

Spoon the polenta into a large serving bowl, top with the chard and mushrooms, sprinkle with the remaining cheese, and serve.

30

SAUTÉED ASIAN GREENS

serves 2–4

Cooking greens, like chard or choy sum, are darker than salad greens, indicating the presence of more vitamins and other nutrients. Here, Asian greens are seasoned with garlic and soy. Serve with brown rice and steamed fish for a lean but flavorful meal.

1 lb (500 g) Chinese mustard greens, bok choy, or choy sum

2 tsp Asian sesame oil

1 clove garlic, minced

1–2 tsp soy sauce

Trim the ends from the greens and cut the greens crosswise into 1½-inch (4-cm) pieces. Place in a colander and rinse well under cold running water.

In a large frying pan, heat the oil over medium heat. Add the garlic and cook, stirring, until fragrant but not browned, about 30 seconds. Add the greens and ¼ cup (2 fl oz/60 ml) water. Cover and cook, shaking pan occasionally, until the greens are tender, 3–4 minutes. Remove from heat, stir in the soy sauce to taste, and serve.

31

SAUTÉED BRUSSELS SPROUTS WITH OLIVE OIL & LEMON ZEST

serves 4

When treated right, Brussels sprouts are peppery and tender. Bring out their best by cooking them quickly, with nothing more than a little good olive oil, lemon, and sea salt. Use the largest frying pan you have for this recipe so that the Brussels sprouts have room to brown properly.

1 lb (500 g) Brussels sprouts

2 Tbsp olive oil

1 tsp grated lemon zest

Sea salt and freshly ground pepper

3 Tbsp fresh lemon juice

Trim the stem ends from the Brussels sprouts and cut the sprouts lengthwise into slices ¼ inch (6 mm) thick.

In a large frying pan, heat the oil over medium-high heat. Add the sprouts, the lemon zest, ½ tsp salt, and a few grinds of pepper. Cook, stirring frequently and reducing heat as necessary to prevent scorching, until the sprouts are tender and slightly browned, 7–8 minutes. Stir in the lemon juice and cook for 1 minute. Remove from the heat and serve.

February is an in-between time for vegetables: the ground will begin to thaw soon, but any spring harvest is still weeks away. Rely on robust roots, nutritious crucifers, and brawny greens to see you through the end of the winter season. Take the edge off any late cold snaps with piping-hot potatoes: roasted in a gratin with celery root, fried with paprika and red chile, or shredded and panfried into crispy galettes. Or, look to more unexpected menu contenders, such as jewel-toned beets; tender, sweet parsnips; and starchy, flavorful celery root.

1
ROASTED FINGERLINGS WITH GARLIC
page 36

2
SHALLOTS IN RED WINE SAUCE
page 36

3
RAINBOW CHARD GRATIN WITH RICOTTA & GRUYÈRE
page 39

8
VEGETABLE MINESTRONE
page 41

9
SWEET POTATO & GREEN CHILE QUESADILLAS WITH ARUGULA
page 42

10
CELERY ROOT RÉMOULADE
page 42

15
PATATAS BRAVAS WITH ALIOLI
page 47

16
SHAVED CARROTS WITH OLIVES & ALMONDS
page 47

17
NEW POTATOES STUFFED WITH CHEESE & HERBS
page 48

22
SAUTÉED HARICOTS VERTS
page 50

23
TURNIP GREENS WITH BACON
page 53

24
ROASTED VEGETABLES WITH PARMESAN BREAD CRUMBS
page 53

february

1

ROASTED FINGERLINGS WITH GARLIC

serves 4

1 lb (500 g) small fingerling potatoes, halved lengthwise

¼ cup (2 fl oz/60 ml) olive oil

Leaves from 4 fresh rosemary sprigs, minced

Salt and freshly ground pepper

3 cloves garlic, thinly sliced

Garlic and rosemary have a natural affinity for potatoes, especially the dense yellow flesh of fingerlings. Halve and roast the potatoes in a hot oven until the skin wrinkles and crisps, then serve with a saucy pot roast or with salmon fillets cooked on a stove-top grill pan.

Preheat the oven to 400°F (200°C).

Place the potatoes in a bowl. Add the oil and rosemary, sprinkle generously with salt and pepper, and turn the potatoes to coat with the seasonings. Arrange the potatoes in a single layer on a rimmed baking sheet.

Roast the potatoes for 10 minutes. Stir the potatoes and roast for 10 minutes more. Scatter the garlic over the potatoes and roast until the potatoes are golden brown and tender when pierced with a knife, about 10 minutes. Transfer to a platter, season with salt, and serve.

2

SHALLOTS IN RED WINE SAUCE

serves 4

3 Tbsp unsalted butter

1 lb (500 g) shallots, peeled (see note)

2½ cups (20 fl oz/625 ml) dry red wine

1 cup (8 fl oz/250 ml) vegetable or chicken broth

¼ cup (2 fl oz/60 ml) balsamic vinegar

½ tsp sugar

1 tsp chopped fresh tarragon (optional)

Salt and freshly ground pepper

Shallots recall the flavor of both onions and garlic. To peel them, trim off the stem ends. Bring a large saucepan three-fourths full of water to a boil. Add the shallots and blanch for 2 minutes. Drain, plunge into cold water, and leave for 5 minutes. Drain again. Squeeze gently to slip off the skins. Use a paring knife to remove any stubborn skins. This elegant dish is an excellent accompaniment to grilled steak or fish. You can also use small pearl or pickling onions in place of the shallots.

In a frying pan, melt 1½ Tbsp of the butter over low heat. Add the shallots and sauté until slightly softened and evenly coated with the butter, 6–8 minutes.

Add 2 cups (16 fl oz/500 ml) of the wine, the broth, vinegar, sugar, and tarragon (if using), raise the heat to high, and bring to a boil. Reduce the heat to medium and simmer uncovered, stirring occasionally, until the shallots are cooked through and almost translucent, 10–15 minutes. The liquid should be thick and syrupy. If it cooks down too much and becomes too dark, it will be bitter, so adjust the heat if it seems to be reducing too quickly. Add the remaining ½ cup (4 fl oz/125 ml) wine and continue to simmer for a few minutes longer until reduced to a concentrated sauce; there should be ½–¾ cup (4–6 fl oz/125–180 ml) liquid.

Remove the pan from the heat and add the remaining 1½ Tbsp butter, stirring briskly to incorporate the butter and give the sauce a nice gloss. Season with salt and pepper and serve.

3

*This update
on a gratin takes
advantage of
rainbow chard,
with its beautiful
tricolored stems and
flavorful crinkled
leaves. Ricotta and
Gruyère melt and
bind the ingredients
together, sparing
you from whisking
over a hot stove.*

RAINBOW CHARD GRATIN WITH RICOTTA & GRUYÈRE

serves 4–6

3 lb (1.5 kg) rainbow chard

1 Tbsp olive oil

1 yellow onion, thinly sliced

1 clove garlic, minced

1½ tsp minced fresh thyme

Salt and freshly ground pepper

2 cups (1 lb/500 g) ricotta cheese

1 cup (4 oz/125 g) shredded Gruyère cheese

1 Tbsp Dijon mustard

1 cup (2 oz/60 g) fresh bread crumbs

Preheat the oven to 375°F (190°C). Butter a 12-inch (30-cm) oval gratin dish.

Cut the chard leaves from the stems. Keeping the leaves and stems separate, cut both into 1-inch (2.5-cm) pieces. In a large frying pan, warm the oil over medium heat. Add the chard stems and sauté for 2 minutes. Add the onion, garlic, and thyme and sauté until the onion softens, about 6 minutes. Add the chard leaves and cook, stirring, until wilted, about 4 minutes. Season with salt and pepper. Transfer the chard leaves and stems to a colander and drain well, pressing with a spoon to remove excess liquid.

In a bowl, stir together the cheeses and mustard. Add the chard and stir to mix well. Spread the chard mixture in the prepared dish and scatter the bread crumbs on top. Bake until the bread crumbs are golden and the gratin is heated through, about 20 minutes, then serve.

4

*Panfried potatoes
are a welcome
vehicle for smoky
cured fish, especially
with a spoonful of
sour cream and a
sprinkle of chives.
After shredding the
potatoes, press out
as much moisture as
possible. This both
firms the texture
of the galettes and
protects you from
spatters while
working over
a hot pan.*

POTATO GALETTES WITH SMOKED SALMON

serves 4

2 russet potatoes, about ¾ lb (375 g) total, peeled

2 Tbsp canola or olive oil

Salt and freshly ground pepper

3 oz (90 g) thinly sliced smoked salmon, cut into 2-inch (5-cm) squares

1 Tbsp snipped fresh chives

1–2 Tbsp sour cream for garnish (optional)

Shred the potatoes on the large holes of a grater-shredder to make long shreds. Squeeze the potatoes dry, one handful at a time, with a kitchen towel.

In a frying pan, warm 2 tsp of the oil over medium-high heat. For each galette, put 1 heaping Tbsp potato shreds in the pan, making 4 at a time. Using a spatula, firmly flatten the potatoes into 3-inch (7.5-cm) pancakes, repeatedly pressing to compact the potatoes and pushing in the loose edges to prevent them from burning. Work the spatula under each galette to keep it from sticking. Continue pressing and lifting the galettes until the tops look translucent, about 3 minutes. Turn and cook, continuing to press and lift, until the galettes are well browned, about 3 minutes. Season with salt and pepper. Remove the galettes from the pan and keep warm.

Wipe out the pan. Add the oil 1 tsp at a time as needed, and repeat to cook the remaining galettes in 2 more batches. As the pan gets hotter, the potatoes will cook more quickly; reduce the heat if necessary.

Top each galette with a square of smoked salmon and a sprinkle of chives. Dot with sour cream, if desired, and serve.

5

Roasting brings out the best in broccoli. The tips of the florets char lightly while the stems stay nicely crisp. Instead of sesame and soy, you could vary the flavors with garlic oil: Omit the peanut and sesame oils, sesame seeds, soy sauce, and rice vinegar. In a small bowl, stir together 3 Tbsp olive oil and the garlic. Arrange the broccoli on the baking sheet. Season with salt and pepper and brush with the garlic oil. Roast for about 15 minutes. Drizzle 2 tsp fresh lemon juice over the broccoli and serve.

ROASTED BROCCOLI WITH SOY, RICE VINEGAR & SESAME SEEDS

serves 4

1 lb (500 g) broccoli stalks with florets, tough ends trimmed

Salt and freshly ground pepper

2 Tbsp peanut oil

1 Tbsp Asian sesame oil

1 large clove garlic, finely chopped

1 Tbsp sesame seeds

1 Tbsp soy sauce

1 Tbsp rice vinegar

Preheat the oven to 475°F (245°C).

If the broccoli stalks are large, split them in half or thirds lengthwise. Arrange the broccoli stalks in a single layer on a rimmed baking sheet. Season lightly with salt and pepper. In a small bowl, stir together the peanut and sesame oils and the garlic. Brush the broccoli stalks on all sides with the oil mixture.

Roast the broccoli, turning once, until the stems are nearly tender-crisp and the florets are beginning to brown, about 10 minutes. Remove the broccoli from the oven and sprinkle with the sesame seeds. Continue to roast until the seeds are toasted, the stems are tender-crisp, and the florets are browned, about 5 minutes.

Remove from the oven and arrange the broccoli on a platter. Drizzle with the soy sauce and vinegar, and serve warm or at room temperature.

6

Roasted beets are delicious on their own or tossed in salads. You can roast them a day ahead, let them cool in their skins, and then peel them when you're ready to serve. Slice them thinly for this salad, then take the time to arrange them attractively on a platter before finishing with a vinaigrette, goat cheese, and fresh herbs.

ROASTED BEETS WITH LEMON-THYME VINAIGRETTE

serves 4–6

8 golden, red, white, and/or Candy Cane beets, in any combination

2 Tbsp olive oil

FOR THE VINAIGRETTE

Grated zest and juice from ½ lemon

½ cup extra-virgin olive oil

¼ cup white wine vinegar

1½ tsp fresh thyme leaves

Salt and freshly ground pepper

5 oz (155 g) fresh goat cheese, crumbled

Salt and freshly ground pepper

1 Tbsp julienned fresh mint

2 tsp coarsely chopped fresh tarragon

2 tsp fresh chervil leaves

Preheat the oven to 400°F (200°C).

Trim the greens from the beets if still attached, leaving 1 inch (2.5 cm) of the stem intact. Place the beets on a large piece of foil. Drizzle with the oil. Gather up the edges of the foil and seal tightly. Place the foil packet on a rimmed baking sheet. Roast until the beets are tender when pierced with a knife, 45–60 minutes. Remove the packet from the oven, unwrap the beets, and let cool.

Meanwhile, make the vinaigrette. In a small bowl, whisk together the lemon zest and juice, oil, vinegar, and thyme. Season to taste with salt and pepper.

When the beets are cool enough to handle, rub them between paper towels to remove the skins. Beginning with the light-colored beets, cut each beet into slices ⅛ inch (3 mm) thick. Arrange the slices in an overlappping pattern on a platter. Sprinkle with the goat cheese and drizzle with the vinaigrette. Season with salt and pepper. Sprinkle with the mint, tarragon, and chervil and serve.

7

Here, cauliflower is sautéed with tomatoes and hints of cinnamon and bay, and then baked with feta cheese until golden. Look for a superb Greek feta to grace this rustic plate.

BAKED CAULIFLOWER WITH TOMATOES & FETA

serves 6

4 Tbsp (2 fl oz/60 ml) olive oil

1 large yellow onion, chopped

2 cloves garlic, minced

2 cups (12 oz/370 g) canned diced tomatoes, with juice

6 ripe plum tomatoes, halved, seeded, and finely chopped

1 head cauliflower, about 2½ lb (1.25 kg), trimmed and cut into 1-inch (2.5-cm) florets

Juice of ½ lemon

¼ tsp ground cinnamon

1 bay leaf

2 oz (60 g) feta cheese, crumbled

Salt and freshly ground pepper

Preheat the oven to 375°F (190°C).

In a large frying pan, heat 2 Tbsp of the oil over medium-high heat. Add the onion and garlic and cook, stirring frequently, until the onion is softened, about 5 minutes. Add the tomatoes, cover, and simmer, stirring occasionally, until softened, about 5 minutes. Add the cauliflower, cover, and cook until the florets are tender-crisp, about 10 minutes.

Transfer the cauliflower and tomatoes to an ovenproof baking dish just large enough to hold the cauliflower in a single layer. In a small bowl, whisk together the lemon juice, cinnamon, remaining 2 Tbsp oil, and ¼ cup (2 fl oz/60 ml) water. Pour evenly over the cauliflower. Break the bay leaf in half and add to the dish. Sprinkle with the feta cheese. Season with salt and pepper. Cover the dish with foil.

Bake until the cauliflower is tender when pierced with a knife, about 50 minutes. Uncover and continue baking until the cauliflower is golden on top, about 10 minutes. Let stand for 15 minutes before serving.

8

Minestrone—brimming with pasta, legumes, and vegetables—is a great informal meal. Serve it as a casual supper to guests of any age, rounding out the menu with crusty bread and a green salad. Save the rinds from Parmesan cheese and drop a chunk into the soup pot to add complexity to the broth. You can also use a light vegetable broth in place of the water.

VEGETABLE MINESTRONE

serves 8–10

1 Tbsp olive oil, plus more for drizzling

2 large cloves garlic

2 carrots, chopped

1 small yellow onion, chopped

1 celery rib, thinly sliced

Salt and freshly ground pepper

1 cup (6 oz/185 g) canned diced tomatoes, with juice

1 bay leaf

2 large fresh sage leaves

2 cups (15 oz/470 g) drained and rinsed canned cannellini beans

2 cups (6 oz/185 g) packed shredded kale or chard

1 cup (4 oz/125 g) tubettini or other small dried pasta shape

Grated Parmesan cheese for garnish

In a large soup pot, heat the oil over medium-high heat. Add the garlic and sauté until the garlic is toasted and the oil is fragrant, about 1 minute. Add the carrots, onion, and celery and sauté until the vegetables start to soften and brown, 3–4 minutes. Season with salt and pepper.

Add the tomatoes, bay leaf, and sage, along with enough water to cover the vegetables by 2 inches (5 cm). Simmer, uncovered, for 30 minutes. Add the beans and kale and continue to simmer for 20–30 minutes. Season with salt and pepper.

Just before the soup is ready, bring a saucepan of salted water to a boil. Add the pasta, stir well, and cook until al dente, according to the package directions. Drain well and place in soup bowls. Discard the bay leaf from the soup, then ladle over the pasta. Drizzle with oil, sprinkle generously with Parmesan, and serve.

9

SWEET POTATO & GREEN CHILE QUESADILLAS WITH ARUGULA

serves 4

2 sweet potatoes, about 1 lb (500 g) total, peeled and cut into ½-inch (12-mm) pieces

4 Tbsp (2 fl oz/60 ml) olive oil, plus 2 tsp

8 flour or corn tortillas, about 9 inches (23 cm) in diameter

3 cups (12 oz/375 g) shredded Monterey jack cheese

1 can (4 oz/125 g) roasted green chiles, drained

⅓ cup (½ oz/15 g) fresh cilantro leaves

4 oz (125 g) baby arugula

Juice of ½ lemon

Salt and freshly ground pepper

A perfect balance of flavors, this fresh dish combines sweet and spicy vegetables with crisp, cool arugula leaves. This recipe is a great way to use up any leftover sweet potato. Serve with a crisp white wine or Mexican beer.

Preheat the oven to 450°F (230°C). Line a baking sheet with parchment paper. Place the sweet potato pieces on the prepared baking sheet, drizzle with 2 Tbsp of the oil, and spread out in a single layer. Roast, stirring once, until the potatoes are caramelized and very tender, about 25 minutes. Let cool, transfer to a bowl, and, using a potato masher or a fork, mash slightly.

Place 4 tortillas on a work surface. Cover each tortilla with one-fourth of the sweet potatoes, cheese, green chiles, and cilantro. Cover with the remaining 4 tortillas.

In a large frying pan, warm about ½ tsp of the oil over medium heat. Fry each quesadilla, turning once, and adding ½ tsp more oil for each, until the cheese is melted and the tortillas are golden brown, about 3 minutes. Transfer the quesadillas to a cutting board and cut into quarters.

Put the arugula in a bowl and drizzle with the remaining 2 Tbsp oil and the lemon juice. Season with salt and pepper and toss to combine. Serve the quesadillas topped with the arugula.

10

CELERY ROOT RÉMOULADE

serves 4

1 celery root, about 1½ lb (750 g)

1 tsp fresh lemon juice

Salt

¼ cup (2 oz/60 g) Dijon mustard

3 Tbsp boiling water

⅓–½ cup (3–4 fl oz/80–125 ml) mild extra-virgin olive oil

2 Tbsp white wine vinegar or Champagne vinegar

3 Tbsp minced fresh chives

Celery root has a rough, shaggy exterior, but beneath it lies ivory white flesh with an intense celery flavor. The French cut it into matchsticks and toss it with a creamy vinaigrette, for a crisp cold-weather salad. Celery root rémoulade is frequently served as one of a trio of salads, alongside shredded carrots and cooked beets.

Using a sharp knife, cut the top from the celery root and discard. Cut away the rough, knobby skin and discard. Using a mandoline, cut the celery root crosswise into very thin slices. Then, using the knife, cut the slices into thin matchsticks.

In a large bowl, combine the celery root, lemon juice, and 1 tsp salt, and toss to coat. Let stand for 30 minutes. Rinse the celery root under cold running water, drain, and pat dry.

Warm a large heatproof bowl with hot water, then dry it completely. Put the mustard in the bowl and slowly drizzle in the boiling water, whisking until incorporated. Whisking continuously, slowly drizzle in enough oil to make a thick sauce. Slowly drizzle in the vinegar, whisking until incorporated.

Add the celery root and toss gently to coat. Cover and refrigerate for at least 3 hours or up to overnight. Transfer to a serving bowl, garnish with the chives, and serve.

11

CHARD WITH CRÈME FRAÎCHE & CUMIN

serves 4

This recipe riffs on classic creamed spinach, substituting coarser chard leaves and tangy crème fraîche and adding cumin and paprika. Pair this dish with lamb chops or a roasted whole fish in place of the traditional steak.

1½ lb (750 g) red chard

2 Tbsp olive oil

½ cup (4 oz/125 g) crème fraîche

2 Tbsp fresh lemon juice

1 tsp ground cumin

1 tsp sweet paprika

Salt and freshly ground pepper

Tear the chard leaves from the center ribs and stems. Chop the ribs and stems together. Coarsely chop the leaves separately.

In a large frying pan, heat the oil over medium-high heat. Add the ribs and stems and cook, stirring frequently, for 2 minutes. Add the leaves and cook until the leaves are wilted and tender and any liquid has evaporated, about 3 minutes.

In a bowl, whisk together the crème fraîche, lemon juice, cumin, and paprika. Season with ½ tsp salt and a few grinds of pepper. Stir into the chard and cook until the sauce is slightly thickened, 1–2 minutes. Transfer to a bowl and serve.

12

BAKED EGGS WITH SPINACH & CREAM

serves 4

A perfect Sunday supper, these easy baked eggs need just biscuits or crusty bread and pan-grilled sausages to complete the menu. For extra flavor, sprinkle each egg with a spoonful of grated Asiago cheese before slipping the ramekins into the oven.

1 Tbsp plus 2 tsp unsalted butter

1½ lb (750 g) baby spinach, tough stems removed

4 eggs

Salt and freshly ground pepper

4 tsp heavy cream

Preheat the oven to 350°F (180°C). Coat four ½-cup (4–fl oz/125-ml) ramekins with the 1 Tbsp butter.

Bring a large saucepan of salted water to a boil. Add the spinach and cook until limp but still bright green, about 4 minutes. Drain well and rinse under cold running water. Drain again and squeeze to remove excess water. Coarsely chop the spinach.

Divide the chopped spinach evenly among the prepared ramekins. Make an indentation in the center of each spinach portion, and dot each portion with ½ tsp of the remaining butter. Break an egg into each ramekin, sprinkle with ½ tsp salt and ¼ tsp pepper, and drizzle with 1 tsp of the cream. Place the ramekins on a rimmed baking sheet.

Bake until the whites are set and the yolks are firm around the edges but still soft in the center, about 15 minutes. Remove from the oven and serve.

13

BOILED POTATOES WITH CREAMY ONION SAUCE

serves 6

This hearty dish of boiled potatoes dressed with a creamy cheese and onion sauce is inspired by a traditional South American recipe. Peeling strips of the skin from the potatoes gives the dish added visual interest. If you can find small purple potatoes in the market, they would work here as well. Look for achiote paste in Latin markets or specialty stores.

2 lb (1 kg) small red or yellow-fleshed potatoes

1 Tbsp unsalted butter

1 Tbsp olive oil

½ cup (2 oz/60 g) thinly sliced yellow onion

4 green onions, white and tender green parts, thinly sliced

½ cup (3 oz/90 g) canned diced tomatoes

1 small clove garlic, minced

¼ tsp achiote paste

¼ tsp ground cumin

Salt and freshly ground pepper

½ cup (4 fl oz/125 ml) whole milk

½ cup (4 fl oz/125 ml) heavy cream

1 cup (4 oz/125 g) shredded queso blanco or farmer cheese, plus 2 Tbsp cheese for serving

Bring a saucepan of salted water to a boil. Using a vegetable peeler, peel off half of the potato skins in strips about ½ inch (12 mm) wide, creating a striped design. Cut potatoes that are larger than 1½ inches (4 cm) in diameter in half.

Add the potatoes to the boiling water and cook until tender when pierced with a knife, about 20 minutes. Drain and rinse under cold running water. Drain again and pat dry.

In a frying pan, melt the butter with the oil over medium-low heat. Add the yellow and green onions and sauté until softened, about 2 minutes. Add the tomatoes, garlic, achiote, and cumin and season with ½ tsp salt and ⅛ tsp pepper. Cook until the onions are tender, 25–30 minutes. Add the milk, cream, and 1 cup cheese and cook, stirring to melt the cheese, until the sauce is well blended and smooth.

Arrange the potatoes on a platter and top with the sauce. Garnish with the 2 Tbsp cheese and serve.

14

SAUTÉED DINOSAUR KALE WITH ANCHOVIES

serves 8

Dinosaur kale can be slowly braised until meltingly tender, but many vegetable lovers instead like to cook it briefly to retain more bite. Sauté it lightly in a hot pan with a few boldly flavored Italian-style ingredients—garlic, pepper flakes, and anchovy—to showcase its texture.

4 bunches dinosaur kale, about 2 lb (1 kg) total

2 Tbsp olive oil

2 cloves garlic, minced

8 olive oil–packed anchovy fillets, drained and minced

Salt

½ tsp red pepper flakes

2 tsp grated lemon zest

1 Tbsp fresh lemon juice

Trim the tough stem ends from the kale. Coarsely chop the kale into bite-sized pieces.

In a large frying pan, heat the oil over medium-high heat. Add the garlic and anchovies and cook, stirring, just until the garlic is golden, about 1 minute. Add the kale, ½ tsp salt, and 1 cup (8 fl oz/250 ml) water. Cook, stirring occasionally, until the kale is tender to the bite, about 10 minutes. Stir in the red pepper flakes and lemon zest and juice. Transfer to a platter and serve.

FEBRUARY

16

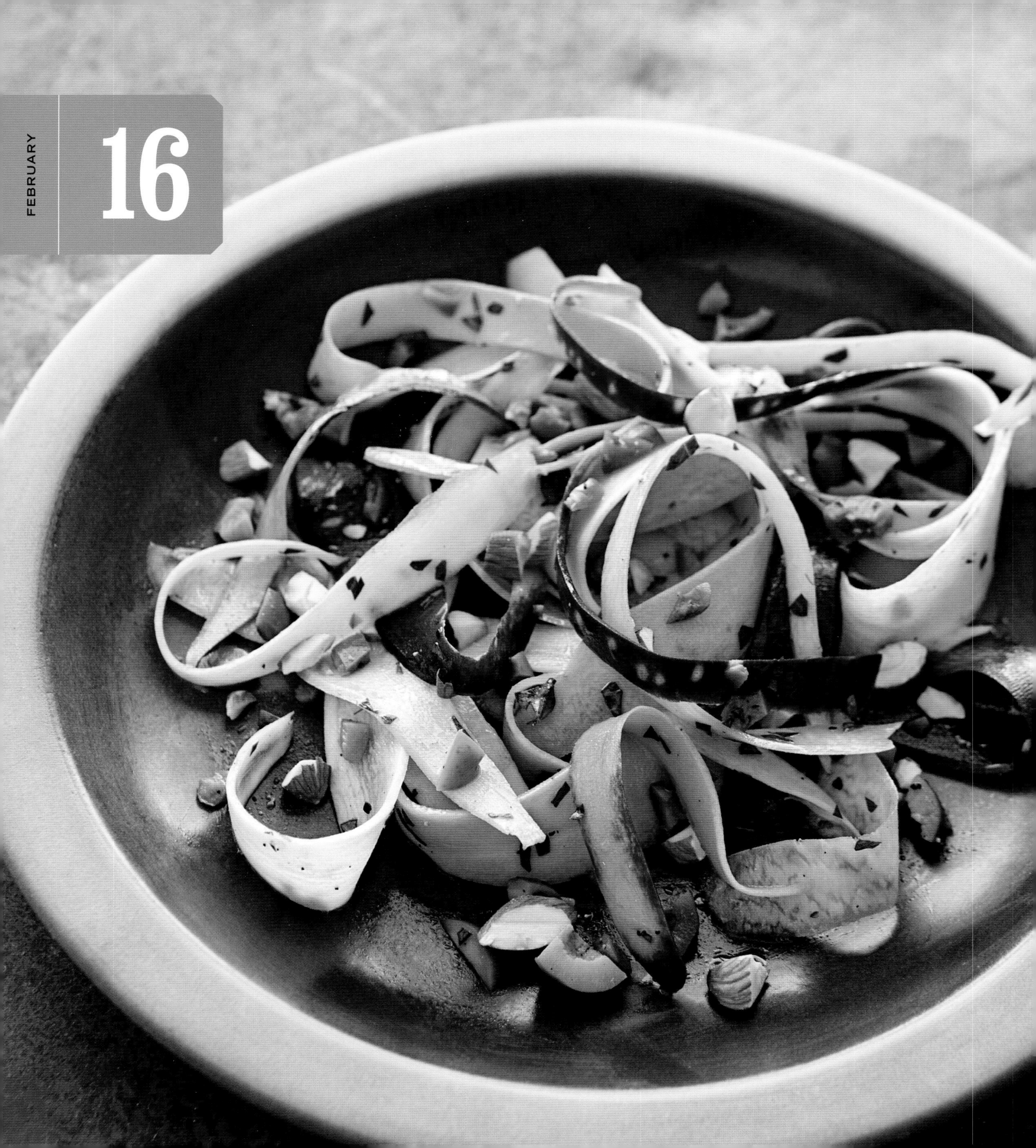

15

These addictive wedges are a mainstay of Spanish tapas. Many bars serve them with alioli, a mayonnaise thickened with egg and sometimes flavored with mustard and lemon juice. Use mild olive oil cut with canola oil, which keeps the flavor from over-whelming the sauce. Look for creamy yellow-fleshed potatoes, which go particularly well with the spicy paprika.

PATATAS BRAVAS WITH ALIOLI

serves 6

FOR THE ALIOLI

⅓ cup (3 fl oz/80 ml) canola oil

⅓ cup (3 fl oz/80 ml) extra-virgin olive oil

4 cloves garlic, chopped

1 egg, at room temperature

1 tsp sherry vinegar

Salt

1½ lb (750 g) yellow-fleshed potatoes such as Yukon gold

½ cup (4 fl oz/125 ml) olive oil

1 tsp Spanish smoked paprika

½ tsp ground cumin

¼ tsp ground cayenne pepper

Salt and freshly ground black pepper

To make the alioli, combine the oils in a measuring cup. In a food processor, process the garlic until finely chopped. Add the egg, vinegar, and 1 tsp salt and process until well blended. With the motor running, slowly drizzle in the oils until a thick mayonnaise forms; you may not need all the oil.

Place the potatoes in a saucepan with water to cover by 2 inches (5 cm) and bring to a boil. Reduce the heat to medium and cook until tender when pierced with a knife, about 10 minutes. Drain the potatoes and let cool slightly. Peel the potatoes and let cool completely. Cut the potatoes into quarters or wedges.

In a large frying pan, warm the oil over medium-high heat for about 3 minutes. Add the potatoes in a single layer and fry, turning as needed, until browned in several places, about 8 minutes. Transfer to paper towels to drain and then transfer to a wide bowl. Sprinkle with the paprika, cumin, and cayenne pepper. Toss gently to coat the potatoes with the spices. Season with salt and pepper and toss again. Serve accompanied by the alioli.

16

Gather purple, yellow, and white varieties of carrots together for this chic salad, elevating the humble root vegetable. The shavings are as delicious as they are pretty, curled around briny green olives and toasty almonds, and sprinkled with fragrant cumin.

SHAVED CARROTS WITH OLIVES & ALMONDS

serves 4

1 lb (500 g) multicolored carrots

¼ cup (1 oz/30 g) pitted green olives

¼ cup (⅓ oz/10 g) lightly packed fresh flat-leaf parsley leaves

2 Tbsp extra-virgin olive oil

1 tsp fresh lemon juice

½ tsp cumin seeds, toasted

Salt and freshly ground pepper

¼ cup (1 oz/30 g) almonds, toasted and crushed

Using a mandoline, shave the carrots lengthwise into thin ribbons. Transfer to a bowl.

On a cutting board, coarsely chop together the olives and parsley. Transfer to a small bowl. Add the oil, lemon juice, and cumin seeds and stir to combine. Season with salt and pepper.

Add the olive mixture to the carrots and toss well. Arrange on plates, sprinkle with the almonds, and serve.

17

Spring is time for tender green leaves, including bundles of lush herbs. The Mediterranean's combination of fines herbes, featured here, can include parsley, chives, chervil, tarragon, marjoram, even lemon balm, but there are no hard and fast rules. Stuff these potatoes with whatever greenery looks and smells the most heavenly at market.

NEW POTATOES STUFFED WITH CHEESE & HERBS

serves 4

⅓ cup (½ oz/15 g) snipped fresh chives

⅓ cup (⅓ oz/10 g) loosely packed fresh flat-leaf parsley leaves

¾ cup (6 oz/185 g) fromage blanc

4 fresh basil leaves

1 shallot, very finely minced

Salt and freshly ground pepper

6 new potatoes, each about 1½ inches (4 cm) in diameter, preferably 2 red, 2 white, and 2 purple

Finely chop the chives and parsley. Transfer to a bowl, add the cheese, and stir well to combine. Stack the basil leaves, roll up lengthwise, and cut crosswise into fine slivers, and then chop. Add the basil to the cheese mixture along with the shallot. Stir to mix well and season with ¼ tsp salt and a generous amount of pepper.

Place the potatoes in a large saucepan with water to cover by 2 inches (5 cm). Bring to a boil, reduce the heat to medium-low, cover, and simmer until the potatoes are tender when pierced with a knife, 12–15 minutes. Let cool.

Halve the potatoes crosswise. Using a melon baller, scoop out about half of the flesh from each potato half, leaving a shell about ½ inch (12 mm) thick. Cut a thin slice off the bottom of each half. Using a small spoon, fill the hollow in each potato half with about 1 Tbsp of the cheese mixture, mounding it generously. Transfer the stuffed potatoes to a plate and serve.

18

Peppery watercress is excellent in creamy soups, both hot and chilled. If you opt to serve this soup hot, top it with crisp croutons. If you prefer to serve it cold, a swirl of heavy cream or crème fraîche makes a nice garnish. Offer this pale green soup as a first course preceding grilled or panfried lamb chops or roasted chicken. Or, pair with a fruit salad and a cheese plate for a weekend lunch.

WATERCRESS SOUP

serves 4

¼ cup (2 fl oz/60 ml) olive oil

1 yellow onion, coarsely chopped

2 large Yukon gold potatoes, peeled and diced

1 lb (500 g) leeks, white and pale green parts, thinly sliced

4 cups (32 fl oz/1 l) chicken broth or water

Fine sea salt and freshly ground pepper

2 bunches watercress, stems removed

1 cup (8 fl oz/250 ml) heavy cream

In a large saucepan, warm the oil over medium heat. Add the onion and cook, stirring occasionally, until soft, about 5 minutes. Stir in the potatoes and cook for 2 minutes. Add the leeks, raise the heat to medium-high, and cook, stirring occasionally, until the leeks begin to soften and wilt, about 4 minutes. Add the broth and season with salt and pepper. Raise the heat to high and bring to a boil. Reduce the heat to medium-low and simmer, uncovered, until the vegetables are very soft, about 25 minutes.

Using an immersion blender, purée the soup in the pan until smooth. Or, transfer the soup to a canister blender or a food processor and purée until smooth.

To serve the soup hot, pour into a clean saucepan, stir in the cream, and reheat gently over medium heat. To serve the soup cold, pour into a bowl, stir in the cream, cover, and refrigerate until well chilled, about 4 hours. Adjust the seasonings just before serving.

19

SAUTÉED SPINACH WITH FETA & PINE NUTS

serves 4–6

2 Tbsp golden raisins

3 Tbsp olive oil

2 cloves garlic, chopped

Pinch of red pepper flakes

2 lb (1 kg) spinach, tough stems removed

Salt

¼ cup (1 oz/30 g) pine nuts, toasted

½ cup (2½ oz/75 g) crumbled feta cheese

1 lemon wedge

This simple dish of sautéed spinach is dressed up with sweet, salty, and spicy accents from the addition of raisins, feta, and red pepper flakes, respectively. Toasted pine nuts contribute crunch and a rich flavor. To toast the nuts, put them in a small dry frying pan over medium-low heat and shake the pan often until they are fragrant and golden. Pine nuts are high in oil and can burn easily, so watch them closely.

Put the raisins in a small bowl and add hot water to cover. Let stand until plumped.

In a frying pan, warm 2 Tbsp of the oil over medium heat. Add the garlic and red pepper flakes and sauté until fragrant. Add as much spinach as will fit in the pan. Raise the heat to high and add the remaining spinach as the first batch wilts. Cook until all the spinach has wilted and the water has evaporated, about 5 minutes. If the pan gets too dry before the spinach has cooked fully, add a splash of water. Remove from the heat.

Drain the raisins and add to the spinach along with the remaining 1 Tbsp oil. Season with salt. Transfer to a platter and top with the pine nuts and cheese. Squeeze the lemon wedge over the top and serve right away.

20

PAN-SEARED BROCCOLI

serves 4–6

Ice water

Salt and freshly ground pepper

1½ lb (750 g) broccoli, cut into florets

2 tbsp olive oil

1 lemon, halved

Here is a tasty alternative to steamed broccoli—and it comes together just as quickly. Blanching takes the raw edge off the broccoli and leaves it bright green, searing gives it an irresistible crispy quality, and the lemon juice brings out its natural essence. You can also add these florets to freshly steamed rice or to a salad.

Have ready a large bowl of ice water. Bring a large saucepan of lightly salted water to a boil. Add the broccoli and blanch for 30 seconds, but no longer; the broccoli should remain bright green and crunchy. Drain the florets and plunge them into the ice water. Let stand until the broccoli is cool to the touch. Drain well.

In a large frying pan, warm the oil over medium-high heat. Add the broccoli florets and toss to coat with the oil. Sear the florets quickly on one side until they have some golden brown spots and begin to caramelize, about 30 seconds. Toss again and sear quickly on the second side, about 30 seconds. Remove from the heat.

Squeeze the lemon halves over the broccoli, season with 1 tsp salt and ½ tsp pepper, and toss to mix. Transfer to a platter and serve.

21

Escarole, a member of the chicory family, is bitter and even a little tough when raw, but turns mellow, nutty, and tender when cooked. Cook the filling completely to avoid a soggy pie. This is impressive as a side dish or can be served as a light main course accompanied with cheeses and salumi.

ESCAROLE & OLIVE PIE

serves 8

3 Tbsp olive oil

1 yellow onion, finely chopped

3 cloves garlic, minced

1 lb (500 g) escarole, thinly sliced crosswise

1 lb (500 g) spinach, tough stems removed

1 cup (5 oz/155 g) coarsely chopped pitted Gaeta or Kalamata olives

¼ tsp cayenne pepper

Salt

2 Tbsp fresh lemon juice

1 sheet frozen puff pastry, about ½ lb (250 g), thawed

½ cup (2 oz/60 g) shredded pecorino romano cheese

1 egg yolk, lightly beaten with 1 Tbsp water

In a large frying pan, warm the oil over medium-low heat. Add the onion and garlic and sauté until the onion is soft and translucent, 7–8 minutes. Add as much of the escarole and spinach as will fit in the pan. Raise the heat to medium and cook, stirring occasionally, until wilted, about 3 minutes. Add the remaining greens and turn to coat with the oil. Add the olives, cayenne, and ¼ tsp salt and cook, stirring occasionally, until the greens are tender, about 4 minutes. Stir in the lemon juice and cook for 2 minutes. Let cool to room temperature. While cooling, spoon the greens to one side and tilt the pan to the opposite side to collect and discard excess liquid.

Preheat the oven to 400°F (200°C).

Cut the puff pastry sheet in half crosswise. On a lightly floured work surface, roll one half into a 12-by-5-inch (30-by-12-cm) rectangle. Transfer the rectangle to a baking sheet. Spoon the filling over the top, leaving a ¼-inch (6-mm) border. Sprinkle with the cheese. Roll the second half into a 11-by-4-inch (28-by-10-cm) rectangle. Carefully center it over the tart. Bringing the edges of the bottom piece of dough up to the top piece of dough, pinch the edges together to seal. Brush the top with the egg mixture. Using a knife, make 3 large slits in the top crust. ⤔

Bake until the crust is golden brown, 30–35 minutes. Transfer to a wire rack and let cool for about 15 minutes. Invert a large platter over the tart, carefully flip both the platter and the pan, and remove the pan, then invert again onto a serving platter. Cut into pieces and serve warm or at room temperature.

22

Haricots verts are long, slender green beans popular in France. They cook quickly, so be careful not to boil them too long, as you want them to retain some snap. You can also coat these tender beans in a warm vinaigrette in place of the butter.

SAUTÉED HARICOTS VERTS

serves 6

1½ lb (750 g) haricots verts or other young, slender green beans, trimmed

1 Tbsp unsalted butter

Salt

Bring a saucepan of salted water to a boil. Add the beans and cook until barely tender, about 5 minutes. Drain and rinse under cold running water until cool. Drain again.

In a frying pan, melt the butter over medium heat. Add the beans and 2 tsp salt and sauté, gently, just until heated through, about 2 minutes.

Transfer to a platter and serve.

23

TURNIP GREENS WITH BACON

serves 4

1½ lb (750 g) turnip greens

1½ Tbsp olive oil

3 thick-cut slices bacon, diced

2 cloves garlic, minced

⅛ tsp red pepper flakes

Salt

To dress up these nutrient-rich turnip greens, sauté 1 yellow onion, chopped, with the bacon until translucent, before adding the garlic and red pepper flakes. Or, substitute a chunk of salt pork, diced, for the bacon. Collard greens and mustard greens can be cooked in the same manner.

Remove the stems and tough center ribs from the turnip greens and discard. Coarsely chop the leaves.

In a large frying pan, heat the oil over medium-high heat. Add the bacon and cook, stirring frequently, until beginning to brown and crisp, 2–3 minutes. Add the garlic and red pepper flakes and cook and stir for 30 seconds. Add the greens, 1 cup (8 fl oz/ 250 ml) water, and ¼ tsp salt and bring to a boil. Reduce the heat to a gentle simmer, cover, and cook, shaking the pan occasionally, until the greens are tender, about 10 minutes.

Adjust the seasonings if necessary and serve.

24

ROASTED VEGETABLES WITH PARMESAN BREAD CRUMBS

serves 4–6

3 slices crusty sourdough bread, each about ½ inch (12 mm) thick

2 cloves garlic

2 Tbsp olive oil

⅓ cup (1½ oz/45 g) grated Parmesan cheese

3 lb (1.5 kg) root vegetables, peeled and cut into ½-inch (12-mm) pieces

½ tsp minced fresh thyme or ¼ tsp dried thyme

¼ tsp freshly grated nutmeg

Salt and freshly ground pepper

Choose any combination of roots for this gratin; parsnips, sweet potatoes, carrots, turnips, golden beets, and rutabagas are all good candidates. For the best flavor, seek out imported Parmigiano-Reggiano cheese and grate it just before you mix it with the bread crumbs.

Preheat the oven to 300°F (150°C).

Place the bread slices on a baking sheet and bake until crisp and dry, 20–25 minutes. Cut 1 garlic clove and rub the cut side of each slice. Let the bread cool and then tear into chunks. Place the slices in a food processor, and process to form coarse crumbs. Transfer to a bowl and mix with 1 Tbsp of the oil and the Parmesan.

Raise the oven temperature to 400°F (200°C). Mince the remaining garlic clove. In a large ovenproof frying pan, heat the remaining 1 Tbsp oil over medium-high heat. Add the vegetables, minced garlic, thyme, and nutmeg to the pan. Season with ½ tsp salt and a few grinds of pepper. Cook, stirring occasionally, until the vegetables begin to brown, 4–6 minutes. Add ¼ cup (2 fl oz/ 60 ml) water, cover, and simmer until the vegetables are tender when pierced with a knife, about 10 minutes.

Remove the pan from the oven and sprinkle the vegetables evenly with the crumb mixture. Return to the oven and bake until the top is golden brown, 10–12 minutes. Remove from the oven and serve.

25

SPINACH & BLACK BEAN ENCHILADAS

serves 4–6

12 tomatillos, husked and halved

3 poblano chiles, halved lengthwise and seeded

1½ white onions, chopped

2 cloves garlic

1½ cups (1½ oz/45 g) fresh cilantro leaves

Salt and freshly ground pepper

3 Tbsp canola oil

½ red bell pepper, seeded and chopped

1 Tbsp plus 1 tsp ground cumin

10 oz (315 g) spinach, tough stems removed

2 cans (15 oz/470 g each) black beans, drained and rinsed

2 cups (8 oz/250 g) finely shredded Monterey jack cheese

10 flour tortillas

2 avocados, halved, pitted, peeled, and sliced, for garnish (optional)

Enchiladas originated in Mexico, where they are typically made with corn tortillas and filled with a seemingly endless variety of meats, cheeses, or vegetables. For this vegetarian version, use soft flour tortillas instead and trade out the black beans for pinto beans and queso blanco, a good melting cow's milk cheese, for the jack cheese. If you like, pass a bowl of crema (tangy, lightly thickened cream) or sour cream at the table.

Preheat the broiler. Arrange the tomatillos and poblanos, cut side down, on a baking sheet. Broil until charred, about 7 minutes. Let cool briefly.

Working in batches, place the tomatillos, poblanos, two-thirds of the onions, the garlic, and 1 cup (1 oz/30 g) of the cilantro in a blender and purée. Transfer to a bowl and season with salt and pepper.

Preheat the oven to 350°F (180°C).

In a frying pan, heat the oil over medium-high heat. Add the remaining onions and the bell pepper and sauté until the onions are translucent, about 5 minutes. Add the cumin, season generously with salt, and stir to combine. Add the spinach in batches and cook, stirring occasionally, until wilted. Remove from the heat, tilt the pan, and using a spoon, press against the spinach and discard as much liquid as possible. Let the spinach cool slightly and transfer to a large bowl. Add the beans, 1 cup (4 oz/125 g) of the cheese, and ¾ cup (6 fl oz/180 ml) of the tomatillo sauce. Roughly chop the remaining cilantro leaves, add to the bowl, and stir to combine.

Cover the bottom of a 9-by-13-inch (23-by-3-cm) baking dish with a few tablespoons ⟫⟫

of the tomatillo sauce. Place ½ cup (4 fl oz/125 ml) of the spinach mixture on each tortilla, roll up tightly, and arrange, seam side down, in the dish. Cover the enchiladas with the remaining tomatillo sauce and sprinkle with the remaining 1 cup cheese.

Cover the dish with foil and bake for 30 minutes. Uncover and continue baking until the cheese is lightly browned, about 10 minutes. Top the enchiladas with the avocado slices, if using, and serve.

26

BRAISED FENNEL WITH PARMESAN

serves 4

4 fennel bulbs

⅓ cup (3 fl oz/80 ml) olive oil

Salt and freshly ground pepper

½ cup (4 fl oz/125 ml) chicken broth

⅓ cup (1½ oz/45 g) shaved Parmesan cheese

Fennel is native to the sunny Mediterranean, but thrives during the cool months of the year. Its delicate anise flavor lends itself to simple preparations: served thinly sliced and raw, baked, or braised, as here. Try it alongside fish, such as halibut or sea bass.

Cut the stalks and feathery leaves from each fennel bulb; discard or reserve for another use. Peel away the tough outer layer of the bulbs and then cut the bulbs lengthwise into wedges. If the cores seem very tough, trim them, but do not cut them away fully or the wedges will fall apart.

In a large frying pan, heat the oil over medium-high heat. Add the fennel, season with salt and pepper, and cook until browned on both sides, about 5 minutes.

Reduce the heat to low. Add the broth, cover, and cook until the fennel is tender, about 10 minutes. Transfer the fennel wedges to a bowl, sprinkle with the Parmesan, and serve.

27

PURÉED CELERY ROOT & POTATO GRATIN

serves 6

1 lb (500 g) celery root, peeled and cut into 1-inch (2.5-cm) cubes

1 lb (500 g) russet potatoes, peeled and cut into 1-inch (2.5-cm) cubes

Salt and freshly ground pepper

½ cup (4 fl oz/125 ml) heavy cream

¼ cup (2 fl oz/60 ml) whole milk

2 Tbsp unsalted butter

⅓ cup (1½ oz/45 g) grated Parmesan cheese

Celery root matches potatoes in starchiness, and adds a hint of celery flavor to this homey gratin. Instead of slicing and layering the root vegetables, this recipe whips the two together like a mash and bakes them to a crusty golden finish. Serve with seared lamb chops.

Preheat the oven to 400°F (200°C). Butter a baking dish.

In a saucepan, combine the celery root and potatoes. Add 1 tsp salt and water to cover by 2 inches (5 cm), and bring to a boil. Cover, reduce the heat to medium, and cook until the vegetables are very tender, 10–15 minutes.

Drain the vegetables thoroughly and return to the warm saucepan. Add the cream, milk, butter, and 1 tsp pepper. Using a potato masher or an electric mixer, beat until smooth and creamy. Spread the celery root mixture evenly in the prepared dish and sprinkle with the Parmesan.

Bake until the top is lightly browned, 15–20 minutes. Serve hot.

28

ROASTED CURRIED PARSNIPS

serves 4

2 Tbsp unsalted butter

1 lb (500 g) parsnips, peeled and cut lengthwise into slices ¼ inch (6 mm) thick

1 tsp Madras curry powder

Salt and freshly ground pepper

4 lime wedges

Parsnips are the forgotten root of the vegetable family, typically passed over in favor of their flashier golden carrot and ruby beet cousins. However, when roasted with aromatic spices, as they are here, they easily win new converts. The curry powder heightens the natural sweetness of the vegetable.

Preheat the oven to 400°F (200°C). Put the butter in a roasting pan just large enough to hold the parsnips in a single layer and place in the preheating oven. Watch carefully to prevent burning.

When the butter has melted, remove the pan from the oven, add the parsnip slices, and stir to coat them evenly. Sprinkle with the curry powder and season with salt and pepper. Stir again, and then spread the parsnips in a single layer. Roast the parsnips, stirring 2 or 3 times, until they are a rich gold and tender when pierced with a fork, 30–40 minutes.

Transfer the parsnips to a bowl and serve, passing the lime wedges at the table for diners to squeeze over the parsnips.

Early spring unfolds in stages. Little new potatoes, stubby fingerlings, baby carrots, spicy radishes, and sweet, cream-colored turnips ringed with violet are among the first vegetables to break ground. A steady chain of March showers encourages a wealth of earthy mushrooms to shoot up, from frilly oysters, apricot-hued chanterelles, and curling black trumpets to ridged, conical morels. Partner them with the season's first leeks, green onions, and shallots, all members of the Allium family.

march

1

MUSHROOMS WITH GARLIC BUTTER & PINE NUTS

serves 4

March showers bring wild mushrooms. Take in the season's offerings with a mix of flavors and textures. Oyster, shiitake, portobello, and cremini can all be readily found at the grocery store, but also look for chanterelles, porcini, matsutakes, black trumpets, and musky-flavored morels, a favorite of foragers.

1 lb (500 g) mixed mushrooms such as morel, portobello, shiitake, oyster, cremini, and white button, stems trimmed

4 Tbsp (2 oz/60 g) unsalted butter, at room temperature

3 cloves garlic, chopped

Salt and freshly ground pepper

2 Tbsp dry white wine

⅓ cup (2 oz/60 g) pine nuts or slivered blanched almonds

1–2 Tbsp chopped fresh chives or flat-leaf parsley

Preheat the oven to 450°F (230°C). Cut the larger mushrooms into pieces so that all the mushrooms, whole and cut, are about the same size. Arrange the mushrooms in a single layer in a large roasting pan.

In a bowl, mix together the butter and garlic to taste. Season with salt and pepper. Dot the mushrooms with the butter mixture. Sprinkle the wine over the mushrooms.

Roast the mushrooms until they begin to sizzle and brown, about 15 minutes. Remove from the oven, sprinkle with the pine nuts, and continue roasting until the mushrooms are cooked through and browned in places, about 10 minutes. The total roasting time depends on the types of mushrooms; certain varieties will take longer than others to cook. Adjust the seasoning if necessary.

Transfer the mushrooms to a bowl, sprinkle with the chives, and serve.

2

ROSEMARY-ROASTED FINGERLING POTATOES WITH WHOLE-GRAIN MUSTARD

serves 4

A moderately high temperature is ideal for roasting waxy potatoes such as fingerlings, red, or Yukon gold, as the intense heat nicely colors their skin. All these varieties hold their shape well, making them prime targets for tossing with dressings.

1 lb (500 g) fingerling or small red or Yukon gold potatoes, 1–2 inches (2.5–4 cm) in diameter

1 Tbsp chopped fresh rosemary

1 Tbsp olive oil

1 Tbsp whole-grain Dijon mustard

Salt and freshly ground pepper

Preheat the oven to 400°F (200°C).

If the potatoes are larger than 1½ inches (4 cm) in diameter, cut them in half. Arrange the potatoes in a single layer on a rimmed baking sheet. Sprinkle with the rosemary. In a small dish, stir together the oil and mustard. Drizzle the mixture over the potatoes. Season with salt and pepper. Toss to coat the potatoes and then spread them out evenly in the pan.

Roast the potatoes, turning them two or three times, until the skin is golden and the flesh is tender when pierced with a fork, 40–45 minutes.

Transfer the potatoes to a serving dish and serve.

3

BRAISED TURNIPS WITH PEAS & MUSHROOMS

serves 4

6 oz (185 g) white or cremini mushrooms, thinly sliced

2 cloves garlic, minced

Salt and freshly ground pepper

2 Tbsp chopped fresh flat-leaf parsley

2 tsp grapeseed or canola oil

4 small white turnips, about 1 lb (500 g) total, peeled and cut into ½-inch (12-mm) wedges

⅔ cup (5 fl oz/160 ml) chicken broth

1 cup (5 oz/155 g) frozen peas

Small turnips are mild, and simmering them with chicken broth helps to further mellow their taste. Cook the mushrooms separately over medium-high heat so they brown well. This recipe calls for frozen peas, but when spring arrives, make this dish with fresh peas for unrivaled seasonal flavor.

In a dry frying pan, sauté the mushrooms over medium-high heat until they release their liquid. Add the garlic and season with salt and pepper. Continue to cook until the liquid has evaporated and the mushrooms are tender, 3–5 minutes. Stir in the parsley and keep warm.

In a large frying pan, heat the oil over medium-high heat. Add the turnips, stir to coat with the oil, and sauté for 1 minute; do not let the turnips take on color.

Add ½ cup (4 fl oz/125 ml) of the broth. When it boils, reduce the heat to medium and cook the turnips for 3 minutes. Turn the turnips and continue to cook until the pan is almost dry. Add the remaining broth and cook until the turnips are fork-tender, about 3 minutes longer. Add the peas and cook for about 1 minute to heat through.

Transfer the turnips and peas to a bowl, top with the mushrooms, and serve.

4

LENTIL, POTATO & SPINACH CURRY

serves 4

1 cup (7 oz/220 g) small French green lentils, picked over and rinsed

1 carrot, cut into 3 pieces

1 celery rib, cut into 3 pieces

1 yellow onion, halved

5 fresh flat-leaf parsley sprigs

2 Tbsp canola oil

2 cloves garlic, minced

1 Tbsp garam masala

2 tsp ground cumin

1 tsp ground coriander

Salt and freshly ground pepper

2 large red potatoes, cut into 1-inch (2.5-cm) cubes

2 cups (3 oz/90 g) packed baby spinach

Cooked white or brown basmati rice for serving

¼ cup (2 oz/60 g) plain yogurt

This warming vegetarian curry features bright green spinach leaves. Chopped mustard greens or kale can be used instead. Serve with steamed basmati rice or toasted naan.

In a large, heavy pot, combine the lentils, carrot, celery, 1 onion half, and the parsley sprigs. Pour in 4 cups (32 fl oz/1 l) water and bring to a boil over medium-high heat. Reduce the heat to medium-low, cover, and simmer until the lentils are tender, about 35 minutes. Remove and discard the vegetables. Drain the lentils; reserve the lentils and cooking liquid separately.

In the pot, warm the oil over medium-high heat. Chop the remaining onion half then add it to the pan and sauté until browned, about 8 minutes. Add the garlic, garam masala, cumin, coriander, 1 tsp salt, and ¼ tsp pepper, and stir until the spices are toasted and fragrant, about 1 minute.

Add the potatoes, reserved lentils, and 2 cups (16 fl oz/500 ml) of the reserved cooking liquid (if necessary, use water to supplement). Bring to a boil, reduce the heat to medium-low, and simmer, covered, until the potatoes are tender, 15–18 minutes. Stir in the spinach and cook until it wilts, about 2 minutes. Season with salt and pepper. Serve the curry over the rice, garnished with the yogurt.

5

ASIAN EDAMAME, CUCUMBER & RED BELL PEPPER SALAD

serves 6

Toasted sesame seeds and sesame oil lend a nutty, earthy flavor and just a touch of bitterness to this colorful salad. In it, a sweet-sour-salty dressing inspired by Asian pickled vegetables melds with the mild taste of edamame, the coolness of cucumbers, and the satisfying crunch of red bell peppers. This is an easy recipe to prepare and a great vegetable dish to tote to a picnic.

½ cup (4 fl oz/125 ml) rice vinegar

4 tsp tamari

5 Tbsp (2½ oz/75 g) sugar

Salt and freshly ground pepper

⅓ cup (3 fl oz/80 ml) canola oil

2 tsp Asian sesame oil

1 lb (500 g) frozen shelled edamame, thawed

1½ English cucumbers, cut into ½-inch (12-mm) dice

2 red bell peppers, seeded and cut into ½-inch (12-mm) dice

3 Tbsp sesame seeds, toasted

In a bowl, whisk together the vinegar, tamari, sugar, 1½ tsp salt, and a few grinds of pepper until the sugar dissolves. Slowly whisk in the canola and sesame oils until well blended to make a dressing. Adjust the seasoning if necessary.

Pat the edamame dry with paper towels and place in a large bowl. Add the cucumbers and bell peppers.

Whisk the dressing and drizzle it over the vegetables. Sprinkle with the sesame seeds and toss well. Cover and refrigerate for at least 1 hour or up to 1 day to blend the flavors. To serve, drain the salad and discard the dressing. Transfer to a bowl and serve.

6

STEAMED ARTICHOKES WITH MEYER LEMON AIOLI

serves 4

Celebrate the start of artichoke season by steaming the globes and dunking the leaves in a tempting sauce. In Provence, this earthy vegetable is often served with aioli, the region's popular and addictive garlic-flavored mayonnaise.

FOR THE MEYER LEMON AIOLI

¼ cup (2 fl oz/60 ml) canola oil

¼ cup (2 fl oz/60 ml) extra-virgin olive oil

3 egg yolks

1 Tbsp Dijon mustard

3 cloves garlic

Salt and freshly ground white pepper

3–4 Tbsp fresh Meyer lemon juice

4 artichokes

½ lemon

To make the aioli, pour the canola and olive oils into a measuring cup with a spout. In a blender or food processor, combine the egg yolks, mustard, and garlic. Add ½ tsp salt and ¼ tsp pepper. Pulse several times until the garlic is pulverized. With the motor running, slowly add the oils in a steady stream. Stir in 3 Tbsp of the lemon juice. Stir in the remaining 1 Tbsp lemon juice if needed to thin the aioli; it should be the consistency of mayonnaise. Transfer to a bowl, cover, and refrigerate.

Cut off the stem of each artichoke flush with the base. Snap off the tough outer leaves. Cut off the top one-third of the artichoke, then cut the artichoke in half lengthwise. Rub the cut surfaces of each artichoke with the lemon half to prevent them from turning brown.

Select a wide saucepan large enough to hold the artichokes in a single layer. Place a steamer rack in the pan and add water to reach the bottom of the rack. Place the artichokes, cut side down, on the rack. Bring the water to a simmer over medium heat. Cover and cook until the base of an artichoke is easily pierced with a fork, about 20 minutes.

Transfer the artichokes to a platter. Serve warm, at room temperature, or chilled, passing the aioli at the table.

7

Although the fried prosciutto pieces that garnish this soup are small, their impact is big. The meaty richness of the famous ham creates chewy-crisp pockets of saltiness.

LEEK & YUKON GOLD POTATO SOUP WITH FRIED PROSCIUTTO

serves 6–8

8 leeks, about 4 lb (2 kg) total

¼ cup (2 fl oz/60 ml) olive oil

6 slices prosciutto, about 3 oz (90 g) total, cut into ribbons

Salt and freshly ground pepper

1½ tsp minced fresh thyme

2 Tbsp all-purpose flour

8 cups (64 fl oz/2 l) chicken broth

5 Yukon gold potatoes, about 2½ lb (1.25 kg) total, cut into 1-inch (2.5-cm) chunks

2 bay leaves

¼ cup (½ oz/15 g) minced fresh chives

Trim off and discard the dark green tops of the leeks. Cut the leeks in half lengthwise and then cut each half crosswise into pieces ½ inch (12 mm) thick.

In a large, heavy pot, warm the oil over medium heat. Add the prosciutto and sauté until crisp, about 6 minutes. Using a slotted spoon, transfer the prosciutto to paper towels to drain. Add the leeks and ½ tsp salt to the pot and stir to coat with the fat. Reduce the heat to medium-low, cover, and cook, stirring occasionally, until the leeks begin to soften, about 10 minutes. Add the thyme and the flour and cook, stirring constantly, until the flour is incorporated.

Raise the heat to medium-high and, stirring constantly, slowly add the broth. Add the potatoes and the bay leaves, season with pepper, cover, and bring to a boil. Reduce the heat to medium-low and simmer until the potatoes just start to become tender, about 6 minutes. Let stand, covered, off the heat until the potatoes are tender all the way through when pierced with a knife, about 15 minutes. Discard the bay leaves and return the soup to a simmer over medium-high heat. If desired, use the back of a large spoon to mash some of the potatoes against the side of the pot and stir them into the soup to thicken it.

Ladle the soup into bowls, garnish with the prosciutto and chives, and serve.

8

Gorgeonzola dolce is mild and creamy, making it perfect for this flavorful dip. Serve with a selection of colorful seasonal vegetables, such as crisp radishes, slender carrots, cauliflower florets, and asparagus. Snap peas, red pepper slices, and cucumber spears also make good accompaniments.

GORGONZOLA DIP WITH CRUDITÉS

serves 8

16 thin asparagus spears, ends trimmed

8 medium or 12 baby radishes with some green leaves attached

8 small or 4 medium carrots

1 cup (3 oz/90 g) cauliflower florets

12 green onions (optional)

5 oz (155 g) soft, creamy Gorgonzola cheese

¼ cup (2 fl oz/60 ml) heavy cream, or as needed

¼ tsp freshly ground pepper

Bring water to a boil in a steamer pan, put the asparagus in a steamer rack over the water, cover, and steam until tender-crisp, 3–4 minutes. Remove the asparagus from the pan and let cool completely. Cut the spears in half on the diagonal or leave whole.

Cut the radishes lengthwise into quarters or leave whole, depending on their size. Peel the carrots. Leave small carrots whole; halve larger carrots crosswise and then in half again lengthwise. Break or cut the cauliflower florets into small pieces. Trim the root ends and tough green tops off the green onions, if using.

In a small bowl, using a fork, mash together the cheese and cream, adding more cream if needed to make a good dipping consistency. Stir in the pepper.

Arrange the vegetables on a platter and serve with the dip.

9

TWO-PEA SAUTÉ WITH BASIL & PECORINO

serves 4

1 Tbsp unsalted butter

1 Tbsp olive oil

½ lb (250 g) sugar snap peas, strings removed

1 lb (500 g) English peas, shelled

Salt and freshly ground pepper

1 lemon

Leaves from 4 fresh basil sprigs, cut into thin ribbons

Small chunk pecorino romano cheese

A speedy sauté brings out the natural sweetness of sugar snap peas and enhances their crunch. Fresh English peas also gain an intriguing sweetness from quick cooking. In this recipe, the vegetable cousins are tossed with aniselike basil, tart lemon zest, and tangy pecorino cheese for a delicious, fast side.

In a large frying pan, melt the butter with the oil over medium heat. Add both types of peas, ¼ cup 2 fl oz/60 ml) water, and a pinch of salt. Cover and cook for 2 minutes. Uncover and sauté until the water evaporates, about 2 minutes. The peas should be tender-crisp and still bright green.

Finely grate 2 tsp zest from the lemon, then halve the lemon. Remove the pan from the heat and squeeze the juice from 1 lemon half over the peas (reserve the remaining half for another use). Add the lemon zest, basil, and a pinch each of salt and pepper. Grate some cheese over the top, stir well to mix, and serve.

10

LEEK, PANCETTA & GRUYÈRE TART

serves 4–6

2 Tbsp olive oil

2 leeks, white and pale green parts, sliced into rounds

2 slices pancetta, coarsely chopped

1 sheet frozen puff pastry, about ½ lb (250 g), thawed

½ cup (2 oz/60 g) shredded Gruyère cheese

½ tsp ground cumin

Easy, quick, and delicious, this tart goes together with just a handful of ingredients. It makes a wonderful first course, or cut into smaller pieces, an irresistible hors d'oeuvre. Comté, Emmentaler, or fontina can be substituted for the Gruyère. Look for all-butter puff pastry for the best flavor.

In a sauté pan, warm 1 Tbsp of the oil over medium heat. Add the leeks and sauté until softened, about 2 minutes. Transfer to a plate and set aside. In the same pan, warm the remaining 1 Tbsp oil over medium heat. Add the pancetta and cook, stirring occasionally, until browned, about 5 minutes. Using a slotted spoon, transfer to paper towels to drain and set aside.

Preheat the oven to 400°F (200°C). On a lightly floured work surface, roll out the pastry sheet into a 9-by-13-inch (23-by-33-cm) rectangle about ⅛ inch (3 mm) thick. Cut in half lengthwise to form 2 rectangles. Transfer the 2 rectangles to a rimmed baking sheet. Using a fork, prick each rectangle evenly over its entire surface. Fold in ½ inch (12 mm) along all 4 sides of each rectangle to create a border.

Arrange the leeks evenly on top of the pastry rectangles, and then sprinkle evenly with the Gruyère and pancetta. Bake until puffed and golden brown, about 20 minutes. Remove from oven, cut each tart into 4 pieces, and serve.

11

Baby carrots, seasoned with sweet and spicy ginger, glazed in butter and honey, and then garnished with mint, are a beautiful accompaniment to roast lamb or chicken. Use a fragrant honey, such as orange blossom or swap out the mint for thyme or tarragon. If you cannot find baby carrots, cut full-sized carrots into slender 3-inch (7.5-cm) lengths.

GINGERED BABY CARROTS

serves 4

2 Tbsp unsalted butter

1 Tbsp honey

1 Tbsp finely chopped crystallized ginger

1 lb (500 g) small, slender carrots

Salt and freshly ground pepper

2 Tbsp chopped fresh mint

2 tsp fresh lemon juice

Preheat the oven to 400°F (200°C). Put the butter in a roasting pan just large enough to hold the carrots in a single layer. Place in the preheating oven. Watch carefully to prevent the butter from burning. When the butter melts, remove the pan from the oven and stir in the honey and ginger. Add the carrots and stir to coat them evenly. Season with salt and pepper and sprinkle with 1½ Tbsp of the chopped mint. Stir again and then spread the carrots out in a single layer.

Roast the carrots, stirring two or three times, until golden, glazed, and tender when pierced with a fork, 35–45 minutes.

Remove the pan from the oven and season the carrots with salt and pepper. Sprinkle evenly with the remaining chopped mint and the lemon juice, toss to coat, and serve.

12

Cornichons are tart, salty, and full of briny flavor. Along with the mustard, they add zip to the tender potatoes and crunchy radishes and celery in this simple salad. A spoonful of crème fraîche on individual servings adds a luxurious touch.

POTATO & RADISH SALAD WITH MUSTARD-DILL VINAIGRETTE

serves 6

6 Tbsp (3 fl oz/90 ml) cider vinegar

7 cornichons, minced

¼ cup (⅓ oz/10 g) minced fresh dill, plus 2 Tbsp coarsely chopped

1 shallot, minced

3 Tbsp Dijon mustard

1 Tbsp sugar

Salt

½ cup (4 fl oz/125 ml) plus 1 Tbsp extra-virgin olive oil

Ice water

2 lb (1 kg) red new potatoes of uniform size

4 celery ribs, chopped

8 large radishes, finely chopped

⅓ cup (2½ oz/75 g) crème fraîche

In a small bowl, whisk together the vinegar, cornichons, minced dill, shallot, mustard, and sugar. Season with ½ tsp salt and stir until the sugar dissolves. Slowly whisk in the oil until well blended to make a vinaigrette.

Have ready a bowl of ice water. In a large saucepan, combine the potatoes, 1 Tbsp salt, and water to cover by 2 inches (5 cm) and bring to a boil. Reduce the heat to medium, cover partially, and simmer until the potatoes are just tender when pierced with a knife, 7–9 minutes.

Drain the potatoes and transfer to the ice water. Let stand until cool, then drain again. Cut each potato into quarters and transfer to a large bowl.

Whisk the vinaigrette and drizzle it over the potatoes. Add the celery and radishes and toss gently. Adjust the seasonings if necessary. Sprinkle with the chopped dill. Serve, passing the crème fraîche at the table.

13

BABY SPINACH WITH LEMON ZEST & CREAM

serves 4

1 cup (8 fl oz/250 ml) heavy cream

1 lemon

2 lb (1 kg) baby spinach

1 tsp sugar

Salt and freshly ground pepper

Lemon zest captures the fruit's bright flavor without any bitterness. Used first in strips to infuse the cream sauce, then finely grated and mixed with the cooked spinach, the layers of lemon lighten this rich, creamy dish.

Pour the cream into a saucepan. Using a vegetable peeler, peel 2 strips of zest, each 2 inches (5 cm) long, from the lemon. Reserve the lemon. Add the zest strips to the cream and bring to a simmer over medium heat. Simmer the cream, stirring occasionally, until reduced by half, about 8 minutes; watch that the cream does not boil too vigorously. Remove the zest strips and discard. Remove the cream from the heat.

Heat a large frying pan over medium heat. Add the spinach, sprinkle with the sugar, toss well, cover, and cook for 3 minutes. Uncover, toss the leaves well, and continue to cook, uncovered, until the spinach is wilted and tender, 1–2 minutes.

Transfer the spinach to a colander and press on it firmly with a wooden spoon to remove all the excess liquid. Chop the drained spinach coarsely and add it to the pan with the reduced cream. Finely grate the remaining zest from the lemon and add to the spinach (reserve the fruit for another use). Season the spinach with a pinch of salt and about ½ tsp pepper and stir well to combine. Place over medium heat and cook, stirring occasionally, until just heated through, 2–3 minutes. Transfer the spinach to a bowl and serve.

14

BROCCOLINI WITH GARLIC & ANCHOVIES

serves 6

2 bunches broccolini, about 10 oz (315 g) each, ends trimmed

2 Tbsp olive oil

2 large cloves garlic, thinly sliced

Pinch of red pepper flakes

6 olive oil–packed anchovy fillets

2 Tbsp capers, rinsed and drained

Broccolini, with its slim stems and small flowering heads, has a sweet flavor, and requires only minimal trimming. Here, it is prepared in the style of southern Italy, with garlic, anchovies, and capers. Serve alongside a big dish of pasta and pour a tart Pinot Grigio.

Bring a large pot of salted water to a boil. Add the broccolini and cook for 2 minutes. Drain and rinse under cold running water. Drain again.

In a large frying pan, warm the oil over medium heat. Add the garlic and red pepper flakes and sauté until the garlic is lightly golden, about 2 minutes. Add the anchovies and capers and stir until the anchovies dissolve, 1–2 minutes.

Add the broccolini and stir gently to coat with the oil. Cover and cook until the broccolini is tender, 5–10 minutes. Transfer the broccolini to a platter and serve.

15

FLASH-FRIED BOK CHOY

serves 6–8

1 Tbsp Asian sesame oil

10 heads baby bok choy, halved lengthwise

1 cup (8 fl oz/250 ml) chicken broth

2 cloves garlic, thinly sliced

1 Tbsp soy sauce

½ tsp red pepper flakes

Halved or quartered baby bok choy heads wilt in a flash in a hot wok. Start a pot of rice, get some teriyaki chicken or salmon broiling, and then cook the bok choy just before everything goes to the table.

Heat a wok or frying pan over high heat. Add the sesame oil and heat until the oil shimmers. Add the bok choy and cook, stirring and tossing constantly, until it starts to wilt on the leafy ends, about 2 minutes. Add the broth, garlic, and soy sauce, bring to a simmer, and cook until the greens are just tender when pierced with a knife, 2–3 minutes. Stir in the red pepper flakes. Transfer to a platter and serve.

16

CARROT-ZUCCHINI LATKES WITH PEAR-APPLE SAUCE

serves 4–6

This is a beautiful dish with lots of possibilities for serving. For an appetizer, serve small latkes with a glass of Prosecco. Or, prepare bigger latkes as a main course alongside grilled vegetables. This recipe also works well as a side dish with thick-cut grilled pork chops. You can make the apple-pear sauce a couple days ahead. Don't fry the latkes until just before serving time, as they tend to get soggy when made too far in advance.

FOR THE PEAR-APPLE SAUCE

3 Anjou pears, peeled, cored, and chopped

2 Granny Smith apples, peeled, cored, and chopped

1 cup (8 fl oz/250 ml) apple juice

3 Tbsp sugar

3 large carrots

3 small zucchini

1 small yellow onion

2 eggs, beaten

¼ cup (1½ oz/45 g) all-purpose flour, plus more as needed

Salt and freshly ground pepper

2 Tbsp unsalted butter

¼ cup (2 oz/60 g) sour cream (optional)

To make the pear-apple sauce, combine the pears, apples, apple juice, and sugar in a heavy pot. Bring to a boil over medium heat, reduce the heat to low, partially cover, and simmer, stirring occasionally, until the fruit is tender, about 15 minutes. Let cool completely in the pan. Transfer to a food processor and pulse to form a chunky sauce. Pour into a small bowl.

Grate the carrots, zucchini, and onion on the large holes of a grater-shredder. Place the vegetables on a kitchen towel, wrap up tightly, and squeeze to remove the excess water. Transfer to a large bowl. Add the eggs, ¼ cup flour, 1 tsp salt, and ½ tsp pepper and mix to combine well.

Heat a frying pan over medium-high heat. Add 1½ tsp of the butter and melt. Add 2 heaping Tbsp of the batter and cook, turning once, until golden brown, about 4 minutes per side. If the latke does not hold together, add 1 tsp flour to the batter, mix well, and cook another latke. Add more butter to the pan as needed and fry the latkes in batches, transferring them to a plate as they are done.

Serve the latkes with the pear-apple sauce and the sour cream, if using.

17

BALSAMIC-BRAISED RED CABBAGE

serves 4–6

The honeyed, mildly tangy quality of balsamic vinegar stands in for harsher red wine vinegar in this new twist on a classic recipe. Green apples lend both sweetness and brightness, red wine adds depth, and a sprinkle of orange zest contributes tartness to this hearty side dish.

3 Tbsp olive oil

1 yellow onion, thinly sliced

Salt and freshly ground pepper

1 Tbsp honey

1 tart green apple such as Granny Smith, halved, cored, and thinly sliced

¼ cup (2 fl oz/60 ml) balsamic vinegar

1 cup (8 fl oz/250 ml) dry red wine

1 head red cabbage, about 2 lb (1 kg), cored and finely shredded

1 orange

In a large frying pan, warm the oil over medium heat. Add the onion and a pinch of salt and sauté until the onion is soft and translucent, 5–7 minutes. Add the honey and cook for 1 minute. Add the apple slices and vinegar, raise the heat to medium-high, and scrape up any browned bits from the bottom of the pan. Bring the liquid to a boil, and add the wine and 1 cup (8 fl oz/ 250 ml) water. Season with a generous pinch each of salt and pepper, and bring to a boil. Reduce the heat to medium-low and simmer until the liquid begins to reduce, about 10 minutes.

Add the cabbage and toss well to coat with the liquid in the pan. Cover and cook the cabbage, stirring occasionally, until it begins to wilt, 25–30 minutes. Uncover and cook until the cabbage is tender and most of the liquid has evaporated, 25–30 minutes.

Remove the pan from the heat and finely grate the zest from the orange over the cabbage (reserve the fruit for another use). Stir well, transfer the cabbage to a bowl, and serve.

18

Carrots and jicama, both crunchy and juicy, are a winning combination in this citrusy salad, which is light on calories and offers lots of fiber. Serve as an accompaniment to a smoked turkey sandwich or grilled chicken, shrimp, or fish.

CARROT & JICAMA SALAD WITH LIME VINAIGRETTE

serves 4–6

2 tsp ground cumin

3 Tbsp fresh lime juice

2 Tbsp canola oil

1 Tbsp seeded and minced jalapeño chile

1 tsp minced garlic

Salt

1 large or 2 medium jicamas, about ¾ lb (375 g) total

3 carrots, about 10 oz (315 g) total

¼ cup (⅓ oz/10 g) finely chopped fresh cilantro

In a small, dry frying pan, warm the cumin over medium-low heat just until fragrant, about 20 seconds. Transfer to a small bowl. Add the lime juice, oil, jalapeño, garlic, and ½ tsp salt and whisk until blended to make a vinaigrette.

Trim the stem and root ends from the jicama and then cut into 4 or 6 wedges. Cut and lift up a small piece of the brown skin near the stem end and pull down to remove. Use a vegetable peeler to remove any tenacious pieces of skin and the tough layer underneath.

Using a food processor fitted with the shredding disk or the large holes on a grater-shredder, shred the jicama and carrots. In a large bowl, combine the jicama, carrots, and cilantro. Pour the vinaigrette over the vegetables, toss gently to mix, and serve.

19

Sturdy, assertive greens take well to braising, and white wine and olives match the bold flavor of broccoli rabe. This is a versatile side dish, pairing well with sausages, roast chicken, or pork chops, or you can toss it with cooked pasta or scrambled eggs.

WHITE WINE–BRAISED BROCCOLI RABE WITH OLIVES

serves 4

1¼ lb (625 g) broccoli rabe, tough stems removed

2 large cloves garlic, minced

3 Tbsp olive oil

½ cup (2½ oz/75 g) coarsely chopped cured black olives

2 olive oil–packed anchovy fillets, finely chopped

1 small fresh hot chile, seeded and minced, or generous pinch of red pepper flakes

1 cup (8 fl oz/250 ml) dry white wine

Salt

Bring a large saucepan of water to a boil. Add the broccoli rabe and cook just until wilted, 3–4 minutes. Drain and let cool for 5 minutes. Chop very coarsely.

In a large frying pan, warm the garlic in the oil over medium-low heat, stirring often, until the garlic is softened but not browned, about 7 minutes. Stir in the olives, anchovies, and chile and sauté until fragrant, about 1 minute.

Increase the heat to medium and add the broccoli rabe to the pan, stirring to combine with the olives and anchovies. Pour in the wine, raise the heat to medium-high, and bring to a simmer. Reduce the heat to medium-low, cover partially, and cook until the broccoli rabe is tender and most of the liquid is absorbed, 15–20 minutes. Season with salt, if needed, and serve.

SPRING ONIONS & ASPARAGUS WITH ROMESCO SAUCE

serves 4

Fat and juicy spring onions resemble giant green onions. When cooked over a charcoal fire, they become deliciously charred and prime candidates for pairing with grilled asparagus and accompanying them both with nut-thickened, spicy romesco sauce. Leeks can be substituted for the spring onions but only if they are pencil-thin and tender.

FOR THE ROMESCO SAUCE

2 ancho chiles

Boiling water

2 red bell peppers

1 ripe tomato

1 Tbsp olive oil

1 slice coarse country bread, crust removed

2 large cloves garlic, chopped

¼ cup (1½ oz/45 g) almonds, toasted

¼ cup (1½ oz/45 g) hazelnuts, toasted and skinned

1 Tbsp red wine vinegar

1 tsp sweet paprika, preferably Spanish

¼ tsp cayenne pepper

Salt and freshly ground black pepper

16 spring onions or thin baby leeks, about ¾ inch (2 cm) in diameter

16 thick asparagus spears, ends trimmed

¼ cup (2 fl oz/60 ml) extra-virgin olive oil

Salt and freshly ground black pepper

To make the sauce, preheat the oven to 500°F (260°C).

Place the ancho chiles in a heatproof bowl, pour in boiling water to cover, and soak until softened, about 20 minutes.

Place the bell peppers and tomato on a baking sheet. Roast until the tomato is soft but still holds its shape, about 10 minutes. Using tongs, transfer the tomato to a bowl, cover, and let steam. Continue roasting the bell peppers until they are soft but still hold their shape, 25–30 minutes longer.

Peel and seed the tomato, chop it coarsely, and place in a blender or food processor. Drain the chiles and remove the stems, seeds, and ribs. Gently scrape away the skin and add the flesh to the blender. When the bell peppers are done, transfer them to the bowl that held the tomato, cover, and let steam for 20 minutes. Peel, seed, and chop the bell peppers coarsely. Add to the blender. ⇻

In a small frying pan, warm the oil over medium heat. Add the bread and fry, turning once, until crisp and golden, 3–5 minutes. Let cool slightly. Break into pieces and add to the blender. Add the garlic, almonds, hazelnuts, vinegar, paprika, and cayenne and process to a coarse purée. Season with salt and black pepper. Pour into a bowl.

Prepare a charcoal or gas grill for direct-heat grilling over high heat. Oil the grill rack.

Trim the roots from the onions or leeks. Trim off the top 1–2 inches (2.5–5 cm) of the greens. Bring a saucepan of salted water to a boil. Add the onions and cook until tender-crisp, 8–12 minutes. If using leeks, cook until the white part yields but is not soft when squeezed, 5–8 minutes. Drain and rinse under cold running water. Drain again.

Refill the saucepan with salted water and return to a boil. Add the asparagus and cook until bright green, about 3 minutes. Drain and rinse under cold running water. Drain again.

Brush the onions or leeks and asparagus lightly with the oil and season with salt and pepper. Place on the grill rack and grill, turning as needed, until the asparagus spears are well browned and charred in places and the onions or leeks are blackened on the outside and tender inside. Transfer the asparagus and onions or leeks to a platter. Serve, passing the romesco sauce at the table.

21

WASABI-CHIVE MASHED POTATOES

serves 4

4 large russet potatoes, about 3½ lb (1.75 kg) total, peeled and quartered

Salt and freshly ground pepper

4 Tbsp (2 oz/60 g) unsalted butter

½ cup (4 fl oz/125 ml) heavy cream

½ cup (4 fl oz/125 ml) whole milk

2–3 tsp wasabi paste or powder

¼ cup (⅓ oz/10 g) minced fresh chives

Potent wasabi paste elevates plain mashed potatoes— just a couple of small spoonfuls adds a lot of fire. Pungent chives lend another boost of flavor as well as vibrant color. Rich cream and butter help all the ingredients shine.

Place the potatoes in a saucepan. Add a generous pinch of salt and water to cover. Bring to a boil, reduce the heat to low, and cook until the potatoes are tender when pierced with knife but not falling apart, 20–30 minutes.

Meanwhile, in a small saucepan, warm the butter, cream, and milk over medium-low heat, stirring to melt the butter. Add 2 tsp of the wasabi paste and a pinch each of salt and pepper and stir well. For a bolder, spicier flavor, add the remaining 1 tsp wasabi paste. Keep warm off the heat.

Drain the potatoes and return them to the hot pan. Place the pan over medium heat and cook for 1–2 minutes to cook away any remaining moisture. Transfer the potatoes to a stand mixer fitted with the paddle attachment, and mix on low speed just to break them up. Gradually increase the speed to medium and continue to mix. When the potatoes are almost smooth, turn off the mixer and add half of the warm milk mixture. Mix on medium speed to blend, adding more of the milk mixture as needed to achieve a creamy consistency.

Stir the chives into the potatoes. Adjust the seasoning if necessary, and serve.

22

CELERY & HERB SALAD WITH HARD-BOILED EGGS & ANCHOVY VINAIGRETTE

serves 4

FOR THE VINAIGRETTE

1 small shallot, chopped

1 Tbsp Dijon mustard

Juice of 1 lemon

4 olive oil–packed anchovy fillets

Salt and freshly ground pepper

½ cup (4 fl oz/125 ml) extra-virgin olive oil

1 head celery, leaves trimmed, ribs thinly sliced

1 bunch radishes, trimmed and thinly sliced

½ cup (¾ oz/20 g) coarsely chopped fresh flat-leaf parsley

2 Tbsp coarsely chopped fresh tarragon

2 Tbsp coarsely chopped fresh dill

Salt and freshly ground pepper

4 eggs, hard-boiled and halved or quartered lengthwise

This refreshingly crisp and flavorful salad would be wonderful served as part of a buffet along with grilled fish or chicken. The recipe calls for parsley, dill, and tarragon, but you can use any combination of fresh leafy herbs you have on hand, such as cilantro, basil, and mint.

To make the vinaigrette, combine the shallot, mustard, lemon juice, anchovies, ½ tsp salt, and ¼ tsp pepper in a blender. Purée until smooth. With the motor running, add the oil in a slow, steady stream and process until blended.

In a large bowl, combine the celery, radishes, parsley, tarragon, and dill. Drizzle with some of the vinaigrette and toss to coat. Transfer to a platter and nestle the eggs in the salad. Using a spoon, top each egg with some of the vinaigrette, season with pepper, and serve, passing additional vinaigrette at the table.

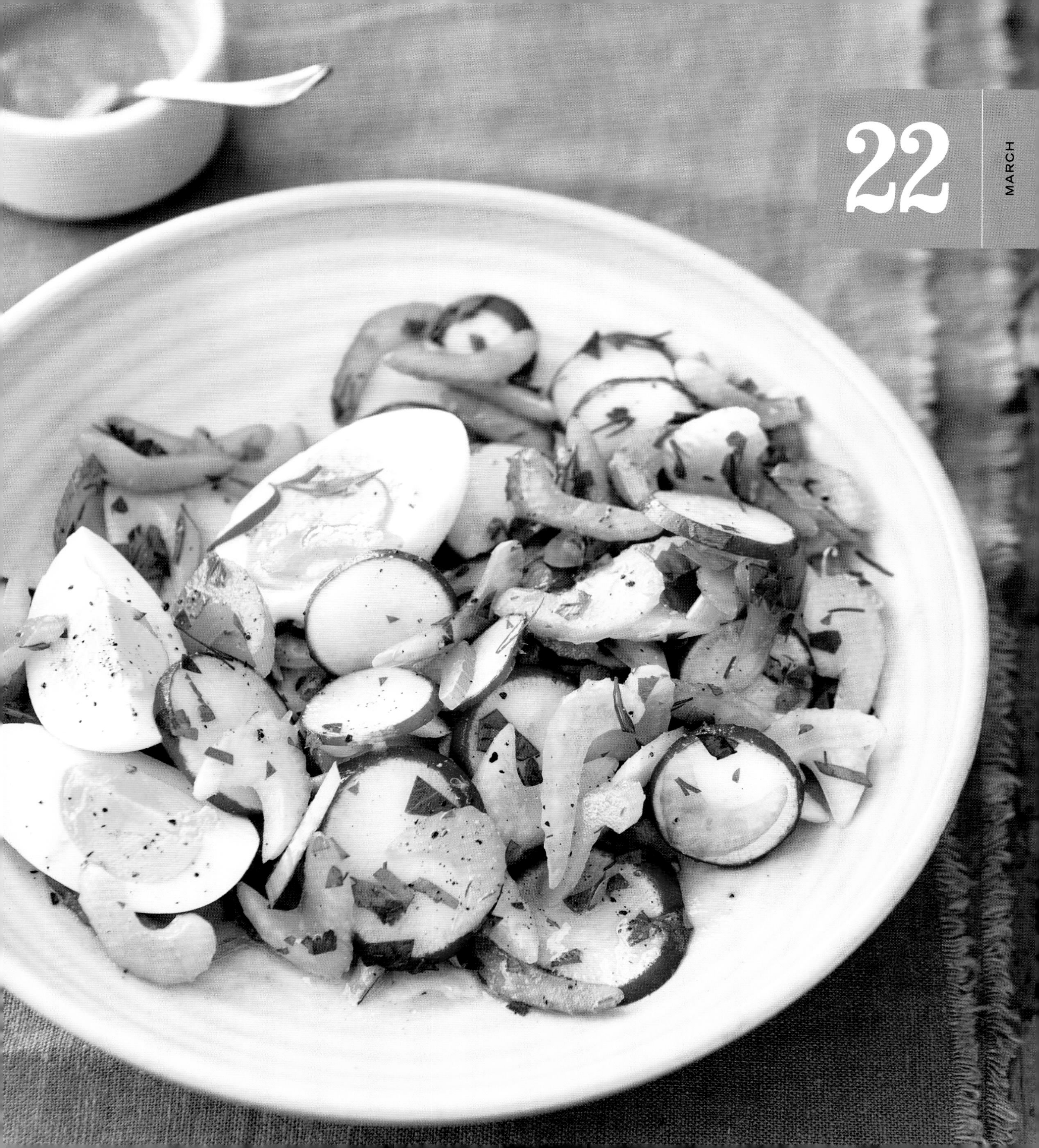

23

French, Italians, Greeks, and others around the Mediterranean eat artichokes both raw and cooked. This salad uses raw artichokes, which must be freshly harvested and not too large. Slice them as thinly as possible for the best flavor and texture. Choose a high-quality, not-too-piquant blue cheese, such as Gorgonzola, Roquefort, Saga, or Cambozola.

SHAVED ARTICHOKES WITH BLUE CHEESE DRESSING

serves 4

2 lemons, halved

8 small to medium artichokes

4 Tbsp (2 fl oz/60 ml) extra-virgin olive oil

¼ cup (½ oz/15 g) frisée

Salt and freshly ground pepper

2 Tbsp crumbled blue cheese

⅓ cup (2 oz/60 g) almonds, toasted and chopped

Squeeze the juice of 2 lemon halves into a large bowl of cold water, then add the spent halves. Snap off the tough outer leaves of each artichoke until you reach the tender inner leaves. Using a small knife, trim the dark green portions from the stem and base and trim the stem. Cut 1 inch (2.5 cm) off the top of the artichoke. Halve the artichoke lengthwise. Using a small spoon, remove the fuzzy choke from each half. As each artichoke is trimmed, add it to the lemon water.

When all of the artichokes are trimmed, drain them, pat them dry, and thinly slice them lengthwise. Put them in a bowl, drizzle with 2 Tbsp of the oil, and toss well. Add the frisée and season with salt and pepper. Drizzle with the remaining 2 Tbsp oil, squeeze in the juice from the remaining 2 lemon halves, and toss gently. Adjust with more salt if necessary.

Transfer to a platter, scatter the blue cheese and almonds over the top, and serve.

24

This quick, flavorful spring side dish brings together three elements that make a beautiful composition on the plate. The orange zest will caramelize deliciously. Be sure to stir the asparagus once or twice during roasting to keep the zest from burning.

ROASTED ASPARAGUS WITH WALNUTS & ORANGE ZEST

serves 4

1½ lb (750 g) asparagus, ends trimmed

1 Tbsp olive oil

1 Tbsp thin orange zest strips

Salt

¼ cup (1 oz/30 g) chopped walnuts, toasted

Preheat the oven to 425°F (220°C).

Place the asparagus spears in a baking dish. Sprinkle with the oil, orange zest, and ⅛ tsp salt. Toss to coat and mix well. Spread the asparagus in a single layer.

Roast the asparagus, stirring well once or twice, until tender when pierced with a knife, about 10 minutes.

Transfer to a platter, sprinkle with the toasted walnuts, and serve.

CARROT & CUMIN TART

serves 4–6

Toasty cumin seeds can complement either savory or sweet dishes, making them an ideal companion for spring carrots, which possess both qualities. The thinly sliced carrots are layered with grated cheese and a rich custard to make this tart a memorable main course. Blind baking the pastry ensures a golden, flaky crust.

FOR THE TART PASTRY

1½ cups (7½ oz/235 g) all-purpose flour

Salt

10 Tbsp (5 oz/155 g) chilled unsalted butter, cut into small pieces

4–5 Tbsp (2–2½ fl oz/60–75 ml) ice water

2 Tbsp unsalted butter

5 or 6 green onions, white and tender green parts, thinly sliced

Salt and freshly ground pepper

½ tsp sugar

3–4 cups (12–16 oz/ 375–500 g) thinly sliced carrots

½ tsp cumin seeds

2 eggs, plus 1 egg yolk

1⅓ cups (11 fl oz/340 ml) heavy cream

Pinch of freshly grated nutmeg or ground mace

1½ cups (6 oz/185 g) shredded Gruyère, Emmentaler, or Jarlsberg cheese

To make the pastry, in a bowl, stir together the flour and ½ tsp salt. Add the butter and, using a pastry blender or 2 knives, cut the butter into the flour until the mixture has the consistency of coarse crumbs. Slowly add the ice water, stirring and tossing with a fork until the dough just holds together. Gently form the dough into a ball, flatten into a disk, place in a plastic bag, and refrigerate for at least 30 minutes.

Preheat the oven to 400°F (200°C).

On a floured work surface, roll the dough into a 14-inch (35-cm) round. Transfer to a 9- or 9½-inch (23- or 24-cm) tart pan, preferably with a removable bottom. Ease the dough into the pan and trim off any excess. Press the dough against the sides to extend it slightly above and just over the rim, so that a tiny lip of pastry rests on the rim.

Line the pastry with a sheet of parchment paper and weigh it down with pie weights or dried beans. Bake until just set, about 10 minutes. Remove the weights and parchment. Prick the bottom of the crust with a fork and continue to bake until the crust sets and colors slightly, 5–10 minutes. Let cool on a wire rack. ⟩⟩

To make the filling, heat a large frying pan over medium heat until hot but not smoking. Add the butter. When it begins to foam, add the green onions and sauté until wilted, about 1 minute. Season with salt and pepper. Remove from the heat.

Bring a saucepan of salted water to a boil. Add the sugar and the carrots and cook until the carrots are bright orange, 1–2 minutes. Drain and let cool. In a small frying pan, toast the cumin seeds over medium heat until fragrant, 2–3 minutes. Pour onto a plate and let cool.

In a bowl, whisk together the whole eggs, egg yolk, cream, and nutmeg until blended. Season with salt and pepper.

Position a rack in the upper third of the oven and preheat to 375°F (180°C). Place a baking sheet on the rack below to catch any drips.

Sprinkle half of the cheese evenly over the bottom of the cooled pastry crust. Arrange as many of the carrot slices on the crust as will fit tightly, sprinkling them with the cumin and green onions as you add them. Pour the cream mixture over the carrots, filling the tart pan almost to the rim. Top with the remaining cheese.

Bake until the top is golden brown and the filling is set, 25–30 minutes. Let the tart stand for at least 10 minutes. Remove the pan sides, if necessary, and serve.

MARCH 26

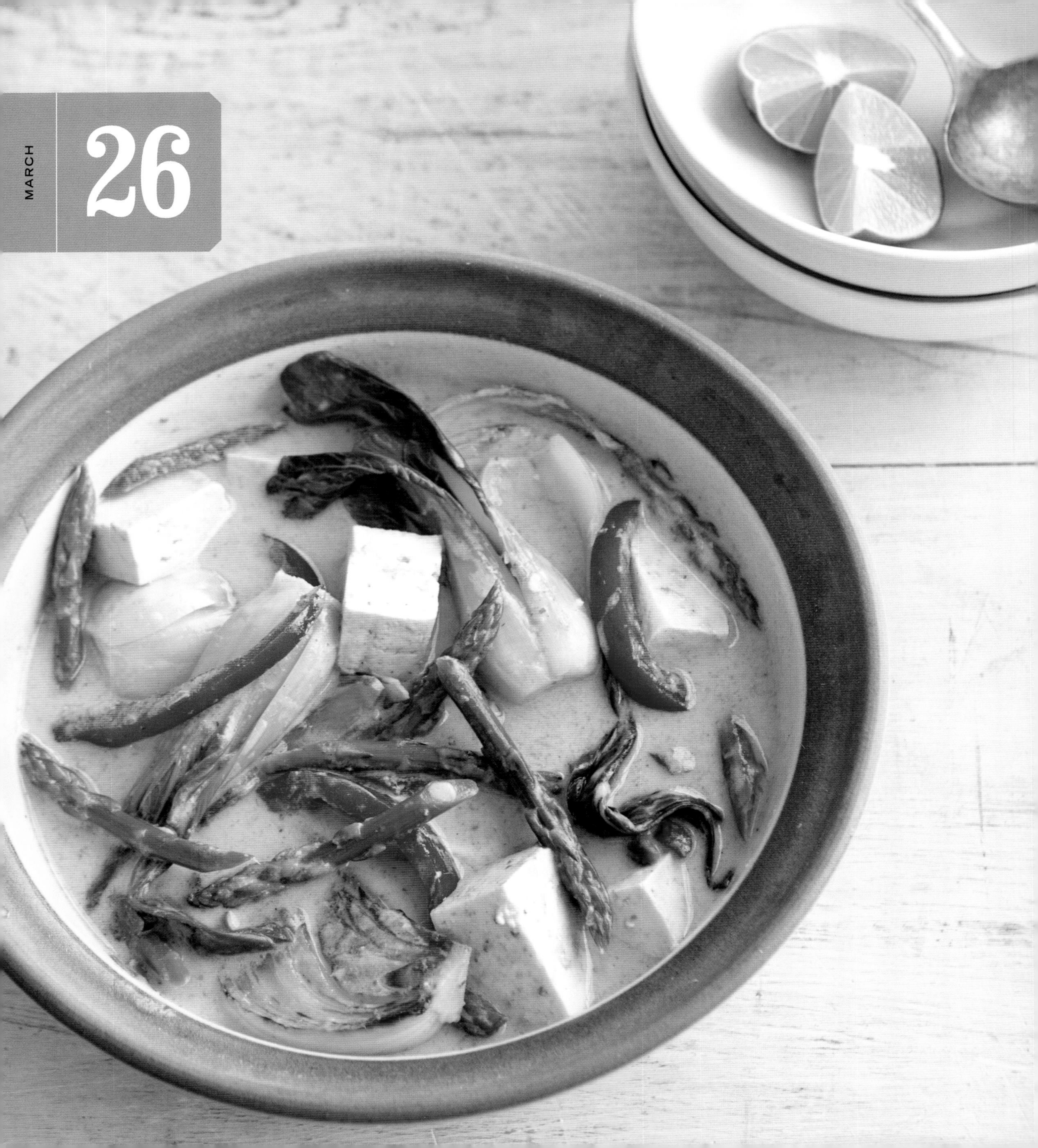

26
MARCH

Thai green curry paste has an incredibly bold, concentrated taste as well as a spicy heat. Here, it is tempered by rich, creamy coconut milk. A sprinkle of fragrant Thai basil over the curry just before serving adds a freshness that perks up all of the complex flavors in the dish.

THAI GREEN CURRY WITH TOFU, ASPARAGUS & BABY BOK CHOY

serves 4–6

1½ lb (750 g) asparagus, ends trimmed

3 baby bok choy, halved lengthwise

2 Tbsp peanut or grape seed oil

1 yellow onion, cut into 8 wedges

1 red bell pepper, seeded and cut into strips 1½ inches (4 cm) long and ¼ inch (6 mm) wide

1-inch (2.5-cm) piece fresh ginger, peeled and minced

2 cloves garlic, thinly sliced

1 can (14 oz/430 ml) coconut milk

3 Tbsp Thai green curry paste

1 cup (8 fl oz/250 ml) chicken or vegetable broth

2 Tbsp Asian fish sauce

1 lb (500 g) firm tofu, cut into 1-inch (2.5-cm) cubes

½ cup (½ oz/15 g) loosely packed fresh Thai basil leaves

1 lime, cut into 8 wedges

Bring a saucepan of lightly salted water to a boil over high heat. Add the asparagus and bok choy and cook just until tender-crisp, about 2 minutes. Drain well and rinse under cold running water until cool. Pat dry.

Heat the oil in a large heavy-bottomed saucepan over medium-high heat until hot. Add the onion and bell pepper and sauté, stirring occasionally, until the vegetables begin to soften, about 4 minutes. Stir in the ginger and garlic and sauté until fragrant, about 30 seconds. Transfer the mixture to a plate. Take care to remove all the garlic and ginger from the pan or it will burn, creating a bitter curry.

Open the can of coconut milk (do not shake it) and scoop out 3 Tbsp of the thick coconut cream on the top. Return the pan to medium-high heat. Add the coconut cream and curry paste to the frying pan and stir well. Whisk in the remaining coconut cream and milk, the broth, and the fish sauce. Return the vegetable mixture to the pan, stir in the tofu, and bring to a gentle boil. Reduce the heat to medium-low and simmer briskly, stirring occasionally, until the sauce has reduced slightly and the vegetables are tender-crisp, about 5 minutes. Stir in the ⇒

reserved asparagus and bok choy and cook until heated through, about 3 minutes. Adjust the seasoning if necessary.

Scatter the basil over the curry. Divide the curry evenly among bowls and serve. Pass the lime wedges at the table.

27
MARCH

When permitted, pop open a peapod and taste before you buy. Choose peas that are tender and sweet rather than starchy. A garnish of crème fraîche adds a silky smoothness and tart flavor to this soup, while sorrel gives it a lemony tang. As days warm up, you can also opt to serve this soup cold: cool it to room temperature, cover, and chill for up to 1 day.

SWEET PEA SOUP WITH SORREL

serves 4

3 lb (1.5 kg) peas

3½ cups (28 fl oz/875 ml) chicken broth

2 Tbsp olive oil

1 cup (3 oz/90 g) thinly sliced leeks

Salt and freshly ground pepper

½ cup (½ oz/15 g) packed sorrel leaves

¼ cup (2 oz/60 g) crème fraîche

Remove the peas from the pods. Reserve 3–4 handfuls of the freshest-looking pods. Rinse the pods well and coarsely chop. In a saucepan, combine the broth and pods and bring to a boil. Reduce the heat to low, cover, and simmer for 15 minutes. Strain the broth into a bowl and discard the pods.

In a large pot, warm the oil over medium heat. Add the leeks and ½ tsp salt and cook, stirring frequently and reducing the heat as necessary to keep the leeks from browning, until softened, 5–8 minutes. Add the peas, broth, and ½ cup (4 fl oz/125 ml) water and bring to a boil. Reduce the heat to low and simmer, uncovered, until the peas are tender, 8–10 minutes. Stir in the sorrel and cook until wilted, about 1 minute.

Working in batches, purée the soup in a blender or food processor. Season with salt and pepper. Ladle into bowls, garnish with the crème fraîche, and serve.

28

ARTICHOKE BOTTOMS WITH WARM CANNELLINI BEAN SALAD

serves 4

1 cup (7 oz/220 g) dried cannellini beans, picked over and rinsed, then soaked overnight in water to cover and drained

6 cups (48 fl oz/1.5 l) chicken broth

4 fresh rosemary sprigs

4 fresh thyme sprigs

4 cloves garlic, crushed

Salt and freshly ground pepper

2 lemons, halved

4 large artichokes

1 bay leaf

½ cup (4 fl oz/125 ml) extra-virgin olive oil

1 Tbsp white wine vinegar

1 Tbsp minced fresh chives

16 marinated white anchovy fillets

1 cup (3 oz/90 g) shaved pecorino cheese

½ cup (½ oz/15 g) fresh flat-leaf parsley leaves

During their high season, devour artichokes in as many ways as possible. In this salad, the tender hearts are paired with buttery white beans and a quartet of fresh herbs. Artichokes and chicken have a special affinity, which makes this a great salad to serve with a roast bird.

In a large saucepan, combine the beans, broth, 2 of the rosemary sprigs, 2 of the thyme sprigs, and 2 of the garlic cloves. Season well with salt and pepper. Bring to a boil, reduce the heat to medium-low, cover partially, and simmer until the beans are tender, about 1 hour. Let the beans cool in the cooking liquid and then drain.

Meanwhile, fill a bowl with water and squeeze in the juice from the lemons. Cut off the stem of each artichoke flush with the base. Snap off the tough outer leaves until you reach the tender inner leaves. Using a vegetable peeler, trim off the stringy layers where the stem and leaves were removed. As each artichoke is trimmed, drop it in the lemon water.

Drain the artichokes, transfer to a saucepan, and add water to cover. Add the bay leaf and the remaining rosemary sprigs, thyme sprigs, and garlic cloves. Season with 1 tsp salt. Bring to a boil, reduce the heat to a simmer, and cook until the artichoke bottoms are tender when pierced with a knife, 20–30 minutes. Let cool in the cooking liquid. ⟫

In a large bowl, whisk together the oil and vinegar. Add the drained beans and chives and toss to combine. Season with salt and pepper.

Remove the artichokes from the cooking liquid and pat dry. Using a spoon, scoop out and discard the furry chokes. Place the artichokes on plates. Top with the bean mixture. Garnish with the anchovies, pecorino, and parsley, and serve.

29

SAUTÉED NEW POTATOES WITH SPRING PEAS

serves 6

2 lb (1 kg) small new potatoes of uniform size such as fingerlings, red, or white

Salt and freshly ground pepper

2 cups (10 oz/315 g) shelled young peas

2 Tbsp unsalted butter

2 Tbsp olive oil

5 or 6 green onions, white and tender green parts, thinly sliced

New potatoes, the first potatoes dug in spring and early summer, are low in starch, with thin, tender skins and delicate flesh. Small round red or white potatoes (also called creamers), fingerlings, and Yellow Finns are among the most common varieties available as new potatoes. Unlike mature potatoes, new potatoes should be eaten within a few days of purchase. If you like, substitute sugar snap or snow peas for the English peas.

Put the potatoes in a large saucepan with water to cover by 2 inches (5 cm). Add a large pinch of salt. Bring to a boil, reduce the heat to medium, and cook until the potatoes are tender when pierced with a knife, 15–20 minutes. Drain the potatoes.

Bring a saucepan of water to a boil. Add a pinch each of salt and sugar and the peas, and cook until the peas turn bright green, about 30 seconds. Drain and rinse under cold running water.

In a frying pan, melt the butter with the oil over medium-low heat. Add the green onions and sauté until wilted, about 3 minutes. Add the potatoes and peas and toss together until heated through, about 5 minutes. Season with salt and pepper and serve.

30

In cooking, celery, which is high in vitamins C and K, is more often treated as a healthful bit player than as the star of a dish. Here, it takes central stage in a simple braise that showcases its fresh, bright flavor.

BRAISED CELERY WITH LEMON

serves 4–6

2 lb (1 kg) celery

1½ cups (12 fl oz/375 ml) chicken broth

¼ cup (2 oz/60 g) finely chopped yellow onion

2 Tbsp unsalted butter

Salt and freshly ground pepper

¼ cup (2 fl oz/60 ml) dry white wine

1–2 tsp fresh lemon juice

Remove any tough outer strings along the curved edges of the celery ribs. Trim the bottom off the celery. Cut the ribs into sections about 4 inches (10 cm) long, discarding any of the smaller white ribs in the middle.

In a frying pan over medium-high heat, combine the broth and onion. Bring to a boil, reduce the heat to medium-low, and simmer until reduced by half, about 5 minutes. Add the butter and ½ tsp salt and stir until the butter melts. Add the celery pieces, cover, and simmer until tender, 20–25 minutes. Transfer the celery to a platter, leaving the liquid in the pan.

Add the wine and lemon juice to the liquid in the pan, return to medium-high heat, and boil until the liquid thickens, 2–3 minutes. Season with salt and pepper. Pour the sauce over the celery and serve.

31

Spring brings delectable young shoots and leaves. Any combination of greens, such as arugula, frisée, spinach, and/or red-leaf lettuce, can be used in this warm salad. With their firm texture and mildly earthy flavor, chanterelles are the ideal complement to the crisp greens, but oyster or shiitake mushrooms make a flavorful substitute.

SPRING GREENS WITH SAUTÉED MUSHROOMS

serves 4

½ lb (250 g) mushrooms

2 tsp unsalted butter

3 Tbsp olive oil

Salt and freshly ground pepper

2 tsp minced shallots

1 Tbsp minced fresh chives

2 tsp red wine vinegar

5 cups (5 oz/155 g) mixed salad greens

Halve or quarter any large mushrooms; leave the small ones whole.

In a small frying pan, melt the butter with 1 Tbsp of the oil over medium-high heat. Add the mushrooms and ¼ tsp salt and sauté until the mushrooms are soft and have released their juices, 2–3 minutes.

In a bowl, whisk together the remaining 2 Tbsp oil, the shallots, half of the chives, ¾ tsp salt, ½ tsp pepper, and the vinegar. Add the greens and toss well to coat.

Arrange the greens on plates. Top with the warm mushrooms. Garnish with the remaining chives and serve.

Brisk but sunny days help all things green and flourish. By April, many of the hallmarks of spring are in their full glory, such as verdant asparagus, nutty artichokes, and a variety of peas and beans. Munch sugar snaps and snow peas whole, or release sweet English peas and earthy favas from their pods. Treat all of these springtime favorites with a light hand—a squeeze of lemon, a pat of butter or splash of olive oil, a generous grating of Parmesan—to set off the iconic flavors of the season.

1
PEA SHOOTS & SHIITAKE MUSHROOMS WITH SOBA NOODLES
page 82

2
HONEY-MUSTARD LEEKS
page 82

3
GRILLED ASPARAGUS & ENDIVE WITH FAVAS, ORANGE & MINT
page 85

8
ASPARAGUS WITH FRIED EGGS & BREAD CRUMBS
page 87

9
BRAISED ARTICHOKES WITH THYME
page 88

10
SMASHED FINGERLINGS WITH FROMAGE BLANC
page 88

15
VEGETABLE STIR-FRY WITH TOFU
page 93

16
SAUTÉED GARDEN BEANS WITH PEA SHOOTS
page 93

17
TABBOULEH
page 94

22
FAVA BEAN SAUTÉ WITH MARJORAM & FETA
page 97

23
BAKED LEEKS WITH BREAD CRUMBS
page 99

24
HERBED MASHED POTATOES
page 99

29
SNOW PEA & RADISH SALAD
page 102

30
ASPARAGUS WITH LEMON & PARMESAN
page 102

4

STEAMED POTATOES
WITH CHIVE OIL
page 85

5

KALE, CREMINI MUSHROOM
& GOAT CHEESE HAND PIES
page 86

6

RADISHES WITH
BUTTER & SEA SALT
page 86

7

BROCCOLI RABE &
PARMESAN FRITTERS
page 87

11

BEET GREEN & PARMESAN TART
page 90

12

ROASTED PORTOBELLO MUSHROOMS
WITH PARMESAN & BASIL
page 90

13

ARTICHOKE RAGOUT WITH
SAFFRON & ORANGE ZEST
page 91

14

FAVA BEAN & RICOTTA CROSTINI
page 91

18

GREEN ONION PANCAKES
page 94

19

LEEK & ASPARAGUS VICHYSSOISE
page 96

20

STIR-FRIED BROCCOLI WITH
CASHEWS & DARK SOY SAUCE
page 96

21

STEAMED BABY ARTICHOKES
WITH GARLIC OIL, BALSAMIC
SYRUP & PINE NUTS
page 97

25

PURPLE CARROTS GLAZED
WITH RED WINE
page 100

26

GRILLED ASPARAGUS
WITH TAPENADE
page 100

27

SPICY POTATOES WITH COOL
YOGURT DIPPING SAUCE
page 101

28

QUICK BROCCOLI WITH
SOY-SESAME DRESSING
page 101

april

1

PEA SHOOTS & SHIITAKE MUSHROOMS WITH SOBA NOODLES

serves 4–6

Pea shoots, the young, tender leaves and curly, delicate tendrils of the English pea plant, can be eaten raw or cooked and are ideal for fast-cooking dishes like stir-fries. Choose pea shoots that are bright green and show no sign of wilting, and be sure to remove any yellowed or tough stems before using. This simple stir-fry can also be made with rice or udon noodles, or it can be served over steamed brown or white rice.

Salt

½ lb (250 g) dried soba noodles

½ cup (4 fl oz/125 ml) chicken or vegetable broth

3 Tbsp oyster sauce

1 Tbsp plus 2 tsp soy sauce

1 Tbsp plus 2 tsp rice vinegar

1 tsp sugar

½ tsp cornstarch

3 Tbsp canola oil

1 tsp Asian sesame oil

2 cloves garlic, minced

1-inch (2.5-cm) piece fresh ginger, peeled and minced

3 green onions, light green and white parts only, chopped

¾ lb (375 g) shiitake mushrooms, stems removed, caps sliced

3 cups (3 oz/90 g) pea shoots

⅓ cup (⅓ oz/10 g) fresh Thai basil leaves, chopped

Bring a pan of lightly salted water to a boil. Add the soba noodles and cook, stirring occasionally, for 4 minutes. Drain, rinse the noodles under cold water, and set aside.

In a bowl, stir together the chicken broth, oyster sauce, soy sauce, vinegar, sugar, and cornstarch.

In a wok or large frying pan, heat the canola oil and sesame oil over high heat. Add the garlic, ginger, and green onions and cook, stirring constantly, just until aromatic, about 30 seconds. Add the shiitakes and sauté until softened and browned on the edges, about 3 minutes. Add the oyster sauce mixture and bring to a boil. Add the noodles and toss to coat with the sauce. Add the pea shoots and cook, stirring, just until wilted.

Remove from the heat, stir in the basil, and serve.

2

HONEY-MUSTARD LEEKS

serves 4

¼ cup (2 fl oz/60 ml) extra-virgin olive oil

2 Tbsp white wine vinegar

2 tsp Dijon mustard

1 tsp honey

Salt and freshly ground pepper

1 lb (500 g) leeks, preferably no more than ½–¾ inch (12 mm–2 cm) in diameter

Update the braised leeks of classic French cuisine with a touch of smoke and sweet. The leeks are grilled and then left to marinate in the honey-mustard dressing for a half hour so that these contrasting flavors can be absorbed. That allows just enough time to throw some pork chops on the grill.

Prepare a charcoal or gas grill for direct-heat grilling over medium heat. Oil the grill rack.

In a bowl, whisk together the oil, vinegar, mustard, honey, ½ tsp salt, and several grinds of pepper to make a dressing.

Bring a large frying pan of lightly salted water to a boil. If using small leeks, trim the tough green parts and root ends. If using slightly larger leeks, remove any tough or bruised outer leaves, trim, and then cut down 2–3 inches (5–7.5 cm) through the length, without cutting into the white base. Add the leeks to the boiling water and cook until softened slightly, about 5 minutes. Drain thoroughly.

Brush the leeks lightly with oil and sprinkle with salt and pepper. Arrange on the grill rack and grill, turning often, until lightly browned, 10–12 minutes. Transfer to a platter. Pour the dressing over the leeks and turn gently to coat thoroughly. Let stand for 30 minutes before serving.

3

GRILLED ASPARAGUS & ENDIVE WITH FAVAS, ORANGE & MINT

serves 4

3 lb (1.5 kg) fava beans, shelled

1 lb (500 g) slender asparagus, ends trimmed

2 heads Belgian endive, preferably red, cut lengthwise into slices about ⅛ inch (3 mm) thick

Salt and freshly ground pepper

1 orange

½ cup (4 fl oz/125 ml) extra-virgin olive oil

½ cup (½ oz/15 g) fresh mint leaves

Belgian endive has an easy elegance, crunchy texture, and subtle taste, here paired with spring vegetables and shards of bright citrus. You can substitute peas for the fava beans, or grilled fennel for the endive. If it is still too cold to grill outdoors, you can cook these vegetables on a stove-top ridged grill pan with similar results. Pair this dish with a crisp white wine such as Sauvignon Blanc or Pinot Grigio.

Bring a pot of lightly salted water to a boil. Add the beans to the boiling water and cook for 1 minute. Drain, rinse under cold running water, and drain again. Pinch each bean to slip it from the skin. Transfer the beans to a bowl.

Preheat a charcoal or gas grill for direct-heat grilling over high heat. Oil the grill rack. Arrange the asparagus and endive slices on the rack perpendicular to the bars. Grill, turning occasionally, until evenly charred, 2–3 minutes. Transfer to a platter and season with salt and pepper.

Working over a bowl, grate the zest from the orange. Cut a thick slice from the top and bottom of the orange. Stand the orange upright and cut off the peel in thick strips, removing the white pith and membrane. Again working over the bowl, cut the segments from the membranes, allowing them and any juices to fall into the bowl. Add the oil and, using a fork, break up the orange segments into bite-sized pieces. Season with salt and pepper.

Scatter the fava beans and mint on top of the grilled vegetables. Drizzle with the oranges and dressing and serve.

4

STEAMED POTATOES WITH CHIVE OIL

serves 4

2 lb (1 kg) small potatoes such as fingerling, Yukon gold, or baby red, each about 1½ inches (4 cm) in diameter

Ice water

1 bunch fresh chives

⅓ cup (3 fl oz/80 ml) extra-virgin olive oil

Salt and freshly ground pepper

Grated zest of 1 lemon

For this recipe, using a fruity olive oil (as opposed to a peppery one) with the chives helps balance the oniony flavor in the bold-tasting, vibrant green drizzling oil. The infused oil forms an innovative sauce for simply steamed new potatoes, which are accented by the brightness of lemon zest.

If necessary, halve any large potatoes so that they are all about the same size. In a saucepan fitted with a steamer basket, bring 1–2 inches (2.5–5 cm) of water to a boil. Add the potatoes, cover, and cook until tender when pierced with a knife, 15–17 minutes.

Meanwhile, bring a small saucepan of water to a boil. Have ready a small bowl of ice water. Coarsely chop three-fourths of the chives. Add to the boiling water and cook for 1 minute. Drain the chives and immediately plunge them into the ice water. Let stand for 1–2 minutes, and then drain and pat dry. Place the chives in a blender. With the motor running, pour in the oil and blend until smooth. Pass the chive oil through a fine-mesh sieve lined with a paper towel into a small bowl.

Cut the remaining chives into 1-inch (2.5-cm) pieces. When the potatoes are done, transfer to a bowl. Add the chive pieces and chive oil and toss gently to mix. Season with salt and pepper. Sprinkle with the lemon zest and serve.

KALE, CREMINI MUSHROOM & GOAT CHEESE HAND PIES

makes 22 hand pies; serves 6–8

FOR THE DOUGH

2½ cups (12½ oz/390 g) all-purpose flour

Salt

1 cup (8 oz/250 g) cold unsalted butter,
cut into small pieces

4–8 Tbsp (2–4 fl oz/60–120 ml) ice water

2 Tbsp unsalted butter

1 Tbsp olive oil

½ yellow onion, chopped

2 cloves garlic, minced

½ lb (250 g) cremini mushrooms,
coarsely chopped

1 bunch kale, ribs removed, leaves
chopped into ½-inch (12-mm) pieces

½ cup (4 fl oz/125 ml) chicken or
vegetable broth

3 oz (90 g) fresh goat cheese

1 egg

You can trade out the kale for chard or spinach and the goat cheese for fontina or Gruyère. Or, you can create an entirely different filling, savory or sweet, for tucking into this versatile dough. Be sure to cook the filling first, as it may not cook through in the oven. Pricking the tops of the pies with fork tines helps prevent the pies from bursting in the oven. If you have any vegetable filling leftover, fold it into an omelet.

To make the dough, combine the flour and 1 tsp salt in a food processor and pulse to mix. Scatter the butter over the flour and process until the mixture resembles coarse crumbs. With the machine running, add the ice water, 1 Tbsp at a time, and process just until the dough comes together. You will probably use only 4 or 5 Tbsp; do not overmix. Turn the dough out onto a lightly floured work surface and pat it into a disk. Wrap tightly in plastic wrap and refrigerate for at least 30 minutes or up to overnight.

To make the filling, in a large frying pan, melt the butter with the oil over medium-high heat. Add the onion and the garlic and cook, stirring occasionally, until the vegetables soften, about 5 minutes. Add the mushrooms and cook, stirring frequently, until they caramelize, about 7 minutes. Add the kale, toss to coat with the other vegetables, and cook until the kale begins to soften, 3–4 minutes. Add the broth and cook until it is absorbed, about 4 minutes. Transfer to a bowl and let cool completely.

Position 1 rack in the center and a second rack in the bottom third of the oven and preheat to 400°F (200°C). Line 2 baking sheets with parchment paper. Cut the ⟫→

dough disk in half and rewrap and return half to the refrigerator. On a floured work surface, roll out the dough ⅛ inch (3 mm) thick. Using a 4-inch (10-cm) round cookie or biscuit cutter, cut out as many circles as possible. Gather up the scraps and set aside.

Place a heaping teaspoon of the goat cheese in the center of each circle, top with 1½ Tbsp of the kale mixture, and fold the circle in half to enclose the filling. Using fork tines, crimp the edges firmly to seal and then prick the top. As the pies are formed, transfer them to a prepared baking sheet. Repeat with the remaining dough half, then press together all of the dough scraps, flatten into a disk, and roll out, cut out, and fill more circles.

In a small bowl, whisk the egg with 1 Tbsp water. Using a pastry brush, brush the top of each pie with the egg wash. Bake the pies, switching the pans between the racks and rotating them back to front about halfway through baking, until they are golden brown, about 20 minutes. Let cool briefly before serving.

RADISHES WITH BUTTER & SEA SALT

serves 8

40 radishes, trimmed,
with a few leaves left intact

Ice water

½ cup (4 oz/125 g) unsalted butter,
at room temperature

Coarse sea salt

This addictive starter calls for young, white-tipped radishes—the freshest you can find. A bit of butter is spread on the tip of the radish, which is then dipped in coarse sea salt. The flavors make for an unforgettable pairing.

Trim the root of each radish just to the base without cutting into the base. Put the radishes in a bowl of ice water and let stand for at least 20 minutes or up to 4 hours before serving.

Pack the butter into a small ramekin and place on a small plate with a butter knife. Pour a layer of salt onto another small plate. Drain the radishes, pat dry, and arrange in a bowl or on a platter.

Serve the radishes accompanied with the butter and salt.

7

In these tasty fritters, pleasantly bitter broccoli rabe is mixed with tangy buttermilk and sharp cheese and then panfried until golden. Serve them alongside lamb chops, preferably rubbed with Italian-inspired seasonings.

BROCCOLI RABE & PARMESAN FRITTERS

serves 4–6

Ice water

1½ cups (4 oz/125 g) chopped broccoli rabe

2 cups (10 oz/315 g) stone-ground cornmeal

½ cup (2 oz/60 g) grated Parmesan cheese

1 Tbsp all-purpose flour

1 tsp baking soda

1 tsp baking powder

Salt

⅓ cup (1 oz/30 g) minced green onions, white and tender green parts only

1 egg, separated, plus 2 egg whites

1½ cups (12 fl oz/375 ml) buttermilk

Canola oil for frying

Bring a pot of salted water to a boil. Have ready a large bowl of ice water. Add the broccoli rabe to the boiling water and cook for 1 minute. Drain and transfer to the ice water. Drain again and spread on paper towels to dry.

In a bowl, combine the cornmeal, cheese, flour, baking soda, baking powder, and 1 tsp salt and mix well. Add the green onions, egg yolk, and buttermilk and stir until well combined. Stir in the broccoli rabe. In a bowl, using an electric mixer, beat the egg whites until stiff peaks form. Fold into the batter.

Pour oil into a large saucepan to a depth of about 2 inches (5 cm) and heat to 325°F (165°C). Working in batches, drop in the batter by the tablespoonful and fry until golden brown, 3–5 minutes. Using a slotted spoon, transfer the fritters to paper towels to drain. Let the oil return to 325°F before frying the next batch. Serve hot.

8

Grass-green asparagus becomes even more tempting when it is garnished with a sunny-side-up egg and crispy crumbs. To make fresh bread crumbs, use slices from a baguette or coarse country loaf about 2 days old, or leave the slices at room temperature overnight to dry out. Tear the slices into pieces and pulse in a food processor to make crumbs. Store in an airtight container in the freezer for up to 4 months.

ASPARAGUS WITH FRIED EGGS & BREAD CRUMBS

serves 4

1 lb (500 g) asparagus, ends trimmed

2 Tbsp unsalted butter

4 eggs

Salt and freshly ground pepper

1 Tbsp minced shallot

2 Tbsp panko or fresh bread crumbs

Fill a frying pan with water to a depth of 1 inch (2.5 cm) and bring to a boil. Add the asparagus, cover, and cook until tender-crisp, 3–4 minutes. Drain the asparagus and arrange on plates. Wipe out the pan.

In the same pan, melt the butter over medium heat. Carefully break each egg into the pan. Season with salt and pepper. Cook until the whites are set and the yolks have thickened but are still soft, about 4 minutes. Using a wide spatula, place an egg on each serving of asparagus. Add the shallot and panko to the pan and sauté until the crumbs are golden, about 2 minutes. Sprinkle over the eggs and serve.

9

In this classic Provençal dish, artichoke hearts are braised, and then served with the cooking broth in a bowl as a first course, along with an abundance of crusty bread. Serve as an opener to a meal of a butter-rubbed roast chicken and oven-roasted fingerling potatoes.

BRAISED ARTICHOKES WITH THYME

serves 4–6

2 or 3 lemons, halved

6 artichokes

¼ cup (2 fl oz/60 ml) olive oil

1 clove garlic, minced

2 Tbsp minced fresh thyme

⅔ cup (5 fl oz/160 ml) chicken broth

Salt

Crusty bread for serving

Fill a large bowl with water and squeeze in the juice of 1 lemon. Cut off the stem of each artichoke flush with the base. Snap off the small tough outer leaves around the base. Cut off the top one-third of the artichoke. Rub the cut surface with a lemon half. Continue to snap off the layers of leaves until you reach the tender, pale inner leaves. Cut off the top one-third of the artichoke again and rub with the lemon half. If the choke in the center has prickly tips, scoop it out with a spoon. If the choke is furry, leave it intact. Cut the artichoke lengthwise into 6 pieces and drop into the lemon water. When all the artichokes have been trimmed, drain them and pat dry.

In a large saucepan, warm the oil over medium heat. Add the artichokes and sauté until lightly golden, 4–5 minutes. Add the garlic and sauté until fragrant, about 2 minutes. Add the thyme, broth, and ½ tsp salt. Reduce the heat to low, cover, and simmer until the base of an artichoke is easily pierced with a fork, 15–20 minutes.

Transfer the artichokes and broth to a bowl and serve with bread.

10

Fromage blanc is a decadently creamy fresh cheese. It is delicious swirled into soups, drizzled with honey, or served with roasted vegetables, like these tender fingerling potatoes. Serve the fromage blanc alongside the potatoes as a dip or dollop a spoonful right on top for a more rustic presentation.

SMASHED FINGERLINGS WITH FROMAGE BLANC

serves 6

2 lb (1 kg) fingerling potatoes

Salt and freshly ground pepper

2 Tbsp unsalted butter

¼ cup (2 oz/60 g) fromage blanc

1 Tbsp minced fresh chives

Place the potatoes in a large saucepan and add water to cover by 2 inches (5 cm). Add 1 tsp salt. Bring to a boil, reduce the heat to medium, cover, and cook until the potatoes are tender when pierced with a knife, 20–25 minutes.

Drain the potatoes and return them to the pan. Add the butter and stir to combine. Using a fork or the back of a wooden spoon, crush the potatoes, breaking them into large, fluffy chunks. Season generously with salt and pepper and transfer to a serving platter. Sprinkle with chives and serve with the fromage blanc on the side.

11

Reconsider composting the leafy tops of beets. They are packed with vitamin A, potassium, iron, and other nutrients and are a delicious addition to soups, sauces, and egg dishes, like this crustless savory tart. Aged Parmesan, salty and sharp, complements the full-flavored dark leaves.

BEET GREEN & PARMESAN TART

serves 8–12

5 Tbsp (3 fl oz/80 ml) extra-virgin olive oil

4 cloves garlic, thinly sliced

1 lb (500 g) beet greens, tough stems removed, leaves and tender stems coarsely chopped

5 eggs

2 Tbsp all-purpose flour

1 cup (4 oz/125 g) grated Parmesan cheese

Salt and freshly ground pepper

In a large frying pan, warm 3 Tbsp of the oil and the garlic over medium-low heat, stirring often, until softened, about 7 minutes. Add half of the beet greens and toss to coat with the oil. Raise the heat to medium, cover, and cook until wilted, about 1 minute. Add the remaining greens, again tossing to coat with the oil. Cover and cook, tossing occasionally, until all the greens are wilted and tender, about 15 minutes. Let cool.

Preheat the broiler.

In a bowl, whisk together the eggs, flour, and cheese. Season with ½ tsp salt and a sprinkling of pepper. Gently fold in the cooled greens.

In a 12-inch (30-cm) cast-iron or other heavy-bottomed ovenproof frying pan, heat the remaining 2 Tbsp oil over medium heat. Pour in the egg mixture and reduce the heat to medium-low. Cook until lightly browned on the bottom and the middle is almost set, about 7 minutes.

Slip the pan under the broiler 4 inches (10 cm) from the heat source and broil until the top is lightly browned and the tart is sizzling hot, 2–3 minutes. Let cool for 5 minutes. Use a spatula or knife to loosen the tart from the pan and slide onto a platter. Cut into wedges and serve warm or at room temperature.

12

With their rich flavor and dense texture, roasted portobello mushrooms make a satisfying vegetarian main course. You can also put the roasted caps between toasted slices of coarse country bread for a hearty sandwich, or slice them and stir them into a pan sauce for spooning over grilled chicken breasts or steaks.

ROASTED PORTOBELLO MUSHROOMS WITH PARMESAN & BASIL

serves 4

3 Tbsp extra-virgin olive oil

1 large clove garlic, finely chopped

4 large portobello mushrooms, about 6 oz (185 g) each, stems removed

Salt and freshly ground pepper

2 Tbsp finely shredded fresh basil, plus 4 sprigs

2 Tbsp shaved Parmesan or Asiago cheese, plus more for garnish

1 Tbsp balsamic or sherry vinegar

Preheat the oven to 450°F (230°C). Lightly oil a baking sheet.

In a small bowl, whisk together 2 Tbsp of the oil and the garlic. Brush the mushrooms all over with the garlic oil. Season generously with salt and pepper. Place the mushrooms, gill side down, on the prepared pan.

Roast for 10 minutes. Remove the pan from the oven, turn the mushrooms, return to the oven, and roast until tender when pierced with a fork, about 8 minutes. Meanwhile, in a small bowl, stir together the shredded basil and the 2 Tbsp cheese. Remove the pan from the oven and sprinkle the cheese mixture evenly over the mushrooms. Continue to roast the mushrooms until the cheese begins to melt, about 2 minutes.

In a small bowl, stir together the remaining 1 Tbsp oil and the vinegar. Remove the pan from the oven and transfer the mushrooms to a platter. Leave whole or cut into thick slices. Drizzle with the vinegar mixture and garnish with basil sprigs. Sprinkle with cheese and serve.

13

ARTICHOKE RAGOUT WITH SAFFRON & ORANGE ZEST

serves 4

1 lemon, halved

6 artichokes

1 orange

2 Tbsp olive oil

½ yellow onion, finely chopped

Salt and freshly ground pepper

2 cloves garlic, minced

1 cup (8 fl oz/250 ml) dry white wine

6–8 saffron threads

Artichokes absorb flavor from marinades and sauces especially well. Here, wedges simmer in a broth of fragrant saffron, sweet orange juice, and tart white wine. When the cooking liquid reduces to a glaze, the saffron shines through.

Fill a large bowl with water. Squeeze the juice from the lemon halves into the water and add the lemon halves. Cut off the stem of each artichoke about 1 inch (2.5 cm) from the base. Snap off the tough outer leaves. Using a paring knife, trim off the dark green flesh from the base and stem. Cut the artichoke in half lengthwise and scoop out the fuzzy choke. Cut the halves into 1-inch wedges and add to the lemon water.

Grate the zest from the orange and then squeeze the juice to measure about ½ cup (4 fl oz/125 ml). Set aside.

In a frying pan, warm the oil over medium-low heat. Add the onion and a pinch of salt and sauté until the onion is soft and translucent, 6–7 minutes. Add the garlic and sauté for 1 minute. Drain the artichokes, pat dry, and add to the pan along with the orange juice, wine, and ½ cup (4 fl oz/125 ml) water. Crumble the saffron threads into the pan. Bring the mixture to a boil and then reduce the heat to low. Add a generous pinch each of salt and pepper, cover the pan, and simmer until the artichokes are just tender when pierced with a knife, about 25 minutes.

Uncover the pan, raise the heat to medium-high, and simmer vigorously until the liquid reduces to a glaze, 6–7 minutes. Stir in half of the orange zest. Transfer the artichokes to a serving dish and sprinkle with the remaining zest. Serve warm or at room temperature.

14

FAVA BEAN & RICOTTA CROSTINI

serves 4

1½ lb (750 g) fava beans, shelled

1 baguette

½ cup (4 oz/125 g) whole-milk ricotta cheese

½ cup (2 oz/60 h) grated pecorino romano cheese

1½ Tbsp chopped fresh mint

½ Tbsp grated lemon zest

2 Tbsp extra-virgin olive oil, plus more for drizzling

Salt and freshly ground pepper

Creamy ricotta cheese makes a perfect foil for the "green" flavor of the fava beans in this colorful, tasty topping for crostini. Fresh mint and fava beans are classic partners in a number of Mediterranean cuisines. Their refreshing taste is set off here by sharp pecorino and lemon zest.

Preheat the oven to 400°F (200°C).

Bring a pot of lightly salted water to a boil. Add the beans to the boiling water and boil until tender, about 5 minutes. Drain, rinse under cold running water, and drain again. Pinch each bean to slip it from the skin. You should have about 1 cup (5½ oz/170 g) skinned beans. Finely chop the beans and add them to a bowl.

Cut the baguette on the diagonal into 16 slices each ½ inch (12 mm) thick. (You will not need the entire loaf.) Arrange the baguette slices on a baking sheet. Bake until golden, about 5 minutes. Remove from the oven and set aside.

Add the ricotta, pecorino, 1 Tbsp of the mint, the lemon zest, and the 2 Tbsp oil to the fava beans. Using a fork, mash the ingredients together until well blended. Season with salt and pepper.

Arrange the toasts on a platter. Spoon the bean mixture onto the toasts. Drizzle lightly with oil, sprinkle with the remaining 1½ tsp mint, and serve.

15

The secret to success with any stir-fry is to cook the ingredients quickly in hot oil over high heat, so always have everything you need cut, measured, and next to the stove top before you begin cooking. You can vary the vegetables here according to what you have on hand, such as trading out the wedges of yellow squash and sugar snap peas for cabbage. To do so, core 1 head of cabbage and cut it into large dice. You can also add a tangle of pea shoots or fresh herbs just before removing the pan from the heat.

VEGETABLE STIR-FRY WITH TOFU
serves 4

¾ lb (375 g) firm tofu, drained

Cornstarch for dusting

3 Tbsp canola oil

2–4 cloves garlic, chopped

1 Tbsp peeled and chopped fresh ginger

1 carrot, sliced on the diagonal, or 3 or 4 small, slender carrots, cut into 1½-inch (4-cm) lengths

1 red bell pepper, seeded and diced

1 yellow onion, sliced lengthwise

1 yellow squash, sliced into ½-inch (1.2-cm) rounds and halved

½ lb (250 g) sugar snap peas, strings removed

Salt

¼–½ tsp Chinese five-spice powder

3–4 Tbsp chicken broth

1 Tbsp sugar

3–4 Tbsp hoisin sauce

Few dashes of soy sauce

Few dashes of chile oil

Few dashes of rice vinegar

½ tsp Asian sesame oil

1½ cups (10½ oz/330 g) white rice, cooked according to package directions

Cut the tofu into 1-inch (2.5-cm) cubes and blot dry with paper towels. Dust the cubes with cornstarch and blot again.

In a deep frying pan or a wok, heat 1 Tbsp of the oil over medium-high heat, swirling it to coat the pan. Add the tofu and cook until lightly browned on the first side, 2½–4 minutes. Turn the tofu cubes, being careful not to break them up, and cook until browned on the opposite side, 2½–4 minutes. Transfer to a plate.

Wipe the pan clean, place over high heat, and add 1 Tbsp of the oil, again swirling to coat the pan. Add the garlic, ginger, carrot, and bell pepper and stir-fry for 1 minute. Add to the tofu.

Return the pan to high heat and heat the remaining 1 Tbsp oil. Add the onion and stir-fry for 1 minute. Add the squash ⟩⟩

and peas and a pinch of salt and stir and toss to coat with the oil. Mix in the five-spice powder and 3 Tbsp broth and stir-fry until the vegetables have begun to soften, 2–3 minutes. Add the sugar, hoisin, soy sauce, and chile oil and stir. Add another 1 Tbsp stock if the mixture seems dry. Cover and cook over high heat until the vegetables are almost tender-crisp, about 4 minutes.

Uncover and add the carrot mixture and tofu. Stir to blend and heat through, about 3 minutes. The liquid should be almost fully evaporated. Season with the vinegar to balance the flavors.

Mound the vegetables onto a platter and sprinkle with the sesame oil. Serve with the hot rice.

16

Pea shoots, the tender leaves and spiraled tendrils of the pea plant, add a peppery accent to sautéed green and wax beans. Look for them at farmers' markets, tucked among the legumes. If unavailable, substitute watercress.

SAUTÉED GARDEN BEANS WITH PEA SHOOTS
serves 4

½ lb (250 g) slender small green beans

½ lb (250 g) slender yellow wax beans

4 Tbsp (2 oz/60 g) unsalted butter

6 green onions, including tender green tops, chopped

½ lb (250 g) pea shoots or watercress, tough stems removed

Salt and freshly ground pepper

Bring a large pot of salted water to a boil over high heat. Add the green and yellow beans and boil until half-cooked, 3–4 minutes. Drain the beans, rinse under cold running water, and pat dry.

In a large frying pan, melt the butter over medium heat. Add the green onions and sauté for 2 minutes. Add the pea shoots and cooked beans and sauté until the beans are warmed through and the pea shoots are just tender, about 3 minutes. Season with salt and pepper. Transfer to a bowl and serve.

17

If you have a surplus of parsley on hand, this classic Levantine salad is the ideal way to use it up. Bursting with nutrients and fiber, it has a refreshing taste that is the perfect foil for the richly spiced kebabs and other meats and sauces of the eastern Mediterranean table.

TABBOULEH

serves 4–6

1 cup (6 oz/185 g) bulgur

Salt and freshly ground pepper

1 cup (8 fl oz/250 ml) boiling water

1 English cucumber, seeded and chopped

1 cup (6 oz/185 g) cherry tomatoes, halved

1 cup (1½ oz/45 g) chopped fresh
flat-leaf parsley

¼ cup (⅓ oz/10 g) chopped fresh mint

¼ cup (¾ oz/20 g) thinly sliced green onion,
white and tender green parts

¼ cup (2 fl oz/60 ml) fresh lemon juice

3 Tbsp extra-virgin olive oil

¼ tsp ground allspice

Place the bulgur in a heatproof bowl. Dissolve 1 tsp salt in the boiling water and pour over the bulgur. Cover tightly and let stand at room temperature for 30 minutes. The bulgur will absorb the water, swell, split, and fluff.

Add the cucumber, tomatoes, parsley, mint, green onion, lemon juice, oil, and allspice to the bulgur and stir and toss to mix well. Season with salt and pepper, holding back a little on the salt. Cover and set aside at room temperature for at least 1 hour to allow the flavors to blend, then serve.

18

These savory pancakes, made of unleavened dough, are layered with green onions and pan-fried until flaky. To prevent the green onion tops from breaking through as you form the pancakes, and to ensure that they cook properly, chop the onions finely. Serve as a first course on an Asian-inspired menu, or cut into smaller wedges and serve with cocktails.

GREEN ONION PANCAKES

serves 4–6

2 cups (10 oz/315 g) all-purpose flour

1 cup (8 fl oz/250 ml) boiling water

3 tablespoons Asian sesame oil

Coarse sea salt for sprinkling

1¼ cups (3¾ oz/110 g) chopped
green onion tops

Canola oil for frying

Sift the flour into a bowl, make a well in the center, and pour the boiling water into the well. Using a wooden spoon, quickly work the water into the flour to make a fairly stiff, though not dry, dough. Knead the dough lightly in the bowl until it forms a ball. Remove the dough from the bowl and brush lightly with some of the oil. Invert the bowl over the dough and leave to cool, about 6 minutes.

Knead the dough very lightly until smooth and elastic, brush with a little more oil, and place in a plastic bag. Set aside for 30–60 minutes.

Using your palms, roll the dough back and forth to form a log about 10 inches (25 cm) long. Cut the log into 6 equal pieces, and form each piece into a ball. Roll out each ball into a very thin round about 7 inches (18 cm) in diameter. Brush generously with the oil, sprinkle with salt, then cover each pancake evenly with one-sixth of the green onion tops. Roll up the round into a cigar shape, twist it into a tight coil, and brush the top with oil. On a lightly oiled work surface, flatten each coil with a rolling pin into a round about 5 inches (13 cm) in diameter. Try to avoid having the onions break through the dough.

Pour oil to a depth of 1 inch (2.5 cm) into a large, wide, shallow frying pan and place over medium-high heat. When the oil is hot, add 2 or 3 pancakes and cook, turning once, until golden brown, about 3 minutes per side. Transfer to a cutting board and keep warm. Repeat with the remaining pancakes. Sprinkle the pancakes with salt, cut into quarters, and serve.

19

LEEK & ASPARAGUS VICHYSSOISE

serves 6–8

5 leeks, about 2½ lb (1.25 kg), dark green tops removed

2 Tbsp unsalted butter

2 Tbsp canola oil

1 tsp minced fresh thyme

5 cups (40 fl oz/1.25 l) chicken broth

1 small russet potato, peeled and coarsely chopped

2 lb (1 kg) asparagus, ends trimmed, spears coarsely chopped

1 cup (1½ oz/45 g) packed baby spinach

1 cup (8 fl oz/250 ml) half-and-half, plus 3 Tbsp for garnish

Salt and freshly ground pepper

Leeks are milder, earthier, and yet somehow more substantial than their onion kin. Here, they are paired with young asparagus and baby spinach to create a variation on the classic vichyssoise. If a springtime cold snap hits, you can skip the chilling step and serve the soup piping hot.

Cut the leeks in half lengthwise and then cut each half crosswise into pieces ¼ inch (6 mm) thick.

In a large, heavy pot with a lid, melt 1 Tbsp of the butter with 1 Tbsp of the oil over medium-high heat. Set aside 1 cup (3 oz/90 g) of the leeks and add the rest to the pot along with the thyme. Reduce the heat to low, cover, and cook, stirring occasionally, until the leeks are softened, about 10 minutes. Add the broth and potato, raise the heat to medium-high, cover, and bring to a boil. Reduce the heat to medium-low and simmer until the potato is tender, about 10 minutes.

Add the asparagus to the pot, cover, and cook until bright green and just tender, about 3 minutes. Stir in the spinach and cook just until it wilts, about 45 seconds.

Working in batches, transfer the mixture to a blender and purée. Pour into a bowl. Stir in the 1 cup (8 fl oz/250 ml) half-and-half and 1 tsp salt. Season with pepper. Let cool to room temperature. Cover and refrigerate until well chilled, at least 4 hours or up to 12 hours.

Just before serving, in a frying pan, melt the remaining 1 Tbsp butter with the remaining 1 Tbsp oil over medium heat. Add the 1 cup leeks and ¼ tsp salt and sauté until the leeks are crisp, about 8 minutes. Transfer to paper towels to drain. Ladle the soup into bowls, drizzle with the 3 Tbsp half-and-half, garnish with the fried leeks, and serve.

20

STIR-FRIED BROCCOLI WITH CASHEWS & DARK SOY SAUCE

serves 4

⅓ cup (2 oz/60 g) cashews

½ cup (4 fl oz/125 ml) chicken broth

2 Tbsp oyster sauce

2 Tbsp dark soy sauce

2 Tbsp mirin

1 tsp cornstarch

2 Tbsp canola oil

1 lb (500 g) broccoli, cut into 1-inch (2.5-cm) florets

1 clove garlic, minced

Dark soy sauce has a molasses-like consistency and adds both sweetness and complexity to this dish. Mirin lends a measure of brightness, oyster sauce an intriguing savory flavor, and cashews a delightful nuttiness. Together, they're a tasty way to perk up everyday broccoli florets in a quick stir-fry.

Preheat the oven to 375°F (190°C).

Spread the cashews in a small baking pan and toast in the oven until the nuts turn a shade or two darker and are fragrant, 6–8 minutes. Pour onto a plate to cool.

In a small bowl, stir together the broth, oyster sauce, soy sauce, and mirin. Add the cornstarch and stir to dissolve.

In a large frying pan or wok, heat the oil over medium-high heat. Add the broccoli and cook, tossing and stirring constantly, until the florets are well coated with oil and turn a vibrant green, about 3 minutes. Add the garlic and cook, stirring, for 1 minute. Stir the soy sauce mixture briefly to recombine, then add to the pan. Bring to a boil, and cook, tossing, until the sauce thickens and the broccoli is tender-crisp, about 4 minutes.

Add the cashews and stir well. Transfer to a bowl and serve.

21

Reducing balsamic vinegar over high heat concentrates its flavor, yielding an intense sweet-tart syrup, the ultimate condiment for spring's baby artichokes. The garlic oil in the dressing adds a savory character, and toasted pine nuts bring a soft crunch with woodsy accents.

STEAMED BABY ARTICHOKES WITH GARLIC OIL, BALSAMIC SYRUP & PINE NUTS

serves 4–6

3 large cloves garlic, thinly sliced

¼ cup (2 fl oz/60 ml) plus 3 Tbsp extra-virgin olive oil

1 cup (8 fl oz/250 ml) balsamic vinegar

2 large lemons, halved

32 baby artichokes, about 4 lb (2 kg)

1 Tbsp coarsely chopped fresh flat-leaf parsley or mint

1 tsp sugar

Salt and freshly ground pepper

½ cup (2½ oz/75 g) pine nuts, toasted

2 oz (60 g) Parmesan cheese, shaved (optional)

In a small bowl, stir together the garlic slices and oil. Cover and let stand at room temperature for 1 hour.

Meanwhile, in a small nonreactive saucepan, bring the vinegar to a boil over high heat and cook until thick, syrupy, and reduced to about ¼ cup (2 fl oz/60 ml), 10–12 minutes. Let cool to room temperature.

Fill a large bowl with water. Squeeze the juice from a lemon half into the water and add the spent half. Juice the remaining 3 halves to measure ¼ cup (2 fl oz/60 ml) juice; add the spent halves to the water. Working with 1 artichoke at a time, cut off the stem flush with the base. Snap off the dark green outer leaves until you reach the pale green center. Cut about ½ inch (12 mm) off the top. Cut the artichoke in half lengthwise and add the halves to the lemon water.

In a large pot fitted with a steamer basket, bring 1–2 inches (5–7.5 cm) of water to a boil. Drain the artichokes and arrange in a single layer in the steamer basket. Cover, reduce the heat to medium, and steam until the artichokes are tender, 14–16 minutes. Transfer to a bowl.

Pour the garlic-oil mixture through a sieve into a small bowl. Discard the garlic. In another small bowl, whisk together the lemon juice, parsley, sugar, ¼ tsp salt, and several grinds of pepper until the sugar dissolves. »→

Slowly whisk in the garlic oil until well blended. Adjust the seasoning if necessary.

Add the dressing and 2½ Tbsp of the balsamic syrup (reserve the remaining syrup for another use) to the artichokes. Season with a large pinch of salt. Toss well. In a small bowl, stir together the pine nuts and a scant ¼ tsp salt and sprinkle over the artichokes. Top with the cheese, if using, and serve.

22

This simple recipe celebrates the spring fava bean harvest by using ingredients that enhance the fresh flavor and buttery texture of the legume. Feta cheese adds a bright tanginess, shallot delivers an oniony accent, lemon juice adds tartness, and marjoram's floral fragrance brings all the elements together. This dish is excellent alongside lamb, chicken, or fish.

FAVA BEAN SAUTÉ WITH MARJORAM & FETA

serves 4

2 lb (1 kg) fava beans, shelled

1 Tbsp olive oil

1 shallot, thinly sliced

Salt and freshly ground pepper

2 tsp minced fresh marjoram

½ lemon

1 oz (30 g) feta cheese

Bring a pot of lightly salted water to a boil. Add the beans and blanch for 1–2 minutes. Drain, rinse under cold running water, and drain again. Pinch each bean to slip it from the skin. Place the beans in a bowl and pat dry.

In a frying pan, warm the oil over medium heat. Add the shallot and a pinch of salt and sauté until the shallot is soft and translucent, 3–4 minutes. Add the beans and another pinch of salt and sauté for 2 minutes. Add the marjoram and sauté until the beans are just tender, 1–2 minutes.

Remove the pan from the heat. Squeeze the juice from the lemon half over the beans and stir to mix. Season with pepper. Transfer the beans to a serving dish. Crumble the cheese over the beans and serve.

23

Springtime leeks are the royalty of the onion family and have pride of place in French cuisine, where they appear with vinaigrettes and in quiches, stews, and gratins, such as this one. Bursting with flavor, this dish works well as a first course, a main course, or a side, and it can be baked in individual baking dishes or a single large one. Serve alongside a roast leg of lamb for a special occasion.

BAKED LEEKS WITH BREAD CRUMBS

serves 6

6 Tbsp (3 oz/90 g) unsalted butter

2 Tbsp minced shallots

6–8 leeks, about 3 lb (1.5 kg) total, white and pale green parts, chopped

Salt and freshly ground white pepper

2 cups (16 fl oz/500 ml) whole milk, plus more as needed

3 Tbsp all-purpose flour

¼ tsp cayenne pepper

½ cup (2 oz/60 g) shredded Gruyère cheese

½ cup (1 oz/30 g) fresh bread crumbs

Preheat the oven to 400°F (200°C).

In a frying pan, melt 2 Tbsp of the butter over medium-high heat. Add the shallots, leeks, and ½ tsp each salt and white pepper. Reduce the heat to medium and cook, stirring often, until the leeks are translucent and very soft, about 15 minutes.

In a small saucepan, warm the 2 cups (16 fl oz/500 ml) milk over medium heat until small bubbles appear around the edge of the pan. Cover and remove from the heat.

In a saucepan, melt 3 Tbsp of the butter over medium-high heat. Remove from the heat and whisk in the flour, ½ tsp salt, ¼ tsp white pepper, and the cayenne. Return the pan to medium-low heat and cook, stirring often, for 2 minutes. Slowly whisk in the hot milk and simmer, stirring, until the sauce thickens, about 15 minutes. If the sauce is too thin, increase the heat; if it is too thick, whisk in a little more milk. Stir in the leek mixture.

Pour the mixture into a baking or gratin dish. Sprinkle evenly with the cheese and the bread crumbs and dot with the remaining 1 Tbsp butter. Bake until the cheese and bread crumb topping are golden and the gratin is bubbly, 20–30 minutes. Remove from the oven and serve.

24

Light, buttery mashed potatoes taste best when eaten shortly after cooking, so whip them just before serving. You can slip in any combination of herbs you like. They go well with roast chicken or seared salmon or halibut.

HERBED MASHED POTATOES

serves 8

4 lb (2 kg) Yukon gold, red, or russet potatoes, peeled and cut into 1-inch (2.5-cm) cubes

Salt and freshly ground pepper

½ cup (4 oz/125 g) sour cream

½ cup (4 oz/125 g) unsalted butter, at room temperature, cut into 1-inch (2.5-cm) pieces

½ cup (¾ oz/20 g) mixed chopped fresh herbs such as chives, dill, tarragon, and/or thyme

1 cup (8 fl oz/250 ml) half-and-half, heated

In a large saucepan, combine the potatoes, 2 tsp salt, and water to cover by 2 inches (5 cm). Bring to a boil, reduce the heat to medium, and cook, uncovered, until the potatoes are tender when pierced with a knife, about 20 minutes.

Drain the potatoes and transfer to a large bowl. Using a potato masher, mash them while they are still piping hot.

Add the sour cream, butter, and herbs to the potatoes and stir them together while slowly pouring in the warm half-and-half. Continue to stir until the potatoes are light and creamy. Season with salt and pepper and serve.

25

Visit the farmers' markets of the season and you might spy carrots in a variety of colors. If you do, put together a bundle of colorful roots, from bright orange to sunny yellow to deep red to jewel-toned purple to lunar white, and use in place of the purple carrots called for here. If only large carrots are available, cut them on the diagonal into slices ½ inch (12 mm) thick.

PURPLE CARROTS GLAZED WITH RED WINE

serves 4

2 tsp unsalted butter or canola oil

24 young, slender purple or orange carrots

½ cup (4 fl oz/125 ml) fruity red wine

⅓ cup (3 fl oz/80 ml) chicken broth

1 tsp peppercorns, coarsely cracked

Melt the butter in a frying pan over medium-high heat. Add the carrots, stir to coat with the butter, and cook for 2 minutes. Add the wine, broth, and peppercorns. Reduce the heat to medium and cook until most of the liquid has evaporated and the carrots are fork-tender, about 10 minutes. Serve hot or warm.

26

When it is still too chilly to fire up the outdoor grill, a stove-top grill pan is a great stand-in. Quick-cooking asparagus over high heat deepens and concentrates its flavor. Dip the spears into tapenade, the classic Provençal olive spread, for an exceptional appetizer. Any leftover tapenade can be used as a sandwich spread.

GRILLED ASPARAGUS WITH TAPENADE

serves 4–6

FOR THE TAPENADE

1 cup (5 oz/155 g) pitted Kalamata olives

4 olive oil–packed anchovy fillets

½ cup (¾ oz/20 g) chopped fresh flat-leaf parsley

1 clove garlic

1 Tbsp salted capers

1 Tbsp fresh lemon juice

¼ cup (2 fl oz/60 ml) olive oil

1½ lb (750 g) thin asparagus, ends trimmed

¼ cup (2 fl oz/60 ml) olive oil

2 cloves garlic, crushed and then finely chopped

Salt and cracked pepper

To make the tapenade, in a food processor, combine the olives, anchovies, parsley, garlic, capers, and lemon juice. With the motor running, add the ¼ cup (2 fl oz/60 ml) oil in a thin, steady stream and process until a chunky paste forms. Spoon into a small serving bowl.

Heat a ridged grill pan on the stove top over medium-high heat. In a shallow bowl, toss the asparagus with the ¼ cup (2 fl oz/60 ml) oil and garlic. Season with salt and pepper.

When the pan just begins to smoke, add the asparagus and cook, turning once, until the spears are tender and well browned, 6–9 minutes. Transfer to a plate and serve with the tapenade for dipping.

27

SPICY POTATOES WITH COOL YOGURT DIPPING SAUCE

serves 4

¼ cup (2 fl oz/60 ml) canola oil

2 Tbsp prepared harissa

¼ tsp cayenne pepper

1 Tbsp sesame seeds

Salt and freshly ground pepper

3 lb (1.5 kg) russet potatoes, peeled and cut into 2-inch (5-cm) chunks

1 cup (8 oz/250 g) Greek-style plain yogurt

Leaves from ½ bunch fresh mint, finely shredded

1 Tbsp fresh lemon juice

These potato chunks get a toasty, nutty accent from a light coating of sesame seeds, and a double dose of heat from cayenne pepper and North African harissa. To counter their bold flavor, they are dipped into a cooling sauce of thick, creamy yogurt seasoned with lemon juice and mint. Serve alongside simply grilled chicken or fish.

Preheat the oven to 425°F (220°C). Drizzle the oil evenly over the bottom of a roasting pan just large enough to hold the potatoes in a single layer, and place the pan in the oven as it preheats.

In a large bowl, combine the harissa, cayenne, sesame seeds, and 1 teaspoon salt. Add the potatoes and toss to coat evenly with the seasonings.

When the oven is preheated and the roasting pan is hot, remove the pan from the oven and carefully add the potatoes, tossing them gently in the oil to coat evenly. Arrange the potatoes in a single layer in the pan. Roast until the undersides of the potato chunks are nicely browned, 25–30 minutes. Using a spatula, flip the potatoes and then continue to roast until tender when pierced with a fork and browned and crisp on the outside, about 15 minutes longer.

While the potatoes are roasting, in a small bowl, stir together the yogurt, mint, and lemon juice, mixing well. Season with salt and black pepper.

Transfer the roasted potatoes to a platter. Serve warm with the yogurt sauce on the side for dipping.

28

QUICK BROCCOLI WITH SOY-SESAME DRESSING

serves 4

1 Tbsp Asian sesame oil

1 Tbsp soy sauce

1 tsp miso

2 tsp fresh lemon juice

1 tsp sugar

Salt

1½ lb (750 g) broccoli, cut into 2-inch (5-cm) florets

2 tsp sesame seeds, toasted

Broccoli, which is found in the produce section of nearly every market, is rich in vitamins, minerals, and fiber. It also adapts well to a wide variety of seasonings, which makes it easy to put this healthful vegetable on your dinner table. Here, it is treated to a light sesame-soy dressing that lets its bright green taste shine through.

In a large bowl, stir together the sesame oil, soy sauce, miso, lemon juice, and sugar until well blended.

Bring a large pot of lightly salted water to a boil. Add the broccoli and cook just until tender-crisp, about 2 minutes. Drain well.

Add the broccoli to the sesame-soy mixture and toss well to coat. Sprinkle with the sesame seeds and serve.

29

Cutting radishes into thin slivers tempers their peppery bite. The tart honey-vinegar dressing provides a contrast to the spicy radishes and complements the sweetness of the snow peas in this crisp salad.

SNOW PEA & RADISH SALAD

serves 4

Ice water

½ lb (250 g) snow peas, strings removed

5 radishes

1½ Tbsp rice vinegar

½ tsp honey

Salt and freshly ground pepper

¼ cup (2 fl oz/60 ml) canola oil

Leaves from 2 fresh mint sprigs, roughly chopped

Bring a large pot of salted water to a boil. Have ready a large bowl of ice water.

Add the snow peas to the boiling water and cook for 1½ minutes. Drain the peas and then immediately plunge them into the ice water. Let stand for 1–2 minutes. Drain the peas and pat dry.

Cut the snow peas on the diagonal into 1-inch (2.5-cm) pieces and place in a bowl. Thinly slice the radishes, then cut the slices into thin strips. Add the radishes to the bowl.

In a small bowl, whisk together the vinegar, honey, and a pinch each of salt and pepper. Add the oil in a slow, steady stream and whisk to blend. Adjust the seasoning if necessary.

Add enough dressing to coat the snow peas and radishes and toss well to coat; you may not need all the dressing. Add the mint, toss gently to mix, and serve.

30

In this simple starter, Parmesan cheese provides a suitably bold contrast to the natural acidity of lemon and the unique flavor of asparagus. Extra-virgin olive oil, preferably a fruity one, binds together all of the elements.

ASPARAGUS WITH LEMON & PARMESAN

serves 6

Ice water

3½ lb (1.75 kg) pencil-thin asparagus, ends trimmed, spears cut into 1½-inch (4-cm) pieces

1 Tbsp grated lemon zest

1 Tbsp fresh lemon juice

Salt and freshly ground pepper

2 Tbsp extra-virgin olive oil

5-oz (155-g) chunk Parmesan cheese

Bring a large saucepan of salted water to a boil. Have ready a large bowl of ice water.

Add the asparagus pieces to the boiling water and cook until the asparagus is tender-crisp and bright green, about 2½ minutes. Drain and then immediately plunge the asparagus into the ice water. Let stand until cool, about 2 minutes. Drain again and transfer the asparagus pieces to a platter.

In a small bowl, whisk together the lemon zest and juice, ¼ tsp salt, and ¼ tsp pepper. Slowly whisk in the oil until well blended. Adjust the seasoning if necessary. Drizzle the dressing evenly over the asparagus. Using a vegetable peeler, shave the cheese over the asparagus and serve.

As days lengthen—a signal that summer is just around the corner—put together inspired mixes of what's in the market, such as asparagus and leeks on a puff-pastry crust. When the weather warms, enjoy classic springtime fare, like peas with mint, cold potato and leek soup, or a tangle of peppery arugula and shaved fennel topped with a lemony vinaigrette. Dress up May dishes with a garnish of bright green pea shoots or watercress, and add welcome crunch to salads and sandwiches with thin cucumber slices.

1
GRILLED BABY ARTICHOKES WITH SPICY GARLIC BUTTER
page 106

2
FAVA BEAN & CORN SALAD WITH MINT
page 106

3
GOAT CHEESE & POTATO GRATIN
page 109

8
STIR-FRIED ASPARAGUS WITH SHIITAKE MUSHROOMS & SESAME SEEDS
page 111

9
PROSCIUTTO-WRAPPED HARICOTS VERTS WITH LEMON AIOLI
page 112

10
SHAVED FENNEL, PARMESAN & ARUGULA SALAD
page 112

15
SPRING VEGETABLE TART
page 117

16
SAUTÉED FRESH PEAS WITH SHREDDED ROMAINE & MINT
page 117

17
FAVA BEANS WITH PECORINO
page 117

22
ROASTED ASPARAGUS & MORELS WITH SHALLOT BUTTER
page 121

23
MASHED POTATOES WITH TOMME CHEESE
page 121

24
GRILLED BABY LEEKS WITH CHERVIL & CHIVES
page 123

29
SWEET & SOUR VIDALIA ONIONS
page 126

30
CRUSHED RED POTATOES
page 126

31
FRESH PEAS WITH ONION & BASIL
page 126

may

1

GRILLED BABY ARTICHOKES WITH SPICY GARLIC BUTTER

serves 4–6

4 Tbsp (2 oz/60 g) unsalted butter

3 cloves garlic, minced

2 Tbsp fresh lemon juice

1/8 tsp red pepper flakes, or more to taste

Hot-pepper sauce

Salt and freshly ground pepper

20 baby artichokes, about 1 lb (500 g) total

A gently steamed artichoke leaf dipped in melted butter is exquisite, but grilled baby artichokes only improve on a good thing. Don't worry if they are on the grill for what seems like too long. They need time to properly cook. Once you strip away the burnt outer leaves, you'll find a fork-tender center. Grill artichoke halves on the grill rack or thread them onto skewers for easy turning.

Prepare a charcoal or gas grill for direct-heat grilling over medium heat. Oil the grill rack. The artichokes can be grilled on skewers. If using wooden skewers, soak in water for at least 30 minutes.

In a small saucepan, melt the butter over medium-low heat. Add the garlic, lemon juice, red pepper flakes, and 1 or 2 dashes of hot-pepper sauce, and stir to mix. Season with salt and pepper. Reduce the heat to low and keep the mixture warm.

Hit each artichoke on a countertop a couple of times; this will loosen the outer leaves and let the butter mixture penetrate. Cut the artichokes in half lengthwise and trim the stems. Using a small spoon, scoop out the hairy chokes. Slide the artichoke halves onto the skewers, if using, with the cut sides facing the same way.

Place the artichokes, cut sides down, on the grill rack and cook for about 5 minutes. Brush with the butter mixture and cook for another 5 minutes. Turn the artichokes, brush the cut sides with the butter mixture, and continue cooking, turning and brushing with the butter mixture about every 5 minutes, for 20–25 minutes longer, taking care not to burn the artichokes. The artichokes are done when the middle of the cut side gives easily.

Transfer the artichokes to a platter, pour any remaining butter mixture over them, and serve.

2

FAVA BEAN & CORN SALAD WITH MINT

serves 4

2 cups (12 oz/375 g) frozen corn kernels

1 1/2 lb (750 g) fava beans, shelled

2 Tbsp extra-virgin olive oil

1 1/2 Tbsp cider vinegar

8 radishes, trimmed and thinly sliced

2 Tbsp coarsely chopped fresh mint

Salt and freshly ground pepper

Corn and fresh fava beans are a perfect pair in this simple salad. If the favas are very young and small, you can skip the peeling step and reduce the cooking time to just 2 minutes. Serve this salad with warm sourdough bread and sweet butter.

Bring a pot of lightly salted water to a boil. Add the corn and cook for 1 minute. Using a sieve, scoop the corn out of the water and transfer to a bowl.

Return the water to a boil, add the fava beans, and cook just until tender, 3–5 minutes. Drain, rinse under cold running water, and drain again. Pinch each bean to slip it from the skin.

In a bowl, whisk together the oil and vinegar. Stir in the corn, beans, radishes, and mint. Season with 1/2 tsp salt and a few grinds of pepper, and serve.

3

GOAT CHEESE
& POTATO GRATIN

serves 6

Olive oil

1½ lb (750 g) small, round white potatoes

2 Tbsp finely chopped fresh
flat-leaf parsley

1 tsp fresh thyme leaves,
plus more for garnish

1 Tbsp all-purpose flour

Salt and freshly ground pepper

3 oz (90 g) very cold fresh goat cheese,
crumbled

1¼ cups (10 fl oz/310 ml) whole milk

1 Tbsp grated Parmesan cheese

*This updated gratin
is made especially
tempting by the
addition of tangy
goat cheese. Look
for soft fresh goat
cheese, without
a rind and free of
any herb or pepper
seasoning.*

Preheat the oven to 350°F (180°C). Oil an
8-inch (20-cm) square or other shallow,
1½-qt (1.5-l) baking dish.

Using a food processor fitted with the slicing
blade or a large, sharp knife, cut the potatoes
into paper-thin slices.

In a small bowl, stir together the parsley
and 1 tsp thyme. In another small bowl, stir
together the flour, ¼ tsp salt, and a grind of
pepper. Place the goat cheese in a third bowl.

Arrange one-third of the potato slices,
slightly overlapping them, in the prepared
dish. Sprinkle with half of the herb mixture,
half of the flour mixture, and one-third of the
goat cheese. Arrange half of the remaining
potato slices on top, again overlapping them
slightly. Sprinkle with the remaining herb
mixture, the remaining flour mixture, and
half of the remaining cheese. Arrange the
remaining potato slices in a layer on top and
sprinkle with the remaining cheese. Pour
the milk evenly over the top.

Cover the dish tightly with foil. Bake until
the potatoes are tender when pierced with
a knife, about 1 hour. Uncover, sprinkle
with the cheese, and continue baking until
golden, about 15 minutes. Let stand for
15 minutes. The moisture in the dish will
thicken and be reabsorbed by the potatoes.
Garnish the gratin with thyme leaves
and serve.

4

ROASTED CARROTS & FENNEL

serves 4

1 large or 2 medium fennel bulbs

½ lb (250 g) multicolored baby carrots

1½ Tbsp olive oil

3 or 4 fresh thyme sprigs

Salt

1½ Tbsp Pernod

*This is a memorable
dish, beautifully
accented by the
colorful hue of the
carrots and elevated
by the anise essence
of the fennel. A quick
flambé burns off the
alcohol in the liquor
and concentrates
the flavor. Once you
learn the trick, strike
the match at the table
for an impressive
presentation.*

Preheat oven to 375°F (190°C).

Cut the stalks and feathery leaves from the
fennel bulb; discard or reserve for another
use. Cut the bulb in half lengthwise, and cut
each half into wedges about ½ inch (12 mm)
thick. Cut the carrots in half crosswise if
they are long. Place the carrots and fennel in
a baking dish or a cast-iron frying pan just
large enough to hold them in a single layer.
Drizzle with the oil, add the thyme, and
sprinkle with ½ tsp salt, and turn to coat
evenly. Spread the vegetables out evenly.

Roast until the fennel has caramelized lightly
and the carrots have begun to wrinkle
slightly, about 35 minutes. Remove from the
oven, drizzle with the Pernod, and carefully
light with a long match. Shake the pan slightly
until the flames go out, and then serve.

5

LEMON-ROASTED POTATOES WITH OREGANO

serves 4

2 lb (1 kg) large russet potatoes, peeled

½ cup (4 fl oz/125 ml) olive oil

¼ cup (2 fl oz/60 ml) fresh lemon juice

1 clove garlic, minced

2 tsp dried oregano

Salt and freshly ground pepper

Bright splashes of lemon and herb hint at sunnier days. Lemon is used liberally and often in Greek cooking. Here, it gives the potatoes a citrusy sharpness that pairs well with the oregano. Be sure to use a russet or other floury baking potato, and cut the potatoes into large pieces, to keep them airy and light inside yet golden and brown outside.

Preheat the oven to 400°F (200°C).

Cut the potatoes in half lengthwise, and then cut each piece in half crosswise. Arrange the potatoes in a baking dish just large enough to hold them in a single layer. Add the oil, lemon juice, garlic, and oregano. Season with salt and pepper. Using your hands, toss the potatoes to coat thoroughly with the oil and seasonings. Spread the potatoes out evenly. Pour 1 cup (8 fl oz/250 ml) water into the pan.

Bake, uncovered, for 30 minutes. Turn the potatoes and continue to bake until tender when pierced with a knife, 15–30 minutes. The potatoes will be just lightly browned in places. Let stand for 10 minutes before serving.

6

FAVA BEAN SOUP

serves 6

3 lb (1.5 kg) fava beans, shelled

2 fresh winter savory sprigs

1 fresh thyme sprig, plus more for garnish

Salt and freshly ground pepper

1½ cups (12 fl oz/375 ml) whole milk

¼ cup (2 fl oz/60 ml) crème fraîche

2 Tbsp unsalted butter

In spring, French cooks use fava beans in countless ways, whole and puréed, in soups, side dishes, salads, and braises. This simple soup calls for just half a dozen ingredients and goes together quickly. The addition of crème fraîche, a French kitchen staple, gives it a smooth, creamy finish.

Pour 4 cups (32 fl oz/1 l) water into a large saucepan and bring to a boil. Add the beans and cook for 1–2 minutes. Using a slotted spoon, transfer the beans to a colander and rinse under cold running water, and then drain. Pinch each bean to slip it from the skin. Transfer the beans to a bowl.

Remove all but 1 cup (8 fl oz/250 ml) of the water from the pan and reserve it. Add the beans, winter savory sprigs, and 1 thyme sprig to the pan. Season with 1 tsp salt and bring to a boil. Reduce the heat to medium, cover partially, and cook until the beans are easily crushed with a fork, about 15 minutes.

Working in batches, purée the beans and their cooking liquid in a blender or food processor. Return to the pan and place over medium heat. Slowly whisk in 1¼ cups (10 fl oz/310 ml) of the milk. The soup will be creamy but somewhat stiff. Whisk in the crème fraîche and butter. If desired, whisk in more milk or some of the reserved cooking liquid until the soup reaches the desired consistency. Adjust the seasoning if necessary.

Ladle the soup into bowls. Garnish with thyme sprigs and pepper and serve.

7

In spring and again in fall, artichokes fill the markets, so eat them every chance you can get. In Rome, small, tender artichokes are lightly cloaked in bread crumbs before they are fried, yielding a crisp result. A squeeze of fresh lemon juice heightens the sweetness of the artichokes.

FRIED ARTICHOKES WITH LEMON & BREAD CRUMBS

serves 4–6

2 lemons

12 baby artichokes

3 eggs

¼ cup (1 oz/30 g) grated pecorino romano cheese

Salt and freshly ground pepper

2 cups (8 oz/250 g) fine dried bread crumbs

Olive oil for frying

Fill a large bowl with water. Cut 1 lemon in half and squeeze the juice of both halves into the water. Snap off the tough outer leaves of each artichoke to reveal the pale inner leaves. Cut off the top ¾ inch (2 cm) of the leaves. Cut a thin slice off the base of the stem, and then peel off the tough, dark outer flesh around the base of the leaves and along the length of the stem, leaving the stem attached. Cut the artichoke in half or quarters lengthwise, and then cut out the fuzzy choke, if any. Drop the wedges into the lemon water. Let stand for about 10 minutes.

Drain the artichokes and pat dry. In a shallow bowl, beat together the eggs and cheese, and season with salt and pepper. Spread the bread crumbs on a plate. One at a time, dip the artichoke pieces into the egg mixture, and then roll in the bread crumbs. Place on a wire rack and let dry for 15 minutes.

Preheat the oven to 200°F (95°C). Pour oil to a depth of 1 inch (2.5 cm) into a deep, heavy frying pan and heat to 375°F (190°C) on a deep-frying thermometer. Add a few artichoke pieces at a time to the hot oil and fry, turning once or twice, until golden brown, about 4 minutes. Using a slotted spoon, transfer the artichokes to a paper towel–lined platter to drain and keep warm in the oven. Fry the remaining artichoke pieces, allowing the oil to return to 375°F between batches.

Cut the remaining lemon into wedges. Arrange the artichokes on a platter, season with salt and pepper, and serve with the lemon wedges.

8

This quick dish pairs tender spring asparagus with pleasantly chewy shiitake mushrooms for a filling and satisfying vegetable stir-fry. Sesame seeds—especially the black variety— lend a savory flavor and subtle crunch to countless Asian dishes.

STIR-FRIED ASPARAGUS WITH SHIITAKE MUSHROOMS & SESAME SEEDS

serves 4–6

3 Tbsp peanut oil

1 clove garlic, minced

1 Tbsp peeled and grated fresh ginger

6 oz (185 g) shiitake mushrooms, stems trimmed, caps thinly sliced

1 lb (500 g) asparagus, ends trimmed, spears cut into 2-inch (5-cm) pieces

¼ cup (2 fl oz/60 ml) dry white wine or sake

¼ cup (2 fl oz/60 ml) chicken broth

1½ Tbsp soy sauce

2 tsp white and/or black sesame seeds

In a large, deep frying pan or a wok, heat the oil over high heat. Add the garlic and ginger and cook, stirring frequently, until fragrant but not browned, about 30 seconds. Add the mushrooms and cook, stirring frequently, until they begin to brown, about 2 minutes. Add the asparagus and cook, stirring constantly, until bright green and tender-crisp, about 3 minutes.

Pour in the wine, broth, and soy sauce and cook until the liquid is reduced and the vegetables are tender, 2–3 minutes. Stir in the sesame seeds and serve.

9

PROSCIUTTO-WRAPPED HARICOTS VERTS WITH LEMON AIOLI

serves 4

This is a stunning presentation for spring and summer entertaining. The bundles of beans can be assembled a day ahead and then grilled just before serving. For a vegetarian option, use a long blanched chive in place of the prosciutto to tie the haricots verts into bundles.

FOR THE LEMON AIOLI

1 clove garlic

Salt

1 egg, plus 1 egg yolk

1 cup (8 fl oz/250 ml) canola oil

1 Tbsp grated lemon zest

1 Tbsp fresh lemon juice

1 lb (500 g) haricots verts, trimmed

2 oz (60 g) prosciutto, cut into 8 pieces each about 1 inch (2.5 cm) wide and 4 inches (10 cm) long

Olive oil for brushing

Salt and freshly ground pepper

To make the aioli, place the garlic and ¼ tsp salt in a blender and process until finely chopped. Add the egg and the egg yolk and process until combined. With the motor running, slowly add the oil, just a few drops at first and then in a steady stream until the oil is completely incorporated. Add the lemon zest and juice and season with salt. Transfer to a bowl.

Bring a pot of generously salted water to a boil. Add the haricots verts and cook until just tender, about 2 minutes. Drain the beans and rinse under cold running water. Transfer to paper towels and let cool and dry completely.

Divide the beans into 8 equal stacks. Lay a piece of prosciutto on a work surface. Put 1 stack of beans at one end and roll up the prosciutto to enclose the beans in a tight bundle. Repeat to make 7 more bundles.

Heat a ridged grill pan over high heat. Lightly brush each bundle with oil and season with salt and pepper. Working in batches if necessary, cook the bundles, turning as needed, until the prosciutto is caramelized, about 2 minutes per side. Serve accompanied with the lemon aioli.

10

SHAVED FENNEL, PARMESAN & ARUGULA SALAD

serves 4–6

If you've only enjoyed fennel cooked, try this Italian method for serving it raw. The thinly shaved, faintly anise-flavored vegetable is transformed when tossed with a rich olive oil vinaigrette and peppery arugula and crowned with Parmesan shavings.

2 fennel bulbs

3 Tbsp extra-virgin olive oil

1½ tsp fresh lemon juice, or as needed

1 tsp Champagne vinegar

Salt and freshly ground pepper

4 cups (4 oz/125 g) baby arugula leaves

2 oz (60 g) piece Parmesan cheese

Cut the stalks and feathery leaves from each fennel bulb. Reserve a few of the leaves for garnish; reserve the remainder and the stems for another use. Trim off the base. If the outer layer is tough or discolored, discard it. Cut each bulb lengthwise into paper-thin slices. Then cut each slice lengthwise into several pieces.

In a large bowl, stir together the oil, 1½ tsp lemon juice, and the vinegar. Season with ½ tsp salt and ½ tsp pepper. Add more lemon juice, if desired. Add the fennel and toss to coat. Let stand for 10–15 minutes. Add the arugula and toss to coat.

Arrange the salad on plates. Using a vegetable peeler, shave the Parmesan into thin slices or curls over the salad. Garnish with fennel leaves and serve.

11

MUSHROOM BRUSCHETTA

serves 4

3 Tbsp olive oil, plus more for brushing and drizzling

2 Tbsp fresh lemon juice

1 clove garlic, crushed

Salt and freshly ground pepper

1 lb (500 g) portobello mushrooms, stems removed, caps cut into slices ¼ inch (6 mm) thick

8 slices coarse country bread, cut on the diagonal into slices ½ inch (12 mm) thick

¼ cup (1 oz/30 g) crumbled feta cheese

2 Tbsp thinly sliced fresh basil

Grill-marked and garlic-rubbed, bruschetta can be the vehicle for many delicious vegetables. In place of the traditional tomatoes, try meaty portobellos, whose big caps are easy to flip on the grill. If you'd like to use smaller mushrooms, you can skip the grill and sauté them in a pan with white wine and herbs.

In a bowl, stir together the 3 Tbsp oil, the lemon juice, garlic, ½ tsp salt, and several grinds of pepper. Add the mushroom slices and turn to coat evenly. Let stand for at least 10 minutes or up to 1 hour.

Prepare a charcoal or gas grill for direct-heat grilling over medium-high heat. Oil the grill rack. Brush the bread slices on both sides with oil and grill until lightly grill-marked, about 1 minute per side. You may need to press the bread onto the rack to get nice grill marks. Transfer to a platter, cover with foil, and place near the grill to keep warm.

Arrange the mushroom slices in a single layer in an oiled grill basket or on oiled heavy-duty foil. Grill, turning once, until softened and richly browned, about 3 minutes per side. Arrange the mushrooms on the grilled bread slices. Drizzle with oil, sprinkle with the feta and basil, and serve.

12

NORTH AFRICAN SPICED CARROT SALAD

serves 4

¾ lb carrots (375 g), cut on the diagonal into slices ¼ inch (6 mm) thick

¼ tsp caraway seeds

1 clove garlic, minced

½–1 tsp prepared harissa

1 Tbsp red wine vinegar

2 Tbsp extra-virgin olive oil

Salt and freshly ground pepper

1 or 2 eggs, hard-boiled, peeled, and quartered lengthwise

8 oil-cured black olives

1 Tbsp chopped fresh cilantro

In North Africa, meals often start with three or more small plates, such as this refreshing salad of springtime carrots. The piquant dressing relies on harissa, a paste of dried chiles, garlic, cumin, and oil. Caraway seeds add another spicy note.

Bring a small saucepan of salted water to a boil. Add the carrots and cook until almost tender, about 2½ minutes. Drain the carrots and transfer to a bowl.

Using a mortar and pestle or a spice grinder, crush the caraway seeds until finely ground. Add the ground seeds to the carrots. Add the garlic, harissa, and vinegar. Toss to mix well. Add the oil and toss until the carrots are evenly coated. Season with salt and pepper.

Transfer the carrot salad to a platter. Arrange the eggs and olives over and around the carrots. Garnish with the cilantro and serve.

13

STUFFED BAKED ARTICHOKES WITH CHILE & MINT

serves 4

Thistle-shaped artichokes have lots of nooks and crannies, perfect for stuffing with bold seasonings like the garlic and two forms of chile in this recipe. The refreshing quality of mint counteracts the spice from the jalapeño and the richness of the oil-coated bread crumbs.

1 lemon

4 large artichokes

1 Tbsp unsalted butter

1 Tbsp extra-virgin olive oil, plus oil for drizzling

1 yellow onion, finely chopped

Salt and freshly ground pepper

1 jalapeño chile, seeded and minced

2 cloves garlic, minced

½ tsp red pepper flakes

1½ cups (3 oz/90 g) fresh bread crumbs

1 egg

Leaves from ½ bunch fresh mint, cut into thin ribbons

Bring a large pot of salted water to a boil. Halve the lemon, squeeze the juice into the boiling water, and carefully drop in the lemon halves. Cut off the stem of each artichoke flush with the base. Cut off the top one-fourth of the artichoke. Using kitchen scissors, snip off any thorny tips that remain on the leaves. Lower the artichokes into the boiling water and cook, turning occasionally, until the bottoms are almost tender when pierced with a knife and the leaves come off when pulled firmly, 15–20 minutes. Drain the artichokes upside down on a rack set over a baking sheet.

In a saucepan, melt the butter with the 1 Tbsp oil over medium heat. Add the onion and a pinch of salt and sauté until the onion is soft and translucent, 5–6 minutes. Add the chile, garlic, and red pepper flakes and sauté for 2 minutes. Turn off the heat, stir in the bread crumbs, and transfer the mixture to a bowl. Add the egg and beat well with a fork until the mixture is well moistened. Add the mint along with a generous pinch each of salt and pepper and stir to blend.

Preheat the oven to 350°F (180°C). Gently open the leaves of each artichoke away from the center. Using a spoon, remove the tough chokes and small yellow leaves. Fill the cavity and the spaces between some of the leaves with the crumb mixture. Arrange the artichokes upright in a baking dish ⟫→

in which they fit snugly and drizzle the tops with oil. Cover with foil and bake until a leaf can be easily pulled from the artichoke, about 20 minutes. Remove the foil and bake until the top of the filling is lightly browned, about 10 minutes. Remove from the oven and serve.

14

ROASTED BROCCOLINI WITH GARLIC & LEMON

serves 3 or 4

Long and lean broccolini is more flavorful than conventional broccoli, but it too benefits from the tart flavor of lemon. Dice the lemon with the peel still on and add it to the roasting pan. The heat of the oven will temper its bitterness, resulting in a potent but pleasing tartness.

1½ Tbsp olive oil

2 cloves garlic, minced

1 bunch broccolini, ends trimmed, coarsely chopped

½ lemon, peel intact, seeded and cut into ¼-inch (6-mm) dice

Salt

Preheat the oven to 350°F (180°C).

In a frying pan, heat 1 Tbsp of the oil over medium-high heat. Add the garlic and sauté until lightly golden, about 1 minute. Add the broccolini, lemon, and ½ tsp salt. Sauté just until the color of the broccolini deepens, about 1 minute.

Transfer the broccolini to a baking dish, drizzle with the remaining 1½ tsp oil, and turn to coat. Roast until the broccolini is tender-crisp, 10–12 minutes. Serve hot or at room temperature.

15

SPRING VEGETABLE TART
serves 4

1 sheet frozen puff pastry,
about ½ lb (250 g), thawed

1 cup (4 oz/125 g) shredded fontina cheese

15–20 thin asparagus spears, ends trimmed

1 small leek, white part only,
halved and thinly sliced

2 eggs

¼ cup (2 fl oz/60 ml) whole milk

Salt and freshly ground pepper

Celebrate the bounty of the season with an all-purpose tart, easy to load with whatever vegetables are stacked highest at the farmers' market. This recipe pairs elegant leeks and asparagus with pungent fontina cheese. Serve it with a tangle of frisée and a glass of crisp white wine, preferably for a weekend lunch on the deck or patio.

Preheat the oven to 400°F (200°C). Line a baking sheet with parchment paper. Lay the puff pastry on the prepared sheet. Fold over the sides to make a 1-inch (2.5-cm) rim, overlapping the pastry at the corners and pressing it lightly. Inside the rim, prick the pastry all over with a fork.

Sprinkle half of the cheese over the bottom of the pastry inside the rim. Top with the asparagus, laying the spears vertically in a row from one side of the pastry to the other. Sprinkle the leeks over the asparagus. Bake for 15 minutes.

Meanwhile, in a bowl, beat the eggs, milk, ½ tsp salt, and several grinds of pepper until well combined. Remove the pastry from the oven. Pour the egg mixture evenly over the asparagus and leeks and sprinkle on the remaining cheese. Bake until the pastry is puffed and golden brown, about 10 minutes. Let the tart stand for 10 minutes before serving.

16

SAUTÉED FRESH PEAS WITH SHREDDED ROMAINE & MINT
serves 3 or 4

1 Tbsp unsalted butter

2 Tbsp minced shallot

2 lb (1 kg) English peas, shelled

½ head romaine lettuce, cut crosswise into very thin strips

½ cup (4 fl oz/125 ml) chicken broth

Salt and freshly ground pepper

¼ cup (⅓ oz/10 g) finely chopped fresh mint

Spring peas are considered a delicacy and are among the most sought-after early spring vegetables. Small, sweet, and tender, they require only brief cooking and minimal seasonings. Their classic companion is fresh mint, which subtly highlights their flavor.

In a large saucepan, melt the butter over medium-high heat. Add the shallot and sauté until translucent, about 1 minute. Add the peas, lettuce, and broth. Cover and cook until the peas are tender to the bite and the lettuce has wilted, about 5 minutes. Season with salt and pepper. Stir in the mint.

Using a slotted spoon, transfer the vegetables to a bowl and serve.

17

FAVA BEANS WITH PECORINO
serves 4

3 lb (1.5 kg) fava beans, shelled

6 oz (185 g) pecorino cheese,
cut into ½-inch (12-cm) cubes

¼ cup (2 fl oz/60 ml) extra-virgin olive oil

Salt and freshly ground pepper

In Italy, fava beans are one of the first vegetables of the spring garden. The young beans are so tender that they are eaten raw, straight out of their pods. For this easy dish, select a medium-aged pecorino that will hold its shape when cut.

Bring a pot of lightly salted water to a boil. Add the beans and cook for 1–2 minutes. Drain, rinse under cold running water, and drain again. Pinch each bean to slip it from the skin. Transfer the beans to a bowl.

Add the cheese to the beans. Drizzle with the oil and season with salt and pepper. Toss to mix well and serve.

18

MARINATED MUSHROOMS

serves 4

¾ lb (375 g) small white mushrooms

⅔ cup (5 fl oz/160 ml) dry red wine

¼ cup (2 fl oz/60 ml) red wine vinegar

⅛ tsp ground allspice

4 cardamom pods, crushed

2 whole cloves

1 bay leaf

¼ tsp peppercorns

1 tsp granulated sugar

⅓ cup (3 fl oz/80 ml) olive oil

Salt

Marinating vegetables in oil and vinegar has an established place in French cooking, and champignons à la grecque remain a great hors d'oeuvre for retro-inspired cocktail parties. Use small whole mushrooms, and have guests spear them with picks. White wine and herbs are the usual marinade ingredients, but the red wine and warm spices are used here in an enticing variation.

Cut off the stem flush with the bottom of each mushroom cap. Place the mushrooms in a saucepan. Add the wine, vinegar, allspice, cardamom, cloves, bay leaf, peppercorns, sugar, oil, and ½ tsp salt. Pour in ½ cup (4 fl oz/125 ml) water. Bring to a boil over medium-high heat, reduce the heat to medium-low, and simmer until the center of a mushroom is easily pierced with a knife, about 10 minutes. Let the mushrooms cool completely in the cooking liquid.

Using a slotted spoon, transfer the mushrooms to a bowl and serve.

19

STUFFED PIQUILLO PEPPERS

serves 6–8

10 oz (315 g) fresh goat cheese

3–4 Tbsp finely chopped fresh chives, plus more for garnish

3–4 Tbsp finely chopped fresh basil

Salt and freshly ground pepper

1 jar (12 oz/375 g) roasted piquillo peppers (about 24 peppers)

1 Tbsp extra-virgin olive oil

FOR THE VINAIGRETTE

⅓ cup (3 oz/80 ml) extra-virgin olive oil

3½ Tbsp balsamic vinegar

1 small shallot, minced

Salt and freshly ground pepper

Spanish piquillo peppers are traditionally hand-picked, then roasted in wood-fired ovens, peeled, and packed into jars or cans. The flavor of wood smoke enhances the distinctive, slight spiciness of these small, triangular, intensely red peppers. They are often stuffed with meat or seafood, but here the filling is herbed fresh goat cheese.

Preheat the broiler.

To make the filling, in a small bowl, use a wooden spoon to mash the goat cheese together with the chives and basil. Season with salt and pepper.

Drain the peppers, but do not rinse them. With your fingers, gently open the stem end of each pepper. Remove any seeds and ribs you can from the insides without cutting or tearing the pepper walls.

With a small spoon or your fingers, carefully stuff about 1 Tbsp of the goat cheese mixture inside each pepper. The cheese mixture should fill the peppers but should not be bursting out.

Arrange the peppers in a single layer on a baking sheet. Brush them with the oil. Slip the pan under the broiler 4–6 inches (10–15 cm) from the heat source and broil until the cheese is soft and bubbly, about 7 minutes. Let cool slightly.

To make the vinaigrette, in a small bowl, whisk together the oil, vinegar, shallot, ½ tsp salt, and ¼ tsp pepper.

Transfer the peppers to a serving dish. Drizzle liberally with the vinaigrette, sprinkle with chives, and serve.

20

Versions of these small, fried or baked pastries are turned out in kitchens throughout South America, where they are filled with everything from seasoned meats, pot beans, or cubed potatoes to pumpkin, cheese, or fruit. Here, a mix of corn, peas, and tomato is spiked with a little jalapeño chile for a satisfying snack or appetizer.

CORN & PEA EMPANADITAS

serves 4–6

FOR THE DOUGH

2 cups (10 oz/315 g) all-purpose flour

1 tsp baking soda

Salt and freshly ground pepper

FOR THE FILLING

1½ Tbsp olive oil

1 white onion, minced

1 small green bell pepper, seeded and minced

1 Tbsp seeded and minced jalapeño chile

2 cloves garlic, minced

1½ cups (9 oz/280 g) frozen corn kernels, thawed

½ cup (2½ oz/75 g) shelled fresh green peas

½ cup (4 fl oz/125 ml) tomato sauce

¼ cup (⅓ oz/10 g) chopped fresh cilantro

Canola oil for frying

To make the dough, in a food processor, combine the flour, baking soda, 1 tsp salt, and ½ tsp pepper and pulse to blend. Add ½ cup (4 fl oz/125 ml) water in a slow stream, pulsing 2 or 3 times until a soft dough forms that sticks together when pinched. If the mixture is still crumbly, drizzle about 2 Tbsp water over the dough and pulse several times. Remove the dough, roll into a log, and wrap tightly in plastic wrap. Refrigerate for 30 minutes.

In a frying pan, warm the olive oil over medium heat. Add the onion, bell pepper, chile, and garlic and cook, stirring, until softened, about 2 minutes. Add the corn and peas and cook, stirring, until tender, about 5 minutes. Add the tomato sauce and cook, stirring frequently, until the mixture thickens, about 5 minutes. Let cool. Stir in the cilantro.

Unwrap the dough, divide into 16 equal pieces, and gently shape each into a ball. On a lightly floured work surface, roll out each ball into a 4-inch (10-cm) circle. Brush the edges of the dough with water. Place about 1 Tbsp of the filling in the center of each circle. Fold the dough in half over the filling and pinch to seal, fluting the edges or crimping them with a fork. ⤳

Pour oil to a depth of 1 inch (2.5 cm) into a heavy frying pan over medium-high heat and heat to 350°F (180°C) on a deep-frying thermometer. Working in batches, place a few pastries in the hot oil and fry, turning as needed with tongs, until crisp and well browned on all sides, 3–5 minutes. Transfer to paper towels to drain. Serve warm or at room temperature.

21

Large portobello mushrooms are so meaty and flavorful that they are easily prepared with just fresh parsley, some garlic, and a little olive oil. Serve these as a first course, side dish, or even as a main, with a green salad, crusty bread, and wedges of aged cheese alongside.

PARSLEY PORTOBELLOS

serves 4

4 portobello mushrooms, stems removed

3 Tbsp olive oil, plus more if needed

6 cloves garlic, coarsely chopped

1½ cups (1½ oz/45 g) fresh parsley leaves, plus sprigs for garnish

Salt and freshly ground pepper

Preheat the oven to 375°F (190°C). Lightly oil a baking dish just large enough to hold the mushrooms in a single layer. Rub the mushroom caps with 1 Tbsp of the oil.

In a food processor, combine the remaining 2 Tbsp oil, the garlic, parsley leaves, ½ tsp salt, and ½ tsp pepper and process until smooth. If the mixture seems too thick, add more oil, a few drops at a time.

Arrange the mushrooms, gill side up, in the prepared dish. Spread the parsley mixture on the mushrooms, covering the gills all the way to the edges. Roast until the mushrooms are juicy and tender when pricked with a fork, about 20 minutes. Transfer to a platter, garnish with parsley sprigs, and serve.

22

Look for thin asparagus spears for this dish; they are generally more tender than fat spears, and the stalks do not require peeling before cooking. Morels, with their honeycomb-patterned exterior, have a special affinity for asparagus, but if you are unable to find them, oyster or cremini mushrooms can be substituted.

ROASTED ASPARAGUS & MORELS WITH SHALLOT BUTTER

serves 6

1½ lb (750 g) thin asparagus, ends trimmed

4 oz (125 g) morel mushrooms

4 Tbsp (2 oz/60 g) unsalted butter

2 shallots, minced

1 Tbsp chopped fresh tarragon

Salt and freshly ground pepper

Preheat the oven to 450°F (230°C).

Arrange the asparagus in a single layer on a baking sheet. If the morels are large, cut them crosswise into rings ¼ inch (6 mm) wide. Leave small ones whole. Add the mushrooms to the baking sheet.

In a small saucepan, melt the butter over low heat. Add the shallots and sauté for 1 minute. Drizzle the shallot butter over the asparagus and morels. Scatter the tarragon over the top and season with salt and pepper. Toss the asparagus and morels in the butter and tarragon until evenly coated and then spread in a single layer.

Roast until the asparagus is lightly browned but still crisp and the morels are dark brown, about 10 minutes. Transfer the asparagus and morels to a platter. Drizzle any pan juices over the top and serve.

23

This French-style preparation of mashed potatoes, known as aligot, is a specialty of the Auvergne region. Tomme fraîche, a fresh cheese, is beaten into hot potatoes. Finish the dish with a drizzle of garlic butter, and serve with sausages for a hearty main dish.

MASHED POTATOES WITH TOMME CHEESE

serves 6

5 Tbsp (2½ oz/75 g) unsalted butter

2 cloves garlic, minced

6 waxy potatoes, about 2 lb (1 kg) total

Salt and freshly ground pepper

½ cup (4 fl oz/125 ml) whole milk

¼ cup (2 fl oz/60 ml) heavy cream

6 oz (185 g) fresh tomme cheese, cubed

In a small frying pan, melt the butter over medium-high heat. Add the garlic, reduce the heat to low, and sauté until barely golden, about 3 minutes. Remove from the heat.

Place the potatoes in a large saucepan with water to cover by 2 inches (5 cm) and bring to a boil. Add 1 tsp salt, reduce the heat to medium, and cook until the potatoes are easily pierced with a fork, 20–25 minutes. Drain the potatoes and return to the hot pan.

In a small saucepan, warm the milk and cream over medium-high heat to just below the boiling point. Gradually pour into the potatoes, mashing them with a potato masher or fork. Stir in the cheese, 1 tsp salt, and ½ tsp pepper. Pour in the garlic-butter mixture and stir until the cheese is melted. Transfer to a bowl and serve.

24

GRILLED BABY LEEKS
WITH CHERVIL & CHIVES

serves 4

16 baby leeks

2 Tbsp sherry vinegar

1 tsp Dijon mustard

Salt and freshly ground pepper

1½ Tbsp minced fresh chives

1 Tbsp minced fresh chervil or flat-leaf parsley, plus more for sprinkling

½ cup (4 fl oz/125 ml) olive oil

Anise-scented chervil contributes fresh flavor to this dish of smoke-tinged baby leeks. The sweet young onions are accented by slightly tart sherry vinegar, spicy Dijon mustard, and peppery olive oil, a mixture that doubles as both marinade and sauce.

Trim the root ends from the leeks, leaving just enough attached to keep the leeks from falling apart.

In a rectangular glass baking dish, combine the vinegar, mustard, a pinch each of salt and pepper, 1 Tbsp of the chives, and the 1 Tbsp minced chervil. Whisk together until well blended. Add the oil in a slow, steady stream, whisking constantly to blend. Place the leeks in the dish and toss to coat. Cover the dish and marinate the leeks at room temperature for at least 1 hour or in the refrigerator for up to overnight.

Prepare a charcoal or gas grill for direct-heat grilling over medium-high heat. Oil the grill rack. Remove the leeks from the marinade, shaking off any excess, and reserve the marinade. Arrange the leeks on the rack and grill, turning occasionally, until tender and nicely browned, 5–6 minutes.

Transfer the leeks to a platter and drizzle lightly with some of the remaining marinade. Sprinkle with the remaining 1½ tsp chives and with minced chervil. Serve hot, warm, or at room temperature.

25

GREEN & YELLOW BEANS
WITH OLIVE-SHALLOT BUTTER

serves 4

10 Kalamata olives, pitted and chopped

1 shallot, chopped

1 clove garlic, chopped

2 Tbsp unsalted butter, at room temperature

5 or 6 fresh basil leaves

½ lb (250 g) young, slender yellow wax beans, trimmed

½ lb (250 g) young, slender green beans, trimmed

Freshly ground pepper

This recipe can also become a sauce for pasta: Cut the beans into short lengths before boiling, and double the amounts for the olive butter. Cook 10 oz (315 g) short macaroni, drain, toss with the butter-coated beans, and garnish with ribbons of fresh basil. Look for crisp beans that make an audible snapping sound when broken.

In a food processor, combine the olives, shallot, garlic, butter, and basil, and process to mix well.

Bring a saucepan of salted water to a boil. Add the yellow beans and cook until tender-crisp, 5–6 minutes. Using a slotted spoon, transfer to a colander and rinse under cold running water. Transfer to a bowl. Return the water to a boil, add the green beans, and cook until tender-crisp, 3–5 minutes. Drain, rinse under running cold water, and drain again.

In a large frying pan, warm 2 Tbsp water over medium heat. Add the beans and toss until heated through. Add the olive butter and toss until the butter coats the beans but has not melted into a puddle. Season with pepper. Transfer the beans to a platter and serve.

26

Combining fava beans and chickpeas with the usual corn and lima beans creates a succotash far different from what many remember in their grade-school cafeteria or on their grandmother's table. If fresh fava beans are unavailable, substitute frozen shelled edamame.

SUCCOTASH SALAD

serves 8–10

FOR THE CHAMPAGNE VINAIGRETTE

½ cup (4 fl oz/125 ml) grape seed oil

¼ cup (2 fl oz/60 ml) extra-virgin olive oil

2 Tbsp Champagne vinegar

2 Tbsp Dijon mustard

1 shallot, minced

Salt and freshly ground white pepper

6 ears corn, husks and silk removed

Ice water

3–4 Tbsp unsalted butter, melted

Salt and freshly ground pepper

1½ lb (750 g) fava beans, shelled

1 can (15 oz/470 g) chickpeas, drained and rinsed

1 can (15 oz/470 g) lima beans, drained and rinsed

3 ripe tomatoes, seeded and diced

10–12 grape or cherry tomatoes, halved lengthwise

2 Tbsp chopped fresh basil

2 Tbsp chopped fresh chervil

2 Tbsp chopped fresh flat-leaf parsley

2 Tbsp chopped fresh tarragon

½ cup (2 oz/60 g) thinly sliced red onion

1 head butter lettuce, torn into large, cup-shaped pieces

To make the vinaigrette, pour the grape seed and olive oils into a measuring cup with a spout. In a bowl, whisk together the vinegar, mustard, shallot, 1 tsp salt, and ½ tsp white pepper. Whisking constantly, add the oils in a slow, steady stream.

Soak the corn in ice water to cover for 10 minutes. Drain the corn and pat dry. Brush the corn with some of the melted butter and season with salt and pepper.

Bring a pot of lightly salted water to a boil. Add the fava beans and cook for 1–2 minutes. Drain, rinse under cold running water, and drain again. Pinch each bean to slip it from its skin.

Prepare a charcoal or gas grill for direct-heat grilling over medium-high heat. Oil the grill rack. Grill the corn, turning often and basting with the melted butter, until lightly charred and caramelized on all sides, ⟶

about 15 minutes. Transfer the corn to a cutting board and let cool. Holding each ear upright and using a sharp knife, cut down along the ear, stripping off the kernels and rotating the ear a quarter turn with each cut.

In a large bowl, combine the corn kernels, favas, chickpeas, lima beans, tomatoes, basil, chervil, parsley, tarragon, and onion. Drizzle with ¼ cup (2 fl oz/60 ml) of the vinaigrette and toss gently to coat. Adjust the seasoning if necessary.

Arrange the lettuce leaves on a platter. Top with the succotash and serve, passing the remaining vinaigrette at the table.

27

These rustic "little toasts" are a crowd-pleasing antipasto, easy to create using canned cannellini beans from your pantry. But best of all, of course, is home-cooked beans, so if you prepare a pot of white beans as a side dish, cook extra and use about 2 cups (14 oz/440 g) to make these crostini the next day.

WHITE BEAN & ARUGULA CROSTINI

serves 6

3 Tbsp extra-virgin olive oil, plus more for brushing and drizzling

2 Tbsp finely chopped yellow onion

2 Tbsp finely chopped carrot

2 Tbsp finely chopped celery

1 can (15 oz/470 g) cannellini beans, rinsed and drained

Salt and freshly ground pepper

1 baguette

2 cups (2 oz/60 g) baby arugula leaves

Preheat the oven to 375°F (190°C).

In a frying pan, warm the 3 Tbsp oil over medium heat. Add the onion, carrot, and celery and sauté until the onion is golden and the carrots and celery are softened, 3–4 minutes. Add the beans, season with salt and pepper, and stir well to combine. Let cool to room temperature.

Meanwhile, cut the baguette on the diagonal into 18 slices each ½ inch (12 mm) thick. (You will not need the entire loaf.) Arrange the bread slices on a baking sheet and brush the tops lightly with oil. Bake until golden, about 5 minutes.

Arrange the toasts on a platter. Spoon the beans on the toasts. Drizzle generously with oil, top with the arugula, and serve.

CURRIED SAMOSAS WITH TAMARIND CHUTNEY

serves 8–10

Here, sweet-hot curry powder and pungent garlic and onion contribute their flavors to a creamy butternut squash filling enclosed in a crisp pastry shell. The tart tamarind chutney balances the sweetness of the filling. Serve these savory pastries at cocktail parties or as a starter for a contemporary Indian menu. Look for the tamarind paste in South Asian or Southeast Asian food shops.

FOR THE TAMARIND CHUTNEY

½ tsp ground cumin

½ tsp garam masala

½ tsp ground ginger

¼ cup (2 oz/60 g) seedless tamarind paste

Salt

Sugar

1 butternut squash, about 1½ lb (750 g)

3 Tbsp olive oil

2 Tbsp chopped white onion

2 cloves garlic, chopped

1 Tbsp Madras curry powder

1 tsp sugar

Salt

1 egg

1 package (1 lb/500 g) square wonton wrappers

Canola or rice bran oil for deep-frying

To make the chutney, in a small, dry saucepan, toast the cumin, garam masala, and ginger over medium-low heat, shaking the pan occasionally, until fragrant, 30–60 seconds. Remove from the heat and let cool in the pan for about 2 minutes.

Break up the tamarind paste with your fingers, and remove any errant seeds. Add the tamarind and 2 cups (16 fl oz/500 ml) water to the spice mixture and return to medium heat. Simmer, stirring and mashing the tamarind constantly, until reduced by one-half, about 15 minutes. Taste and adjust the seasoning with salt and sugar. Pour the chutney into a small bowl, let cool, cover, and set aside at room temperature. You should have about 1 cup (8 fl oz/250 ml).

Preheat the oven to 400°F (200°C). Cut the squash in half lengthwise and scoop out and discard the seeds. Place the halves, cut sides up, on a rimmed baking sheet and drizzle with 1 Tbsp of the olive oil. Bake the squash until tender when pierced with a knife, about 40 minutes. Let cool until easy to handle, then scoop the cooled flesh into a bowl and discard the skins. ⋙

In a saucepan, warm the remaining 2 Tbsp oil over medium heat. Add the onion and garlic and sauté until the onion is soft, 3–5 minutes. Remove from the heat and stir in the curry powder. Add the squash flesh and mash with a potato masher until almost smooth. Stir in the sugar and 1 tsp salt, then adjust the seasoning if necessary.

In a small bowl, beat the egg with a fork until blended. Lay about 5 wonton wrappers on a work surface; keep the remaining wrappers covered with a slightly damp kitchen towel. Spoon a scant 1 Tbsp of the squash filling in the center of each wrapper and flatten with the bottom of the spoon. Brush the edges of the wrapper with the egg. Fold each wrapper in half on the diagonal, forming a triangle, then press the edges together to seal the filling inside; set aside. Repeat with the remaining wrappers and filling.

Preheat the oven to 200°F (95°C). Set a wire rack on a large baking sheet and place near the stove. Pour oil to a depth of 3 inches (7.5 cm) into a deep, heavy frying pan and heat over medium-high heat until hot but not smoking. Working in batches, add the samosas to the oil and fry, turning once, until golden brown on both sides, about 2 minutes on each side. Using a slotted spoon, transfer to the rack to drain and then keep warm in the oven. Cook the remaining samosas in the same way, adding more oil to the pan if needed. You should have about 40 samosas.

Arrange the samosas on a platter, set the chutney alongside for dipping, and serve.

29

SWEET & SOUR VIDALIA ONIONS
serves 4

4 Vidalia onions

Salt and freshly ground pepper

1 clove garlic, crushed

3 fresh thyme sprigs

1 bay leaf

1 Tbsp olive oil

1 cup (8 fl oz/250 ml) chicken broth, plus more as needed

3 Tbsp red wine vinegar

2 Tbsp sugar

Vidalia onions are full of natural sugars. Slow-cooking them in red wine vinegar and chicken broth accentuates their sweetness. The liquid doubles as a sauce, accented with mellow roasted garlic and woodsy fresh thyme. If you like, use a mixture of Vidalias and small, saucer-shaped cipollini onions, cutting the cipollini in half through the stem end.

Preheat the oven to 350°F (180°C).

Peel and quarter each onion, leaving just enough of the root end attached to keep the wedges together. Arrange the onions in a baking dish in a single layer and sprinkle lightly with salt and pepper. Add the garlic, thyme sprigs, and bay leaf to the dish. Drizzle the oil over the onions.

In a small saucepan, bring the 1 cup broth to a boil over medium-high heat. Add the vinegar and sugar and cook, stirring occasionally, until the sugar dissolves, 2–3 minutes.

Pour the broth mixture over the onions. There should be enough to come halfway up the sides of the onions. Add a bit more broth, if needed. Cover the dish tightly with foil.

Bake the onions, stirring occasionally, until they release some of their juices and begin to soften, 30–40 minutes. Carefully remove the foil, raise the oven temperature to 400°F (200°C), and continue to bake the onions, stirring occasionally, until the liquid is reduced to about 2 Tbsp and the onions are very soft, 1–1¼ hours.

Transfer the onions to a serving dish and serve hot or at room temperature.

30

CRUSHED RED POTATOES
serves 4–6

2 lb (1 kg) red new potatoes

Salt and freshly ground pepper

1 Tbsp extra-virgin olive oil

2 Tbsp unsalted butter

Fresh chives, cut into 1-inch (2.5 cm) lengths, for garnish

New potatoes boil quickly, and you can leave the thin skins on for simple mashes. The recipe calls for red potatoes, but other varieties, such as Yukon gold or Yellow Finn, can be substituted. For an extra touch of flavor, stir in minced fresh flat-leaf parsley, thyme, or rosemary leaves.

Place the potatoes in a large saucepan and add water to cover by 2 inches (5 cm) and 1 tsp salt. Bring to a boil, reduce the heat to medium, cover, and cook until the potatoes are tender when pierced with a fork, 20–25 minutes.

Drain the potatoes and return them to the pan. Add the oil and butter. Using a fork or the back of a wooden spoon, crush the potatoes, breaking them into large, fluffy chunks and mixing in the oil and butter. Season with salt and the pepper. Transfer to a bowl, garnish with the chives, and serve.

31

FRESH PEAS WITH ONION & BASIL
serves 4

6 Tbsp (3 fl oz/90 ml) olive oil

1 small yellow onion, finely chopped

4 lb (2 kg) English peas, shelled

Salt and freshly ground pepper

Handful of fresh basil leaves

Shell the peas immediately before cooking to preserve their sweetness, and cook them just until they are bright green. Slowly and gently sautéing the onion will render it mellow, especially when combined with fragrant basil.

In a saucepan, warm the oil over medium heat. Add the onion and sauté until translucent and golden, about 10 minutes.

Add the peas and stir well. Pour in just enough water to cover the peas. Cover the pan and cook until the peas begin to soften, 3–4 minutes. Season with salt and pepper, and stir in the basil. Continue cooking until the peas are tender but still firm, about 2 minutes longer. Remove from the heat and serve.

Plunge into the first days of summer with picnic-perfect dishes, such as creamy potato salads or crunchy slaws packed with slivered carrots and cabbage. As the weather warms, eggplants and tomatoes make their first appearance in local farmers' markets. Green tomatoes sliced, dusted with cornmeal, and fried, or red tomatoes stuffed with white beans and tuna and baked are both delicious this time of year. So, too, are young eggplants, sliced, grilled, and then glazed with miso or dressed with a heady mix of feta, yogurt, and hot-pepper sauce.

4

STEAMED SUGAR SNAP PEAS
WITH BLACK SESAME SEEDS
page 132

5

MISO-GLAZED GRILLED
ASIAN EGGPLANT
page 133

6

TOMATOES WITH
BASIL VINAIGRETTE
page 133

7

BUTTERMILK COLESLAW
WITH CARROTS & RAISINS
page 135

11

FRIED GREEN TOMATOES
WITH RÉMOULADE
page 138

12

ROASTED POTATO SALAD
WITH GREEN ONION DRESSING
page 138

13

GRILLED EGGPLANT,
CORN & BREAD SALAD WITH
TOMATO-BASIL VINAIGRETTE
page 139

14

FRIED ZUCCHINI
WITH CURRY DIP
page 139

18

GRILLED FINGERLING POTATOES
WITH MUSTARD & HERBS
page 142

19

PANZANELLA
page 143

20

CUCUMBER, CILANTRO & JALAPEÑO
SALAD WITH GOAT CHEESE
page 143

21

PEPERONATA
page 144

25

GARLICKY ZUCCHINI SOUP
WITH BASIL GREMOLATA
page 148

26

GRILLED SUMMER SQUASHES
WITH FRESH MINT VINAIGRETTE
page 148

27

EGGPLANT CAPONATA
page 149

28

YELLOW TOMATOES WITH
MINT & PECORINO
page 149

june

1

MEDITERRANEAN CHICKPEA & POTATO SALAD

serves 4

Ice water

4 oz (125 g) young, slender green beans, trimmed

1¼ lb (625 g) red potatoes, quartered

1 cup (7 oz/220 g) drained and rinsed canned chickpeas or kidney beans

1 small red onion, finely chopped

½ cup (¾ oz/20 g) chopped fresh flat-leaf parsley

½ cup (¾ oz/20 g) roughly chopped fresh mint

4 green olives, pitted and coarsely chopped

1 Tbsp capers, chopped

1 Tbsp whole-grain mustard

1 Tbsp red wine vinegar

Salt and freshly ground pepper

1 Tbsp olive oil

Add a little excitement to the picnic table with this mixed-vegetable salad. Skip the typical mayo-based dressing in favor of a mustardy vinaigrette with accents of capers and olives, and lots of fresh herbs. For a more substantial salad, fold in some chopped hard-boiled eggs: Bring water to a full boil in a saucepan, lower the eggs into the water with a slotted spoon, reduce the heat to medium-low, and simmer for 10 minutes. Remove from the heat and place in a bowl of ice water until cool.

Bring a large pot of salted water to a boil. Have ready a bowl of ice water. Add the green beans to the boiling water and cook until bright green and tender-crisp, about 3 minutes. Using a slotted spoon, transfer to the bowl of ice water. Drain the beans and place in a large bowl. Add the potatoes to the boiling water and cook until just tender, 10–15 minutes. Drain the potatoes and add to the bowl.

Add the chickpeas, onion, parsley, mint, olives, and capers to the green beans and potatoes. In a small bowl, whisk together the mustard, vinegar, 1 tsp salt, and ½ tsp pepper. Whisk in the oil. Pour the dressing over the vegetables, toss until well coated, and serve.

2

BAKED TOMATOES WITH TUNA, WHITE BEANS & BREAD CRUMBS

serves 2

2 slices coarse country bread, each about ½ inch (12 mm) thick

1 clove garlic, halved

2 Tbsp olive oil

2 Tbsp chopped fresh flat-leaf parsley

4 large or 8 small ripe but firm tomatoes

1 can (5 oz/155 g) water-packed albacore tuna, drained

½ cup (3½ oz/105 g) drained and rinsed canned cannellini or butter beans

2 Tbsp minced red onion

1 Tbsp capers, drained

1 tsp sherry vinegar

These plump stuffed tomatoes, which rely on basic ingredients probably already in your pantry, are an easy-to-assemble and satisfying main course that needs only a green salad and crusty bread to complete the menu. For a striking presentation, look for uniformly shaped tomatoes with their stems attached, then reserve the tops, slip them into the baking dish about 10 minutes before the tomatoes are ready, and put them back on the tomatoes just before serving.

Preheat the oven to 300°F (150°C). Lightly oil a baking dish.

Place the bread slices on a baking sheet and bake until crisp and beginning to brown, about 15 minutes. Rub the cut side of the garlic on one side of each warm bread slice. Let the bread cool. Tear the bread into chunks, put in a food processor, and process to make uniform coarse crumbs. Transfer the crumbs to a bowl and toss with 1 Tbsp of the oil and 1 Tbsp of the parsley. Raise the oven temperature to 375°F (190°C).

Cut a thin slice off the top of each tomato. Using a melon baller, gently scoop out the core and seeds of each tomato, leaving the side walls intact. Arrange the tomatoes, cut side up, in the prepared dish.

In a large bowl, combine the tuna, beans, onion, capers, vinegar, the remaining 1 Tbsp olive oil, and the remaining 1 Tbsp parsley. Stir to mix, using a fork to break up the tuna. Spoon the filling into the tomatoes, dividing it evenly and mounding it slightly on top. Cover the filling generously with the bread crumbs.

Bake until the bread crumbs are golden and the sides of the tomatoes are soft and the skins have just begun to split, 20–25 minutes. Let cool slightly before serving.

3

GRILLED FENNEL WITH ROMESCO SAUCE

serves 6

2 large fennel bulbs

¼ cup (2 fl oz/60 ml) olive oil, plus oil for brushing

Salt and ground pepper

2 dried ancho or pasilla chiles

1 red bell pepper, quartered lengthwise and seeded

2 plum tomatoes, quartered lengthwise and seeded

1 yellow onion, quartered

4 cloves garlic

¼ cup (1 oz/30 g) slivered blanched almonds

2 Tbsp sherry vinegar

2 Tbsp dry white wine

2 tsp Spanish smoked paprika

Fennel's anise flavor mellows when grilled. Here, the crisp, refreshing bulbs are paired with a Spanish-inspired romesco sauce, a blend of peppers, chiles, and tomatoes, with a handful of almonds for texture. The rustic red sauce is as versatile as it is flavorful. Use it as a condiment for other grilled vegetables, fish, or steak.

Trim the stalks ½ inch (12 mm) above each fennel bulb; discard or reserve for another use. Trim away any bruised parts from the bulbs. Cut the bulbs lengthwise into quarters, removing the thickest part of the central core but keeping the layers intact and attached. In a large bowl, combine the fennel and ¼ cup oil and toss to coat. Season with salt and pepper.

In a small bowl, soak the chiles in warm water to cover until soft and pliable, about 10 minutes. Drain, reserving the soaking liquid. Pat the chiles dry with paper towels. Halve and seed each chile.

Prepare a charcoal or gas grill for direct-heat grilling over medium-high heat. Oil the grill rack and a grill basket.

Brush the chiles, bell pepper, tomatoes, onion, and garlic with oil. Arrange the vegetables, including the fennel, on the grill or in the grill basket. Grill, turning often, until lightly charred on all sides, 2–3 minutes for the garlic, about 5 minutes for the chiles, 6–8 minutes for the tomatoes, 8–10 minutes for the onion and bell pepper, and 10–15 minutes for the fennel. Transfer all the vegetables except the fennel to a bowl, cover, and let steam for 10 minutes. Transfer the fennel to a platter. ↠

Peel the bell pepper and tomatoes. In a blender or a food processor, combine the bell pepper, tomatoes, chiles, onion, garlic, almonds, vinegar, wine, and paprika. Process to a pourable sauce, adding the reserved chile soaking liquid as needed. Season the romesco sauce with salt and pepper, transfer to a bowl and serve with the fennel.

4

STEAMED SUGAR SNAP PEAS WITH BLACK SESAME SEEDS

serves 4

1 lb (500 g) sugar snap peas, strings removed

2 green onions, white and tender green parts, cut into slices ¼ inch (6 mm) thick

1½ tsp Asian sesame oil

1 tsp black sesame seeds

Salt

As the days warm, sugar snap peas are showing up in greater abundance in markets. The sweet, crunchy pods are wonderful eaten raw as a snack, or parboiled or steamed for a few minutes and served hot or cold. Here, a double dose of sesame— black seeds and oil—produces a fragrant, colorful side dish with wide appeal.

In a saucepan fitted with a steamer rack, bring 1–2 inches (5–7.5 cm) of water to a boil. Arrange the sugar snap peas in the rack, cover, and steam until tender-crisp, about 3 minutes. Transfer the peas to a bowl.

Add the green onions, sesame oil, and sesame seeds. Season with a pinch of salt and toss to coat the peas evenly. Serve warm or at room temperature.

5

MISO-GLAZED GRILLED ASIAN EGGPLANT

serves 4

Slender Asian eggplants thrive in hot weather, just like their globe-shaped brothers, but their size and shape makes them easier to split lengthwise and handle over the grill. The cut side offers a porous surface for basting with Asian flavors and allows the smoke to penetrate.

¼-inch (6-mm) piece fresh ginger, peeled and coarsely chopped

1 clove garlic, coarsely chopped

¼ cup (2 oz/60 g) white miso

½ tsp Asian chile sauce such as Sriracha

2 Tbsp rice vinegar

2 tsp sugar

1 Tbsp mirin

4 Asian eggplants, halved lengthwise

Salt and freshly ground pepper

Canola oil for brushing

3 green onions, white and tender green parts, cut on the diagonal into slices ¼ inch (6-mm) thick

Prepare a charcoal or gas grill for direct-heat grilling over medium-high heat. Oil the grill rack.

In a blender, combine the ginger, garlic, miso, chile sauce, vinegar, sugar, and mirin. Add 1 Tbsp water and process to form a smooth purée.

Sprinkle the eggplant halves lightly with salt and pepper. Lightly brush all over with the oil.

Arrange the eggplant halves, cut side down, on the grill rack, cover the grill, and cook until the flesh just starts to char and soften, 6–8 minutes. Turn the eggplants and grill, covered, until just tender, 3–4 minutes. Brush the cut sides of the eggplant with the miso mixture and cook, covered, until the eggplant is tender and the glaze has browned in spots, 3–4 minutes.

Transfer the eggplant halves to a platter, sprinkle with the green onions, and serve.

6

TOMATOES WITH BASIL VINAIGRETTE

serves 4

Once you've had some hot days, scout the farmers' market for multicolored and delightfully misshapen heirloom tomatoes in a variety of sizes for this late-spring salad. Look for teardrop-shaped chive blossoms at the same time. Their mild onion flavor and bright lavender color make an especially attractive and tasty garnish.

FOR THE BASIL VINAIGRETTE

1 cup (1 oz/30 g) lightly packed fresh purple basil leaves

1 small clove garlic, coarsely chopped

1 Tbsp red wine vinegar

1 Tbsp balsamic vinegar

Salt

⅓ cup (3 fl oz/80 ml) extra-virgin olive oil

1 lb (500 g) mixed heirloom tomatoes, cut into slices ¼ inch (6 mm) thick

1 cup (6 oz/185 g) cherry tomatoes, halved

1 Tbsp snipped green onions, white part only, or chive blossoms

Freshly ground pepper

To make the vinaigrette, in a food processor, combine the basil, garlic, vinegars, and ½ tsp salt and pulse until the basil is coarsely chopped. With the motor running, drizzle in the oil and process just until the vinaigrette is emulsified. Transfer to a small bowl.

Arrange the tomatoes on a platter and pour the vinaigrette over them (you may not need all of it). Sprinkle the onions over the tomatoes, grind a little pepper over the top, and serve.

7

BUTTERMILK COLESLAW WITH CARROTS & RAISINS

serves 4–6

Picnics and barbecues call for crunchy, creamy coleslaw. This version offers rich and tangy flavor with a homemade buttermilk dressing and a touch of sweetness with a big handful of golden raisins. A duo of red and green cabbage provides the prettiest look.

FOR THE BUTTERMILK DRESSING

¾ cup (6 fl oz/180 ml) mayonnaise

½ cup (4 fl oz/125 ml) buttermilk

¼ cup (2 oz/60 g) sour cream

½ bunch fresh flat-leaf parsley, leaves and tender stems, finely chopped

½ bunch fresh chives, finely chopped

Salt and freshly ground white pepper

½ cup (3 oz/90 g) golden raisins

1 large carrot, cut into thin matchsticks

½ red onion, thinly sliced

2 shallots, thinly sliced

3 Tbsp white vinegar

½ head green cabbage, cored and finely shredded

½ head red cabbage, cored and finely shredded

Salt and ground white pepper

Chopped fresh flat-leaf parsley leaves and chives for garnish

To make the dressing, in a bowl, stir together the mayonnaise, buttermilk, and sour cream. Stir in the parsley and chives. Season with salt and pepper.

In a small bowl, soak the raisins in warm water to cover until plump, about 30 minutes. Drain the raisins. In another small bowl, combine the carrot, onion, shallots, and vinegar and toss to coat.

In a large bowl, toss together the green and red cabbage. Add the raisins, carrot-vinegar mixture, and buttermilk dressing and toss to coat. Season with salt and pepper. Garnish with the parsley and chives and serve.

8

SAUTÉED ZUCCHINI WITH OLIVE OIL, GARLIC & BASIL

serves 4

This easy side calls for a trio of Italian kitchen staples: olive oil, garlic, and fresh basil. The garlicky zucchini can also double nicely as a pasta sauce. Boil 1 lb (500 g) pasta, such as penne or rigatoni, according to package directions. Drain, add to the frying pan, and toss with the zucchini. Serve with plenty of grated Parmesan.

2 lb (1 kg) zucchini

⅓ cup (3 fl oz/80 ml) olive oil

2 cloves garlic, finely chopped

2 Tbsp finely chopped fresh basil

Salt and freshly ground pepper

Cut the zucchini in half lengthwise and then cut crosswise into slices about ½ inch (12 mm) thick.

In a large, heavy frying pan, warm the oil over medium heat. Add the garlic and sauté until fragrant and golden, about 2 minutes. Add the zucchini and cook, stirring frequently, until the zucchini slices are tender, about 5 minutes. Sprinkle the basil over the zucchini toward the end of the cooking time.

Season with salt and pepper, transfer to a bowl, and serve.

9

Celebrate summer's bounty with this colorful bean salad, a perfect companion to grilled meat or seafood and a welcome dish on a barbecue or picnic table. You can blanch and marinate the beans in advance; top with the almonds just before serving.

SUMMER BEANS WITH LEMON & ALMONDS

serves 4

¼ cup (1½ oz/45 g) almonds

½ lb (250 g) green beans, trimmed

½ lb (250 g) yellow wax beans, trimmed

Ice water

1 Tbsp extra-virgin olive oil

2 Tbsp chopped fresh tarragon

Grated zest and juice from 1 lemon

Salt and freshly ground pepper

Preheat the oven to 350°F (180°C). Spread the almonds on a baking sheet and toast until lightly browned and fragrant, about 10 minutes. Pour onto a cutting board and let cool. Coarsely chop the nuts.

Cut the beans in half on the diagonal, if desired. Bring a large saucepan of lightly salted water to a boil. Have ready a large bowl of ice water. Add the beans to the boiling water and cook just until tender, 3–4 minutes. Drain the beans and transfer to the ice water to cool. Drain well and put in a large bowl.

Add the oil, tarragon, and lemon zest and juice to the beans. Stir to mix well, then season with salt and pepper. Transfer the dressed beans to a platter, top with the almonds, and serve.

10

Simple and versatile, this side dish is essentially a warm broccoli salad dressed with a tangy vinaigrette. High-heat roasting brings out a deliciously sweet flavor. If you buy broccoli tops with the stems already trimmed away, buy 1½ pounds (750 g).

ROASTED BROCCOLI WITH PINE NUTS & BALSAMIC VINAIGRETTE

serves 4–6

2 lb (1 kg) broccoli, cut into 1-inch (2.5-cm) florets

3 Tbsp olive oil

Salt and freshly ground pepper

2 Tbsp balsamic vinegar

1 tsp Dijon mustard

¼ cup (2 oz/60 g) pine nuts, toasted

Preheat the oven to 400°F (200°C).

In a large baking pan, toss the broccoli with 2 Tbsp of the oil and ¼ tsp salt until well coated. Spread in a single layer. Roast, stirring frequently, until browned and tender, 18–25 minutes.

In a large bowl, stir together the vinegar, mustard, and remaining 1 Tbsp oil. Add the warm broccoli and pine nuts and toss to coat. Season with salt and pepper and serve.

11

Southern cooks never pass up an opportunity to serve crusty, tangy fried green tomatoes. Make sure to purchase hard, unripened tomatoes, not ripe green-skinned heirloom varieties. These tomatoes are great with baked ham, and make a tasty breakfast topped with crisp bacon, especially if you add the bacon fat to the pan when you fry the tomatoes.

FRIED GREEN TOMATOES WITH RÉMOULADE

serves 6–8

FOR THE RÉMOULADE

1 cup (8 fl oz/250 ml) mayonnaise

1 Tbsp minced cornichons

1 Tbsp capers, rinsed

1 Tbsp minced fresh flat-leaf parsley

2 tsp minced fresh tarragon

1 tsp spicy brown mustard

½ tsp anchovy paste

1 small clove garlic, minced

¾ cup (4 oz/125 g) all-purpose flour

Salt and freshly ground black pepper

⅛ tsp cayenne pepper

1 cup (8 fl oz/250 ml) milk

2 eggs

1 cup (5 oz/155 g) yellow cornmeal, preferably stone-ground

3 unripened green tomatoes, about 7 oz (220 g) each, cut crosswise into slices about ¼ inch (6 mm) thick

1 cup (8 fl oz/250 ml) canola oil

To make the rémoulade, in a bowl, stir together the mayonnaise, cornichons, capers, parsley, taragon, mustard, anchovy paste, and garlic until well blended. Cover and refrigerate for 1 hour before serving.

In a shallow dish, stir together the flour, 2 tsp salt, ½ tsp black pepper, and the cayenne. In a second shallow dish, whisk together the milk and eggs. Spread the cornmeal in a third shallow dish. Have ready a baking sheet.

One at a time, dip the tomato slices into the flour mixture to coat evenly, shaking off the excess. Dip into the egg mixture, letting the excess drip back into the bowl, and then place in the cornmeal, patting gently to help it adhere. Transfer to the baking sheet.

Preheat the oven to 200°F (95°C). Set a large wire rack on another baking sheet and place near the stove. In a large frying pan, heat the oil over medium-high heat until it shimmers. Working in batches, add the coated tomato slices to the hot oil and fry until golden ⟶

brown, about 2 minutes. Turn the slices and fry until browned on the second sides, about 2 minutes. Using a slotted spatula, transfer the slices to the rack and keep warm in the oven while you fry the remaining tomatoes. Serve hot, passing the rémoulade at the table.

12

Roasting adds unexpected texture to this salad, producing potatoes with crispy skin and a creamy interior. The rich, pale green dressing contrasts perfectly with the golden brown potatoes.

ROASTED POTATO SALAD WITH GREEN ONION DRESSING

serves 10–12

3 lb (1.5 kg) baby Yukon gold potatoes, each about 1 inch (2.5 cm) in diameter

3 Tbsp olive oil

Salt

FOR THE GREEN ONION DRESSING

½ cup (½ oz/15 g) fresh cilantro leaves, plus sprigs for garnish

3 green onions, white and tender green parts, chopped

1 clove garlic, chopped

½ cup (4 oz/125 g) sour cream

¼ cup (2 fl oz/60 ml) mayonnaise

4 tsp red wine vinegar

4 tsp Dijon mustard

Salt and freshly ground pepper

Preheat the oven to 400°F (200°C). Put the potatoes on a rimmed baking sheet, drizzle with the oil, sprinkle with 1 Tbsp salt, and toss them to coat evenly. Roast, tossing every 15 minutes, until the skins are crisp and golden brown, about 45 minutes. Let cool.

To make the dressing, in a food processor or blender, combine the cilantro leaves, green onions, garlic, sour cream, mayonnaise, vinegar, and mustard, and process until smooth. Season with salt and pepper.

Transfer the cooled potatoes to a bowl, add the dressing, and toss to coat. Garnish with the cilantro sprigs and serve, or cover and refrigerate for up to 4 hours before serving.

13

GRILLED EGGPLANT, CORN & BREAD SALAD WITH TOMATO-BASIL VINAIGRETTE

serves 6–8

This nontraditional take on a classic Italian bread salad showcases other warm-weather vegetables: smoky grilled eggplant and toasty charred corn. A tangy tomato dressing brings the flavors into focus and basil's aniselike character accents the aromas from the grill.

2 large ripe tomatoes, about 1 lb (500 g), peeled, seeded, and chopped

6 Tbsp (½ oz/15 g) shredded fresh basil leaves

2 Tbsp balsamic vinegar

8 Tbsp (½ cup/125 ml) olive oil

2 large cloves garlic, minced

Salt and freshly ground pepper

3 ears corn, husks and silk removed

2 large eggplants, about 2½ lb (1.25 kg) total, cut crosswise into slices ½ inch (12 mm) thick

1 loaf coarse country Italian bread such as pugliese, about ¾ lb (375 g), cut into 1-inch (2.5-cm) cubes

In a blender, combine the tomatoes, 2 Tbsp of the basil, the vinegar, 1 Tbsp of the oil, the garlic, ½ tsp salt, and several grinds of pepper. Pulse to form a chunky vinaigrette.

Prepare a charcoal or gas grill for direct-heat grilling over medium-high heat. Oil the grill rack. Brush the ears of corn on all sides with 1 Tbsp of the oil, and season with salt and pepper. Brush the eggplant slices on both sides with the remaining oil, and season both sides with salt and pepper.

Arrange the eggplant slices on the grill and grill, turning once, until softened and grill-marked on both sides, about 12 minutes. Transfer to a cutting board. Grill the corn, turning frequently, until charred in spots, 10–12 minutes. Transfer to the cutting board. Cut the eggplant slices into ¾-inch (2-cm) pieces. Hold each ear of corn upright. Using a sharp knife, cut down along the ear, stripping off the kernels and rotating the ear a quarter turn after each cut.

In a large bowl, combine the eggplant, corn, bread cubes, and the remaining basil. Pour in the tomato vinaigrette, toss well, and serve.

14

FRIED ZUCCHINI WITH CURRY DIP

serves 4–6

Here, the zucchini is fried in a shallow layer of oil to ensure it stays crisp. For a pretty presentation, use a mix of green zucchini and yellow squash. The dip, which can be made up to 3 days in advance, is also good served with steamed artichokes or roasted red potatoes.

FOR THE CURRY DIP

1 cup (8 fl oz/250 ml) mayonnaise

1 tsp curry powder

1 tsp fresh lemon juice

Salt

1 cup (4 oz/125 g) shredded Parmesan cheese

¾ cup (2 oz/60 g) panko

2 Tbsp finely chopped fresh flat-leaf parsley

Salt and freshly ground pepper

2 eggs

3 zucchini, cut into pieces 3 inches (7.5 cm) long and 1 inch (2.5 cm) wide

Olive oil for frying

To make the dip, in a small bowl, stir together the mayonnaise, curry powder, and lemon juice. Season with ⅛ tsp salt and stir to combine.

Preheat the oven to 200°F (95°C). Line a large platter with paper towels. Pour oil to a depth of ½ inch (12 mm) into a deep, heavy frying pan and heat to 350°F (180°C) on a deep-frying thermometer or until a piece of zucchini slipped into the hot oil sizzles on contact.

Have ready a baking sheet. In a small bowl, stir together the Parmesan, panko, and parsley. Season with 1 tsp salt and ¼ tsp pepper and mix well. In another small bowl, beat the eggs just until blended. One at a time, dip each piece of zucchini into the eggs, allowing the excess to drip back into the bowl. Then dip it into the Parmesan mixture, coating evenly on all sides. Transfer to the baking sheet.

Working in batches of 5 or 6 pieces, fry the zucchini, turning as needed, until golden brown, about 2 minutes per side. Using a slotted spoon, transfer the zucchini to the towel-lined platter to drain and keep warm in the oven. Allow the oil to return to 350°F (180°C) between batches. Serve the zucchini hot with the dip.

15

Even partisans of traditional burgers will be won over by these healthful vegetarian patties, and slathering them with a smoky mayonnaise makes them even more appealing. Set out paper-thin red onion slices for those who might want them and garnish each plate with pickle slices or wedges.

CHICKPEA & ROASTED RED PEPPER BURGERS WITH SMOKED PAPRIKA MAYONNAISE

serves 5

FOR THE SMOKED PAPRIKA MAYONNAISE

5 Tbsp (3 fl oz/80 ml) mayonnaise

1 tsp Spanish smoked paprika

2 tsp fresh lemon juice

Salt

1 small red potato

Salt and freshly ground pepper

1 Tbsp olive oil, plus more for frying

1 clove garlic, minced

1 tsp seeded and minced jalapeño chile

1 tsp ground cumin

¼ tsp chili powder

1 can (15 oz/470 g) chickpeas, drained and rinsed

¼ cup (2 oz/60 g) chopped roasted red bell pepper

2 eggs, lightly beaten

5 Tbsp (1 oz/60 g) panko

2 Tbsp minced fresh flat-leaf parsley

5 brioche buns, split

Lettuce leaves for serving (optional)

To make the paprika mayonnaise, in a small bowl, stir together the mayonnaise, smoked paprika, and lemon juice. Season with salt.

Put the potato in a small saucepan. Add water to cover by 1 inch (2.5 cm) and a generous pinch of salt. Bring to a boil over medium-high heat, reduce the heat to medium, and cook until the potato is fork-tender, about 15 minutes. Drain the potato and let cool, then cut into small dice.

In a small frying pan, warm the 1 Tbsp oil over medium heat. Add the garlic, jalapeño, cumin, and chili powder and cook, stirring, just until the garlic begins to soften and the spices are fragrant, about 1 minute.

In a food processor, pulse the chickpeas until finely chopped; do not purée. Transfer them to a large bowl and add the roasted pepper, eggs, panko, parsley, potato, and garlic mixture. Season with ½ tsp salt and ¼ tsp pepper. Using your hands, mix until well combined and then form into 5 patties. »→

Pour enough oil into a large frying pan to coat the bottom, and heat over medium-high heat. Add the patties and cook, turning once, until golden brown and heated through, about 3 minutes per side. Place a lettuce leaf (if using) on the bottom half of each bun, top with a burger and a generous dollop of the mayonnaise, and serve.

16

Charred onions are a delicious companion to grilled meats or poultry. The Italian kitchen is the inspiration for this treatment, which features a punchy anchovy dressing. Pass it at the table so anchovy lovers can get their fill.

GREEN ONIONS WITH ANCHOVY SAUCE

serves 4

1 can (2 oz/50 g) olive oil–packed anchovy fillets

2 cloves garlic, crushed

2 pitted green olives

1 Tbsp red wine vinegar

2 Tbsp extra-virgin olive oil

Freshly ground pepper

16–20 green onions

In a food processor or blender, combine the anchovies and their oil, garlic, olives, vinegar, and olive oil, and process until smooth. Season with pepper. Transfer the sauce to a small bowl. Cover and refrigerate for 2 hours to meld the flavors.

Prepare a charcoal or gas grill for direct-heat grilling over medium heat. Oil the grill rack.

Trim the roots from the onions, and then trim off the dark green tops, leaving the pale green portion intact. Arrange the onions on the rack, placing them perpendicular to the bars, and grill, turning frequently, until softened and lightly browned, about 7 minutes. Transfer the onions to a plate and serve, passing the sauce at the table.

17

GRILLED ZUCCHINI & FAVA BEANS WITH SEA SALT

serves 4

16 young, tender fava bean pods

3 zucchini, sliced lengthwise

3 Tbsp extra-virgin olive oil, plus more for drizzling

Salt and freshly ground fine pepper

Freshly ground coarse pepper

Quality salt helps to heighten the flavor of grilled vegetables. A coarse sea salt is best, preferably used together with a flavorful olive oil. When using young vegetables, you can skip the fuss of peeling fava beans in favor of charring the pods on the grill. Serve them at your next outdoor gathering, where guests can enjoy shelling their own beans.

Prepare a charcoal or gas grill for direct-heat grilling over medium-high heat. Oil the grill rack.

Rub the fava bean pods and zucchini slices with the 3 Tbsp oil and season with 1 tsp salt and ½ tsp fine pepper. Arrange the pods and zucchini slices on the grill rack and grill, turning frequently, until the pods are evenly charred and the zucchini slices are tender, about 5 minutes.

Transfer the vegetables to a platter, drizzle with oil, and sprinkle with salt and coarse pepper.

18

GRILLED FINGERLING POTATOES WITH MUSTARD & HERBS

serves 6–8

3 lb (1.5 kg) fingerling potatoes or any thin-skinned new potato

½ cup (4 fl oz/125 ml) dry white wine plus 2 Tbsp

Olive oil for brushing

½ cup (4 fl oz/125 ml) mayonnaise

1 Tbsp whole-grain mustard

2 Tbsp minced fresh flat-leaf parsley

2 Tbsp minced fresh tarragon

Salt and freshly ground pepper

Once you've fired up the coals for a prime piece of meat, there's no reason to exclude potatoes from the grill. Waxy fingerlings are firm enough that they won't fall apart, and lengthier ones, angled correctly, won't escape through the grate. Select potatoes of uniform size with smooth skins. Parboiling for a short time before grilling helps to ensure tenderness.

Bring a pot of salted water to a boil. Add the potatoes, cover, and cook over medium-high heat until they can be pierced with a knife but are not completely tender, about 10 minutes. Drain. In a large bowl, combine the warm potatoes and the ½ cup (4 fl oz/125 ml) wine and toss to coat. Let cool to room temperature, tossing often. Cut the potatoes in half lengthwise and brush with oil.

Prepare a charcoal or gas grill for direct-heat grilling over medium-high heat. Oil the grill rack or a grill basket.

In a bowl, stir together the mayonnaise, mustard, the 2 Tbsp wine, the parsley, and tarragon. Let the dressing stand for 10 minutes.

Arrange the potatoes on the grill or in a grill basket, and grill, turning once, until grill marks appear, about 5 minutes per side. Transfer to a large bowl, add the dressing, and toss to coat. Seasoning with salt and pepper. Serve warm, or cover tightly, refrigerate for about 1 hour, and serve cold.

19

*This riff on a classic
Italian salad is a
good way to rescue
day-old bread.
The recipe calls for
rosemary focaccia,
but you can
substitute any
good-quality country
or sourdough loaf.
As long as you have
some flavorful
tomatoes on the
counter and a good
oil and vinegar
tucked away in the
pantry, all of the
ingredients should
be within easy reach.*

PANZANELLA

serves 6

FOR THE BALSAMIC VINAIGRETTE

¼ cup (2 fl oz/60 ml) grape seed oil

1 Tbsp extra-virgin olive oil

1 Tbsp balsamic vinegar

1 Tbsp red wine vinegar

1 Tbsp Dijon mustard

1 clove garlic, minced

Salt and freshly ground pepper

6 tomatoes, about 3 lb (1.5 g) total

¾ lb (12 oz/375 g) small pear-shaped heirloom tomatoes

Salt and freshly ground pepper

6 slices rosemary focaccia

Olive oil for brushing

6 cloves garlic

¼ cup (2 fl oz/60 ml) balsamic vinegar

10 fresh basil leaves, finely shredded

3 Tbsp minced fresh flat-leaf parsley

3 cups (3 oz/90 g) arugula, tough stems removed

2 cups (2 oz/60 g) coarsely chopped romaine lettuce hearts

1 red onion, thinly sliced

To make the vinaigrette, combine the grape seed and olive oils in a measuring cup. In a bowl, whisk together the balsamic and red wine vinegars, the mustard, garlic, ½ tsp salt, and ¼ tsp pepper. Whisking constantly, add the oils in a slow, steady stream.

Cut all the tomatoes in half. Place in a colander over a bowl and generously season with salt. Let stand for 10 minutes to drain. Reserve the liquid released by the tomatoes.

Prepare a charcoal or gas grill for direct-heat grilling over medium-high heat. Oil the grill rack.

Brush the focaccia slices on both sides with oil. Arrange the slices on the grill rack and grill, turning once, until nicely charred, about 4 minutes per side. Transfer the focaccia to a cutting board and let cool slightly. Tear or cut into ¾-inch (2-cm) chunks.

With the flat side of a chef's knife, crush the garlic cloves into a paste. In a large bowl, stir together the reserved tomato liquid, ⟩⟩

the vinegar, ¼ cup (2 fl oz/60 ml) water, and 1 Tbsp of the balsamic vinaigrette. Add the garlic and bread chunks and toss to soak the bread. Add the tomatoes, basil, and parsley. Adjust the seasoning if necessary and toss again.

In another large bowl, combine the arugula, romaine, and red onion and season with salt and pepper. Add the balsamic vinaigrette, 1 Tbsp at a time, and toss to coat. Add the tomato and bread mixture, toss again, and serve.

20

*Quintessentially
cool, cucumber has
a refreshing quality
that's welcome on
balmy days. This
light and refreshing
salad is punctuated
with heat from
jalapeño chile and
tanginess from
soft goat cheese.*

CUCUMBER, CILANTRO & JALAPEÑO SALAD WITH GOAT CHEESE

serves 4

2 medium cucumbers or 1 English cucumber

1 cup (1½ oz/45 g) coarsely chopped fresh cilantro

1 red or green jalapeño chile, seeded and very thinly sliced

Salt

¼ cup (2 fl oz/60 ml) fresh lime juice

2 Tbsp canola oil

4–6 oz (125–185 g) fresh goat cheese

Peel the cucumbers and cut in half lengthwise. Use a spoon to scrape out the seeds. Cut crosswise into half-moons about ¼ inch (6 mm) thick.

In a nonreactive bowl, combine the cucumbers, cilantro, and chile. Sprinkle with ½ tsp salt, add the lime juice and oil, and stir to mix well. Let stand to allow the flavors to blend, about 30 minutes.

Transfer the salad to bowls or plates. Crumble the goat cheese over the top and serve.

21

Italy's peperonata—a blend of bell peppers, onions, and tomatoes—is found in many variations throughout the country but especially in the sunny south. The braised vegetables are versatile: try them topped with a fried egg, heaped next to a grilled steak, or spooned onto an antipasto platter and served with plenty of garlicky crostini.

PEPERONATA

serves 4

¼ cup (2 fl oz/60 ml) olive oil

1 yellow onion, halved and thinly sliced

1 clove garlic, thinly sliced

4 red, yellow, and/or green bell peppers, halved, seeded, and thinly sliced crosswise

2 tomatoes, peeled, seeded, and chopped

Salt and freshly ground pepper

2 Tbsp chopped fresh basil or flat-leaf parsley

In a large frying pan, warm the oil over medium heat. Add the onion and sauté until tender, about 5 minutes. Add the garlic and sauté until fragrant, about 1 minute.

Stir in the bell peppers and cook, stirring occasionally, just until they begin to brown, about 10 minutes. Add the tomatoes and cook until the peppers are tender and the sauce thickens, about 20 minutes.

Season with salt and pepper, transfer to a serving dish, and sprinkle with the basil. Serve hot or at room temperature.

22

When eggplants are cooked on a grill over a hot fire, they take on an intense smokiness without a touch of bitterness. Globe eggplant slices and slender Asian eggplants, split lengthwise, can be grilled and served the same way. Dress the eggplant with bold Mediterranean ingredients that marry well with mild flavor and meaty texture.

GRILLED ASIAN EGGPLANT WITH FETA DRESSING

serves 4–6

FOR THE FETA DRESSING

¼ cup (2 oz/60 g) Greek-style plain yogurt

1 Tbsp mayonnaise

¼ cup (1½ oz/45 g) crumbled feta cheese

1 Tbsp fresh lemon juice

8 large fresh basil leaves, chopped

3 cloves garlic, finely chopped

Hot-pepper sauce

Salt and freshly ground pepper

About 2 Tbsp whole milk, if needed

2 eggplants, cut crosswise into slices ½ inch (12 mm) thick, or 4 Asian eggplants, split lengthwise

2 Tbsp canola or olive oil

To make the dressing, in a bowl, stir together the yogurt, mayonnaise, feta, lemon juice, basil, and garlic. Add 1 or 2 dashes of hot-pepper sauce, and season with salt and pepper. Using the milk, thin the dressing to the desired consistency.

Prepare a charcoal or gas grill for direct-heat grilling over medium heat. Oil the grill rack.

Generously brush the eggplant slices on both sides with the oil. Arrange the slices on the grill rack and grill, turning once, until the slices are tender but still hold their shape, about 6 minutes per side.

Transfer the eggplant slices to a platter, spoon the dressing over the top, and serve.

23

Cooks in the American South have long known that pickled okra is delicious and versatile. You can roll it in prosciutto and serve it as an hors d'oeuvre, chop it and add it to egg salad, slip a pod into a Bloody Mary, or even snack on it straight from the jar. The key to this recipe is to use perfectly fresh okra so the pickled pods will be crisp.

PICKLED OKRA

makes 6 one-pint (16–fl oz/500-ml) jars

3½ cups (28 fl oz/875 ml) cider vinegar

Kosher salt

2 Tbsp mustard seeds

1 Tbsp cumin seeds

6 dried whole chiles

24 cloves garlic

3 lb (1.5 kg) okra, stem ends trimmed

Have ready six 1-pt (16–fl oz/500-ml) hot, sterilized jars and their lids.

In a large nonreactive saucepan, combine the vinegar and 2 Tbsp plus 1 tsp salt. Add 3½ cups (28 fl oz/875 ml) water and bring to a boil over medium-high heat, stirring to dissolve the salt.

Meanwhile, in each jar, place 1 tsp mustard seeds, ½ tsp cumin seeds, 1 chile, and 4 garlic cloves. Tightly pack the okra, stems ends up, into the jars, filling to within ¾ inch (2 cm) of the rims.

Ladle the hot brine into the jars, leaving ½ inch (12 mm) of headspace. Remove any air bubbles and adjust the headspace, if necessary. Wipe the rims clean and seal tightly with the lids.

Process the jars for 7 minutes in a boiling-water bath. Let the jars stand undisturbed for 24 hours and then set them aside for 2 weeks for the flavors to develop. The sealed jars can be stored in a cool, dark place for up to 1 year. If a seal has failed, store the jar in the refrigerator for up to 1 week.

24

Asparagus is wonderful simply steamed and sprinkled with olive oil, lemon juice, and salt. But on a cool night in early summer, this creamless gratin is a perfect showcase for the pretty spears. Serve with a crisp, dry Pinot Grigio.

ASPARAGUS WITH ASIAGO & BREAD CRUMBS

serves 4

1 lb (500 g) asparagus, ends trimmed

2 Tbsp olive oil

1 cup (4 oz/125 g) shredded Asiago cheese

3 Tbsp dried bread crumbs

1 Tbsp minced fresh flat-leaf parsley

Finely grated zest of 1 small lemon, plus 1–2 Tbsp fresh lemon juice

Salt and freshly ground pepper

Preheat the oven to 450°F (230°C).

Arrange the asparagus in a single layer in a baking dish and drizzle with 1 Tbsp of the oil. Toss the spears gently to coat with the oil.

In a bowl, whisk together the cheese, bread crumbs, parsley, and lemon zest. Season with ½ tsp salt and a grind of pepper. Drizzle in the remaining 1 Tbsp oil and stir until well mixed. Sprinkle the crumb mixture over the asparagus. Bake, uncovered, until the asparagus is just tender and the topping is melted and golden brown, 15 minutes.

Drizzle the asparagus with some lemon juice and serve.

25

Gremolata is an Italian herb condiment with vibrant flavor and color. This version includes some basil to add hints of licorice to parsley's herbal taste. Topped with this simple mixture, a garlic-infused zucchini soup gets a fresh, bold hit of summer.

GARLICKY ZUCCHINI SOUP WITH BASIL GREMOLATA

serves 6

3 leeks, about 1½ lb (750 g) total

2 lemons

3 Tbsp olive oil

3 zucchini, about 1½ lb (750 g) total, cut into ½-inch (12-mm) cubes

3 Tbsp minced garlic

Salt and freshly ground pepper

1 celery rib, finely chopped

8 cups (64 fl oz/2 l) chicken broth

1 russet potato, peeled and finely chopped

3 Tbsp minced fresh flat-leaf parsley

3 Tbsp minced fresh basil

Trim the dark green tops from the leeks. Cut the leeks lengthwise into quarters and then cut crosswise into ¼-inch (6-mm) pieces. Using a vegetable peeler, remove the zest in wide strips from 1 lemon.

In a large, heavy pot, heat 1½ Tbsp of the oil over high heat. Add two-thirds of the zucchini and spread in a single layer. Cook, without stirring, until beginning to brown, about 1½ minutes. Stir and then cook, stirring occasionally, until the zucchini is just tender, about 2 minutes. Stir in 1 Tbsp of the garlic and ¼ tsp salt and cook until fragrant, about 30 seconds. Transfer to a large plate.

Add the remaining 1½ Tbsp olive oil to the pot and heat over medium-high heat. Add the leeks, celery, 1 Tbsp of the garlic, and ¼ tsp salt and stir to mix well. Reduce the heat to low, cover, and cook, stirring occasionally, until the leeks soften, about 10 minutes. Add the broth, potato, lemon zest strips, and remaining zucchini, raise the heat to high, and bring to a boil. Reduce the heat to low, cover partially, and simmer, stirring occasionally, until the potato is tender, about 15 minutes.

Meanwhile, to make the gremolata, finely grate the zest from the remaining lemon. In a small bowl, stir together the grated zest, the remaining 1 Tbsp garlic, the parsley, and the basil. ↠

Discard the lemon zest strips from the pot. Use a large spoon to mash the potato and zucchini against the sides of the pot and stir into the soup to thicken it slightly. Stir in the sautéed zucchini and 1 tsp salt, and season with pepper. Ladle the soup into bowls, garnish with the gremolata, and serve.

26

Folks with a vegetable patch or a CSA box know that at some point they are going to confront more zucchini or other summer squashes than they know what to do with. That's the time to pull out this recipe. Grilled summer squashes are splendid on their own, but top them with this simple mint vinaigrette and you won't mind that garden surplus.

GRILLED SUMMER SQUASHES WITH FRESH MINT VINAIGRETTE

serves 6–8

4 zucchini, about 1½ lb (750 g) total

4 yellow summer squashes, about 1½ lb (750 g) total

2 Tbsp olive oil, plus more for drizzling

2 Tbsp rice vinegar

½ cup (¾ oz/20 g) chopped fresh mint

Salt and freshly ground pepper

1 Tbsp sesame seeds, toasted

Prepare a charcoal or gas grill for direct-heat grilling over medium heat. Oil the grill rack.

Cut all the squashes crosswise on a sharp diagonal into slices about ½ inch (12 mm) thick. Place in a bowl, drizzle with oil, and toss to coat.

Arrange the squashes on the grill and cook, turning, until grill-marked, about 2 minutes per side. Transfer the squashes to a large bowl. Add the 2 Tbsp oil, vinegar, and mint, and toss to coat. Season with salt and pepper. Sprinkle with the sesame seeds and serve.

27

In this classic Sicilian eggplant dish, sweet-and-sour flavors dominate. Salt-preserved capers impart more pungency than brine-cured. Soak them in water to remove excess salt before using. Serve caponata as an antipasto, or use it as a condiment to go with tuna in oil or grilled seafood.

EGGPLANT CAPONATA

serves 6

2 Tbsp capers, preferably salt-packed

¼ cup (2 fl oz/60 ml) olive oil

1 yellow onion, chopped

1 eggplant, about 1½ lb (750 g), peeled and cut into ½-inch (12-mm) cubes

1 clove garlic, minced

1 celery rib, cut into slices ½ inch (12 mm) wide

½ cup (4 fl oz/125 ml) tomato sauce

6 green olives, pitted and chopped

2 Tbsp pine nuts, lightly toasted

Salt and freshly ground pepper

¼ cup (2 fl oz/60 ml) red wine vinegar

3 Tbsp sugar

If using salt-packed capers, place them in a small bowl with cold water to cover and let soak for 20 minutes. Drain, rinse well, and then drain again and pat dry. If using vinegar-packed capers, rinse under cold running water, drain, and pat dry. Chop the capers.

In a large frying pan, heat the oil over medium-high heat. Add the onion and sauté until lightly browned, about 8 minutes. Add the eggplant and cook, stirring occasionally, until the eggplant is soft and lightly browned, about 15 minutes. Add the garlic, celery, and tomato sauce. Stir in ½ cup (4 fl oz/125 ml) water and cook, stirring occasionally, until the eggplant is very soft, about 5 minutes. Stir in the capers, olives, and pine nuts. Season with salt and pepper. Remove from the heat.

In a small saucepan, bring the vinegar and sugar almost to a boil over medium heat and cook until the sugar dissolves, about 2 minutes. Pour the warm liquid over the eggplant mixture. Return the mixture to medium heat and cook until all the liquid is absorbed, 1–2 minutes. Let stand at room temperature for at least 2 hours or in the refrigerator for up to overnight to allow the flavors to blend. Serve at room temperature.

28

Juicy red tomatoes indicate prime summertime eating, but yellow tomatoes can be just as delicious. This method for roasting tomatoes creates something a little different to celebrate the season. Rubbing the cut halves with brown sugar and curry powder causes them to caramelize until wonderfully sweet in the heat of the broiler.

YELLOW TOMATOES WITH MINT & PECORINO

serves 4–6

2 tsp firmly packed golden brown sugar

1 tsp curry powder

Salt and freshly ground pepper

6 large yellow tomatoes, cored and halved lengthwise

1½ oz (45 g) pecorino cheese, coarsely grated

14 fresh mint leaves, finely chopped

2 green onions, tender white and green parts, finely chopped

1 Tbsp extra-virgin olive oil

Preheat the broiler. Line a baking sheet with foil. In a coffee saucer or plate, stir together the sugar, curry powder, 1 tsp salt, and several grinds of pepper. Press the cut surfaces of the tomatoes into the spice mixture and then arrange, coated side up, on the prepared sheet.

Broil the tomatoes 4–6 inches (10–15 cm) from the heat source until the topping bubbles and starts to caramelize, about 10 minutes.

Meanwhile, in a small bowl, stir together the pecorino, mint, green onions, and oil. Transfer the tomatoes to a platter. Sprinkle with the cheese mixture and serve.

29

PICKLED BEETS

makes 4 one-pint (16–fl oz/500-ml) jars

1 lb (500 g) beets

1 white onion, sliced

1 cup (8 fl oz/250 ml) cider vinegar

¼ cup (2 oz/60 g) sugar, or to taste

1 Tbsp cardamom pods

1 Tbsp whole cloves

Salt

Any beet variety—red, white, golden, striped—can be pickled this way. Use these tangy beet slices to add color, texture, and flavor to salads or even sandwiches. For an easy first course or side dish, layer the beet slices with slices of fresh mozzarella and top with a drizzle of olive oil.

Bring 3 cups (24 fl oz/750 ml) water to a boil. If the greens are still attached to the beets, remove them, leaving 1 inch (2.5 cm) of the stem intact. In a large saucepan (if using different-colored beets, place them in separate pans), combine the beets with water to cover by 2 inches (5 cm). Bring to a boil, reduce the heat to medium-low, cover partially, and simmer until the beets are tender, 25–30 minutes. Drain the beets, reserving 2 cups (16 fl oz/500 ml) of the cooking liquid.

Meanwhile, ready four 1-pt (16–fl oz/500-ml) jars hot, sterilized jars and their lids.

When the beets are cool enough to handle, peel them and cut into slices ¼ inch (6 mm) thick. Divide the beet slices and onion slices evenly among the jars.

In a saucepan, combine the reserved cooking liquid, the vinegar, the ¼ cup sugar, the cardamom, the cloves, and a pinch of salt. Bring to a boil over medium heat, stirring until the sugar is dissolved. Taste and adjust with more sugar, if needed.

Ladle the hot vinegar mixture into the jars, evenly distributing the spices and leaving ½ inch (12 mm) of headspace. Remove any air bubbles and adjust the headspace, if necessary. Wipe the rims clean and seal tightly with the lids.

Process the jars for 7 minutes in a boiling-water bath. Let the jars stand undisturbed for 24 hours and then set them aside for 1 week for the flavors to develop. The sealed jars can be stored in a cool, dark place for up to 3 months. If a seal has failed, store the jar in the refrigerator for up to 1 week.

30

FARRO WITH FRESH CORN & SUGAR SNAP PEAS

serves 6–8

2¼ cups (1 lb/500 g) pearled farro

4 cups (32 fl oz/1 l) vegetable broth

Salt and freshly ground pepper

2 tbsp olive oil

1 yellow onion, finely chopped

1 lb (500 g) sugar snap peas, strings removed, cut on the diagonal into ¼-inch (6-mm) pieces

Kernels from 4 ears fresh corn or 2 cups (12 oz/375 g) thawed frozen corn

½ cup (4 fl oz/120 ml) cider vinegar

Pleasantly chewy farro grains are delicious in side dishes and salads year-round. Try them with sweet corn and sugar snaps, just barely cooked so the bright essence and crunch won't be lost. Farro holds exceptionally well, making it ideal picnic fare.

Heat a heavy-bottomed saucepan over medium-high heat. Add the farro and stir frequently until lightly toasted and aromatic, about 3 minutes. Add the broth and 1 Tbsp salt and bring to a boil. Reduce the heat to low, cover, and simmer until all the broth is absorbed and the farro is tender with a bit of a bite remaining at the center, 12–15 minutes. Transfer to a large bowl and let cool.

In a large frying pan, heat the oil over medium-low heat. Add the onion and sauté until softened and translucent, about 10 minutes. Add the peas and corn and sauté until just tender, about 5 minutes.

Add the vegetables to the farro, drizzle with the vinegar, and toss to mix well. Season with salt and pepper. Serve warm or at room temperature.

July means barbecue season. All kinds of vegetables do well on a grill, from onions to zucchini to corn on the cob. Even potatoes become more irresistible when treated to a little char and smoke. If you're digging into sticky-sweet ribs or chicken, round out the menu with a homey potato salad or a slaw that marries cabbage and apple in a creamy dressing. Burgers taste better when accompanied with crunchy homemade pickles, especially if you have used cucumbers harvested from your backyard plot or pulled from your CSA box.

july

1

TOMATO, ZUCCHINI & GOAT CHEESE TART

serves 6–8

This savory tart features a simple combination of peak-of-summer vegetables and fresh goat cheese, all baked in a buttery cornmeal crust. Look for stone-ground cornmeal, which retains more nutrients and flavor. Serve thin slices of this tart for a striking appetizer, or accompany larger slices with a salad for a light lunch.

FOR THE CORNMEAL DOUGH

1 cup (5 oz/155 g) all-purpose flour

½ cup (2½ oz/75 g) fine-grind stone-ground cornmeal

Salt

6 Tbsp (3 oz/90 g) unsalted butter, cut into pieces

1 egg

1 Tbsp olive oil

½ lb (250 g) zucchini, cut crosswise into slices ⅛ inch (3 mm) thick

Salt and freshly ground pepper

5 oz (155 g) fresh goat cheese, crumbled

¾ lb (375 g) tomatoes, one size or a mixture of sizes, sliced or halved, depending on size

1 tsp coarsely torn fresh thyme, plus more for garnish

To make the dough, in a food processor, combine the flour, cornmeal, and ½ tsp salt. Add the butter and pulse until the mixture resembles coarse crumbs. Add the egg and ¼ cup (2 fl oz/60 ml) cold water and pulse just until the dough begins to come together. Flatten the dough into a disk, wrap in plastic wrap, and refrigerate for at least 1 hour or up to 2 days.

In a large frying pan, warm the oil over medium-high heat. Add the zucchini and sprinkle lightly with salt and pepper. Reduce the heat to medium-low and cook, stirring frequently, until the zucchini is softened but not browned, about 5 minutes. Transfer the zucchini to paper towels to drain.

Position a rack in the lower third of the oven and preheat to 375°F (190°C). On a lightly floured work surface, roll out the dough into a 12-inch (30-cm) circle about ¼ inch (6 mm) thick. Carefully transfer the dough to a 9-inch (23-cm) fluted tart pan with removable sides. Press the dough into the bottom and sides of the pan. Fold the edges over and press into the sides of the pan, forming a double thickness around the pan rim. Trim off any excess dough overhanging the rim. ⟫

Sprinkle half of the cheese over the bottom of the crust. Arrange the tomatoes and zucchini in overlapping concentric circles or another attractive pattern on top of the cheese. Season lightly with salt and pepper. Top with the remaining cheese and the thyme.

Bake until the crust is golden brown and the juices are bubbling, 35–40 minutes. Let the tart cool for 10 minutes. Remove the pan sides, sprinkle with thyme, and serve warm.

2

CLASSIC POTATO SALAD

serves 8

If you like hard-boiled eggs in your potato salad, by all means, add them. The same goes for chopped dill pickles or bread-and-butter pickles—you can even use pickle juice in place of the vinegar. You can also cook baking potatoes instead of red ones. They fall apart more easily, but some folks like that.

3 lb (1.5 kg) red potatoes

Salt and freshly ground pepper

3 Tbsp white wine vinegar

1 cup (8 fl oz/250 ml) mayonnaise

2 Tbsp whole-grain mustard

4 celery ribs, finely chopped

4 green onions, white and pale green parts, chopped

2 Tbsp minced fresh flat-leaf parsley

Place the potatoes in a large saucepan, add water to cover by 1 inch (2.5 cm) and a pinch of salt, cover, and bring to a boil. Reduce the heat to medium-low, cover partially, and cook at a brisk simmer until the potatoes are tender, about 25 minutes. Drain the potatoes and rinse under cold running water until they are cool enough to handle.

Cut the potatoes into chunks about ½ inch (12 mm) thick. Place in a large bowl and sprinkle with the vinegar. Let cool completely.

In a small bowl, mix together the mayonnaise and mustard. Add to the potatoes along with the celery, green onions, and parsley and mix gently. Season with salt and pepper. Cover and refrigerate until chilled, at least 2 hours, before serving.

3

CUCUMBER DILL SOUP

serves 6

3 English cucumbers, peeled, halved lengthwise, and seeded

1 cup (8 oz/250 g) Greek-style or other thick, whole-milk plain yogurt

1 Tbsp fresh lemon juice

3 green onions, white and tender parts, chopped

3 Tbsp chopped fresh dill

1 clove garlic, chopped

1 tsp caraway seeds, crushed

Salt and freshly ground white pepper

1 cup (8 fl oz/250 ml) vegetable broth

2 Tbsp extra-virgin olive oil

A chilled soup is a great beginning for a picnic at the beach or on a boat. For foolproof transport, select a container with a tight-fitting lid that permits easy pouring. Pour in the soup, cap tightly, place upright in a cooler, and secure in place with ice. To serve, pour the soup into widemouthed glasses or cups so that guests can sip it without need for a spoon.

Coarsely chop 5 of the cucumber halves and transfer to a large bowl. Add the yogurt, lemon juice, green onions, dill, garlic, and caraway seeds. Season with 1 tsp salt and ¼ tsp white pepper. Stir to combine, cover, and set aside at room temperature for 1 hour to blend the flavors. Chop the remaining cucumber half and set aside for garnish.

In a blender, purée the cucumber mixture until smooth. With the motor running, slowly add the broth and process until fully incorporated, about 30 seconds. Transfer to a pitcher, cover, and refrigerate until chilled, at least 2 hours or up to 12 hours (if the soup separates, stir it until emulsified).

Just before serving, stir in the chopped cucumber and oil. Pour the soup into cups or bowls and serve.

4

MEXICAN-STYLE CORN ON THE COB

serves 6

½ cup (4 oz/125 g) unsalted butter, at room temperature, plus melted butter for brushing

2 Tbsp minced fresh cilantro

Finely grated zest from 1 lime

1 Tbsp fresh lime juice

6 ears corn, husks and silk removed

Ice water

Ancho chile powder or other pure chile powder for serving

Salt

Biting into hot corn on the cob slathered with butter is one of summer's greatest pleasures. Here, that classic is given a Latin accent with the addition of lime and cilantro to the butter and a sprinkle of ground chile at the table. Be careful not to overcook the corn; it tastes best when the kernels still carry some snap.

Using a rubber spatula, in a small bowl, mash together the ½ cup butter, cilantro, and lime zest and juice, mixing well. Cover and set aside while you prepare the corn.

Prepare a charcoal or gas grill for direct-heat grilling over medium heat. Oil the grill rack.

Fill a large bowl with cold water, add the corn, and let stand for 10 minutes.

Drain the corn and pat dry. Grill, turning often and basting with melted butter, until lightly charred on all sides and just tender, 15 to 20 minutes.

Serve the corn piping hot, with the cilantro-lime butter, chile powder, and salt on the side.

5

JULY

Romaine lettuce is both sturdy enough and flavorful enough to stand up to the heat and the char of a grill. Here, it is combined with avocado, tomatoes, and a Caesar-inspired vinaigrette for the perfect accompaniment to a thick grilled steak. To make the roasted garlic for the dressing, remove the loose outer layers of a garlic head, and cut off and discard the top ¼–½ inch (6–12 mm); place the head in a small baking dish; drizzle the cut side with olive oil, cover with foil, and roast in a 400°F (200°C) oven until soft when pressed, 30–40 minutes. Let cool, then squeeze the cloves free of their skins.

GRILLED ROMAINE SALAD

serves 4

FOR THE VINAIGRETTE

¼ cup (2 fl oz/60 ml) white wine vinegar

½ tsp anchovy paste

½ tsp whole-grain mustard

1 Tbsp fresh lemon juice

1 Tbsp fresh oregano leaves, chopped

¼ tsp homemade or store-bought roasted garlic

½ cup (4 fl oz/125 ml) canola oil

½ cup (4 fl oz/125 ml) extra-virgin olive oil

1 tsp honey

Salt and freshly ground pepper

2 heads romaine lettuce, outer leaves removed and stem left intact

Olive oil for drizzling

1 cup (6 oz/185 g) cherry tomatoes, halved

1 avocado, pitted, peeled, and sliced

4 oz (125 g) Asiago cheese

To make the vinaigrette, in a blender or food processor, combine the vinegar, anchovy paste, mustard, lemon juice, oregano, and roasted garlic and pulse to blend. With the machine running, slowly add both oils and process until the dressing emulsifies. Transfer to a bowl, stir in the honey, and season with salt and pepper. You should have about 1¼ cups (10 fl oz/310 ml), which is more than you'll need for this salad; store any extra in an airtight container in the refrigerator for up to 1 week.

Prepare a charcoal or gas grill for direct-heat grilling over medium heat. Oil the grill rack.

Remove the outer leaves from each romaine head, then cut each head in half lengthwise. Trim the base of the stem from each half, but leave the remainder of the stem attached to hold the leaves together. Drizzle the cut side of each half with a little olive oil.

Place the romaine halves, cut side down, on the grill and cook until the leaves develop a little char and have begun to wilt, 2–3 minutes. Turn and cook for about 2 minutes more. You want the lettuce to be a little wilted but still hold its shape. ⇥

Transfer the romaine halves, cut side up, to individual plates, and garnish each plate with one-fourth of the tomatoes and avocado. Using a vegetable peeler, shave the cheese over the salads. Spoon some of the vinaigrette over each salad and serve. Pass additional vinaigrette at the table.

6

JULY

Pickles are a no-fail canning project, and preserving summer's crunchy cukes means you can enjoy them year-round. These sweet-and-sour pickles are addictive, whether served alongside burgers at a barbecue or chopped and added to home-made tartar sauce to accompany pan-fried fish.

BREAD & BUTTER PICKLES

makes 1 qt (1 l)

1 English cucumber or 6 pickling cucumbers, about 1 lb (500 g)

1 white onion, thinly sliced

2 cups (16 fl oz/500 ml) white wine vinegar

¾ cup (6 oz/185 g) sugar

Kosher salt

1 tsp celery seeds

1 tsp mustard seeds

2 bay leaves

Have ready a 1-qt (1-l) canning jar or other glass jar with a lid. Cut the cucumber into slices about ⅛ inch (3 mm) thick. In a nonreactive heatproof bowl, combine the cucumber and onion.

In a small nonreactive saucepan, bring the vinegar, sugar, ¼ cup (1½ oz/45 g) salt, celery and mustard seeds, and bay leaves to a boil, stirring to dissolve the sugar and salt. Immediately pour the vinegar mixture over the cucumber and onion slices. Let cool to room temperature.

Pack the vegetables and liquid into the jar, discarding any excess liquid. Cover tightly and refrigerate. Let sit for 24 hours before serving. The pickles will keep for up to 1 month in the refrigerator.

7

BLACK BEAN, CORN & QUINOA SALAD

serves 4

A South American–inspired salad, this flavorful dish calls for protein-rich quinoa, tiny seeds harvested from a plant native to the Andean region. Ají amarillo paste, made from a hot yellow South American chile, can be found in Latin American stores.

½ cup (3 oz/90 g) quinoa, well rinsed

Salt and freshly ground pepper

2 Tbsp fresh lime juice

3 Tbsp white vinegar

2 Tbsp minced fresh cilantro

¼ tsp aji amarillo paste

¼ tsp dried oregano

½ cup (4 fl oz/125 ml) extra-virgin olive oil

1 cup (7 oz/220 g) drained and rinsed canned black beans

⅔ cup (4 oz/125 g) fresh corn kernels, cut from 2 ears of corn

1 tomato, halved, seeded, and finely chopped

1 small red bell pepper, seeded and finely diced

In a small saucepan, combine the quinoa, ¼ tsp water, and 1½ cups (12 fl oz/375 ml) water. Cover and bring to a boil. Reduce the heat to low and simmer until the quinoa is tender and all the water has been absorbed, about 10 minutes. Transfer the quinoa to a colander and rinse under cold running water. Drain thoroughly and transfer to a large serving bowl.

Meanwhile, in a bowl, whisk together the lime juice, vinegar, cilantro, ají paste, and oregano. Season with ½ tsp salt and ½ tsp pepper. Whisking constantly, add the oil in a thin stream.

Add the beans, corn, tomato, and bell pepper to the quinoa. Pour in the vinaigrette, toss to coat all the ingredients well, and serve.

8

ZUCCHINI-FETA PANCAKES

serves 6–8

Be careful to squeeze out all the excess liquid from the zucchini or the pancakes won't hold together in the frying pan. Serve the pancakes with a green salad for a light lunch, or alongside grilled sausages or lamb chops as a substantial side.

4 cups (1 lb/500 g) shredded zucchini

Salt and freshly ground pepper

⅔ cup (3½ oz/105 g) all-purpose flour

1 tsp baking powder

1 cup (5 oz/155 g) crumbled feta cheese

4 eggs, separated

½ cup (1½ oz/45 g) thinly sliced green onions, white and tender green parts

2 Tbsp chopped fresh flat-leaf parsley

1 Tbsp chopped fresh mint

3 Tbsp olive oil, plus more as needed

Sour cream for serving

Put the zucchini in a fine-mesh sieve, sprinkle with 2 tsp salt, and let stand for 15–30 minutes. Squeeze out any excess liquid.

In a bowl, stir together the flour, the baking powder, ¼ tsp pepper, and 1 tsp salt. In another bowl, stir together the zucchini, feta, egg yolks, green onions, parsley, and mint. Add the flour mixture to the zucchini mixture and stir to combine. In a clean bowl, beat the egg whites until soft peaks form. Fold into the zucchini mixture.

In a frying pan, warm the 3 Tbsp oil over medium heat. Drop a spoonful of the batter into the pan for each pancake and fry, turning once, until crisp, about 1½ minutes per side. Transfer to paper towels, season with salt, and keep warm. Cook the remaining batter the same way, adding more oil to the pan as needed. Serve topped with sour cream.

9

*This recipe makes
excellent use of all of
summer's bounty. It
is the perfect option
for a backyard
get-together when
you can mingle
around the grill.
Due to the large
amount of vegetables
and the long cooking
time, be prepared
to replenish the
coals every 20 or
so minutes if using
charcoal. Use fresh
herbs such as
rosemary, thyme,
oregano, and
marjoram, and serve
with slices of grilled
country bread.*

ANTIPASTO GRILL

serves 8–10

2 globe eggplants, cut crosswise into
slices ½ inch (12 mm) thick, or 4–6 Asian
eggplants, halved lengthwise

Salt and freshly ground pepper

1½ cups (12 fl oz/375 ml) olive oil

½ cup (¾ oz/20 g) chopped mixed fresh
herbs, plus extra for garnish

4 cloves garlic, minced, plus 2 or 3 medium
heads, ½ inch (12 mm) of top trimmed

Balsamic vinegar

2 red bell peppers, seeded and cut
lengthwise into wide strips

2 yellow bell peppers, seeded and
cut lengthwise into wide strips

4–6 mild green chiles, halved lengthwise
and seeded

1½ lb (750 g) asparagus, ends trimmed

2 red onions, quartered

6 green onions, including 2–3 inches
(5–7.5 cm) of tender green tops

2 or 3 yellow squash, halved lengthwise
or thickly sliced and flesh lightly scored

2 or 3 zucchini, halved lengthwise
and flesh lightly scored, or 8–10 baby
zucchini, left whole

4–6 ripe but firm small tomatoes,
halved or left whole

1 cup (6 oz/185 g) mixed oil-cured olives

Place the eggplant slices in a colander,
sprinkle with salt, and let drain.

In a bowl, combine the oil, the ½ cup
herbs, the minced garlic, 1 Tbsp salt,
and 1 tsp pepper.

Prepare a charcoal or gas grill for direct-
heat grilling over medium-high heat.
Oil the grill rack.

Set the garlic heads on a piece of foil, and
drizzle each with 1 Tbsp of the herbed oil
and a few drops of vinegar. Season with salt
and pepper and seal the foil tightly. Place the
foil packet near the edge of the grill where
the heat is less intense, and grill until the garlic
is soft and caramelized, 10–12 minutes.

Meanwhile, working in batches, arrange the
eggplant, bell peppers, chiles, asparagus, red
and green onions, squashes, zucchini, and
tomatoes on the grill rack over the hottest part
of the fire. You may have to work in batches
depending on the size of your grill. ⟫→

Brush the vegetables with the herbed oil and
grill, turning often, until grill marks appear,
about 5 minutes, depending on the type of
vegetable. Move the vegetables to the edge of
the grill where the heat is less intense, and
grill until tender-crisp, about 5 minutes.

Transfer the grilled vegetables to a platter
and garnish with fresh herbs. Serve with
the olives.

10

*These tidy cheese-
filled eggplant
bundles are a fun
presentation. A
big squeeze of
lemon juice and a
scattering of lemon
zest help to highlight
the tang of the
goat cheese.*

GRILLED EGGPLANT
& GOAT CHEESE ROLLS

serves 6

2 eggplants, about 1½ lb (750 g) total

2 Tbsp extra-virgin olive oil,
plus more for brushing

Salt and freshly ground pepper

½ lb (250 g) goat cheese, crumbled

Zest of 1 lemon, plus fresh lemon juice
for drizzling

2 Tbsp chopped fresh flat-leaf parsley

1 tsp fresh thyme leaves

Chopped red onion for garnish

Prepare a charcoal or gas grill for direct-heat
grilling over medium heat. Oil the grill rack.

Cut the eggplants lengthwise into slices about
¼ in (6 mm) thick. Brush the slices on both
sides with oil and sprinkle with salt and
pepper. Arrange the slices on the grill and
cook, turning once, until golden and softened,
4–5 minutes per side. Place the slices in a
paper bag or sealed container to steam. Let
cool to room temperature, about 20 minutes.

In a bowl, stir together the cheese, 2 Tbsp oil,
lemon zest, parsley, and thyme. Place about
2 Tbsp of the cheese mixture along a narrow
end of each eggplant slice and roll up tightly
to enclose. Arrange the rolls, seam side down,
on a platter. Drizzle with oil and lemon juice.
Garnish with red onion and serve.

11

MARINATED SUMMER BEANS WITH TOASTED ALMONDS & DRY JACK CHEESE

serves 4

Green and yellow summer beans shine when cooked just until tender and tossed in a simple dressing of lemon juice and olive oil. Use dry Monterey jack cheese if you can find it. It has a sharp, sweet flavor that brings out the sweetness of the beans.

½ lb (250 g) green beans, trimmed

½ lb (250 g) yellow wax beans, trimmed

Ice water

1 Tbsp olive oil

2 Tbsp chopped fresh tarragon

1 tsp grated lemon zest

3 Tbsp fresh lemon juice

Salt and freshly ground pepper

½ cup (2 oz/60 g) dry Monterey jack or Parmesan cheese shavings

⅓ cup (2 oz/60 g) almonds, toasted and coarsely chopped

Slice the beans in half on the diagonal. Bring a large saucepan of salted water to a boil. Have ready a large bowl of ice water.

Add the beans to the boiling water and cook just until tender, 3–4 minutes. Drain the beans and plunge into the ice water to cool. Drain well and transfer to a serving bowl.

Add the oil, tarragon, lemon zest, and 2½ Tbsp of the lemon juice to the beans. Mix well and season with salt and pepper and additional lemon juice, if desired. Garnish with the cheese and almonds, and serve.

12

GRILLED WHITE CORN SALAD

serves 4–6

Summer corn, full of natural sugars, becomes toasty— tasting almost of caramel when cooked on the grill. Brushing the ears with oil helps create the golden grill marks. Once the kernels are stripped from the cobs, they are tossed with onions, cilantro, and a sweet-spicy-tart dressing that highlights their essence.

Salt and freshly ground pepper

6 ears white corn, husks and silk removed

2 Tbsp olive oil, plus more for brushing

2 Tbsp fresh lime juice

2 cloves garlic, minced

1–2 green chiles, seeded and minced

1 tsp firmly packed golden brown sugar

1 tsp ground cumin

½ tsp red pepper flakes

½ cup (½ oz/15 g) cilantro leaves

2 green onions, including tender green parts, thinly sliced

Prepare a charcoal or gas grill for direct-heat grilling over medium heat. Oil the grill rack.

Fill a bowl with cold water, add 1 tsp salt, and stir to dissolve. Add the corn and let stand for 10 minutes.

In a bowl, combine the 2 Tbsp oil, lime juice, garlic, chile to taste, brown sugar, cumin, and red pepper flakes. Add in ½ tsp salt and several grinds of pepper, and stir to dissolve the sugar.

Drain the corn thoroughly, pat dry, and brush with oil. Grill, turning frequently, until lightly browned and tender, about 15 minutes. Let cool. Hold each ear of corn upright on a cutting board. Using a sharp knife, cut down along the ear, stripping off the kernels and rotating the ear a quarter turn after each cut. Transfer the kernels to a bowl.

Add the cilantro and green onions and toss gently. Add the dressing and toss to coat thoroughly. Adjust the seasoning if necessary. Serve at room temperature.

13

Breading and frying eggplant on the stove top is delicious, but the absorbent flesh does soak up oil. Oven-frying the eggplant is not only healthier, it keeps the texture intact, and produces a custardy finish. Look for an eggplant that feels heavy with a shiny, smooth skin.

EGGPLANT PARMESAN

serves 4–6

FOR THE TOMATO-BASIL SAUCE

3 Tbsp olive oil

5 large cloves garlic

3 lb (1.5 kg) plum tomatoes, cored and quartered

1 bay leaf

2 tsp sugar

Salt and freshly ground pepper

½ cup (1 oz/30 g) firmly packed torn fresh basil

¼ cup (2 fl oz/60 ml) olive oil

1 cup (5 oz/155 g) all-purpose flour

3 eggs, lightly beaten

1¾ cups (7 oz/220 g) dried bread crumbs

Salt and freshly ground pepper

½ cup (2 oz/60 g) grated Parmesan cheese

1 large eggplant, about 1½ lb (750 g), cut crosswise into 18 slices about ¼ inch (6 mm) thick

½ lb (250 g) fresh mozzarella cheese, cut into 18 pieces

To make the sauce, in a large saucepan, warm the oil over medium heat. Add the garlic and cook until golden on all sides, about 4 minutes. Remove from the heat. Working in batches, purée the tomatoes in a blender until smooth, and then strain through a coarse-mesh sieve into the pan with the oil and garlic. Add the bay leaf, the sugar, 1 tsp salt, and a few grinds of pepper. Bring to a boil over medium-high heat, reduce the heat to low, and simmer, uncovered, until thickened, about 45 minutes. Stir the basil into the sauce and simmer for 5 minutes. Season with salt and pepper.

Meanwhile, preheat the oven to 400°F (200°C). Pour the oil onto a rimmed baking sheet and swirl to cover the bottom.

Put the flour, eggs, and bread crumbs into 3 separate shallow bowls. Season each bowl with 1 tsp salt and a few grinds of pepper. Stir ¼ cup (1 oz/30 g) of the Parmesan into the bread crumbs. Dip each eggplant slice first in the flour, then in the eggs, and finally in the bread crumbs, gently tapping or shaking off the excess each time. Place on the prepared pan. ⇥

Bake for 15 minutes. Turn the slices and continue to bake until golden and tender, about 15 minutes. Let cool for 5–10 minutes.

Lightly oil a 9-by-13-inch (23-by-33-cm) baking dish. Overlap the eggplant slices in the prepared dish, alternating each slice with a piece of mozzarella. Spoon the sauce over the top and sprinkle with the remaining Parmesan. Bake until the cheese is melted and the sauce is bubbling, about 30 minutes. Let stand for 10 minutes before serving.

14

A sprinkle of toasted peanuts and bright green cilantro adds crunch and color to this Thai-style salad, which is refreshing, pungent, and spicy at the same time. Marinating the cucumber, onion, and chile in the sweetened vinegar mixture mellows their flavors and softens their textures.

SPICY THAI CUCUMBER SALAD WITH ROASTED PEANUTS

serves 4

⅓ cup (3 fl oz/80 ml) rice vinegar

1½ Tbsp sugar

Salt and freshly ground pepper

1 English cucumber

¼ red onion, thinly sliced

1 jalapeño chile, thinly sliced

Leaves from ½ bunch fresh cilantro, coarsely chopped

2 Tbsp roasted peanuts, coarsely chopped

In a small nonreactive saucepan, combine the vinegar, sugar, and a pinch each of salt and pepper. Bring to a boil. Reduce the heat to low and cook, stirring occasionally, until the sugar dissolves, 2–3 minutes. Let cool completely.

Cut the cucumber into slices about ¼ inch (6 mm) thick. Transfer to a large bowl and add the onion and chile. Pour the vinegar mixture over the vegetables and stir well to coat. Let the vegetables stand at room temperature for at least 30 minutes, stirring occasionally, to blend the flavors.

Stir the cilantro into the salad. Top with the peanuts and serve.

15

FRIED RICOTTA-STUFFED ZUCCHINI BLOSSOMS

serves 4–6

1 cup (8 oz/250 g) ricotta cheese

1½ tsp chopped fresh flat-leaf parsley, plus more for garnish

1 Tbsp chopped fresh basil

Salt and freshly ground pepper

2 eggs

1 cup (5 oz/155 g) all-purpose flour

12 large zucchini blossoms

Olive or canola oil for frying

In Italy, zucchini blossoms are often stuffed with mozzarella and anchovies and fried in a crisp coating. Here, herbed ricotta is tucked into the blossoms with delicious results. If the ricotta is very moist, spoon it into a cheesecloth-lined fine-mesh sieve set over a bowl, and place in the refrigerator to drain overnight. Fresh squash blossoms are highly perishable, so use them as soon as possible.

In a bowl, stir together the ricotta, 1½ tsp parsley, and the basil. Season with salt and pepper. Scrape the mixture into a pastry bag fitted with a large plain tip. In a small, shallow bowl, whisk the eggs until lightly beaten. Spread the flour on a plate.

Gently wipe the zucchini blossoms with damp paper towels, and carefully remove the stamens. Gently spread each flower open, insert the tip of the pastry bag, and pipe about 1 Tbsp of the ricotta mixture into the blossom. Do not overfill the blossoms, or the filling may seep out as they cook. Roll each blossom first in the flour, then in the eggs, and then again in the flour, gently shaking off the excess each time.

Preheat the oven to 200°F (95°C). Line a platter with paper towels. Pour oil to a depth of 1 inch (2.5 cm) into a heavy frying pan and heat to 375°F (190°C) on a deep-frying thermometer.

Add the blossoms, a few at a time, being careful not to crowd the pan. Fry the blossoms, turning once, until lightly golden, 3–4 minutes. Using a slotted spoon, transfer the blossoms to the paper-lined platter to drain and place in the oven to keep warm. Allow the oil to return to 375°F between batches. Garnish with parsley and serve warm.

16

GREEK POTATO SALAD

serves 4–6

1½ lb (750 g) small red potatoes

1 Tbsp capers, preferably salt-packed

2 Tbsp red wine vinegar

1 tsp ground coriander

2 Tbsp extra-virgin olive oil

Salt and freshly ground pepper

¼ cup (⅓ oz/10 g) coarsely chopped fresh flat-leaf parsley

1 tsp grated lemon zest

This Greek-inspired potato salad relies on the bright flavors of capers, vinegar, parsley, and lemon. Be sure to allow the potatoes to stand once dressed with the vinaigrette in order to soak up all that flavor. Pair this salad with grilled lamb chops or lamb burgers.

Place the potatoes in a large saucepan with water to cover by 2 inches (5 cm) and bring to a boil. Reduce the heat to medium and cook until tender when pierced with a knife, 20–25 minutes. Drain the potatoes, let cool, and cut in half. Transfer to a bowl.

Meanwhile, if using salt-packed capers, place them in a small bowl with cold water to cover and let soak for 20 minutes. Drain, rinse well, and then drain again and pat dry. If using vinegar-packed capers, rinse under cold running water, drain, and pat dry. Coarsely chop the capers.

In a small bowl, whisk together the vinegar, coriander, and oil. Season with salt and pepper. Pour the vinaigrette over the potatoes. Scatter the capers, parsley, and lemon zest over the top. Toss until the potatoes are evenly coated with the dressing. Let stand for 20 minutes to let the potatoes soak up the dressing, and then serve.

17

ZUCCHINI "PASTA" WITH FRESH TOMATO SAUCE

serves 4

4 zucchini, about 2 lb (1 kg) total

Salt and freshly ground pepper

4 large tomatoes, about 2 lb (1 kg) total, diced

2 cloves garlic, minced

Leaves from ½ bunch fresh basil, cut into thin ribbons

3 Tbsp extra-virgin olive oil

Small piece Parmesan cheese (optional)

Here, a trio of familiar ingredients, garden-fresh zucchini, juicy tomatoes, and aged Parmesan, come together in a surprising dish that recalls a plate of pasta. Look for Parmesan imported from Italy, labeled Parmigiano-Reggiano. It will lend an especially nutty, almost caramel-like taste to the dish.

Using a mandoline, a sharp knife, or a very sharp vegetable peeler, cut each zucchini lengthwise into slices about ⅛ inch (3 mm) thick. Carefully transfer the slices to a large bowl, sprinkle with 1 Tbsp salt, and toss gently to coat. Let stand for 20 minutes. Gently rinse the slices under cold running water. Pat the slices dry with a kitchen towel and arrange in a loose mound on a platter.

In a large bowl, combine the tomatoes and their juices, the garlic, and the basil and toss gently to mix. Stir 2 Tbsp of the oil and a generous pinch each of salt and pepper into the tomato mixture.

Drizzle the remaining 1 Tbsp oil over the zucchini and season with a few grinds of pepper. Spoon the tomato mixture over the zucchini. Using a vegetable peeler, cut shavings of Parmesan over the top, if desired, and serve.

18

CHARRED EGGPLANT SOUP WITH CUMIN & GREEK YOGURT

serves 6–8

2 large eggplants, about 2½ lb (1.25 kg) total, peeled and cut crosswise into slices 1 inch (2.5 cm) thick

3 ripe tomatoes, about 1¼ lb (625 g) total, halved and seeded

1 Tbsp extra-virgin olive oil, plus more for brushing

3 carrots, finely chopped

5 shallots, finely chopped

3 cloves garlic, minced

¾ tsp minced fresh thyme

¼ tsp ground cumin

1 cup (8 fl oz/250 ml) fruity white wine

5 cups (40 fl oz/1.25 l) chicken or vegetable broth

Salt and freshly ground pepper

½ cup (4 oz/125 g) Greek-style plain yogurt

The supple texture of cooked eggplant is transformed into a soup that needs no cream to achieve its silken consistency. This relatively uncomplicated recipe packs lots of flavor: eggplant asserts its smokiness, shallots and garlic add pungent sweetness, white wine brings brightness, and a touch of musky cumin imparts an exotic taste.

Prepare a charcoal or gas grill for direct-heat grilling over medium-high heat. Oil the grill rack. Brush the eggplant and tomato with oil and arrange on the grill rack. Cook, turning once, until softened and charred, about 8 minutes for the tomatoes and 10 minutes for the eggplant. Transfer to a cutting board and let cool. Remove and discard the skins from the tomatoes. Coarsely chop all but 1 of the eggplant slices. Finely chop the remaining eggplant slice and reserve for garnish.

In a large, heavy pot, heat the 1 Tbsp olive oil over medium-high heat. Add the carrots and sauté until just beginning to soften, about 4 minutes. Add the shallots, garlic, thyme, and cumin and cook, stirring occasionally, until fragrant, about 2 minutes. Add the tomatoes, coarsely chopped eggplant, wine, and broth and bring to a boil. Reduce the heat to low, cover partially, and simmer for 15 minutes to blend the flavors.

Working in batches, transfer the mixture to a blender and process to a coarse purée. Pour the purée back into the pot and season with salt and pepper. Cook gently over medium-low heat, stirring occasionally, until heated through, about 10 minutes. Adjust the seasoning if necessary. Ladle the soup into bowls. Garnish with dollops of yogurt and the finely diced eggplant and serve.

19

GREEN BEAN & YELLOW TOMATO SALAD WITH MINT

serves 4

1 lb (500 g) young, slender green beans, trimmed

½ cup (¾ oz/20 g) chopped fresh mint

2 Tbsp extra-virgin olive oil

Salt and freshly ground pepper

2 yellow tomatoes

½ cup (2 oz/60 g) thin red onion wedges

2 tsp red wine vinegar, or as needed

This simple salad combines tender-crisp green beans and sweet summer tomatoes. Toss in the mint while the beans are steaming hot to release its fragrant oils. Yellow tomatoes have a sweeter, less acidic flavor, but red ones can be substituted, or use an equal amount of each. If using red tomatoes, reduce the amount of vinegar to taste.

Bring a large pot of water to a boil. Add the beans and cook until tender, 5–7 minutes. Drain and transfer the hot beans to a large serving bowl.

Add the mint, oil, and ½ tsp salt to the beans and toss to mix. Let cool to room temperature, about 20 minutes.

Cut the tomatoes into wedges about ½ inch (12 mm) thick. Add the tomatoes, onion, and 2 tsp vinegar to the beans. Season with pepper and toss to mix. Add more vinegar, if desired. Serve at room temperature.

20

ZUCCHINI & PARMESAN FRITTATA

serves 10–12

2 zucchini

6 eggs

2 Tbsp half-and-half

¼ cup (1 oz/30 g) grated Parmesan cheese

Salt and freshly ground pepper

2 Tbsp unsalted butter

1 Tbsp extra-virgin olive oil

2 Tbsp finely chopped yellow onion

1 clove garlic, minced

1 tsp chopped fresh thyme

¼ cup (⅓ oz/10 g) chopped fresh flat-leaf parsley, plus more for garnish

Frittatas are quick and easy to assemble and cook and can be served at room temperature, making them ideal for serving at a cocktail party. They're also well suited for brunch and pair nicely with ham or bacon. This recipe calls for zucchini, but you can use any of your favorite summer squash varieties in its place.

Shred the zucchini on the large holes of a grater-shredder. Lay the shredded zucchini on paper towels to drain briefly.

In a large bowl, whisk together the eggs, the half-and-half, the cheese, ¾ tsp salt, and ½ tsp pepper just until blended. Stir in the drained zucchini.

Preheat the broiler. In a flameproof 10-inch (25-cm) frying pan, melt the butter with the oil over medium-high heat. When the butter foams, add the onion and sauté until translucent, 2–3 minutes. Add the garlic, thyme, and parsley and sauté for 1 minute.

Pour in the egg mixture, reduce the heat to low, and cook until the eggs are just firm around the edges, 3–4 minutes. Using a spatula, lift the edges and tilt the pan to let the uncooked portion flow underneath. Continue cooking until the eggs are nearly set, 4–5 minutes more.

Slip the pan under the broiler about 4 inches (10 cm) from the heat source and broil until the top sets and browns lightly, about 2 minutes. Remove the pan from the broiler and slide the frittata onto a cutting board; let cool. Cut into 1-inch (2.5-cm) pieces, garnish with parsley, and serve at room temperature.

21

SPICY GRILLED BROCCOLI RABE

serves 4

1 bunch broccoli rabe, tough stems removed

3 Tbsp olive oil

Grated zest and juice of 1 lemon

1 tsp red pepper flakes

Olive oil for drizzling

Salt and freshly ground pepper

Moderately bitter broccoli rabe mellows in the high heat of stove-top grilling. If the broccoli rabe has particularly thick stalks, split each stalk lengthwise or blanch the whole stalks in boiling water for a couple of minutes before grilling. Pair this lemony, spicy side dish with grilled or broiled lamb or pork chops.

Rinse the broccoli rabe thoroughly, then shake off the excess water but leave the water clinging to the stems. Put the broccoli rabe into a bowl, add the oil, lemon zest and juice, red pepper flakes, 1 tsp salt, and ½ tsp pepper, and toss to coat evenly. Let the broccoli rabe marinate while the grill pan heats.

Heat a grill pan over medium-high heat until very hot. Arrange the broccoli rabe in a single layer on the hot pan and cook, turning once, until browned, but not black, on both sides, about 4 minutes per side. Serve warm or at room temperature.

22

HOMEMADE SAUERKRAUT

makes 8 one-pint (16–fl oz/500-ml) jars

5 lb (2.5 kg) red or green cabbage, or a mixture (about 4 medium heads)

Kosher salt

Tangy sauerkraut calls for only three ingredients: cabbage, salt, and patience. The fermentation process can take up to a month, depending on the temperature of the surrounding environment. If you would like to flavor the sauerkraut, mix 3 Tbsp caraway seeds with the cabbage before packing it into the crock. Or, for a colorful variation, add 1 cup (5 oz/ 155 g) peeled and shredded carrots to the sauerkraut before you start to remove it from the crock.

Remove and discard any tough leaves from the cabbage heads. Cut the heads into quarters through the stem end, and cut out the core. Using a mandoline, a food processor, or a chef's knife, finely shred the cabbage. Place in a large bowl, sprinkle with 3 Tbsp salt, and toss to combine. Cover and let stand until softened, about 30 minutes.

Working in batches, tightly pack the cabbage into a 4-qt (4-l) ceramic crock or food-grade plastic tub. Add any accumulated liquid from the bowl. Cover the cabbage with cheesecloth, set a plate on the cloth, and top with 1 or 2 heavy weights. Cover the crock with a kitchen towel and let stand at room temperature.

Within 24 hours, the cabbage should be submerged in brine. If it isn't, stir 1 tsp salt into 1 cup (8 fl oz/250 ml) water and add to the crock, then reassemble the cheesecloth, plate, and weights. Check the cabbage every day or two. If scum forms, scrape it off, then rinse the plate and cheesecloth before returning them to the crock and topping with the weights. Depending on the surrounding temperature, the cabbage will ferment in 10 days to 4 weeks. It is ready when bubbles no longer appear and the aroma is pleasantly pungent, usually about 2 weeks. Taste, and if it is too mild, let it continue to ferment.

The flavor will become more concentrated as the weeks pass. Using tongs or a large spoon, remove a serving or a jarful at a time and re-cover the crock. If you remove more than you can use at one time, refrigerate the remainder in a separate container. Each batch will vary, depending on how cool the storage environment is, but after several weeks, the sauerkraut will lose texture and be less tasty. Try to work through your crock within 4 weeks or so.

23

FRESH CORN & GRUYÈRE SOUFFLÉ

serves 4

1 Tbsp grated Parmesan cheese

2 ears corn, husks and silk removed

5 egg whites

½ tsp cream of tartar

4 egg yolks

4 Tbsp (2 oz/60 g) unsalted butter

2 Tbsp minced shallot

¼ cup (1½ oz/45 g) all-purpose flour

Salt and freshly ground pepper

1 cup (8 fl oz/250 ml) whole milk

1 cup (4 oz/125 g) grated Gruyère cheese

Sweet or savory soufflés are a delicious way to showcase seasonal ingredients. They also look wonderful, especially if you get them to the table before they begin to fall. This summery dish makes an excellent main course, for lunch or dinner, accompanied with a green salad and a glass of crisp white wine.

Preheat the oven to 350°F (180°C). Butter the bottom and sides of a 4-cup (32–fl oz/1-l) soufflé dish. Sprinkle with the Parmesan and turn to coat the bottom and sides.

Hold each ear of corn upright on a cutting board. Using a sharp knife, cut down along the ear, stripping off the kernels and rotating a quarter turn after each cut.

In a bowl, using an electric mixer, beat the egg whites and the cream of tartar until stiff peaks form, about 4 minutes. In a small bowl, beat the egg yolks until creamy, about 2 minutes.

In a saucepan, melt the butter over medium-high heat. Add the shallot and sauté until translucent, about 1 minute. Whisk in the flour, ½ tsp salt, and ¼ tsp pepper. Continuing to whisk, slowly add the milk and cook, stirring often, until a smooth, thick sauce forms, about 5 minutes. Let cool briefly.

Whisk the egg yolks into the sauce until well blended. Stir in the corn and the Gruyère. Stir 3 Tbsp of the egg whites into the corn mixture to lighten it. Using a rubber spatula, gently fold in the remaining egg whites just until no white streaks remain. Gently spoon the mixture into the prepared dish.

Bake until the top is puffed and golden brown, about 40 minutes. Remove from the oven and serve.

24

FARRO SALAD WITH TOMATOES, BASIL & RICOTTA SALATA

serves 4

1 cup (6 oz/185 g) farro

Salt and freshly ground pepper

2 Tbsp extra-virgin olive oil

1 Tbsp fresh lemon juice

1 cup (6 oz/185 g) cherry or grape tomatoes, halved

½ cup (2 oz/60 g) crumbled ricotta salata cheese

2 green onions, white and tender green parts, thinly sliced

¼ cup (⅓ oz/10 g) shredded fresh basil

Farro, an ancient strain of wheat, is grown in the Italian provinces of Tuscany, Umbria, Abruzzo, and Lazio, where cooks prepare it in a variety of ways, including soups, stews, side dishes, and salads. In this colorful, summery treatment, the light brown, nutty grains are tossed with a lemony dressing, sweet cherry tomatoes, and pleasantly salty ricotta salata.

In a large saucepan, combine the farro and 2 qt (2 l) water and let stand for 1 hour. Place the pan over medium-high heat, bring to a boil, and add 1 tsp salt. Reduce the heat to medium or medium-low so that the farro simmers steadily, and cook, uncovered, until the farro is tender yet still slightly firm and chewy, about 25 minutes. Drain well.

In a serving bowl, whisk together the oil and lemon juice. Season with salt and pepper. Add the farro and toss well. Add the tomatoes, ricotta salata, green onions, and basil, and stir gently until all the ingredients are evenly distributed. Serve at room temperature.

25

EDAMAME, CORN, TOMATO & AVOCADO SALAD

serves 4

2 ears corn, husks and silk removed, or 1 cup (5 oz/155 g) frozen corn kernels

1½ cups (9 oz/280 g) frozen shelled edamame

12 cherry tomatoes, halved

1 large avocado, pitted, peeled, and cubed

2 Tbsp fresh lime juice

Salt and freshly ground pepper

1 Tbsp canola oil

2 Tbsp chopped fresh cilantro

Toothsome edamame (soybeans), sweet corn kernels, and juicy cherry tomatoes come together in this summery salad that is tossed with a brightly flavored cilantro-lime dressing. This is a vegetable dish that even kids will enjoy.

If using ears of corn, hold each ear of corn upright on a cutting board. Using a sharp knife, cut down along the ear, stripping off the kernels and rotating the ear a quarter turn after each cut.

Bring a saucepan of water to a boil and have ready a bowl of ice water. Add the corn kernels and the edamame to the saucepan and cook for 3 minutes. Using a slotted spoon, transfer the corn and edamame to the bowl of ice water. Drain, pat dry, and place in a large serving bowl. Add the tomatoes and avocado to the bowl.

In a small bowl, whisk together the lime juice, 1 tsp salt, and 1 tsp pepper. Slowly whisk in the oil. Pour the dressing over the salad and toss gently to combine. Garnish with the cilantro and serve.

26

ZUCCHINI WITH ROASTED RED PEPPERS & CHIVES

serves 4

2 red bell peppers

2 cloves garlic, chopped

3–4 Tbsp chopped fresh chives

5–8 fresh basil leaves, thinly sliced

2 Tbsp extra-virgin olive oil

Aged balsamic vinegar

Salt and freshly ground pepper

4 young, tender zucchini, about 1 lb (500 g) total, cut into bite-sized pieces

Break out the high-quality balsamic vinegar for the final touch on this dish of roasted peppers and crisp zucchini. Full of flavor, this vegetable medley pairs well with grilled chicken or steak, or serve it alongside rice or quinoa for a meatless meal.

Preheat the broiler. Arrange the bell peppers on a baking sheet and broil, turning as needed, until blistered and charred on all sides, 10–15 minutes. Transfer the blackened peppers to a bowl, cover, and let cool to the touch. Peel the charred skin from the peppers. Slit them lengthwise and remove the stems and seeds.

Finely chop the peppers and transfer to a large serving bowl. Add the garlic, chives, basil to taste, and oil. Season with vinegar, salt, and pepper.

Bring water to a boil in a steamer pan, put the zucchini in a steamer rack over the water, cover, and steam until tender-crisp, 3–4 minutes. Remove the zucchini from the rack.

Add the zucchini to the bell pepper mixture, toss well, and serve.

27

SPANISH PEPPERS WITH OLIVES & CAPERS

serves 6

3 Tbsp olive oil

½ cup (2 oz/60 g) thinly sliced shallots

1 clove garlic, minced

2 lb (1 kg) red, yellow, and/or orange bell peppers, seeded and cut into 1½-inch (4-cm) pieces

Salt and freshly ground pepper

¼ cup (2 fl oz/60 ml) sherry vinegar

¼ cup (1½ oz/45 g) pitted and coarsely chopped mild green olives

1 Tbsp capers, drained

This colorful mix of sweet bell peppers simmered in olive oil is delicious served warm or at room temperature. Set it out as part of a tapas spread, with serrano ham or slices of chorizo, spicy roasted potatoes, crusty slices of baguette, and a chilled rosé. The peppers are also good atop grilled bread as an appetizer or alongside cold roast chicken.

In a large frying pan, warm the oil over medium-high heat. Add the shallots and garlic and cook, stirring, until fragrant but not browned, 1–2 minutes. Add the bell peppers, ¼ tsp salt, and a few grinds of pepper and cook, stirring frequently, until the peppers are soft, about 8 minutes. Add the vinegar, olives, and capers and cook until most of the liquid has evaporated, 1–2 minutes. Season to taste with additional salt and pepper, and serve.

28

CREAMY COLESLAW WITH GREEN APPLE & PARSLEY

serves 6–8

1 head green cabbage, about 2 lb (1 kg)

2 celery ribs

1 Granny Smith apple, halved and cored

1 small yellow or red onion

2 small carrots

2 Tbsp cider vinegar

2 Tbsp minced fresh flat-leaf parsley

1¼ cups (10 fl oz/310 ml) mayonnaise

Salt and freshly ground pepper

Many barbecue fans argue that a barbecue isn't complete without a big bowl of cool, crisp coleslaw on the table. Nothing tastes better alongside a batch of spicy barbecued ribs. If you turn up your nose at too-sweet slaws, this one is for you. It gets a tart lift from an unexpected source: grated apple.

Cut the cabbage into wedges through the stem end, and cut out the core. Using a food processor fitted with the thin slicing attachment or a sharp knife, slice the cabbage into thin slivers. Transfer to a large bowl. Thinly slice the celery and add to the cabbage.

If using the food processor, replace the slicing attachment with the shredding attachment. Cut the apple halves and the onion into wedges. Shred the apple, onion, and carrots in the processor, or on the large holes of a box grater. Add to the cabbage and celery.

Sprinkle the vegetables with the vinegar and toss to coat. Add the parsley and mayonnaise and mix well. Season with salt and pepper. Cover and refrigerate until chilled, at least 2 hours. Adjust the seasoning if necessary. Serve cold.

29

TOMATO BRUSCHETTA

serves 4

About 1 lb (500 g) cherry tomatoes
or 3 or 4 large tomatoes

About 16 fresh basil leaves,
torn into small pieces

Salt

8 slices coarse country bread,
each about ½ inch (12 mm) thick

2 cloves garlic

¼ cup (2 fl oz/60 ml) extra-virgin
olive oil

Bruschetta, at its simplest, is grilled bread rubbed with garlic and drizzled with olive oil, but it can also be prepared with a variety of toppings. This classic version demands the best-quality ingredients. Use a crusty coarse bread; ripe, red tomatoes harvested at the height of the season; freshly picked basil; and the best extra-virgin olive oil your budget will allow.

Preheat the broiler.

If using cherry tomatoes, cut them in half. If using large tomatoes, core and seed them and cut into ½-inch (12-mm) pieces. In a bowl, combine the tomatoes, basil, and a pinch of salt.

Place the bread slices on a baking sheet and broil, turning once, until crisp and golden on both sides, about 3 minutes.

Immediately rub one side of each slice vigorously with a garlic clove, using 1 clove for 4 slices.

Arrange the bread slices, garlic side up, on a platter. Spoon the tomato mixture on the slices. Drizzle with the oil and serve.

30

SHAVED SUMMER SQUASH & PEAS

serves 4

2 cups (10 oz/315 g) shelled English peas

1 lb (500 g) mixed summer squashes such
as zucchini, yellow squash, and pattypan

¼ cup (1 oz/30 g) shaved ricotta salata cheese

2 green onions, white and tender green
parts, thinly sliced on the diagonal

¼ cup (⅓ oz/10 g) chopped fresh mint

¼ cup (2 fl oz/60 ml) extra-virgin olive oil

Salt and freshly ground pepper

Summertime typically brings a bumper crop of squashes, and this tasty mix of squash and peas is a great way to serve that bounty. Select a mild olive oil so as not to mask the fresh flavors of the vegetables.

Bring a saucepan of generously salted water to a boil. Add the peas and blanch for 1 minute. Using a wire skimmer, scoop out the peas, transfer to a colander, and rinse under cold running water. Drain and transfer to a bowl.

Using a mandoline or vegetable peeler, shave the squash lengthwise into thin ribbons. Add to the bowl with the cheese, green onions, mint, and oil. Toss gently to combine. Season with salt and pepper and serve.

31

CUCUMBER, RED ONION & FRESH DILL SALAD

serves 4

2 English cucumbers

½ red onion, thinly sliced

3 Tbsp chopped fresh dill

2 Tbsp chopped fresh mint

2 Tbsp rice vinegar

¼ cup (2 fl oz/60 ml) extra-virgin olive oil

Salt and freshly ground pepper

On days so hot you can't look at the stove, turn to crisp raw salads. The best tool to use for thinly slicing the cucumbers is a mandoline, but if you lack one, a sharp chef's knife and a steady hand will get the job done.

Using a mandoline or vegetable peeler, shave the cucumbers lengthwise into thin ribbons. In a large serving bowl, toss the cucumbers and onion with the dill, mint, vinegar, and oil. Season with salt and pepper and serve.

During the hottest days of the year, look for the vegetables that thrive in the scorching heat. Rely on the staples of the sun-soaked Mediterranean: tender summer squashes, vibrant, juicy tomatoes, meaty eggplants, and plump peppers, both sweet and hot. Put them together with plenty of aromatic basil and garlic, the flavors of summer, whether you're simmering them in a big pot of ratatouille or puréeing them into a cool, refreshing gazpacho.

1
FRESH CORN, JALAPEÑO & MONTEREY JACK TAMALES
page 178

2
ZUCCHINI & FARRO SALAD WITH LEMON VINAIGRETTE
page 178

3
SUMMER SQUASH WITH TOMATO-BASIL VINAIGRETTE
page 180

8
ROMANO BEANS WITH TOMATOES & PANCETTA
page 183

9
SAUTÉED YELLOW TOMATOES WITH ARUGULA PESTO & FETA
page 184

10
CREAMED CORN WITH CHIPOTLE CHILES
page 184

15
CORN FRITTERS
page 189

16
BREAD SALAD WITH CHARRED TOMATOES, CUCUMBER & OLIVES
page 189

17
SUMMER BEAN & CORN SALAD WITH TARRAGON & CHERVIL
page 190

22
BAKED ZUCCHINI & RED ONIONS WITH MINT & VINEGAR
page 193

23
GIARDINIERA
page 195

24
GRILLED POTATO SALAD WITH CREAMY VINAIGRETTE
page 195

29
GRILLED CHERRY TOMATOES
page 198

30
CARROT SLAW WITH LEMON-HONEY DRESSING
page 198

31
EGGPLANT, ZUCCHINI & SQUASH KEBABS
page 198

august

1

AUGUST

FRESH CORN, JALAPEÑO & MONTEREY JACK TAMALES

serves 4–6

Tamales are actually quite easy to make and this is a fun dish to prepare with your kids, who will love stuffing and rolling the corn husks. The recipe calls for masa harina, a traditional Mexican corn flour used to make tamales and tortillas. Do not confuse this with cornmeal, which is dried ground corn with a coarse texture and will not produce the same quality dough.

2 ears corn, husks intact

2 cups (8 oz/250 g) masa harina

½ cup (4 oz/125 g) unsalted butter, cut into pieces

½ tsp sugar

½ tsp baking powder

Salt and freshly ground pepper

½ cup (4 fl oz/125 ml) chicken or vegetable broth

2 tsp olive oil

1 small jalapeño chile, seeded and minced

¾ cup (3 oz/90 g) shredded Monterey jack cheese

Using a large knife, cut off the bottom ½ inch (12 mm) of each ear of corn so that the husks come free in whole pieces. Set the husks aside, and remove and discard the silk. Hold each ear of corn upright on a cutting board. Using a sharp knife, cut down along the ear, stripping off the kernels and rotating the ear a quarter turn after each cut.

In a food processor, pulse half of the kernels to chop roughly. Add the masa harina, the butter, the sugar, the baking powder, and 1 tsp salt. Process until completely combined. Add the broth and process just until smooth.

In a small frying pan, heat the oil over medium-high heat. Add the remaining corn kernels and the chile, season with salt and pepper, and sauté just until the vegetables begin to soften, about 2 minutes. Let cool.

In a large pot with a steamer rack, add enough water to reach just below the rack. Cover the bottom of the rack with the small corn husks. Set the pot over medium heat.

Place 2–3 Tbsp of tamale dough on each of the largest corn husks. Top with 2 tsp of the corn and jalapeño mixture and 2 tsp of the cheese. Using your hands, slightly flatten 1 tsp of the dough, and then place on the cheese. Wrap the tamale inside the corn husk, completely enclosing it, using 2 corn husks if necessary, and place in the steamer. Arrange any remaining corn husks on top of the tamales, cover the pot, and ⇥

steam until the dough pulls away from the husks, about 1 hour. Occasionally check the water level in the pot and add more if necessary.

Remove the tamales from the pot and serve in the husks.

2

AUGUST

ZUCCHINI & FARRO SALAD WITH LEMON VINAIGRETTE

serves 6

This hearty, summertime salad needs only panfried sausages and a platter of sliced ripe tomatoes to complete the menu. Pour ice-cold pale ale for a fitting beverage.

1½ cups (8 oz/250 g) pearled farro

Salt

2 Tbsp olive oil, plus ½ cup (4 fl oz/125 ml)

1 lb (500 g) zucchini, cut into ½-inch (12-mm) chunks

1 clove garlic

¼ cup (2 fl oz/60 ml) fresh lemon juice

1 small cucumber, about ½ lb (250 g), peeled and cut into ½-inch (12-mm) chunks

5 green onions, white and tender green parts, sliced on the diagonal ¼ inch (6 mm) thick

¼ cup (¼ oz/10 g) chopped fresh basil

¼ cup (¼ oz/10 g) chopped fresh mint

1 cup (5 oz/155 g) crumbled feta cheese

Bring a pot of salted water to a boil. Add the farro and season with salt. Reduce the heat to low and cook until tender, 12–15 minutes. Drain and let cool.

Meanwhile, in a large frying pan, heat the 2 Tbsp oil over medium-high heat. Add the zucchini chunks, season with salt, and sauté until tender-crisp, 3–4 minutes. Transfer to a plate and let cool.

On a cutting board, mash the garlic and a pinch of salt into a paste. In a small bowl, stir together the mashed garlic and lemon juice and let stand for 10 minutes. Whisk in the ½ cup oil.

Combine the farro, zucchini, cucumber, green onions, basil, mint, and feta in a large bowl. Drizzle with the vinaigrette and toss. Season with salt and serve.

3

Zucchini, yellow crookneck, and pattypan squashes are terrific grilled and lightly dressed with a tomato-basil vinaigrette. This same vinaigrette can be used to dress a salad of mixed lettuces or a green bean or a green bean and corn salad. Accompany this squash salad with rustic bread and a bowl of mixed olives.

SUMMER SQUASH WITH TOMATO-BASIL VINAIGRETTE

serves 6

FOR THE TOMATO-BASIL VINAIGRETTE

½ cup (4 fl oz/125 ml) grape seed oil

¼ cup (2 fl oz/60 ml) extra-virgin olive oil

2 oil-packed sun-dried tomatoes, minced

1 Tbsp balsamic vinegar

1 Tbsp red wine vinegar

1 Tbsp maple syrup

1 Tbsp Dijon mustard

5–6 fresh basil leaves, cut into thin ribbons

Salt and freshly ground pepper

5–6 small to medium zucchini, about 1 lb (500 g) total

5–6 yellow crookneck squashes, about 1 lb (500 g) total

10 small pattypan squashes, about 1 lb (500 g) total

2 plum tomatoes, cored, quartered, and seeded

½ cup (4 fl oz/125 ml) olive oil

1 Tbsp minced fresh marjoram

Salt and freshly ground pepper

¼ cup (1½ oz/45 g) pine nuts, toasted

2 Tbsp minced fresh flat-leaf parsley

5 cups (5 oz/150 g) mixed greens

To make the tomato-basil vinaigrette, combine the oils in a measuring cup. In a blender or food processor, combine the sun-dried tomatoes, vinegars, maple syrup, and mustard. Pulse several times to form a thick paste. With the motor running, add the oils in a slow, steady stream. Add the basil, season with salt and pepper, and pulse once to incorporate. Pour the vinaigrette into a small bowl.

Cut the zucchini and other squashes in half lengthwise, and then cut each half into wedges about ¾ inch (2 cm) thick. In a large bowl, combine the squash wedges, tomatoes, oil, and marjoram and toss to coat. Season with salt and pepper.

Prepare a charcoal or gas grill for direct-heat grilling over medium-high heat. Oil the grill rack. Arrange the squashes and tomatoes on the rack or in a grill basket. Grill, turning as needed, until lightly charred on all sides, 8–10 minutes. Move the vegetables ⤞

to the edge of the grill where the heat is less intense, cover, and grill until cooked through, 5–6 minutes.

Return the grilled vegetables to the bowl. Stir in the pine nuts and parsley. Adjust the seasoning if necessary.

In a bowl, season the greens with salt and pepper and dress with 2 Tbsp of the vinaigrette. Arrange the greens on plates and top with the grilled vegetables. Pass the remaining vinaigrette at the table.

4

This dish is a good addition to a backyard grilling get-together. Grill the eggplant first, then let it rest in its vinaigrette while you grill the rest of the menu: chicken or chops, corn on the cob, and stone fruit for dessert.

GRILLED EGGPLANT & GREEN ONIONS WITH HERBS

serves 4

2 Tbsp extra-virgin olive oil, plus more for brushing

2 Tbsp fresh lemon juice

1 Tbsp tahini

2 cloves garlic, minced

4 Asian eggplants, about 1 lb (500 g) total, cut crosswise into slices ¼ inch (6 mm) thick

Salt and freshly ground pepper

2 green onions, white part only, finely chopped

2 Tbsp finely chopped flat-leaf fresh parsley

2 Tbsp finely chopped fresh mint

Prepare a charcoal or gas grill for direct-heat grilling over medium heat. Oil the grill rack or a grill basket. (The slices can easily escape through the grill rack, making the basket a good idea.)

In a small bowl, whisk together the 2 Tbsp oil, lemon juice, tahini, and garlic.

Brush the eggplant slices on both sides with oil, sprinkle with salt and pepper, and place on the grill rack or in the basket. Grill, turning once, until golden and softened, 4–5 minutes per side. Transfer to a bowl, cover, and let steam until cool; this softens the eggplant and makes it more tender.

Add the green onions, parsley, and mint to the bowl with the eggplant. Drizzle with the dressing and toss well. Adjust the seasoning if necessary. Let stand for 30 minutes to meld the flavors, and then serve.

CLASSIC GAZPACHO

serves 4–6

2 lb (1 kg) ripe tomatoes

2 large cloves garlic, chopped

1 cup (6 oz/185 g) seeded canned plum tomatoes, with juice

½ cup (2½ oz/75 g) seeded and chopped English cucumber, plus ¼ cup (1½ oz/45 g) for garnish

½ cup (2 oz/60 g) chopped red onion, plus 2 Tbsp for garnish

1 small red bell pepper or 2–3 gypsy peppers, seeded and chopped

2 slices day-old coarse country bread, crusts removed, torn into 1-inch (2.5-cm) pieces

1 Tbsp red wine vinegar

2 tsp extra-virgin olive oil, plus more for drizzling

Dash of hot-pepper sauce

Sea salt and freshly ground pepper

FOR THE PANFRIED CROUTONS

1 slice day-old coarse country bread, crusts removed

2 tsp olive oil

There are many variations on this Spanish soup, including white and green versions in addition to the more classic red. In all cases, the soups are served cold, and many of them are thickened with bread. Any one of them makes a perfect starter to a summer meal.

Remove the seeds from the tomatoes and chop coarsely. In a blender, combine the fresh tomatoes and the garlic and process to a coarse purée. Add the canned tomatoes and process to a smooth purée. Pass the mixture through a coarse-mesh sieve to remove all the bits of skin and any remaining seeds, and then return the mixture to the blender.

Add the ½ cup cucumber, ½ cup onion, bell pepper, and bread and process until the soup is a finely pulpy purée. Add the vinegar, oil, and hot-pepper sauce and process until combined. Season to taste with salt and pepper. Transfer the soup to an airtight container and refrigerate for at least 3 hours or up to overnight. Refrigerate the cucumber and onion, if desired.

When ready to serve, make the croutons. Cut the bread slices into ½-inch (12-mm) cubes. In a frying pan, warm the oil over medium-high heat. Add the bread cubes and fry, stirring often, until golden on all sides, about 5 minutes. Transfer to a plate and let cool. ≫→

Adjust the seasoning if necessary. Pour into chilled bowls. Top each serving with a sprinkle of cucumber, onion, and croutons. Drizzle with oil and serve at once.

HUSK-GRILLED CORN WITH QUESO AÑEJO & CHILE

serves 6

6 ears corn

2 limes, quartered

Crema or sour cream for drizzling

Crumbled queso añejo or grated Parmesan cheese for sprinkling

Ground pequin or other hot chile powder

Salt

Grilled corn is one of Mexico's favorite street foods. In one of its more elaborate guises, it is doused with lime juice and lavished with crema, a cultured cream similar to sour cream (which can be substituted here), then sprinkled with cheese and chile powder. Serve the corn alongside grilled chicken and a simple green salad.

Carefully pull the husks back from each ear of corn, remove the silk, and put the husks back in place. Soak the ears in cold water to cover for about 30 minutes.

Prepare a charcoal or gas grill for direct-heat grilling over high heat. Oil the grill rack.

Remove the ears of corn from the water and place directly on the grill rack over medium-hot coals. Grill, turning frequently, until the corn is tender, about 20 minutes. If the husks are burned but the corn is not yet tender, wrap the ears in foil and continue roasting until done.

Pull back the husks on the corn and tie them with strips of husk. Rub the corn with the lime quarters, drizzle with crema, and sprinkle with cheese, chile powder, and salt. Transfer to a platter and serve.

POBLANO CHILES STUFFED WITH BLACK BEANS & SUMMER VEGETABLES

serves 4–6

Here, zucchini, yellow summer squashes, and roasted chiles are mixed with black beans and rice to create a memorable and colorful filling for mild heart-shaped poblano chiles. Tangy crème fraîche binds the filling and a garnish of Parmesan adds a salty accent.

8 poblano chiles

2 Tbsp olive oil

½ white onion, finely chopped

Salt and freshly ground black pepper

1 zucchini, chopped

2 yellow summer squashes, chopped

1 ripe tomato, chopped

¼ tsp cayenne pepper

1 can (15 oz/470 g) black beans, drained and rinsed

Leaves from ¼ bunch fresh cilantro, coarsely chopped

1 cup (5 oz/155 g) cooked white rice

½ cup (4 oz/125 g) crème fraîche

Small piece of Parmesan cheese

Preheat the broiler. Line a baking sheet with foil. Place 2 of the chiles on the prepared sheet. Broil, turning occasionally, until charred on all sides, about 15 minutes. Transfer the chiles to a bowl, cover, and let steam for 5 minutes. Peel the charred skin from the chiles. Remove the stems and seeds, and chop the flesh. Preheat the oven to 400°F (200°C).

In each of the remaining chiles, cut a slit 2 inches (5 cm) long. With a paring knife, carefully scrape out the seeds from the insides of the chiles.

In a frying pan, warm the oil over medium heat. Add the onion and a pinch of salt and sauté until the onion is soft and translucent, 5–6 minutes. Add the zucchini and summer squashes, cover, and cook until just tender, 5–6 minutes. Uncover, add the tomato, the cayenne, and a pinch each of salt and black pepper, and sauté for 2 minutes. Let the vegetables cool slightly.

Add the beans, cilantro, rice, and crème fraîche to the pan and mix well. Spoon the bean mixture into the chiles. Place the stuffed chiles, cut side up, in a baking dish, and add enough water to come ½ inch (12 mm) up the sides of the dish. Cover tightly with foil and bake until the stuffing is heated through and the water has evaporated, about 20 minutes. »→

Remove the foil, grate some Parmesan over the tops of the chiles, and bake, uncovered, until the cheese melts, about 5 minutes. Remove from the oven and serve.

ROMANO BEANS WITH TOMATOES & PANCETTA

serves 6

Romano beans, long, flat, wide green beans—sometimes labeled "Italian beans"—are the most common variety of snap bean in Italy. If you cannot find them in your market, regular green beans can be substituted in this simple summer braise.

2 oz (60 g) pancetta, chopped

1 Tbsp olive oil

3 green onions, white and tender green parts, thinly sliced

½ lb (250 g) fresh tomatoes, peeled, seeded, and chopped, or 1 can (14 oz/440 g) plum tomatoes, coarsely chopped, with juice

1 lb (500 g) romano beans or green beans, trimmed

Salt and freshly ground pepper

1 Tbsp finely chopped fresh flat-leaf parsley

In a saucepan large enough to hold the beans, cook the pancetta over medium heat, stirring often, until crisp, about 5 minutes. Using a slotted spoon, transfer the pancetta to paper towels to drain.

Add the oil to the fat remaining in the pan and warm over medium heat. Add the green onions and sauté until softened, about 3 minutes. Add the tomatoes and simmer, stirring occasionally, until reduced slightly, about 10 minutes.

Stir in the beans and season with salt and a few grinds of pepper. Reduce the heat to low, cover, and cook until the beans are tender, about 15 minutes. Check often and add a few Tbsp of hot water if the sauce looks dry.

Stir in the pancetta and transfer to a bowl. Sprinkle with the parsley and serve.

9

Buttery toasted walnuts and peppery arugula meld with the distinctive flavor of basil to create a bold pesto that coats this quick sauté of yellow tomatoes. The tangy richness of feta cheese adds a salty edge to the sweet tomatoes and earthy pesto, bringing all of the flavors together.

SAUTÉED YELLOW TOMATOES WITH ARUGULA PESTO & FETA

serves 4

3 Tbsp walnuts, toasted

Grated zest of 1 lemon

1 clove garlic, coarsely chopped

¼ cup fresh basil leaves

1 cup (2½ oz/75 g) packed baby arugula leaves

5 Tbsp (3 fl oz/80 ml) extra-virgin olive oil

Salt and freshly ground pepper

1½ lb (750 g) bite-sized yellow pear or grape tomatoes

2 oz (60 g) feta cheese

Preheat the oven to 375°F (190°C).

In a food processor, combine the walnuts, lemon zest, and garlic and pulse just to combine. Add the basil and arugula and process until coarsely chopped. With the motor running, slowly pour in 4 Tbsp (2 fl oz/60 ml) of the oil. Continue to process until the mixture is moist and well blended but still slightly chunky. Transfer the pesto to a small bowl. Adjust the seasonings with salt and pepper.

In a frying pan, heat the remaining 1 Tbsp oil over medium-high heat. Add the tomatoes and a pinch of salt and sauté until the tomatoes are warmed through and their skins are just beginning to split, 3–4 minutes. Remove the pan from the heat and stir in the pesto.

Transfer the tomatoes to a shallow serving bowl and crumble the cheese over the top. Serve hot or at room temperature.

10

Naturally sweet summer corn contrasts beautifully with spicy and smoky ingredients, such as the chipotle chiles used here in this updated version of a classic. Rich, silky cream lends a complementary sweetness and pleasing richness to the dish and prevents the spice of the chiles from overwhelming the other ingredients.

CREAMED CORN WITH CHIPOTLE CHILES

serves 4

6 ears corn, husks and silk removed

2 Tbsp unsalted butter

½ white onion, finely chopped

2 chipotle chiles in adobo sauce, seeded and minced, plus 1 tsp adobo sauce

1 tsp dried oregano

½ tsp sugar

Salt and freshly ground pepper

¾ cup (6 fl oz/180 ml) heavy cream

Hold each ear of corn upright on a cutting board. Using a sharp knife, cut down along the ear, stripping off the kernels and rotating the ear a quarter turn after each cut. Transfer the kernels to a bowl. Using the dull edge of the knife, carefully scrape the pulp from the corncobs into the bowl.

In a large frying pan, melt the butter over medium heat. Add the onion and sauté until soft and translucent, 5–6 minutes. Add the chipotle chiles, adobo sauce, corn kernels with pulp, oregano, and sugar. Pour in ½ cup (4 fl oz/125 ml) water and add a generous pinch each of salt and pepper. Bring the mixture to a boil, reduce the heat to low, cover, and cook, stirring occasionally, until the corn is tender but still has a bit of crunch, about 10 minutes. Uncover and cook until the water evaporates, 2–3 minutes.

Add the cream to the pan, raise the heat to medium-low, and cook until the liquid is thick enough to coat the back of a spoon, 2–3 minutes. Adjust the seasoning if necessary and serve.

11

Ratatouille is the iconic countryside stew of Provence, France. The meaty combination of eggplants, tomatoes, zucchini and peppers satisfies even the heartiest appetite. Julia Child, among others, insisted on cooking each vegetable separately, but many home cooks prefer to toss all of the ingredients into the same generous saucepan, as in this recipe.

RATATOUILLE

serves 10

2 tsp olive oil

2 small yellow or white onions, chopped

2 small eggplants, cut into 1-inch (2.5-cm) cubes

4 cloves garlic, minced

2 zucchini, cut into 1-inch (2.5-cm) cubes

2 large red, green, or yellow bell peppers, seeded and cut into 1-inch (2.5-cm) pieces

8–10 large ripe tomatoes, 6–7½ lb (3–3.75 kg) total, peeled, seeded and coarsely chopped

3 fresh thyme sprigs

1 fresh rosemary sprig

1 bay leaf

Salt and freshly ground pepper

¼ cup (⅓ oz/10 g) minced fresh basil

In a large saucepan, warm the oil over medium heat. Reduce the heat to medium-low, add the onions, and sauté until translucent, about 2 minutes. Add the eggplant cubes and garlic and cook, stirring frequently, until the eggplants are slightly softened, 3–4 minutes. Add the zucchini and bell peppers and cook, turning and tossing, until softened, 4–5 minutes. Add the tomatoes, thyme, rosemary, and bay leaf. Season with ½ tsp salt and ½ tsp pepper and cook, stirring, for 2–3 minutes.

Cover, reduce the heat to low, and cook, stirring occasionally, until the vegetables are soft and have somewhat blended together, about 40 minutes. Stir in the basil and remove from the heat. Serve warm or at room temperature.

12

This colorful black bean salad is at its best when the peppers, chiles, and onions are still slightly warm from the grill. The chile- and-cumin-spiked vinaigrette highlights the sweetness of the charred onions and peppers and the earthiness of the chiles.

SPICY BLACK BEAN SALAD

serves 6

FOR THE VINAIGRETTE

¼ cup (2 fl oz/60 ml) extra-virgin olive oil

3 Tbsp fresh lime juice

2 Tbsp red wine vinegar

1 Tbsp ground cumin

1 Tbsp chile powder

Salt and freshly ground pepper

Hot-pepper sauce

2 small yellow onions, quartered

2 yellow bell peppers, quartered and seeded

2 red bell peppers, quartered and seeded

2 Anaheim chiles, halved and seeded

2 jalapeño chiles, halved and seeded

Olive oil for brushing

2 cans (15 oz/470 g each) black beans, drained and rinsed

Leaves from 1 bunch fresh cilantro, chopped

1 red onion, chopped

To make the vinaigrette, in a small bowl, whisk together the oil, lime juice, vinegar, cumin, and chile powder. Season with 1 tsp salt, ½ tsp pepper, and a few dashes of hot-pepper sauce, and whisk again.

Prepare a charcoal or gas grill for grilling over medium-high heat. Oil the grill rack.

Brush the yellow onions, bell peppers, and chiles with oil. Arrange the onions, bell peppers, and chiles on the grill rack or in a grill basket. Grill, turning occasionally, until well charred on all sides, about 10 minutes.

Transfer the grilled vegetables to a large bowl, cover, and let steam for 10 minutes. Pick over the vegetables, removing most of the burned skin and leaving some charred bits. Chop the grilled vegetables to a uniform size and place in a serving bowl.

Add the black beans, cilantro, red onion, and vinaigrette and toss to coat evenly. Serve warm or at room temperature.

13

If you are new to pickling vegetables, start with this straightforward recipe. Make the pickles at the height of summer, when small Kirby cucumbers and heads of fresh dill can be found at local farmers' markets.

CLASSIC DILL PICKLES

makes 6 one-pint (16–fl oz/500-ml) jars

3 cups (24 fl oz/750 ml) distilled white vinegar

Kosher salt

6 Tbsp (1½ oz/45 g) purchased pickling spice

6 large, mature dill heads, or 6 Tbsp (1½ oz/45 g) dill seeds and 24 fresh dill sprigs

24 cloves garlic

36 peppercorns

6 lb (3 kg) Kirby cucumbers, each about 1½ inches (4 cm) in diameter, cut into slices ½ inch (12 mm) thick

Have ready six 1-pt (16–fl oz/500 ml) hot, sterilized jars and their lids.

In a large nonreactive saucepan, combine the vinegar and 2 Tbsp salt. Add 3 cups (24 fl oz/750 ml) water and bring to a boil over medium-high heat, stirring to dissolve the salt.

Meanwhile, in each jar, place 1 Tbsp pickling spice, 1 dill head (or 1 Tbsp dill seeds and 4 dill sprigs), 4 garlic cloves, and 6 peppercorns. Layer the cucumber slices in the jars, making sure to pack them tightly and avoid large gaps. Fill the jars to within ¾ inch (2 cm) of the rims.

Ladle the hot brine into the jars, leaving ½ inch (12 mm) of headspace. Remove any air bubbles and adjust the headspace, if necessary. Wipe the rims clean and seal tightly with the lids.

Process the jars for 7 minutes in a boiling-water bath. Let the jars stand undisturbed for 24 hours and then set them aside for 2 weeks for the flavors to develop. The sealed jars can be stored in a cool, dark place for up to 1 year. If a seal has failed, store the jar in the refrigerator for up to 1 week.

14

Smashing anchovy fillets and garlic cloves into warm olive oil creates a thick, flavorful sauce for roasted zucchini. Anchoïade is also excellent drizzled over other grilled vegetables, or used as a dip for crudités and crusty bread.

ROASTED ZUCCHINI WITH ANCHOÏADE

serves 3–4

2 zucchini

1 Tbsp olive oil

1 tsp fresh thyme leaves

Sea salt and freshly ground pepper

FOR THE ANCHOÏADE

⅓–½ cup (3–4 fl oz/80–125 ml) extra-virgin olive oil

1 can (2½ oz/75 g) anchovy fillets, rinsed and drained

3 cloves garlic, minced

Preheat oven to 400°F (200°C).

Cut each zucchini in half crosswise. Cut each half lengthwise into 3 even slices. Arrange the slices in a baking dish just large enough to hold them in a single layer. Drizzle with the oil and sprinkle with the thyme. Season with salt and pepper and turn to coat evenly.

Roast until the slices are golden brown, 15–20 minutes. Turn and roast until golden on the other sides and tender-crisp, 5–10 minutes.

To make the anchoïade, in a small frying pan, heat ⅓ cup (3 fl oz/80 ml) of the oil over low heat. Add the anchovies and garlic and cook, mashing the anchovies until they dissolve into oil to make a paste, about 3 minutes. If necessary, gradually stir in a little more oil until the sauce has the consistency of a thick vinaigrette.

Serve the zucchini accompanied by the anchoïade.

16

15

When it is time to make these fritters, look for the best local corn in season: yellow or white, standard or super-sweet. For a savory edge, add 2 Tbsp finely chopped fresh cilantro to the batter and serve with lime wedges instead of maple syrup. Or make a spicy dip: Mix together 1 cup (8 oz/250 g) plain yogurt; 1 clove garlic, minced; 1 serrano chile, minced; grated zest of ½ lime; and salt to taste.

CORN FRITTERS

serves 4–6

Canola oil for deep-frying

1½ cups (7½ oz/235 g) all-purpose flour

¾ tsp baking soda

Salt and freshly ground pepper

1½ cups (9 oz/280 g) corn kernels (from about 4 ears)

1 cup (8 fl oz/250 ml) buttermilk

1 egg

Pure maple syrup for serving

Pour oil to a depth of at least 3 inches (7.5 cm) into a large, heavy saucepan and heat to 375°F (190°C) on a deep-frying thermometer. Preheat the oven to 200°F (95°C). Set a large wire rack on a baking sheet and place near the stove.

While the oil is heating, in a bowl, sift together the flour, the baking soda, ¾ tsp salt, and ¼ tsp pepper. In a blender, combine ½ cup (3 oz/90 g) of the corn kernels, the buttermilk, and the egg and process until smooth. Pour into the dry ingredients and stir just until smooth. Fold in the remaining corn kernels.

Working in batches, add the batter by the Tbsp to the hot oil and deep-fry until golden brown, about 3 minutes. Using a slotted spoon, transfer to the rack and keep warm in the oven while you fry the remaining fritters. Serve the fritters hot, passing the maple syrup at the table.

16

Layering pungent, bitter, and salty ingredients adds complexity to vegetable dishes. Kalamata olives offer all three qualities, which makes them a good match for the smoky-sweet charred tomatoes, crisp cucumber, and crusty bread cubes in this summer salad.

BREAD SALAD WITH CHARRED TOMATOES, CUCUMBER & OLIVES

serves 4

½ loaf coarse country Italian bread such as pugliese (about 8 oz/250 g)

3 or 4 large ripe tomatoes, about 2½ lb (1.25 kg) total, preferably a mixture of colors

1 small English cucumber

½ red onion, chopped or thinly sliced

¾ cup (4 oz/125 g) pitted and coarsely chopped Kalamata olives

⅓ cup (3 fl oz/80 ml) extra-virgin olive oil

2 Tbsp red wine vinegar

Salt and freshly ground pepper

Leaves from ½ bunch fresh basil, torn into small pieces

Preheat the oven to 375°F (190°C).

Cut the bread into ½-inch (12-mm) cubes and arrange in a single layer on a baking sheet. Lightly toast in the oven until the cubes are just dry and very light brown, 8–10 minutes. Remove the cubes from the baking sheet.

Preheat the broiler. Line the baking sheet with foil and place the tomatoes on the prepared sheet. Broil until the skins begin to char and blacken, 2–3 minutes. Turn the tomatoes and broil for another 2–3 minutes. Let cool.

Remove and discard any loose skin from the tomatoes (it's fine if a few charred bits remain), and then coarsely chop. Transfer the tomatoes to a large bowl. Cut the cucumber in half lengthwise and scrape out the seeds. Cut the halves crosswise into slices about ½ inch (12 mm) thick. Alternatively, cut the whole cucumber crosswise into slices about ½ inch (12 mm) thick. Add to the bowl with the tomatoes. Add the onion, olives, oil, and vinegar. Season with salt and pepper and stir well to mix. Let stand at room temperature for up to 1 hour to blend the flavors.

Add the toasted bread cubes to the salad and toss gently. Add the basil, toss gently to mix, and serve.

17

Tall stalks of rustling corn and wild tangles of snap beans can dominate the vegetable patch this time of year. Grab the best of each, with both green and yellow varieties of beans for color contrast. A splash of vinegar and the sweet scent of tarragon and chervil round out this dish.

SUMMER BEAN & CORN SALAD WITH TARRAGON & CHERVIL

serves 6

Ice water

2 ears corn, husks and silk removed

¾ lb (375 g) yellow wax beans, trimmed

¾ lb (375 g) green beans, trimmed

1 small red onion, thinly sliced

¼ cup (2 fl oz/60 ml) extra-virgin olive oil

2 Tbsp white wine vinegar

1 tsp minced fresh tarragon

8 fresh chervil sprigs

Salt and freshly ground pepper

Have ready a bowl of ice water. Bring a large pot of salted water to a boil. Add the ears of corn and cook until crisp-tender, about 5 minutes. Remove the corn with tongs and let cool. Add the wax beans to the boiling water and cook for 1 minute. Add the green beans and cook until the beans are crisp-tender, about 2 minutes longer. Drain the beans and transfer them to the ice water to cool.

Hold each ear of corn upright on a cutting board. Using a sharp knife, cut down along the ear, stripping off the kernels and rotating the ear a quarter turn with each cut. Transfer the corn to a bowl.

Drain the beans and add to the bowl holding the corn. Add the onion, drizzle with the oil and vinegar, and toss to combine. Sprinkle with the tarragon and chervil, season with salt and pepper, and toss again. Serve at room temperature, or cover, chill, and serve cold.

18

Spanish Padrón peppers tend to be sweet and mild, and they're easy to prepare on the stove top. You can also roast them over an open flame or in a grill basket. Serve a heap of these addictive peppers, dusted with sea salt, on a rustic board. If possible, use Maldon salt for its exceptional mineral flavor and coarse texture.

GRILLED PADRÓN PEPPERS WITH SEA SALT

serves 4

1 lb (500 g) Padrón peppers

1 Tbsp extra-virgin olive oil

½ tsp sea salt

In a bowl, toss the peppers with the oil.

Heat a ridged grill pan on the stove top over high heat. Add the peppers in a single layer and cook, turning as needed, until the skin is blistered on all sides, 3–4 minutes. Season with ½ tsp salt and serve.

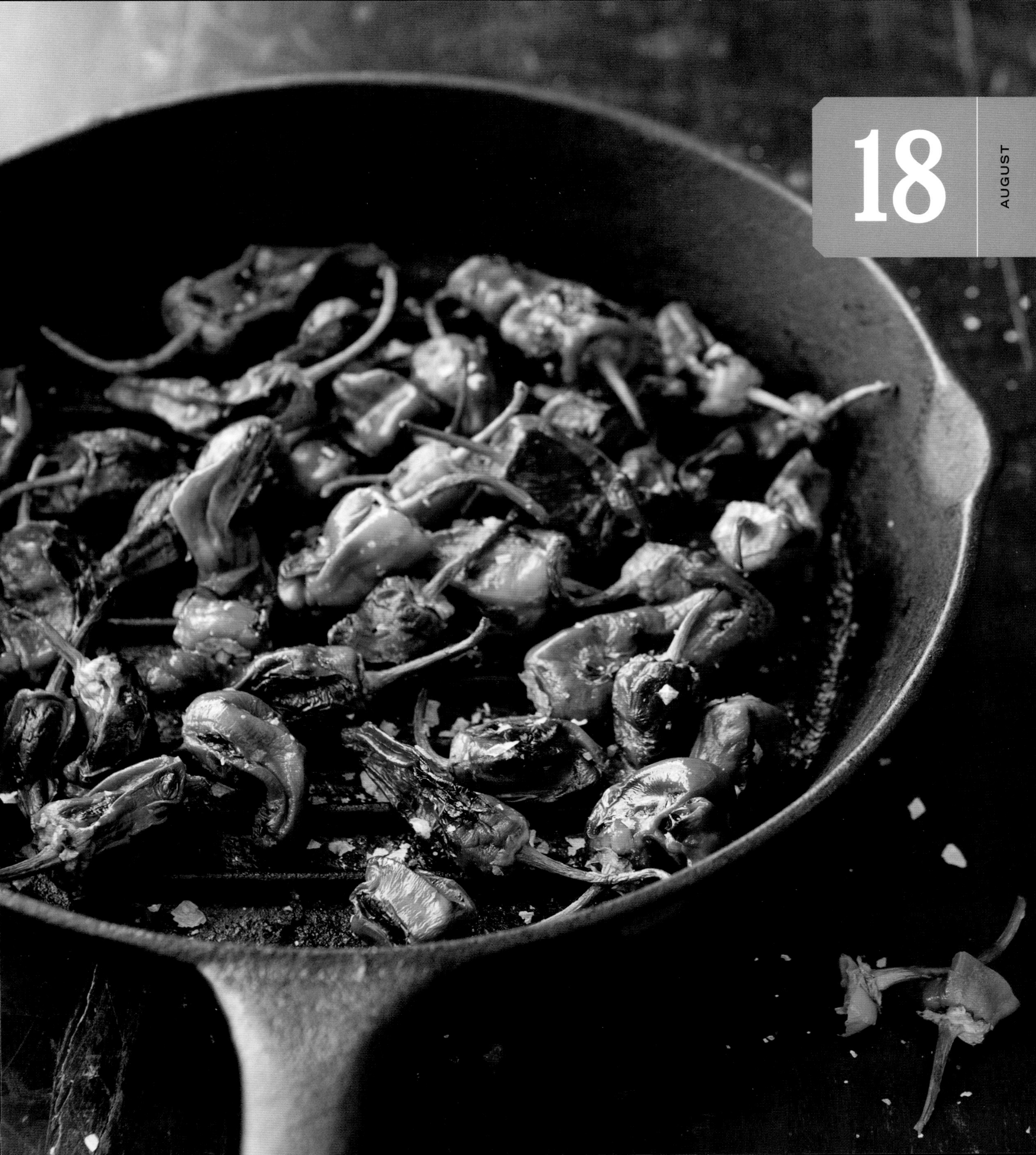

19

BAKED TOMATOES WITH PANKO & ANCHOVIES

serves 4

3 Tbsp extra-virgin olive oil

4 ripe but firm red tomatoes, halved crosswise

2 cloves garlic, halved

Salt and freshly ground pepper

2 olive oil–packed anchovy fillets

½ cup (2 oz/60 g) panko

3 Tbsp chopped fresh flat-leaf parsley

These Provençal-style tomatoes are crowned with a savory mixture of bread crumbs, anchovy, and garlic. The halved tomatoes are first browned in a frying pan, then topped and baked. Searing them on the stove top helps to bring out their natural sweetness. Japanese bread crumbs, known as panko, are flakier and crunchier than conventional bread crumbs, which keeps the topping light and crisp.

Preheat the oven to 400°F (200°C).

In a frying pan, heat 1 Tbsp of the oil over medium-high heat. Add the tomatoes, cut side down, and cook until lightly browned, 3–4 minutes. Oil a baking dish just large enough to hold the tomatoes in a single layer. Arrange the tomato halves, cut side up, in the prepared dish.

In a large mortar, combine the garlic and ½ tsp salt. Using a pestle, and working in a circular motion, grind together until a paste forms. Add the anchovies and continue working the pestle until the anchovies are fully incorporated. Stir in the bread crumbs and parsley. Season with salt and pepper. Spoon the stuffing over the tomatoes. Drizzle with the remaining 2 Tbsp oil.

Bake until the bread crumb mixture is golden and crisp and the tomatoes are soft but maintain their shape, 20–25 minutes. Remove from the oven and let stand for 15 minutes. Serve warm or at room temperature.

20

GRILLED PORTOBELLO BURGERS

serves 4

2 Tbsp olive oil

1 Tbsp balsamic vinegar

1 clove garlic, minced

Salt and freshly ground pepper

4 large portobello mushrooms, stems removed

4 slices Monterey Jack or smoked mozzarella cheese

4 round Italian rolls

2 Tbsp purchased pesto

½ cup (4 fl oz/125 ml) mayonnaise

1 or 2 tomatoes, sliced

These garlic-brushed, cheese-topped grilled portobello burgers will satisfy both vegetarians and carnivores alike. Serve them tucked into crusty rolls with pesto mayonnaise and thick slices of ripe tomatoes. Serve chips and pickles on the side.

Prepare a charcoal or gas grill for grilling over medium-high heat.

In a small bowl, stir together the oil, the vinegar, the garlic, ½ tsp salt, and ⅛ tsp pepper. Using a small spoon, remove the gills from the undersides of the mushrooms. Brush both sides of each mushroom with the oil mixture.

Place the mushrooms, stem side up, on the grill and cook until well marked, about 4 minutes. Turn and cook until tender, about 4 minutes. Place a slice of cheese on top of each mushroom about 2 minutes before you remove them from the grill and cook until melted.

Cut the rolls in half horizontally. Place each half, cut side down, on the cooler part of the grill, and grill until lightly toasted, 2–3 minutes.

In a small bowl, mix together the pesto and mayonnaise and season with salt and pepper. Spread the pesto-mayonnaise on the toasted rolls. Place a grilled mushroom on the bottom of each roll and top with the tomato slices. Close with the top half of the roll, and serve.

21

Here, roasted summer vegetables are bathed in garlicky olive oil before serving. Let the vegetables stand for a while to meld the flavors of the salad. Steaming helps to loosen the skins of the roasted eggplant and peppers: use separate bowls or do as Spanish cooks do and wrap them together in newspaper or parchment paper.

ROASTED SUMMER VEGETABLES WITH GARLIC OIL
serves 6–8

1 eggplant, about 1½ lb (750 g)

2 large red bell peppers

2 ripe tomatoes

2 large cloves garlic, unpeeled

2 red onions, about 1 lb (500 g) total

¼ cup (2 fl oz/60 ml) extra-virgin olive oil, plus olive oil for brushing

Salt and freshly ground pepper

Preheat the oven to 500°F (260°C).

Arrange the eggplant, bell peppers, tomatoes, and garlic cloves on a baking sheet. Remove the papery outer skins of the onions and add the onions to the baking sheet. Brush the vegetables generously with olive oil.

Roast the vegetables, checking them every 10 minutes; use tongs to remove any that are beginning to color and have become soft but are still holding their shape. The timing will depend on the size and ripeness of vegetables. Allow about 10 minutes for the tomatoes, 20–25 minutes for the bell peppers and garlic, 45 minutes for the eggplant, and 50 minutes for the onions. The onions will still be somewhat firm.

As the vegetables are removed from the oven, place each type in a bowl, cover, and let steam for 20 minutes.

Peel the tomatoes, cut lengthwise into quarters, and remove most of the seeds. Arrange the tomato wedges together on a platter. Peel the peppers, slit them open, and remove the stem, seeds, and ribs. Cut each pepper into 4–8 wide strips and add to the platter. Cut the stem from the eggplant and pull off the skin. Cut the eggplant lengthwise into thick strips and remove most of the seeds. Add the eggplant to the platter. Peel away the tough outer layers of the onions, cut them into quarters, and add to the platter.

Peel the garlic and place on a cutting board. Using a chef's knife, alternately chop and, using the side of the knife, press and smear the garlic until a paste forms. Transfer ⟶

the garlic paste to a bowl, add the ¼ cup oil, season with salt and pepper, and mix well. Pour the garlic oil over the roasted vegetables. Let stand at room temperature for 1 hour before serving.

22

Zucchini taste best when they are small, young, and mild. Here, their understated flavor is heightened by roasted red onions and aromatic mint. Serve this easy-to-assemble side dish with grilled fish fillets, or sautéed sea scallops.

BAKED ZUCCHINI & RED ONIONS WITH MINT & VINEGAR
serves 4

1 red onion, halved lengthwise and thinly cut crosswise

1 Tbsp olive oil

4 small zucchini, each 4–5 inches (10–13 cm) long, about 1½ lb (750 g) total, halved lengthwise

Salt and freshly ground pepper

¼ cup (⅓ oz/10 g) finely chopped fresh mint

1 tsp red wine vinegar

Preheat the oven to 400°F (200°C).

Spread the onion slices in a 9-by-13-inch (23-by-33-cm) baking dish. Drizzle with the oil and stir to combine. Spread the slices in an even layer.

Bake until the onion slices begin to brown on the edges, about 15 minutes. Push the onion slices aside. Arrange the zucchini halves, cut side down, in the dish and spoon the onion slices on top. Sprinkle with ¼ tsp salt and season with pepper. Bake for 10 minutes, remove from the oven, and turn the zucchini cut side up. Bake until the zucchini halves are tender when pierced with a knife, 5–10 minutes.

Arrange the zucchini, cut side up, on a plate. Add the mint and vinegar to the onion slices and stir to blend. Spoon the onion over the zucchini and serve.

23

23

This classic Italian pickle, which makes an excellent antipasto, contains an array of summer vegetables, each preserved to maintain its distinctive flavor and texture. The recipe is flexible: use asparagus or green beans instead of any of the vegetables, or lemon thyme for the oregano.

GIARDINIERA

makes 6 one-pint (16–fl oz/500-ml) jars

4 small zucchini, about ¾ lb (375 g) total, cut into rounds ¼ inch (6 mm) thick

10–12 celery ribs, cut into halves

Kosher salt

6 ice cubes

3 cups (24 fl oz/750 ml) white wine vinegar

4 red bell peppers, about 1½ lb (750 g) total, halved lengthwise and seeded

3 or 4 carrots, peeled and halved lengthwise

6 fresh oregano sprigs

18 cloves garlic

6 bay leaves

1 Tbsp peppercorns

1 small head cauliflower, cut into small florets

6 Tbsp (3 fl oz/90 ml) extra-virgin olive oil

In a large nonreactive bowl, combine the zucchini and celery. Add 1 Tbsp salt and the ice cubes. Cover and refrigerate for 2–3 hours. Drain, rinse, and then drain well.

Have ready six 1-pt (16–fl oz/500-ml) hot, sterilized jars and their lids.

In a large nonreactive saucepan, combine the vinegar and 1 Tbsp salt. Add 3 cups (24 fl oz/750 ml) water and bring to a boil over medium-high heat, stirring to dissolve the salt.

Meanwhile, cut each bell pepper half into 4 rectangles. Cut the carrots into sticks about ¼ inch (6 mm) thick and at least ½ inch (12 mm) shorter than the height of the jars.

In each jar, place 1 oregano sprig, 3 garlic cloves, 1 bay leaf, and ½ tsp peppercorns. Divide all the vegetables among the jars, filling them to within 1 inch (2.5 cm) of the rims.

Ladle the hot brine into the jars, leaving ½ inch (12 mm) of headspace. Remove any air bubbles and adjust the headspace, if necessary. Add 1 Tbsp of the oil to each jar. Wipe the rims clean and seal tightly with the lids.

Process the jars for 10 minutes in a boiling-water bath. Let the jars stand undisturbed for 24 hours and then set them aside for 2 weeks for the flavors to develop. The sealed jars can be stored in a cool, dark place for up to 1 year. If a seal has failed, store the jar in the refrigerator for up to 1 week.

24

Here's a new twist on potato salad. The potatoes are grilled instead of boiled then tossed with the dressing while they are still warm. The dressing doesn't completely abandon mayonnaise as a base, but it cuts in plenty of white wine and fresh herbs, transforming it into a creamy vinaigrette.

GRILLED POTATO SALAD WITH CREAMY VINAIGRETTE

serves 6–8

4 lb (2 kg) small new potatoes

Olive oil for brushing

¼ cup (2 fl oz/60 ml) dry white wine, plus 2 Tbsp

Salt and freshly ground pepper

½ cup (1½ oz/45 g) mayonnaise

1 tsp whole-grain mustard

1 tbsp minced fresh flat-leaf parsley

2 Tbsp minced fresh tarragon

2 Tbsp finely chopped fresh chives

Bring a saucepan of water to a boil. Add the potatoes and cook just until they can be pierced with a knife but are not completely tender, 5–7 minutes. Drain and pat dry. Brush the potatoes with oil.

Prepare a charcoal or gas grill for grilling over medium-high heat. Oil the grill rack.

Arrange the potatoes on the rack and grill, turning once or twice, until tender when pierced with a knife, 4–5 minutes. Transfer the potatoes to a cutting board and let cool until they can be handled.

Cut the potatoes into slices or chunks, discarding the small end pieces. Transfer to a large bowl while still warm. Add the ¼ cup wine and season with salt and pepper. Toss gently to coat. Let stand until completely cool, 20–30 minutes.

In a small bowl, stir together the mayonnaise, 2 Tbsp white wine, mustard, parsley, tarragon, and chives. Add the dressing to the potatoes, toss to coat, and serve.

25

AUGUST

Easy to prepare, and infinitely adaptable, tortas, or vegetable pies, are favorite supper dishes in parts of Latin America. This combination of zucchini, fresh corn, and poblano chiles is ideal for summer. Dark green poblano chiles have a wonderful rich flavor, but they can sometimes be a bit fiery. If heat is a concern, substitute mild Anaheim chiles.

ZUCCHINI, POBLANO & CORN TORTA

serves 6–8

1 ear white corn, husk and silk removed

3 Tbsp olive oil

2 large poblano or Anaheim chiles, roasted, peeled, and cut into 1-inch (2.5-cm) pieces

1 white onion, chopped

Salt and freshly ground pepper

1 lb (500 g) zucchini, thinly sliced

½ tsp dried oregano

1½ cups (6 oz/185 g) shredded Monterey jack cheese

4 eggs

¼ cup (1 oz/30 g) crumbled cotija cheese

¼ tsp ancho chile powder (optional)

⅓ cup (2½ oz/75 g) sour cream

1 Tbsp fresh lime juice

¼ cup (⅓ oz/10 g) minced fresh cilantro

1 Tbsp chipotle chiles in adobo, finely chopped

Position a rack in the upper third of the oven and preheat to 325°F (165°C). Butter a 6-cup (48–fl oz/1.5-l) gratin dish or other shallow baking dish.

Hold the ear of corn upright on a cutting board. Using a sharp knife, cut down along the ear, stripping off the kernels and rotating the ear a quarter turn after each cut.

In a frying pan, warm 1 Tbsp of the oil over medium heat. Add the chiles and onion and cook, stirring frequently, until the onion is tender, about 5 minutes. Stir in 1 tsp salt. Scrape into a colander and let cool.

Add the remaining 2 Tbsp oil to the pan and return to medium heat. Add the corn kernels and zucchini and cook, stirring frequently, until the zucchini slices are softened but not breaking up, about 5 minutes. Stir in the oregano, 1 tsp salt, and ¼ tsp pepper and cook for about 30 seconds to blend the flavors. Add to the colander with the chiles. Let the cooked vegetables cool and drain for 15 minutes.

Spread 1 cup (8 oz/250 g) of the zucchini mixture in an even layer in the bottom of the prepared dish. Sprinkle with half of the Monterey jack cheese. Top with half of »→

the remaining vegetables, then with all of the remaining jack cheese, and end with the remaining vegetables.

In a small bowl, beat the eggs with 1 tsp salt and a pinch of pepper. Pour into the dish and use a spatula to spread evenly. Scatter the cotija cheese over the top and dust with the chile powder, if using. Bake until puffed and lightly browned, about 30 minutes.

Meanwhile, in a small bowl, combine the sour cream, lime juice, cilantro, and chipotle, Season with ¼ tsp salt and stir to mix well.

Serve the torta warm or at room temperature with the cilantro-lime sour cream.

26

AUGUST

Slicing eggplants into thin rounds and roasting them in a hot oven yields crisps reminiscent of potato chips. Look for firm Asian eggplants (sometimes called Japanese or Chinese eggplants) for the best results. Laced with cucumber, sun-dried tomato, and garlic, the yogurt sauce is equally delicious spooned over grilled chicken breasts or poached salmon.

EGGPLANT CRISPS WITH YOGURT SAUCE

serves 4

2 very firm Asian eggplants, cut crosswise into slices about ⅛ inch (3 mm) thick

2 Tbsp olive oil

1 cup (8 oz/250 g) plain yogurt

1 cucumber, peeled and coarsely chopped

8 oil-packed sun-dried tomatoes, finely chopped

2 cloves garlic, minced

Salt

Preheat oven to 400°F (200°C).

Arrange the eggplant slices in a single layer on a baking sheet. Use a second baking sheet if necessary. Drizzle with the oil and turn to coat evenly.

Roast the eggplant slices until golden, about 15 minutes. Turn the slices and roast until golden brown on the second sides and crisp, about 15 minutes.

Meanwhile, in a bowl, combine the yogurt, cucumber, sun-dried tomatoes, garlic, and ¼ tsp salt, and stir to mix well.

Transfer the eggplant crisps to paper towels to drain. Sprinkle with 2 tsp salt. Serve warm or at room temperature with the yogurt sauce.

27

SUMMER VEGETABLE ROLLS WITH RICE NOODLES

serves 4

½ lb (250 g) shiitake mushrooms

2 tsp canola or peanut oil

1 clove garlic, minced

1 tsp soy sauce, plus more for serving

7 oz (220 g) thin dried rice noodles

12–16 rice paper wrappers

1 red bell pepper, seeded and thinly sliced

2 avocados, pitted, peeled, and sliced

1 head butter lettuce, torn into bite-sized pieces

2 carrots, peeled and cut into matchsticks

1 cup (1 oz/30 g) loosely packed mixed fresh herb sprigs such as mint, cilantro, and basil

Asian red chile sauce for serving

Asian peanut sauce for serving

Stuffed with shiitake mushrooms, bell pepper, avocado and carrots, these fresh spring rolls make a great starter or a light supper. Arrange a platter of the ingredients and let diners make their own rolls. Or, assemble the rolls up to 30 minutes ahead of serving and keep them at room temperature, covered tightly with plastic wrap.

Trim the stems from the shiitakes and slice the caps. In a large frying pan, heat 1 tsp of the oil over medium-high heat. Add the garlic and cook, stirring, until fragrant but not browned, about 30 seconds. Add the mushrooms and sauté until they release their juices, 3–4 minutes. Add the 1 tsp soy sauce and cook until the mushrooms are dry, about 1 minute. Transfer to a bowl.

Bring a pot of water to a boil. Add the noodles, stir to separate, and cook until tender, 3–5 minutes. Drain and rinse under cold running water. Transfer the noodles to a bowl and toss with the remaining 1 tsp oil.

Fill a large, shallow bowl with very hot tap water. Soak 1 rice paper wrapper in the water until flexible, about 30 seconds. Shake off the excess water and place the wrapper flat on a work surface. Arrange some noodles, mushrooms, bell pepper, avocado, lettuce, carrots, and herbs across the center of the wrapper. Fold the ends in over the filling, then, starting at the edge closest to you, roll up tightly. Repeat to make more rolls. Cut the rolls in half or in thirds and arrange on a plate. Serve with soy sauce, chile sauce, and peanut sauce for dipping.

28

SPICY DILLY BEANS

makes 6 one-pint (16–fl oz/500-ml) jars

3 cups (24 fl oz/750 ml) distilled white vinegar

Kosher salt

6 large, mature dill heads, or 6 Tbsp (1½ oz/45 g) dill seeds and 24 fresh dill sprigs

1½ tsp cayenne pepper

6 cloves garlic

4 lb (2 kg) green beans

Tuck away some summer beans in the pantry with this simple pickling technique. You can enjoy the spicy beans on their own, or use them as a garnish for Bloody Marys. If you like, use small fresh chiles, abundant at farmers' markets in late summer, in place of the cayenne.

Have ready six 1-pt (16–fl oz/500 ml) hot, sterilized jars and their lids.

In a large nonreactive saucepan, combine the vinegar and 6 Tbsp (2½ oz/75 g) salt. Add 3 cups (24 fl oz/750 ml) water and bring to a boil over medium-high heat, stirring to dissolve the salt.

Meanwhile, in each jar, place 1 dill head (or 1 Tbsp dill seeds and 4 dill sprigs), ¼ tsp cayenne, and 1 garlic clove. Trim the beans so they are ½ inch (12 mm) shorter than the height of the jars. Pack the beans as tightly as possible into the jars. It may help to hold the jar horizontally and use a chopstick to compact the beans as you add more.

Ladle the hot brine into the jars, leaving ½ inch (12 mm) of headspace. Remove any air bubbles and adjust the headspace, if necessary. Wipe the rims clean and seal tightly with the lids.

Process the jars for 10 minutes in a boiling-water bath. Let the jars stand undisturbed for 24 hours and then set them aside for 2 weeks for the flavors to develop. The sealed jars can be stored in a cool, dark place for up to 1 year. If a seal has failed, store the jar in the refrigerator for up to 1 week.

29

Exposing juicy little tomatoes to high heat will make them sputter, burst at the seams, shrivel a bit, and become shockingly sweet. Use a grill basket to keep them from falling through the grate.

GRILLED CHERRY TOMATOES

serves 4–6

2½ cups (15 oz/470 g) cherry tomatoes

3 tsp olive oil

½ tsp sugar

½ cup (½ oz/15 g) loosely packed basil leaves, torn

12 fresh mint leaves, thinly sliced

1 tsp balsamic vinegar

Prepare a charcoal or gas grill for direct-heat grilling over medium-high heat. Oil a grill basket.

Put the tomatoes in a bowl. Add 1 tsp of the oil, the sugar, ½ tsp salt, and several grinds of pepper and toss to coat evenly.

Transfer the tomatoes to the grill basket and place on the grill. Grill, shaking the basket frequently, until the tomatoes are softened and lightly browned and the skins are starting to split, about 3 minutes. Do not cook the tomatoes until fully collapsed. Return the tomatoes to the bowl and toss with the basil, mint, vinegar, and remaining 2 tsp oil. Serve warm or at room temperature.

30

In this sweet-and-tangy slaw, raw carrots are mixed with a lemony dressing, and sliced almonds deliver a welcome crunch. Serve with fried chicken or pan-grilled pork chops. Sturdy slaws like this one also pack well in a roast pork sandwich or a chicken wrap.

CARROT SLAW WITH LEMON-HONEY DRESSING

serves 4

2 Tbsp extra-virgin olive oil

2 Tbsp sherry vinegar

2 tsp fresh lemon juice

1½ tsp honey

Salt

1½ lb (750 g) carrots, grated

½ cup (3 oz/90 g) golden raisins

¼ cup (1½ oz/45 g) sliced almonds

1 Tbsp chopped fresh flat-leaf parsley

In a large bowl, whisk together the oil, vinegar, lemon juice, and honey. Season with ¼ tsp salt.

Add the carrots, raisins, almonds, and parsley and stir to mix well. Serve at room temperature.

31

Mix and match pieces of summer squash, eggplant, and red onion on bamboo skewers to create colorful seasonal kebabs. Or, use sturdy rosemary branches in place of the skewers for an even prettier presentation. When the kebabs come off the grill, stack them on a big platter and let guests help themselves to both the skewers and the fragrant herb sauce.

EGGPLANT, ZUCCHINI & SQUASH KEBABS

serves 4

2 Asian eggplants, cut into rounds 1 inch (24 mm) thick

2 yellow summer squashes, cut into rounds 1 inch (24 mm) thick

1 red onion, quartered and thickly sliced

2 zucchini, cut into rounds 1 inch (24 mm) thick

½ cup (¾ oz/20 g) coarsely chopped fresh flat-leaf parsley

½ cup (¾ oz/20 g) coarsely chopped fresh mint

Grated zest and juice of 1 lemon

1 Tbsp capers, drained

½ cup (4 fl oz/125 ml) extra-virgin olive oil, plus more for brushing

Salt and freshly ground pepper

Soak 8 bamboo skewers in water for about 30 minutes. Prepare a charcoal or gas grill for direct-heat grilling over medium-high heat. Oil the grill rack.

Using a sharp knife, score both cut sides of the eggplant, squash, and zucchini rounds. Thread the eggplant, squash, zucchini, and red onion onto the skewers, using 5 or 6 pieces per skewer and alternating the vegetables.

In a small bowl, stir together the parsley, mint, lemon zest and juice, capers, and ½ cup oil. Season with salt and pepper.

Brush the skewers with oil and place on the grill rack. Grill, turning once, until nicely charred, 2–3 minutes per side. Transfer to a platter, drizzle with the herb sauce, and serve.

September brings the last of the summer vegetables, which are slowly replaced by autumn's tough-skinned squashes. As the days cool, it is time to turn on the oven. Roast artichokes stuffed with a mixture of bread crumbs and pine nuts, or bake a strata of potatoes, mushrooms, and Asiago cheese until golden. If you are just back to school or work after a summer vacation, ease into fall by putting comfort food on the table, such as creamy mashed potatoes alongside the first roast of the season.

september

1

SEPTEMBER

GARLICKY SPINACH & PARMESAN FRITTATA

serves 4–6

1¼ lb (625 g) spinach

4 Tbsp (2 fl oz/60 ml) olive oil

1 small yellow onion, thinly sliced

Salt and freshly ground black pepper

6 eggs

4 cloves garlic, finely chopped

¼ cup (1 oz/30 g) grated hard cheese
such as Parmesan

Pinch of cayenne pepper

You can substitute Swiss chard for the spinach in this simple but flavorful frittata. Cut the chard stems crosswise into pieces ¼ inch (6mm) wide and then coarsely chop the leaves. Add the stems to the onion and sauté for about 4 minutes, then add the leaves and sauté for about 3 minutes longer. Serve this frittata with a salad of mixed greens, sliced pears or apples, and toasted walnuts for an easy weeknight supper.

Position a rack in the upper third of the oven and preheat to 350°F (180°C). Trim the tough stems from the spinach, set aside a couple handfuls of whole leaves, and coarsely chop the remainder.

In a large frying pan over medium heat, warm 2 Tbsp of the oil. Add the onion and sauté until tender, about 6 minutes. Add all the spinach, season with salt, and sauté until tender, 2–3 minutes. Transfer to a plate.

In a large bowl, lightly beat the eggs with the garlic and cheese. Season with the cayenne, salt, and black pepper.

Gently squeeze the liquid out of the spinach then stir the spinach into the egg mixture. In an 8-inch (20-cm) ovenproof frying pan over medium-high heat, warm the remaining 2 Tbsp oil. Add the egg mixture, reduce the heat to medium, and cook until the eggs are set around the edges, about 5 minutes. Transfer to the oven and cook until set, 7–9 minutes longer. Let cool briefly.

If desired, invert the frittata onto a large plate. Cut into wedges and serve.

2

SEPTEMBER

FRESH SHELL BEANS WITH BUTTERNUT SQUASH, BACON & SAGE

serves 4

1 lb (500 g) fresh shell beans such
as cranberry beans, shelled

1 small butternut squash,
about 1½ lb (750 g)

2 thick slices bacon

1½ Tbsp minced fresh sage

Olive oil for drizzling

Sea salt and freshly ground pepper

¼ cup (1 oz/30 g) pecan halves, toasted

Woodsy sage pairs nicely with a variety of late-summer vegetables, like creamy cubes of sweet butternut squash and earthy shell beans. Toasted pecans and salty bacon provide contrasting tastes and textures.

Bring a large saucepan of water to a boil. Add the beans, reduce the heat to medium, and simmer until the beans are tender but not falling apart, 25–30 minutes. Drain the beans.

Halve the squash lengthwise and scoop out and discard the seeds. Cut the skin away from the flesh, and cut the flesh into ½-inch (12-mm) cubes.

Heat a frying pan over medium heat. Add the bacon and cook, turning once, until browned and crisp, 7–9 minutes. Transfer to paper towels to drain. Pour off all but 1 Tbsp of the bacon fat from the pan. When the bacon has cooled, crumble it into pieces.

Warm the bacon fat over medium-high heat. Add the squash and cook, stirring frequently, until lightly browned and just tender when pierced with a knife, 8–10 minutes. Add the sage and beans, drizzle with oil, and season lightly with salt and pepper. Cook, stirring frequently, until the beans are heated through and the flavors are blended, about 1 minute. Stir in the bacon and pecans. Transfer to a platter and serve.

3

Rosemary has a resinous flavor that pairs well with sweet roasted peppers and onions and tangy olives. If you like, use 3 large bell peppers, 1 red, 1 yellow, and 1 green, to make this an even more colorful vegetable roast.

ROASTED PEPPERS WITH OLIVES & ROSEMARY

serves 4

2 red bell peppers, quartered lengthwise and seeded

2 yellow or orange bell peppers, quartered lengthwise and seeded

1 large sweet onion, about 10 oz (315 g), cut into 8 wedges

1 Tbsp olive oil

Salt and freshly ground pepper

1 Tbsp chopped fresh rosemary leaves or 1 tsp dried rosemary

About 12 Kalamata olives, left whole or pitted and coarsely chopped

Preheat the oven to 400°F (200°C).

Cut each bell pepper quarter lengthwise into strips ½ inch (12 mm) wide. Combine the bell pepper strips and onion wedges in a 9-by-13-inch (23-by-33-cm) baking dish. Drizzle with the oil and sprinkle with ¼ tsp salt and a few grinds of pepper.

Roast the vegetables, turning them once or twice, until golden and tender, about 50 minutes. If using dried rosemary, sprinkle it over the vegetables halfway through the roasting time. When the vegetables are ready, sprinkle them with the olives and the fresh rosemary, if using, and roast for 5 minutes.

Transfer the vegetables to a bowl and serve.

4

Chopped basil, mint, parsley, and dill give depth to this spinach salad. Ground cumin is toasted in a dry pan over medium-low heat to release its earthy aroma and intensify its flavor before it is stirred into the vinaigrette. Because the corn is added raw, look for the freshest young corn you can find.

SPINACH, CORN & HERB SALAD WITH TOASTED CUMIN

serves 4

2 ears corn, husks and silk removed

1 large tomato, chopped

½ cup (2½ oz/75 g) chopped English cucumber

½ cup (2 oz/60 g) chopped yellow onion

2 Tbsp finely chopped fresh basil

2 Tbsp finely chopped fresh mint

2 Tbsp finely chopped fresh flat-leaf parsley

2 Tbsp finely chopped fresh dill

1 tsp finely chopped garlic

1 tsp ground cumin

¼ cup (2 fl oz/60 ml) extra-virgin olive oil

2 Tbsp red wine vinegar

Salt and freshly ground pepper

5 oz (155 g) baby spinach leaves

Hold each ear of corn upright on a cutting board. Using a sharp knife, cut down along the ear, stripping off the kernels and rotating the ear a quarter turn after each cut. You will have about 1 cup (6 oz/185 g) kernels.

In a large serving bowl, combine the corn, tomato, cucumber, and onion. Add the basil, mint, parsley, dill, and garlic.

In a small, dry frying pan, warm the cumin over medium-low heat just until fragrant, about 20 seconds. Transfer to a small bowl. Add the oil, vinegar, ½ tsp salt, and a grind of pepper, and whisk until blended.

Add the spinach and the dressing to the corn mixture, toss to mix with the vinaigrette, and serve.

5

CREAMIEST MASHED POTATOES

serves 6–8

Salt

4 large Yukon gold or Yellow Finn potatoes, about 2 lb (1 kg) total, peeled and quartered

3 large cloves garlic (optional)

1/2 cup (4 fl oz/125 ml) whole milk

1/2 cup (4 fl oz/125 ml) heavy cream

2 Tbsp unsalted butter

Pinch of freshly grated nutmeg (optional)

Back-to-school season calls for comfort foods, and the first roast dinner of the season wouldn't be complete without mashed potatoes. These are classic, extra-creamy whipped spuds, but you can substitute sour cream or crème fraîche for the milk for a tangier and even more decadent dish. For a touch of green, stir in 1 Tbsp chopped fresh chives or dill just before serving.

Fill a saucepan with water, and add 2 Tbsp salt, the potatoes, and the garlic, if using. Bring to a boil, reduce the heat to a simmer, and cook until the potatoes are tender when pierced with a knife, about 30 minutes. Drain the potatoes and pass through a ricer into a large bowl. The potatoes can also be mashed with a potato masher or a large fork, but will be slightly lumpier in texture. Cover the bowl to keep the potatoes warm.

In a small saucepan, bring the milk, cream, and butter to just below a boil over medium heat. Immediately remove from the heat. Gradually add the milk mixture to the potatoes while stirring with a fork. The potatoes should be smooth and thick. Beat the potatoes a few times with a large spoon to smooth them out. Add the nutmeg, if using. Season with salt and serve.

6

SPICY CAULIFLOWER GRATIN

serves 4

1 medium head cauliflower

1 1/2 Tbsp butter

3 1/2 Tbsp all-purpose flour

1 1/2 cups (12 fl oz/375 ml) milk

Salt and freshly ground pepper

1/3 cup (2/3 oz/20 g) fresh bread crumbs

1 Tbsp capers, drained

1 tsp red pepper flakes

A bubbling béchamel sauce highlights the best qualities of cruciferous vegetables, especially mildly cabbagey, highly nutritious cauliflower florets. Here, the classic sauce is updated with a sprinkling of capers and red pepper flakes, with the latter packing an unexpected kick.

Preheat the oven to 400°F (200°C). Butter a baking dish.

In a large saucepan fitted with a steamer basket, bring 1–2 inches (5–7.5 cm) of water to a boil. Add the cauliflower head, cover, and cook until nearly fork-tender, 15–20 minutes. Transfer to a cutting board and let cool. Cut the cauliflower lengthwise into 8 spearlike wedges and arrange in the prepared dish.

In a saucepan, melt 1 Tbsp of the butter over medium heat. Remove from the heat and whisk in the flour. Return to medium heat and slowly add the milk, whisking constantly. Reduce the heat to low, add 1 tsp salt and 1/2 tsp pepper, and cook, whisking occasionally, until the sauce is thickened and smooth, about 15 minutes.

In a small frying pan, melt the remaining 1/2 Tbsp butter over medium heat. Add the bread crumbs and cook, stirring often, until golden, 3–4 minutes.

Stir the capers and red pepper flakes into the sauce and pour over the cauliflower. Sprinkle evenly with the toasted bread crumbs. Bake until the sauce is bubbling and the edges are golden, about 30 minutes. Remove from the oven and serve.

ARTICHOKES STUFFED WITH GARLIC, PINE NUTS & HERBS

serves 4

Steamed and hot with plenty of melted butter for dipping, or chilled with mayonnaise are both much-loved classic ways to serve artichokes. But many Italian Americans insist that stuffed artichokes, with a garlicky filling of bread crumbs and pine nuts, are the best way to show off these members of the thistle family.

1 lemon, halved

4 artichokes, about 9 oz (280 g) each, with stems

6 Tbsp (3 fl oz/90 ml) olive oil

2 cups (4 oz/125 g) coarse fresh bread crumbs

⅓ cup (2 oz/60 g) pine nuts, toasted

2 Tbsp minced fresh flat-leaf parsley

3 cloves garlic, minced

½ tsp dried oregano

Salt and freshly ground pepper

Mayonnaise for serving

Fill a large bowl with water. Squeeze the juice from 1 lemon half into the water and then add the spent half. Cut 1 inch (2.5 cm) off the top of each artichoke. Using kitchen scissors, snip off any thorny tips that remain on the leaves. Rub the cut areas with the lemon half. Place the artichokes in the bowl of water. Cut off the stem of each artichoke flush with the base. Rub the cut areas with the remaining lemon half. Trim away the thick skin from each stem. Rub the peeled stems with the lemon half and then chop the stems.

In a frying pan, warm 1 Tbsp of the oil over medium heat. Add the chopped stems and ¼ cup (2 fl oz/60 ml) water, reduce the heat to medium-low, cover, and cook until the stems are tender and the water has evaporated, 8–10 minutes. Let cool slightly.

Remove the artichokes from the water and place each upside down on a work surface. Press hard on each bottom to loosen the leaves and force them far enough apart to hold the stuffing.

In a bowl, combine the cooked stems, bread crumbs, pine nuts, parsley, garlic, and oregano. Stir in 2 Tbsp of the oil. Season with salt and pepper. Using one-fourth of the bread crumb mixture for each artichoke, stuff the mixture between the outer few layers of thick leaves. Leave the thin inner leaves intact.

Pour 1 Tbsp of the oil into a saucepan just large enough to hold the artichokes upright in a single layer, and tilt to coat the pan ⟫→

bottom. Arrange the stuffed artichokes, bases down, in the saucepan and drizzle with the remaining 2 Tbsp olive oil. Add water to come ½ inch (12 mm) up the sides of the artichokes without immersing the stuffing. Bring to a boil. Reduce the heat to medium-low, cover, and simmer, adding more boiling water to the pan as needed to maintain the level, until a leaf can be easily pulled from an artichoke, about 1 hour.

Meanwhile, preheat the oven to 400°F (200°C). Lightly oil a baking sheet. When the artichokes are ready, carefully transfer them, bases down, to the prepared sheet. Bake until the stuffing is lightly browned, about 15 minutes. Serve the artichokes with mayonnaise.

ROASTED SWEET POTATOES WITH MOLASSES & CHILI

serves 4

Sweet potatoes are ideal for roasting because their natural sugars, especially when augmented with a little molasses, caramelize to a rich, deep color and flavor. The chili powder adds some heat to produce an appealing sweet-hot taste. For a milder result, substitute ground cumin for the chili powder.

1 lb (500 g) sweet potatoes, peeled, halved lengthwise, and sliced crosswise

3 Tbsp canola oil

1 Tbsp molasses

1 tsp chili powder

Salt and freshly ground pepper

Preheat the oven to 450°F (230°C).

Arrange the sweet potatoes in a single layer on a rimmed baking sheet. In a small dish, stir together the canola oil and molasses. Drizzle the mixture evenly over the sweet potatoes. Sprinkle with the chili powder and then season generously with salt and pepper. Toss to coat the sweet potatoes evenly, then spread them out evenly.

Roast the sweet potatoes, turning them once or twice, until they are browned and crisp but still tender when pierced with a fork, 20–30 minutes.

Transfer the sweet potatoes to a bowl and serve.

9

Buttered bread crumbs crisp into a wonderful golden crust on this comforting gratin of herb-spiked tomatoes. Serve the gratin alongside fried or grilled chicken, or make it the center-piece of a meatless meal, accompanying it with a green salad, corn on the cob, and crusty French bread. To peel the tomatoes, using a sharp knife, make a shallow X on the bottom of each tomato, blanch the tomatoes in boiling water for 30 seconds, and then immerse in cold water. The skin will slip right off.

CREOLE TOMATO GRATIN

serves 4

5 Tbsp (2½ oz/75 g) unsalted butter

2 cloves garlic, minced

2 cups (4 oz/125 g) fresh bread crumbs, preferably from French bread

4 ripe beefsteak or other large tomatoes, peeled and sliced ½ inch (12 mm) thick

Sea salt and freshly ground pepper

2 Tbsp minced fresh basil

2 Tbsp minced fresh flat-leaf parsley

2 Tbsp grated Parmesan cheese

Preheat the oven to 350°F (180°C). Butter a gratin dish or other shallow baking dish about 11 inches (28 cm) long and 9 inches (23 cm) wide.

In a frying pan, melt the butter over medium-low heat. Add the garlic and sauté until tender and fragrant but not at all browned, 2–3 minutes. Remove from the heat and stir in the bread crumbs until evenly coated with the butter mixture.

Spread about one-fourth of the bread crumb mixture evenly in the bottom of the prepared gratin dish. Top with half of the tomato slices, arranging them in a single layer and overlapping them slightly. Sprinkle with salt, pepper, and 1 Tbsp each of the basil and parsley. Top with one-third of the remaining bread crumb mixture and then the remaining tomato slices. Sprinkle with salt and pepper and with the remaining basil and parsley. Top with the remaining bread crumb mixture, and sprinkle the Parmesan evenly over the surface.

Bake, uncovered, until browned and bubbly, about 1 hour. Serve hot, directly from the dish.

10

Skinny, deep green long beans—also known as snake beans, yard-long beans, and asparagus beans—will delight kids and impress adults. Look for them at farmers' markets and Asian groceries, where they are often sold tied in bundles. Cut them into manageable lengths and cook them in a searing-hot wok until the skins wrinkle and brown in spots before adding any seasonings.

DRY-FRIED LONG BEANS

serves 4–6

¼ cup (2 fl oz/60 ml) chicken broth

1 tsp sugar

Salt

½ cup (4 fl oz/125 ml) canola oil

¾ lb (375 g) Asian long beans, cut into 4-inch (10-cm) lengths

2 Tbsp peeled and finely chopped fresh ginger

1 red bell pepper, seeded and chopped

1 Tbsp balsamic vinegar

1 tsp Asian sesame oil

In small bowl, mix together the broth, sugar, and ½ tsp salt.

Heat the oil in a wok or a large, deep frying pan over medium-high heat until almost smoking. Add the beans and cook, alternately stirring them and pressing them against the wok, until the skin wrinkles and brown spots appear, about 3 minutes. Using a slotted spoon, transfer the beans to a plate.

Pour off all but 1 Tbsp oil. Return the wok to medium-high heat, add the ginger, and stir-fry until fragrant, about 30 seconds. Add the broth mixture, return the beans to the pan, and cook until the beans are tender but still crunchy and the pan is almost dry, 3–4 minutes. Stir in the bell pepper, vinegar, and sesame oil. Serve warm or at room temperature.

11

The anise tones of fennel are brought out by the heady combination of Indian spices in this dish. Grilling the spiced fennel leaves it both smokey and aromatic. A cooling cucumber-mint raita tempers the spice. Serve with tandoori-style chicken or fish.

GRILLED INDIAN-SPICED FENNEL WITH RAITA

serves 4

2 medium or 4 small fennel bulbs, about 1 lb (500 g) total

Boiling water

3 Tbsp olive oil

2 tsp mustard seeds

2 tsp ground coriander

½ tsp ground cloves

½ tsp ground cardamom

1¼ tsp ground cumin

Salt and freshly ground pepper

½ cup (4 oz/125 g) plain yogurt

¼ cup (1 oz/30 g) shredded cucumber

1 Tbsp chopped fresh mint

Prepare a charcoal or gas grill for direct-heat grilling over medium heat. Oil the grill rack or a grill basket.

Cut the stalks and feathery leaves from each fennel bulb; discard or reserve for another use. Cut the bulbs lengthwise into thin slices. Place the fennel in a heatproof bowl, add boiling water to cover, and let stand for 2 minutes to soften slightly. Drain thoroughly, pat dry, and return to the bowl. Add the oil, mustard seeds, coriander, cloves, cardamom, 1 tsp of the cumin, ½ tsp salt, and several grinds of pepper. Toss to mix well, then coat the fennel evenly with the spice mixture.

In a small bowl, stir together the yogurt, cucumber, mint, and remaining ¼ tsp cumin.

Arrange the fennel slices on the grill rack or in the basket. Grill, turning occasionally, until softened and lightly browned, about 3 minutes per side. Serve with the raita on the side.

12

Look for very small, freshly harvested artichokes for this recipe. If the artichokes are too large, they will have already begun forming a prickly choke. Look for these "babies" at farmers' markets or specialty produce stores. Serve these savory bites as part of a larger antipasto spread or slice or chop and add to salads or sandwiches.

MARINATED ARTICHOKE HEARTS

makes 1 one-pint (16 fl oz/500 ml) jar

1 bottle (24 fl oz/750 ml) dry white wine

1 cup (8 fl oz/250 ml) white wine vinegar

2 tsp coarse sea salt

10 peppercorns

4 bay leaves

4 whole cloves

2 lb (1 kg) baby artichokes

1 lemon, halved

About 1½ cups (12 fl oz/375 ml) extra-virgin olive oil

Have ready one 1-pt (16–fl oz/500 ml) hot, sterilized jar and its lid.

In a saucepan, combine the wine, vinegar, salt, 4 of the peppercorns, 1 of the bay leaves, and 1 of the cloves. Reduce the heat to low and simmer for 5 minutes.

Meanwhile, snap off the tough outer leaves of each artichoke to reveal the pale inner leaves. Cut off ½ inch (12 mm) of the spiky tips. Cut off the stem 1 inch (2.5 cm) from the bottom and peel the remaining stem. Rub the stem and cut edges of each artichoke lightly with the cut side of a lemon half. When all of the artichokes are ready, drop them into the simmering wine mixture.

Bring the wine mixture back to a simmer and cook the artichokes for 10 minutes. Drain the artichokes and pat dry. Pack the artichokes into the jar, layering them with the remaining peppercorns, bay leaves, and cloves. Fill the jar with the oil, leaving ½ inch (12 mm) of headspace. Remove any air bubbles and adjust the headspace with more oil, if necessary. Wipe the rim and seal tightly with the lid. Store in a cool, dark place for 1 month before eating. Store the jar in the refrigerator once it has been opened.

13

CORN & ROASTED POBLANO SOUP

serves 6

If the weather turns unexpectedly cool in mid-September, this creamy soup is guaranteed to warm you up. Infusing the milk with cumin, chile, and herbs helps to cut some of its richness, and puréeing only one-third of the soup ensures the creaminess is nicely balanced with the texture of whole corn kernels.

8 cups (64 fl oz/2 l) whole milk

2 Tbsp cumin seeds

1–2 chipotle chiles, coarsely chopped

2 bay leaves

1 large fresh rosemary sprig or ½ tsp dried rosemary

8 ears corn, husks and silk removed

2 Tbsp unsalted butter

2 Tbsp olive oil

2 large yellow onions, chopped

Salt

4–6 cloves garlic, minced

2 tsp ground cumin

6 large poblano chiles, roasted, peeled, seeded, and chopped

6 green onions, white and tender green parts, finely chopped

Pour the milk into a heavy saucepan. In a small, dry frying pan, toast the cumin seeds over high heat, shaking the pan constantly, until they begin to change color, about 4 minutes. Immediately add to the milk. Add the chipotle chiles, bay leaves, and rosemary. Cover and bring to a gentle simmer over low heat; do not allow to boil. Remove from the heat and let stand, covered, for about 20 minutes.

Meanwhile, hold each ear of corn upright on a cutting board. Using a sharp knife, cut down along the ear, stripping off the kernels and rotating the ear a quarter turn with each cut. In a large saucepan, melt the butter with the oil over medium heat. Add the yellow onions and 2 tsp salt and sauté until the onions are soft and golden brown, 15–20 minutes. Reduce the heat to medium-low, add the garlic and ground cumin, and sauté until aromatic, about 5 minutes. Stir in the corn and poblano chiles, and cook, stirring, until the corn is lightly browned, about 5 minutes.

Strain the milk through a fine-mesh sieve into the corn mixture. Bring to a gentle simmer and continue to simmer until the flavors are melded, about 15 minutes. Let cool for about 5 minutes. ⋙

In a food processor, purée about one-third of the soup. Return the purée to the saucepan, stirring well. If necessary, place over low heat to reheat gently. Ladle the soup into bowls, garnish with the green onions, and serve.

- -

14

WARM TOMATO & OLIVE BRUSCHETTA

serves 4

Olives and capers infuse robust flavors into the traditional tomato topping for bruschetta, and these bolder elements call for a rustic whole-grain loaf. Follow this first course with pasta tossed with a sauce of wilted greens and sausage and a dessert of gelato and biscotti.

1 Tbsp olive oil

2 cups (12 oz/370 g) chopped fresh plum tomatoes

3 Tbsp green olives, pitted and chopped

2 tsp chopped fresh oregano or ½ tsp dried oregano

1 Tbsp capers, drained and chopped

Freshly ground pepper

4 slices whole-grain coarse country bread, each about ½ inch (12 mm) thick

2 cloves garlic, halved

Preheat the broiler.

In a frying pan, warm the oil over medium-high heat. Add the tomatoes, olives, and oregano and sauté until the tomatoes start to soften, about 1 minute. Remove from the heat and stir in the capers and a few grinds of pepper.

Place the bread slices on a baking sheet and broil, turning once, until crisp and golden on both sides, about 3 minutes.

Immediately rub one side of each bread slice with a garlic clove half. Arrange the slices on a platter, garlic side up. Top with the warm tomato mixture and serve.

15

*For those who can't
get enough of the
tender sweetness of
summer squash (or
those faced with an
overabundance in
their garden), this
simple preparation
borrows from a
classic, eggplant
parmigiana, trading
out the eggplant
for yellow squash.
On warm days,
serve it at room
temperature, with
crusty bread
to mop up the
tomato sauce.*

GRILLED SUMMER SQUASH PARMESAN

serves 4

4 Tbsp (2 fl oz/60 ml) extra-virgin olive oil

2 cloves garlic, crushed

1 can (28 oz/875 g) diced or crushed tomatoes

Salt and freshly ground pepper

10 fresh basil leaves, torn into small pieces

2 lb (1 kg) yellow summer squashes, cut lengthwise into slices ⅓ inch (9 mm) thick

¾ lb (340 g) fresh mozzarella cheese, thinly sliced

¼ cup (1 oz/30 g) grated Parmesan cheese

In a saucepan, warm 1 Tbsp of the oil over medium-low heat. Add the garlic and sauté until fragrant, about 2 minutes. Add the tomatoes and ½ tsp salt, raise the heat to medium-high, and simmer, stirring occasionally, until the sauce thickens, 25–30 minutes. Remove from the heat, discard the garlic, and stir in about half of the basil.

Prepare a charcoal or gas grill for direct-heat grilling over medium-high heat. Oil the grill rack. Preheat the oven to 375°F (190°C).

Place the squash slices on a baking sheet, drizzle with the remaining 3 Tbsp oil, season with salt and pepper, and toss to coat. Arrange the squash slices on the grill rack and cook, turning once, until lightly charred on both sides, 3–4 minutes per side. Transfer to a plate.

Lightly oil a large, shallow baking dish and spread about ¼ cup (2 fl oz/60 ml) of the tomato sauce on the bottom. Arrange one-fourth of the squash in the dish. Top with one-third of the mozzarella slices and a few pieces of basil. Cover with another ¼ cup sauce. Make 2 more layers of squash, mozzarella, basil, and sauce. Top with a final layer of squash and sauce and sprinkle with the Parmesan. Bake, until the juices are bubbling and the top is lightly browned, about 35 minutes. Serve warm or at room temperature.

16

*This Spanish-style
sauté is a great way
to use up a late-
summer bounty of
zucchini. Spanish
cooks sometimes add
beaten eggs to this
sauté, turning it
into a loose frittata.
Serve with a crisp
white wine such
as an Albariño.*

SAUTÉED ZUCCHINI, ONIONS & POTATOES WITH OREGANO

serves 4

5 Tbsp (3 fl oz/80 ml) olive oil

1 yellow onion, quartered and cut into ¾-inch (2-cm) pieces

2 cloves garlic, minced

2 zucchini, halved lengthwise and cut into ¾-inch (2-cm) pieces

1 Tbsp chopped fresh oregano

Salt

2 waxy potatoes, about ½ lb (250 g) total, peeled and cut into ⅓-inch (9-mm) pieces

In a large frying pan, heat 2 Tbsp of the oil over medium-high heat. Add the onion and sauté until translucent, about 3 minutes. Add the garlic and sauté until the onion is tender, about 5 minutes. Using a slotted spoon, transfer the onion mixture to a bowl.

Add 1 Tbsp of the oil to the pan. Add the zucchini and oregano and sprinkle with salt. Cook over medium-high heat, stirring frequently, until the moisture in the zucchini evaporates and the flesh is tender, about 15 minutes. Return the onion mixture to the pan and remove from the heat.

In another frying pan, warm the remaining 2 Tbsp oil over medium heat. Add the potatoes, spreading them in a single layer, and reduce the heat to medium-low. Cook the potatoes, stirring occasionally, until tender and golden, about 8 minutes. Using the slotted spoon, transfer to paper towels to drain.

Add the potatoes to the pan with the squash. Cook the vegetables over medium heat for 5 minutes to blend the flavors. Serve hot or at room temperature.

17

SWEET POTATO FRIES WITH GARLIC & HERBS

serves 4

2 lb (1 kg) orange-fleshed sweet potatoes

2 Tbsp olive oil

Coarse sea salt

3 Tbsp grated Parmesan cheese

2 Tbsp chopped fresh flat-leaf parsley

1 clove garlic, minced

Anyone who likes classic French fries is guaranteed to like these cheese-and-herb-dusted sweet potato fries. They are roasted rather than deep-fried, which cuts calories dramatically without sacrificing flavor. Leaving the peel on adds more taste and texture to the dish as well as more nutrients into your diet. If your pocketbook allows, splurge on either Maldon sea salt or fleur de sel.

Preheat the oven to 450°F (230°C).

Rinse and dry the sweet potatoes. Cut the unpeeled potatoes lengthwise into slices ½ inch (12 mm) thick, and then cut each slice into batons about ¼ inch (6 mm) wide and 3 inches (7.5 cm) long.

Place the potatoes on a baking sheet. Drizzle with the oil, sprinkle with ¼ tsp salt, and toss to coat. Spread the potatoes out evenly. Roast, stirring with a spatula midway through, until the potatoes are tender and browned on the edges, 20–25 minutes.

In a large bowl, stir together the Parmesan, parsley, and garlic. Add the warm fries and mix gently to coat. Season with salt and serve.

18

ROASTED MUSHROOM, SHALLOT & RADICCHIO SALAD

serves 6

1 lb (500 g) mixed wild and cultivated mushrooms such as chanterelle and shiitake

8 Tbsp (4 fl oz/125 ml) olive oil, plus 2 tsp

2½ tsp fresh thyme leaves

Salt and freshly ground pepper

4 large shallots

¼ cup (2 fl oz/60 ml) balsamic vinegar

1 tsp fresh lemon juice

½ tsp sugar

1 head Treviso radicchio, thinly sliced

1 small head red-leaf lettuce, leaves torn into bite-sized pieces

1 cup (1½ oz/45 g) coarsely chopped fresh flat-leaf parsley

Used both in the dressing and in the salad, roasted shallots suffuse this dish with their sweet, mellow onionlike flavor. The roasted mushrooms bring a savory earthiness that pairs nicely with the shallots and the bitter crunch of the radicchio.

Preheat the oven to 400°F (200°C). Trim the tough stems from the mushrooms and thinly slice the caps.

On a rimmed baking sheet, toss together the mushrooms, 3 Tbsp of the oil, 2 tsp of the thyme, ½ tsp salt, and ¼ tsp pepper. In a small baking dish, toss together the shallots, the 2 tsp oil, 2 pinches of salt, and several grinds of pepper. Roast the mushrooms until golden brown and tender, about 15 minutes, stirring once halfway through cooking. Roast the shallots until soft and lightly browned, 25–30 minutes, stirring once halfway through cooking. Trim the root ends from 2 of the roasted shallots and place the shallots in a food processor. Cover the remaining shallots and the mushrooms with foil to keep warm.

Add the remaining 5 Tbsp (3 fl oz/80 ml) oil, remaining ½ tsp thyme, vinegar, lemon juice, and sugar to the food processor. Season with a scant ½ tsp salt and several grinds of pepper. Process until a smooth dressing forms, about 30 seconds.

Thinly slice the remaining 2 roasted shallots. In a large bowl, toss together the radicchio, lettuce, and parsley. Drizzle with about two-thirds of the dressing and toss again. Season with salt and pepper. Arrange the greens on a platter. Top with the warm mushrooms and sliced shallots. Drizzle with the remaining dressing and serve.

19

POLENTA WITH VEGETABLE RAGOUT

serves 4

Quick-cooking polenta is a boon to the busy cook. In less than 10 minutes, you can dish up a piping-hot bowl worthy of topping with all sorts of vegetables or meaty sauces or braises. Here, creamy polenta is crowned with a mixture of late-season bell peppers, eggplant, and zucchini redolent of the Provençal table.

4 Tbsp (2 fl oz/60 ml) olive oil

2 cloves garlic, chopped

1 small Asian eggplant, halved lengthwise and sliced crosswise

1 red bell pepper, seeded and cut crosswise into strips

1 small zucchini, halved lengthwise and thinly sliced crosswise

1 Tbsp chopped fresh thyme

2½ cups (20 fl oz/625 ml) canned plum tomatoes, with juice

4 cups (32 fl oz/1 l) vegetable broth

Salt and freshly ground pepper

1 cup (7 oz/220 g) quick-cooking polenta

In a large frying pan, warm 3 Tbsp of the oil over medium heat. Add the garlic, eggplant, bell pepper, zucchini, and thyme and cook, stirring occasionally, until the vegetables begin to soften, about 5 minutes. Add the tomatoes and ¼ cup (2 fl oz/60 ml) water and cook until the vegetables are soft but still hold their shape, 8–10 minutes, stirring occasionally to break up the tomatoes.

In a deep saucepan, bring the broth to a boil. Add 1 Tbsp salt. Gradually whisk in the polenta. Reduce the heat to medium-low and cook, stirring frequently, until the polenta is thick and soft, 5–8 minutes. Remove the pan from the heat and season with salt and pepper.

Spoon the polenta into bowls, top with the ragout, and serve.

20

POTATO–CELERY ROOT PANCAKES

serves 4–6

Golden, crispy potato pancakes gain some intrigue from celery root, which imparts a mild celery flavor. Choose a high-quality sea salt for sprinkling, which will contribute an appealing mineral taste and additional crunch to the pancakes.

2 small russet potatoes, about 1 lb (500 g)

1 celery root, about ½ lb (250 g)

1 shallot, minced

2 eggs

2 Tbsp all-purpose flour

Salt and freshly ground pepper

Canola oil for frying

Coarse sea salt for serving

Peel the potatoes and celery root. Using a food processor fitted with the shredding disk, shred the potatoes and celery root. (Or, shred the vegetables on the large holes of a grater-shredder.) Line a colander with cheesecloth or a thin kitchen towel. Transfer the potatoes and celery root to the colander, set over a bowl, and twist the cheesecloth tightly into a pouch, squeezing out the moisture. Let the vegetables drain for 15 minutes. Squeeze the cheesecloth again. Carefully pour out the clear liquid from the bowl, leaving behind the white starchy substance that settles in the bottom of the bowl.

Add the shallot, the eggs, the flour, 1½ tsp salt, and 1½ tsp pepper to the bowl and beat with a fork until well blended. Add the shredded potatoes and celery root and toss to combine.

Preheat the oven to 200°F (95°C). Line a baking sheet with paper towels.

Heat a large frying pan over medium-high heat. Pour in oil to a depth of ¼ inch (6 mm). When the oil begins to shimmer, carefully drop the potato mixture by heaping tablespoonful into the pan, spacing the portions 1 inch (2.5 cm) apart. Using a spatula, gently press on the pancakes to flatten them. Cook, turning once, until golden and crisp, 3–4 minutes per side. Transfer to the towel-lined baking sheet and keep warm in the oven. Repeat to cook the remaining potato mixture.

Sprinkle the pancakes with coarse sea salt and serve.

21

PUMPKIN SOUP WITH SWEET & SPICY PUMPKIN SEEDS

serves 6–8

Welcome autumn with smooth, creamy soups made from winter squash. This puréed pumpkin soup is made especially appealing when topped with its own crunchy seeds. The seeds, like the flesh of the pumpkin, take well to sweet partners, such as maple syrup, and to warm spices, such as cayenne pepper and paprika.

½ tsp sugar

½ tsp sweet paprika

¼ tsp cayenne pepper, plus a pinch

Salt and freshly ground pepper

3½ Tbsp unsalted butter

7 Tbsp (3½ fl oz/105 ml) pure maple syrup

½ cup pumpkin seeds, toasted

1 yellow onion, finely chopped

2 celery ribs, finely chopped

2 cloves garlic, minced

½ cup (4 fl oz/125 ml) dry white wine

6 cups (48 fl oz/1.5 l) chicken broth

3 cans (15 oz/470 g each) pumpkin purée

¾ cup (6 fl oz/180 ml) heavy cream

In a small bowl, stir together the sugar, paprika, ¼ tsp cayenne, and ¼ tsp salt. In a frying pan, melt ½ Tbsp of the butter with 1 Tbsp of the maple syrup and 1 tsp water over medium-high heat. Bring to a boil, swirling the pan to blend. Add the pumpkin seeds, stir to coat, and cook until the liquid is almost evaporated, 1–2 minutes. Transfer to the bowl with the spice mixture and toss to coat the seeds. Pour onto a piece of parchment paper, spread in a single layer, and let cool.

In a large, heavy pot, melt the remaining 3 Tbsp butter over medium heat. Add the onion and celery and sauté until softened and beginning to brown, about 7 minutes. Stir in the garlic and cook until fragrant, about 45 seconds. Add the wine, raise the heat to high, and bring to a boil. Cook until the wine is reduced to ¼ cup (2 fl oz/60 ml), about 2 minutes. Add the broth and pumpkin purée, stir to combine, and bring to a simmer. Reduce the heat to low, cover partially, and simmer gently to blend the flavors, about 10 minutes.

Add the remaining 6 Tbsp (3 fl oz/90 ml) maple syrup, the pinch of cayenne, 2 tsp salt, and a few grinds of pepper to the pot. Stir to mix, cover, and simmer to blend the flavors, about 10 minutes. »→

Meanwhile, in a bowl, using a whisk or electric mixer on medium-high speed, beat the cream until it holds soft peaks.

Ladle the soup into bowls, garnish with the cream and spiced pumpkin seeds, and serve.

22

ROASTED GARLIC FENNEL WEDGES

serves 4

Fennel has an anise flavor that pairs well with the assertive character of garlic. Because fennel can dry out easily during roasting, here it is drizzled with a little broth or wine to keep it moist while the edges caramelize. Thyme or oregano may be substituted for the marjoram. Serve with roast pork loin and buttery mashed potatoes.

1 or 2 fennel bulbs, about 1 lb (500 g) total

4 large cloves garlic, sliced

3 Tbsp olive oil

2 Tbsp chicken broth or white wine

Salt and freshly ground pepper

2 Tbsp chopped fresh marjoram, plus sprigs for garnish

Preheat the oven to 375°F (190°C).

Cut the stalks and feathery leaves from the fennel bulb; reserve a few leaves for garnish. Trim away any bruised outer layers and then cut the bulb lengthwise into wedges 1 inch (2.5 cm) wide. Cut out only the toughest part of the central core so the layers remain intact and attached. Combine the fennel and garlic on a rimmed baking sheet. Drizzle with the oil and broth and toss to coat evenly. Season generously with salt and pepper. Spread the fennel wedges out in a single layer.

Roast the fennel, stirring 1 or 2 times, for 20 minutes. Remove the pan from the oven and sprinkle the fennel with the chopped marjoram. Continue to roast until the fennel and garlic are tender when pressed with a fork and lightly browned at the edges, 25–30 minutes.

Transfer the fennel to a bowl, garnish with marjoram sprigs and fennel leaves, and serve.

23

Look for anchovies packed in oil in small jars, which typically offer better flavor and texture than the canned options. This pungent Italian-inspired dressing would also complement sliced tomatoes, grilled squash or eggplant, or a pasta salad with cherry tomatoes.

GREEN BEAN & POTATO SALAD WITH HERBS & ANCHOVIES

serves 6–8

1 lb (500 g) green beans

3 lb (1.5 kg) small potatoes, preferably Yukon gold

6 olive oil–packed anchovy fillets

2 small shallots

1 large clove garlic

½ tsp sugar

1 tsp Dijon mustard

½ cup (½ oz/15 oz) fresh basil leaves

½ cup (½ oz/15 oz) fresh tarragon leaves

½ cup (½ oz/15 oz) fresh flat-leaf parsley leaves

6 Tbsp (3 fl oz/90 ml) white wine vinegar

¾ cup (6 fl oz/180 ml) olive oil

Salt and freshly ground pepper

Bring a saucepan of salted water to a boil. Add the green beans and cook until bright green and just tender-crisp, about 4 minutes. Drain the beans in a colander, rinse under cold running water, and drain again.

In the same saucepan, combine the potatoes and water to cover by 1 inch (2.5 cm) and bring to a boil. Reduce the heat to medium, cover partially, and simmer until the potatoes are just tender when pierced with a knife, 8–10 minutes. Drain and let cool. Cut the potatoes into thick slices or small chunks. Transfer to a large bowl.

In a food processor, combine the anchovies, shallots, and garlic and pulse until minced. Add the sugar, mustard, basil, tarragon, parsley, vinegar, and oil and process until a relatively smooth dressing forms, about 10 seconds.

Add about three-fourths of the dressing to the warm potatoes and toss well to coat. Add the green beans, the remaining dressing, 1¼ tsp salt, and ¼ tsp pepper. Toss well and serve.

24

Enjoy the last of summer's sweet corn with this simple recipe. If possible, use grade B maple syrup for this dish. Its deep amber color and caramel notes will act as a good counterpoint to the spicy cayenne pepper in the butter.

GRILLED CORN WITH MAPLE-CAYENNE BUTTER

serves 4

½ cup (4 oz/125 g) unsalted butter, at room temperature

2 Tbsp pure maple syrup

1 lemon

Pinch of cayenne pepper

Salt and freshly ground black pepper

4 ears corn, husks and silk removed

Canola oil for coating

In a bowl, mix together the butter and maple syrup. Finely grate the zest from the lemon into the bowl. Halve the lemon and squeeze the juice from 1 lemon half into the bowl (reserve the remaining half for another use). Mix well. Add the cayenne and a pinch each of salt and black pepper and stir to blend. Spoon the butter mixture onto a piece of plastic wrap and form it into a log about 1½ inches (4 cm) in diameter. Wrap the log tightly with the plastic wrap and refrigerate it until firm, about 1 hour.

Prepare a charcoal or gas grill for direct-heat grilling over high heat. Oil the grill rack.

Rub each ear of corn evenly with the oil and sprinkle lightly with salt, coating all sides. Grill the corn, turning occasionally, until browned in spots and tender, 12–14 minutes.

Transfer the corn to a platter. Cut slices of the butter from the log and place 1 slice on top of each ear, letting the butter melt and then spreading it over the corn, coating all sides. Serve, passing the remaining butter at the table.

25

SPICY OKRA STEW

serves 4

2 Tbsp canola oil

1 yellow onion, chopped

Salt and freshly ground black pepper

1 lb (500 g) okra, cut into slices
about ¼ inch (6 mm) thick

2 cloves garlic, minced

½ tsp cayenne pepper

½ tsp ground coriander

½ tsp ground cumin

3 large ripe tomatoes, peeled and
coarsely chopped

Leaves from ¼ bunch fresh flat-leaf
parsley, coarsely chopped

*This recipe uses
popular eastern
Mediterranean
seasonings: aromatic
coriander, musky
cumin, and spicy
cayenne. Parsley
adds both bright color
and a fresh herbal
taste that balances
the hearty okra and
tart-sweet tomatoes.*

In a saucepan, warm the oil over medium
heat. Add the onion and a pinch of salt and
sauté until the onion is just beginning to
soften, 2–3 minutes. Add the okra and sauté
until lightly browned, 7–10 minutes. Reduce
the heat to medium-low and sauté until the
okra is just tender, 4–5 minutes.

Add the garlic, cayenne, coriander, and
cumin. Season with salt and black pepper
and cook for 1 minute to blend the flavors.
Add the tomatoes and 1 cup (8 fl oz/250 ml)
water and simmer until the tomatoes have
broken down and the mixture begins to
thicken, 7–9 minutes.

Remove the stew from the heat, stir in the
parsley, and serve.

26

BAKED EGGPLANT WITH YOGURT & POMEGRANATE MOLASSES

serves 4–6

1 cup (8 oz/250 g) Greek-style plain yogurt

1 clove garlic, crushed

6 Tbsp (3 fl oz/90 ml) extra-virgin olive oil

3 Asian eggplants, about 1½ lb (750 g) total,
peeled and cut crosswise into slices ¾ inch
(2 cm) thick

Salt and freshly ground pepper

1 Tbsp pomegranate molasses

*Asian eggplants
are mild and sweet,
which eliminates
the need to salt
the flesh to leach
out the bitterness.
This dish is given
a boost of richness
from a topping
of creamy, thick
Greek-style yogurt
and a tart-sweet
edge from a drizzle
of pomegranate
molasses. It is an
excellent side dish to
a roast leg of lamb,
or a light, satisfying
main course
accompanied with
a green salad and
whole-grain bread.*

In a small bowl, stir together the yogurt
and garlic. Cover and set aside for 1 hour
to allow the flavors to blend.

Preheat the oven to 475°F (245°C). Brush a
rimmed baking sheet with 1 Tbsp of the oil.

Arrange the eggplant slices in a single
layer on the prepared sheet. Brush the slices
evenly with 4 Tbsp (2 fl oz/60 ml) of the oil.
Sprinkle generously with salt and pepper.

Bake the eggplant until tender when pierced
with a knife, about 15 minutes. Transfer the
eggplant to a platter. Remove the garlic clove
from the yogurt. Spoon the yogurt over each
eggplant slice, spreading it with the back of
the spoon to cover evenly.

In a small bowl, whisk together the
pomegranate molasses, ½ tsp salt, and the
remaining 1 Tbsp olive oil. Drizzle over
the eggplant and serve.

LAYERED VEGETABLES ON GARLIC TOAST

serves 4

If you are preparing eggplant for dinner earlier in the week, roast or sauté extra slices, which will save you time when you are ready to make these luscious cheese-topped open-faced sandwiches. Or, use this recipe as a starting point to come up with your own vegetable combination, replacing the eggplant and mozzarella with mushrooms and fontina or sweet peppers and provolone.

1 eggplant, about ¾ lb (375 g), peeled and cut crosswise into 8 slices about ½ inch (12 mm) thick

Salt and freshly ground pepper

4 large, firm plum tomatoes, about 1 lb (500 g) total, halved and seeded

4 Tbsp (2 fl oz/60 ml) olive oil

1 cup (3½ oz/105 g) thinly sliced yellow onion

1 tsp minced garlic, plus 1 clove garlic, halved

5 oz (155 g) spinach

1 Tbsp finely chopped Kalamata olives

4 slices whole-grain coarse country bread, each about ¾ inch (2 cm) thick

4 large fresh basil leaves, finely shredded

4 oz (125 g) mozzarella cheese, shredded

Sprinkle both sides of each eggplant slice lightly with salt and layer the slices in a colander set over a plate. Place a second plate on top to weigh them down and let stand for 1 hour. Rinse the slices well and pat dry.

Preheat the oven to 425°F (220°C). Arrange the tomatoes, cut side up, in a baking dish and drizzle with 1 Tbsp of the oil. Arrange the eggplant slices on a baking sheet, and brush both sides of each slice with 1 Tbsp of the oil. Roast the eggplant for 15 minutes, then turn and roast until lightly browned and soft, about 10 minutes. Roast the tomatoes, turning them occasionally so they cook evenly, until the skins are shriveled and caramelized, 35–45 minutes. Cover the roasted tomatoes with foil, let cool, and peel off any loose skins. Reduce the oven temperature to 350°F (180°C).

Heat a large frying pan over medium heat. Add 1 Tbsp of the oil and the onion and toss to coat. Sprinkle with 2 Tbsp water, cover, reduce the heat to low, and cook until the onion is wilted and tender, about 8 minutes. Uncover the pan, stir in the minced garlic, and cook for 1 minute. Add the spinach, cover, and cook until wilted, about 3 minutes. Remove from the heat and stir in the olives, a pinch of salt, and a grind of pepper. »→

Arrange the bread slices on a baking sheet. Brush evenly with the remaining 1 Tbsp oil. Bake until lightly toasted, about 12 minutes. Rub 1 side of each bread slice lightly with the cut side of a garlic half. Remove from the oven. Preheat the broiler.

Make a layer of the spinach mixture on the toasts. Top each toast with 2 eggplant slices, slightly overlapping them, and then with 2 roasted tomato halves, cut side up. Sprinkle with the basil and top with the cheese. Broil until the cheese is hot and bubbly, about 4 minutes. Transfer to plates and serve.

STEAMED CAULIFLOWER WITH CURRY BUTTER

serves 4

Choose any color of cauliflower—white, purple, sunny orange, lime green—to pair with this brightly flavored curry butter. The butter will also complement other steamed seasonal vegetables, such as broccoli, carrots, or fingerling potatoes.

1 head cauliflower, about 1½ lb (750 g), trimmed and cut into 1-inch (2.5-cm) florets

2 Tbsp finely chopped fresh flat-leaf parsley

FOR THE CURRY BUTTER

4 Tbsp (2 oz/60 g) unsalted butter, at room temperature

2 tsp curry powder

1 tsp grated lemon zest

1 tsp fresh lemon juice

¼ tsp sugar

⅛ tsp ground mace

⅛ tsp hot paprika

Salt

In a large pot fitted with a steamer basket, bring 1–2 inches (2.5–5 cm) of water to a boil. Place the cauliflower florets in a single layer in the basket, reduce the heat to medium, and cook until tender-crisp, about 8 minutes.

While the cauliflower is cooking, make the curry butter. In a small bowl, stir together the butter, curry powder, lemon zest and juice, sugar, mace, paprika, and ½ tsp salt, mixing well. Transfer the butter to a serving bowl.

When the cauliflower is ready, transfer it to the bowl holding the curry butter, add the parsley, toss to coat evenly, and serve.

29

Briefly roasting small tomatoes at a high temperature allows them to retain their moisture and shape while deepening their natural flavors. Chopped fresh rosemary, thyme, or tarragon can be used in place of the basil. Serve the tomatoes as a side dish, add them to a green salad, or toss them with warm penne and grated Parmesan for an easy pasta dish.

FLASH-ROASTED TOMATOES

serves 4

2 cups (12 oz/375 g) cherry, grape or vine-ripened tomatoes

2 Tbsp thinly sliced shallot

Salt and freshly ground pepper

3 Tbsp olive oil

¼ cup (¾ oz/20 g) sliced green onion, white and tender green parts

1½ Tbsp chopped fresh basil (optional)

1½ Tbsp balsamic vinegar

Preheat the oven to 450°F (220°C).

Combine the tomatoes and shallot on a baking sheet or in a shallow baking dish large enough to hold the tomatoes in a single layer. Season with salt and pepper. Drizzle evenly with the oil and stir to coat. Spread the tomatoes out evenly.

Roast the tomatoes, stirring once, for 10 minutes. Gently stir in the green onion and basil, if using, and vinegar. Continue to roast the tomatoes until they are softened but still hold their shape, about 5 minutes.

Transfer the tomatoes to a bowl. Serve warm or at room temperature.

30

Bright and bracing, this pickled fennel can be enjoyed just a day after it is packed into jars. The orange zest and juice and the mirin accentuate the vegetable's sweet anise flavor. The fennel fronds look attractive in the jars and on a serving plate alongside the fennel slices. Pair them both with a fresh goat cheese. Use a citrus zester to remove the orange zest in long, thin curls.

PICKLED FENNEL WITH ORANGE ZEST

makes 3 one-pint (16–fl oz/500-ml) jars

4 large fennel bulbs with leaves attached, about 1 lb (500 g) each

1½ cups (12 fl oz/375 ml) white wine vinegar

1½ cups (12 fl oz/375 ml) fresh orange juice (from 3 or 4 navel oranges)

¼ cup (2 fl oz/60 ml) mirin

1 Tbsp pink peppercorns

Long, thin zest strips of 1 navel orange (about 1 Tbsp)

3 Tbsp olive oil

Have ready three 1-pt (16–fl oz/500-ml) hot, sterilized jars and their lids.

Cut off the fennel stalks and feathery leaves from each fennel bulb. Set aside 12 of the most attractive fronds; discard the remaining fronds or reserve for another use. Trim the base of each bulb and remove the outer layer if bruised. Cut each bulb in half lengthwise. Remove the outermost layer of each half and cut lengthwise into strips about ¾ inch (2 cm) wide. Cut the remainder of each bulb half lengthwise into slices ¾ inch thick.

In a large nonreactive saucepan, combine the vinegar, orange juice, and mirin. Bring to a boil over medium-high heat, then immediately remove from the heat.

In a mortar, using a pestle, crush 1½ tsp of the peppercorns. Divide the crushed pepper evenly among the jars.

Divide the fennel strips evenly among the jars. Press a fennel frond against the side of each jar for visual effect, then pack the jars with the fennel slices, the orange zest strips, and the remaining fronds, alternating them and filling to within ¾ inch (2 cm) of the rims. Place ½ tsp of the remaining whole peppercorns in each jar.

Ladle the vinegar mixture into the jars, leaving ½ inch (12 mm) of headspace. Remove any air bubbles and adjust the headspace, if necessary. Add 1 Tbsp of the oil to each jar. Wipe the rims clean and seal tightly with the lids. Let the jars stand undisturbed for 24 hours, then store in the refrigerator for up to 2 weeks.

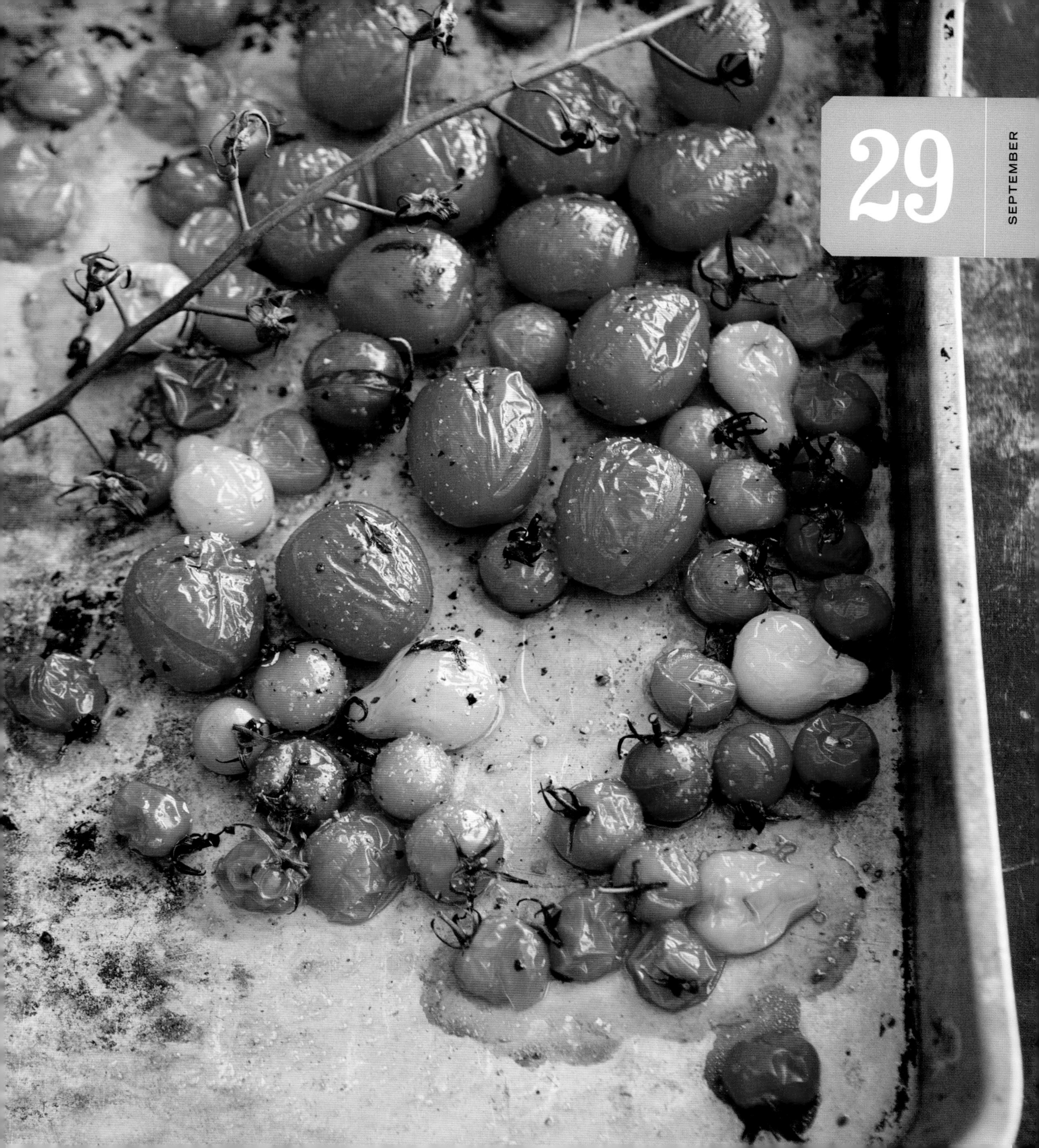

29 SEPTEMBER

In October, roots and tubers, hearty greens and crucifers flood farmers' markets. So, too, does a wide array of hearty, flavorful squashes: ribbed, deep green acorns; pear-shaped, tan butternuts; squat, green kabochas; and bumpy-skinned, mottled green turbans. Enjoy plump, sweet, bright orange pumpkins, as well, along with carrots and parsnips. By now, mushrooms have made a strong return, and it's time to make a simple mushroom ragout enriched with cream, or a mushroom and potato gratin seasoned with thyme for comforting meals.

1
ROOT-VEGETABLE TACOS WITH LIME-CILANTRO CREAM
page 226

2
CHILE-GLAZED SWEET POTATOES
page 226

3
POLENTA CROSTINI WITH CHANTERELLES
page 228

8
BEER-BATTERED ONION RINGS
page 231

9
MUSHROOMS EN PAPILLOTE
page 232

10
TOMATO & EGGPLANT TIAN
page 232

15
MUSHROOM & POTATO GRATIN WITH THYME & PARMESAN
page 237

16
BALSAMIC-ROASTED KABOCHA SQUASH
page 237

17
GRILLED PUMPKIN WITH PUMPKIN SEED DRESSING
page 238

22
BAKED ACORN SQUASH WITH LEMON & BROWN SUGAR
page 240

23
SPICY CORN CAKES WITH BLACK BEANS
page 243

24
AUTUMN MUSHROOM RAGOUT
page 243

29
CIPOLLINE IN AGRODOLCE
page 246

30
PUMPKIN PURÉE WITH TOASTED PUMPKIN SEEDS
page 246

31
SPAGHETTI SQUASH WITH PARMESAN & OREGANO
page 246

4
**CHICKPEA & SWEET
POTATO CURRY**
page 228

5
**BROCCOLI & CAULIFLOWER
WITH PICKLED ONIONS & BACON**
page 229

6
**QUICK BAKED BEANS
WITH PANCETTA**
page 229

7
BROCCOLI GRATIN
page 231

11
**TEMPURA STRING BEANS
WITH GARLIC AIOLI**
page 234

12
**FENNEL, CHICKPEA, DILL
& SUN-DRIED TOMATO SALAD**
page 234

13
**STIR-FRIED BOK CHOY WITH
SHIITAKE MUSHROOMS**
page 235

14
**ROASTED SWEET POTATO SALAD
WITH MAPLE & PECANS**
page 235

18
POMMES FRITES
page 238

19
CHARD WITH RAISINS & PINE NUTS
page 239

20
**ROASTED FENNEL
WITH FENNEL SEED**
page 239

21
**SPICED CARROT
& PARSNIP SALAD**
page 240

25
SPINACH & CHEESE TIMBALES
page 244

26
**SPICED BUTTERNUT
SQUASH TAGINE**
page 244

27
**CAULIFLOWER SOUP
WITH CHERVIL**
page 245

28
**SMASHED TURBAN SQUASH
WITH HONEY BUTTER**
page 245

october

1

ROOT-VEGETABLE TACOS WITH LIME-CILANTRO CREAM

serves 4–6

Root vegetables make this vegetarian main dish hearty and original. Adjust the amount of chili powder based on how much heat you want. In the summer months, substitute grilled seasonal vegetables that have marinated in the spice mixture for the root vegetables. Serve with a pot of beans on the side and ice-cold Mexican beer.

2 sweet potatoes, peeled and chopped

4 parsnips, peeled and cut into ¼-inch (6-mm) dice

2 Tbsp canola oil

1 Tbsp ground cumin

1 tsp ground coriander

½ tsp chili powder

Salt

FOR THE LIME-CILANTRO CREAM

½ cup (4 oz/125 g) sour cream

¼ cup (⅓ oz/10 g) finely chopped fresh cilantro, plus more for garnish

Juice of 1 lime

Salt and freshly ground pepper

FOR THE TOMATILLO SALSA

6 tomatillos, husked and halved

1 jalapeño chile, halved lengthwise and seeded

¼ cup (⅓ oz/10 g) fresh cilantro leaves

¼ white onion, roughly chopped

1 clove garlic

Salt and freshly ground pepper

10–12 small corn tortillas, warmed

Preheat the oven to 450°F (230°C). Line a baking sheet with parchment paper. Put the sweet potatoes and parsnips in a bowl. Add the oil, cumin, coriander, chili powder, and ½ tsp salt. Transfer the vegetables to the prepared sheet and spread in a single layer. Roast, stirring once, until the vegetables are caramelized, about 20 minutes.

Meanwhile, to make the lime-cilantro cream, in a small bowl, stir together the sour cream, cilantro, and lime juice. Season with salt and pepper.

To make the tomatillo salsa, preheat the broiler. Arrange the tomatillos and the jalapeño cut side down on a baking sheet. Broil until charred, about 7 minutes. Let cool briefly. Place the tomatillos, jalapeño, cilantro, onion, and garlic in a blender and purée. Season with salt and pepper. Transfer to a small bowl. ⟫

Top the lime-cilantro cream with cilantro. Place 3 Tbsp of the root vegetables on each tortilla, top with the salsa, and serve, passing the lime-cilantro cream at the table.

2

CHILE-GLAZED SWEET POTATOES

serves 4–6

Look for Beauregard, Jewel, or Hernandez sweet potatoes or the misnamed Garnet yam, all of which boast deep orange flesh. The mixture of citrus and brown sugar accentuates the sweetness of the potatoes, and the sour cream dampens the heat of the smoke-scented chipotles.

2 lb (1 kg) orange-fleshed sweet potatoes, peeled and cut into 1½-inch (4-cm) chunks

2 Tbsp canola oil

Salt

1 Tbsp firmly packed dark brown sugar

1 Tbsp finely chopped chipotle chiles in adobo

1 tsp fresh orange juice

1 tsp fresh lemon juice

¼ cup (⅓ oz/10 g) chopped fresh cilantro

½ cup (4 oz/125 g) sour cream

Preheat the oven to 400°F (200°C).

Combine the potato chunks, oil, and 1 tsp salt on a rimmed baking sheet and toss to coat well. Spread out in a single layer and bake, without turning, until tender-crisp and lightly browned, 35–40 minutes.

Remove from the oven. Using a spatula, carefully loosen the potatoes from the sheet. Sprinkle with the sugar and chipotles and turn gently to coat. Spread out in a single layer again and bake for 5 minutes.

Transfer the potatoes to a bowl and drizzle with the orange juice and lemon juice. Garnish with the cilantro and serve, passing the sour cream at the table.

3

The subtle quality of polenta makes it the perfect bed for sautéed vegetables, such as the chanterelle mushrooms that top these lightly fried polenta crostini. Aficionados insist that these trumpet-shaped golden mushrooms have a fruity aroma that recalls apricots. Be sure to add the polenta to the water slowly and to stir constantly to avoid lumps. Uncork a Merlot or Cabernet Sauvignon to accompany these elegant crostini.

POLENTA CROSTINI WITH CHANTERELLES

serves 8–10

FOR THE POLENTA

1 bay leaf

Salt and freshly ground pepper

2 Tbsp olive oil

1 cup (5 oz/155 g) polenta

1 Tbsp unsalted butter

FOR THE MUSHROOMS

4 Tbsp (2 oz/60 g) unsalted butter

3 shallots, minced

½ lb (250 g) chanterelle mushrooms, roughly chopped

Salt and freshly ground pepper

½ cup (4 oz/125 g) mascarpone cheese

2 Tbsp minced fresh flat-leaf parsley

Wedge of Parmesan cheese

To make the polenta, in a saucepan, bring 4 cups (32 fl oz/1 l) water to boil. Add the bay leaf, 1 Tbsp salt, and 1 Tbsp of the oil. Slowly add the polenta, stirring constantly. Reduce the heat to low and cook, stirring often, until the polenta pulls away from the sides of the pan, about 30 minutes. Remove and discard the bay leaf.

Rinse an 8-by-10-inch (20-by-25-cm) baking dish but do not dry. Immediately pour the polenta into the dish. It should be about ½ inch (12 mm) thick. Set aside to cool until firm, about 30 minutes.

Just before serving, prepare the mushrooms. In a large sauté pan, melt the 4 Tbsp butter over medium heat. Add the shallots and sauté until slightly wilted, about 2 minutes. Add the chanterelles, season with salt and pepper, and sauté until golden brown and tender, about 4 minutes. Remove from the heat and set aside.

Cut the cooled polenta into pieces about 1 by 2 inches (2.5 by 5 cm). In a large frying pan, melt the 1 Tbsp butter with the remaining 1 Tbsp oil over medium-high heat. Working in batches, fry the polenta pieces, turning once, until barely golden on both sides and heated through, about 3 minutes per side. ↠

Arrange the polenta on a platter. Place a small dollop of mascarpone on each piece. Spoon the mushrooms over the mascarpone, dividing them evenly, and garnish with the parsley. Using a vegetable peeler or a cheese plane, shave a little Parmesan over each piece. Serve hot.

4

This South Asian–inspired curry is distinctive on its own or served alongside chicken marinated in yogurt, lemon juice, and spices and broiled or baked. The flavors will deepen if the curry is prepared one day ahead and then reheated. Add a little water or broth to thin it when reheating.

CHICKPEA & SWEET POTATO CURRY

serves 4

2 Tbsp canola oil

1 small yellow onion, chopped

2 cloves garlic, finely chopped

1 Tbsp peeled and chopped fresh ginger

1 Thai or jalapeño chile, seeded and finely chopped

1 Tbsp Madras curry powder

Salt and freshly ground pepper

1 large sweet potato, peeled and cut into ½-inch (12-mm) cubes

1 can (15 oz/470 g) chickpeas, drained and rinsed

1 can (14 fl oz/430 ml) coconut milk

½ cup (2½ oz/75 g) frozen peas

½ cup (3 oz/90 g) canned diced tomatoes, drained

Steamed basmati rice for serving (optional)

In a large saucepan, warm the oil over medium-low heat. Add the onion, garlic, ginger, and chile and cook, stirring occasionally, until the onion is translucent, about 4 minutes. Stir in the curry powder and cook, stirring constantly, until fragrant, about 30 seconds. Season to taste with salt and pepper.

Add the sweet potato, chickpeas, coconut milk, and 1 cup (8 fl oz/250 ml) water to the pan. Raise the heat to medium-high, bring just to a boil, reduce the heat to low, and simmer, uncovered, until the sweet potato is tender, about 10 minutes. Add the peas and tomatoes and cook until heated through, about 5 minutes.

Serve the curry in bowls over steamed rice, if desired.

5

BROCCOLI & CAULIFLOWER WITH PICKLED ONIONS & BACON

serves 6–8

Although the most common cauliflower is snowy white or ivory, you can also occasionally find heads with green, orange, or purple florets. In every case, look for evenly colored, tightly packed, firm florets. The leftover pickled onions can be slipped into sandwiches or tossed into a salad of mixed lettuces and feta cheese.

2 cups (16 fl oz/500 ml) cider vinegar

3 Tbsp sugar

16 peppercorns

10 whole cloves

Salt and freshly ground pepper

1 large red onion, thinly sliced

5 slices bacon

Ice water

1 head cauliflower, cut into 1-inch (2.5-cm) florets (about 4 cups/12 oz/375 g)

1 large head broccoli, cut into 1-inch (2.5-cm) florets (about 6 cups/12 oz/375 g)

¼ cup (2 fl oz/60 ml) extra-virgin olive oil

In a small, nonreactive saucepan, combine the vinegar, sugar, peppercorns, and cloves. Season with ¼ tsp salt and bring to a boil. Reduce the heat to medium-low and simmer for 10 minutes to infuse the flavors. Pour the mixture into a heatproof nonreactive bowl, add the onion, and let stand at room temperature for 1 hour.

Meanwhile, in a large frying pan, cook the bacon over medium heat, turning once, until crisp and browned, about 7 minutes. Transfer to paper towels to drain. Let cool to room temperature and then coarsely chop.

In a large pot fitted with a steamer basket, bring 1–2 inches (5–7.5 cm) water to a boil. Have ready a large bowl of ice water. Stir 1 Tbsp salt into the ice water. Place the cauliflower florets in a single layer in the steamer basket, cover, reduce the heat to medium, and cook until tender-crisp, about 8 minutes. Transfer the cauliflower to the ice water. Let stand until cool. Using a slotted spoon, transfer the cauliflower to a large bowl. Steam the broccoli florets in the same manner until tender-crisp, about 4 minutes, then transfer to the ice water until cool. Drain well and add to the bowl with the cauliflower.

Drizzle the oil over the cauliflower and broccoli, season with salt and pepper, and toss well. Top with some of the pickled onion slices (reserve the remaining slices for another use). Sprinkle with the bacon and serve.

6

QUICK BAKED BEANS WITH PANCETTA

serves 4–6

When you are craving old-fashioned baked beans and it is almost dinnertime, this remarkably easy recipe will put them on the table in record time. Serve with sausages, a green salad, and biscuits.

¼ cup (2 fl oz/60 ml) olive oil, plus 2 Tbsp

4 oz (125 g) pancetta, coarsely chopped

1 small yellow onion, quartered

1 celery rib, cut into thirds

1 carrot, cut into thirds

4 cloves garlic, chopped

3 fresh sage leaves

2 cans (15 oz/470 g each) cannellini beans, drained and rinsed

4–6 cups (32–48 fl oz/1–1.5 l) vegetable broth or water

Salt and freshly ground pepper

2 Tbsp tomato paste

1–2 Tbsp chopped fresh flat-leaf parsley

1 tomato, peeled, seeded, and chopped

In a large, heavy ovenproof pot, warm the 2 Tbsp oil over medium heat. Add the pancetta and sauté until browned but not yet crisp, about 3 minutes. Discard all but 2 Tbsp of the fat in the pot, leaving the pancetta. Add the onion, celery, carrot, garlic, sage, and beans. Add enough broth to cover the vegetables and season with 1 tsp pepper. Bring to a simmer, cover, and transfer to the oven. Bake for 30–45 minutes. Remove from the oven.

In a small bowl, whisk together the tomato paste and 1 cup (8 fl oz/250 ml) of the hot bean cooking liquid. Add to the pot and stir to incorporate. Season with salt and pepper.

Drizzle the beans with the ¼ cup oil, garnish with the parsley and chopped tomato, and serve.

7

You can use this same technique to make a gratin with cauliflower, squash, carrots, or other vegetables. Any leftover bread crumbs can be packed into an airtight container and frozen for up to 3 months.

BROCCOLI GRATIN

serves 4

2–4 slices sourdough or coarse country bread, crusts removed

¼ cup (2 fl oz/60 ml) olive oil

½ cup (2 oz/60 g) grated Parmesan cheese

2 Tbsp capers, drained and finely chopped

2 cloves garlic, crushed

1½ lb (750 g) broccoli, stalks peeled and chopped, heads cut into small florets

3 Tbsp sour cream

Preheat the broiler. Arrange the bread slices on a baking sheet and toast in the broiler, turning once, until golden on both sides, about 2 minutes. Break into large pieces and process in a food processor to form coarse crumbs. Measure 2 cups (6 oz/185 g) crumbs. In a bowl, toss the crumbs with the oil, Parmesan, capers, and garlic.

Bring a saucepan of lightly salted water to a boil. Add the broccoli and cook for 2 minutes. Drain and cool under cold running water. Drain again and arrange in a broiler-proof shallow baking or gratin dish. Spread the sour cream over the broccoli, and sprinkle with the bread crumb mixture.

Place in the broiler and cook until the gratin is heated through and the crumbs are golden and crisp, 4–5 minutes. Remove from the broiler and serve.

8

During football season, serve these classic onion rings alongside a juicy cheeseburger, atop a grilled steak, or as an appetizer. This batter also works well with other vegetables. Try broccoli or cauliflower florets, whole cremini or button mushrooms, or thawed frozen artichoke hearts. Finish with salt and a squeeze of fresh lemon juice.

BEER-BATTERED ONION RINGS

serves 4–6

1 cup (4 oz/125 g) all-purpose flour

1 egg

Salt

¼ tsp cayenne pepper

¾ cup (6 fl oz/180 ml) lager beer

2 large yellow or Vidalia onions, about 1 lb (500 g) total

Canola oil for deep-frying

Ketchup for serving (optional)

In a bowl, whisk together the flour, egg, ½ tsp salt, and the cayenne until blended. Add the beer and whisk just until combined to make a batter. The batter may have some lumps. Let stand for 30 minutes.

Cut the onions into thick rounds, and separate the rounds into rings.

Pour oil to a depth of at least 3 inches (7.5 cm) into a large, heavy saucepan and heat over high heat to 350°F (180°C) on a deep-frying thermometer. Preheat the oven to 200°F (95°C). Set a large wire rack on a baking sheet and place near the stove.

Working in batches, dip the onion rings into the batter to coat, letting the excess drip back into the bowl, and carefully add to the hot oil. Deep-fry until golden brown, about 3 minutes. Using tongs, transfer the fried rings to the rack and keep warm in the oven. Fry the remaining onion rings, letting the oil return to 350°F between batches.

Transfer the onion rings to a platter and sprinkle with salt. Serve with ketchup, if desired.

9

MUSHROOMS EN PAPILLOTE

serves 4–6

2 Tbsp unsalted butter

1 lb (500 g) mushrooms such as chanterelle, shiitake, trumpet, portobello, or a mixture

1 tsp fresh lemon juice

2 Tbsp chopped fresh flat-leaf parsley

Salt and freshly ground pepper

Fall is the most exciting time of the year for foragers of wild mushrooms (or the lucky recipients). Here, they are baked in a parchment packet, or en papillote, which allows them to cook through without browning in their own juices. It's a great dish for entertaining.

Preheat the oven to 375°F (190°C).

Cut an 18-by-11-inch (45-by-28-cm) rectangle of parchment paper. Fold the rectangle in half crosswise. Open the parchment and coat with 1 Tbsp of the butter.

Cut the mushrooms into bite-sized pieces and place in a bowl. Cut the remaining 1 Tbsp butter into pieces and add to the bowl with the lemon juice, parsley, ½ tsp salt, and ¼ tsp pepper. Toss well and then spread the mushrooms over one-half of the prepared piece of parchment paper. Fold the other half of the parchment rectangle over the mushrooms. Starting at one side of the rectangle, fold the long edges over twice and work your way along the edge to end with a twist on both ends. Place the package on a baking sheet.

Bake until the parchment packet is puffed and the mushrooms are cooked through, about 15 minutes. Transfer the packet to a platter, carefully open the packet, and serve.

10

TOMATO & EGGPLANT TIAN

serves 6–8

2 globe or 4 Asian eggplants, cut crosswise into slices ½ inch (12 mm) thick

1–1½ Tbsp olive oil

Salt and freshly ground pepper

6 ripe, juicy tomatoes, about 3 lb (1.5 g) total

1 clove garlic, minced

1 tsp fresh thyme leaves, plus small sprigs for garnish

2–4 Tbsp (⅓ oz/10 g) chopped fresh basil (optional)

¼ cup (1 oz/30 g) coarse dried bread crumbs

1 Tbsp unsalted butter, cut into small pieces

In France, a tian is the name for both a cooking vessel and the vegetable dish that is cooked in it. Here, the last of the year's eggplants and tomatoes are seasoned with fragrant thyme, basil, and garlic in a Provençal–inspired casserole.

Preheat the oven to 400°F (200°C).

Arrange the eggplant slices in a single layer on a baking sheet. Brush both sides with the oil and sprinkle with ½ tsp salt and ¼ tsp pepper. Roast in the oven until the eggplant slices are lightly browned on the undersides and a crust has formed on the tops, about 15 minutes. Turn the slices and cook until the insides are soft and the undersides are browned, about 10 minutes.

Slice the tomatoes and put them in a bowl with their juice. Add the garlic, thyme leaves, ½ tsp salt, and ¼ tsp pepper and toss gently to mix.

Raise the oven temperature to 450°F (230°C). Generously oil a baking or gratin dish.

Arrange the eggplant slices in a layer in the prepared dish, overlapping them slightly. Sprinkle with 2 Tbsp of the basil, if using. Arrange the tomato mixture over the top, lifting the eggplant slices to allow the juices and some of the tomato slices to slip underneath. Sprinkle evenly with the bread crumbs and dot with the butter.

Bake until the tomatoes are bubbling and the bread crumbs are browned, 20–25 minutes. Sprinkle with the remaining basil, if desired, and with the thyme sprigs, and then serve.

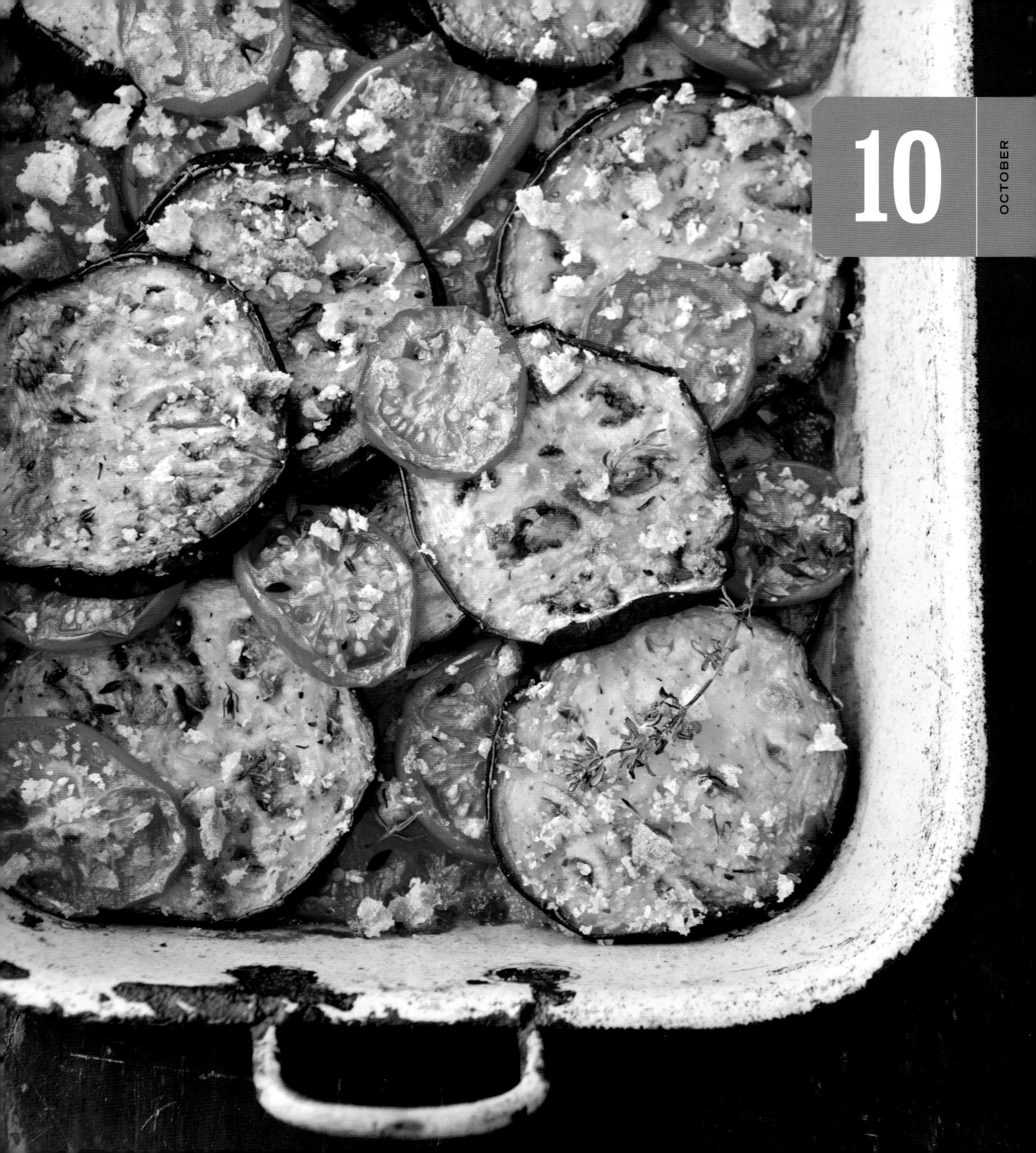

10

OCTOBER

11

TEMPURA STRING BEANS WITH GARLIC AIOLI

serves 4

The secret to creating a tempura batter that produces a light, lacy coating is to use ice water (an ice-cold batter absorbs less oil), to whisk together the ingredients just until blended (the mixture should be lumpy), and to use the batter as soon as it is assembled. Always allow the oil to return to the specified frying temperature before adding each batch of beans. Serve these irresistible green beans as an appetizer or first course.

FOR THE AIOLI

2 cloves garlic, coarsely chopped

Salt

2 eggs

2 Tbsp fresh lemon juice

1 tsp Dijon mustard

1½ cups (12 fl oz/375 ml) extra-virgin olive oil

1 cup (8 fl oz/250 ml) ice water

1 egg, beaten

¾ cup (3 oz/90 g) sifted all-purpose flour, plus more for dusting

2 or 3 ice cubes

Peanut oil for deep-frying

1 lb (500 g) green beans, trimmed

Salt

To make the aioli, in a blender, combine the garlic and ½ tsp salt and pulse until pureed. Add the eggs, lemon juice, and mustard and process until blended. With the motor running, slowly pour in the olive oil in a steady stream and process until the mixture thickens to the consistency of mayonnaise. Transfer to a bowl, cover, and refrigerate until ready to serve. (You will not need all of it; the remainder will keep for up to 4 days.)

To make the batter, in a bowl, whisk together the ice water and egg until blended. Whisk in the ¾ cup flour just until blended; the batter should be quite lumpy. Add the ice cubes. Spread flour for dusting in a shallow bowl.

Preheat the oven to 200°F (95°C). Line a baking sheet with paper towels. Pour oil to a depth of 3 inches (7.5 cm) into a wok or deep saucepan and heat to 350°F (180°C) on a deep-frying thermometer. Working in batches, lightly dust the beans with flour, then dip them in the batter, allowing the excess to drip back into the bowl. Immerse the beans in the oil and fry, stirring gently, until crisp and lightly golden, about 3 minutes. Using tongs or a slotted spoon, transfer the beans to the prepared baking sheet, season with salt, and keep warm in the oven. Arrange the beans on a platter and serve with the aioli for dipping.

12

FENNEL, CHICKPEA, DILL & SUN-DRIED TOMATO SALAD

serves 6

Fresh mozzarella cheese comes in a variety of shapes and sizes. Bocconcini are balls roughly the size of cherry tomatoes and are often marinated in olive oil and herbs and served as hors d'oeuvres. In this salad, they add both color and textural contrast to the salad.

1 can (15 oz/470 g) chickpeas, drained and rinsed

1 cup (5 oz/155 g) oil-packed sun-dried tomatoes, drained and coarsely chopped

7 Tbsp (3½ fl oz/105 ml) extra-virgin olive oil

⅔ cup (¾ oz/20 g) finely chopped fresh dill

1 tsp finely chopped fresh oregano

¼ cup (2 fl oz/60 ml) fresh lemon juice, plus 1 tsp

Salt and freshly ground pepper

1 tsp sugar

2 small fennel bulbs, cored and thinly sliced

1 head romaine lettuce, leaves torn into bite-sized pieces

6 oz (185 g) fresh mozzarella bocconcini, cut into quarters

In a bowl, toss together the chickpeas, sun-dried tomatoes, 1 Tbsp of the oil, 2 Tbsp of the dill, the oregano, 1 tsp lemon juice, ¼ tsp salt, and several grinds of pepper. Let stand at room temperature for 15 minutes.

In a small bowl, whisk together the ¼ cup lemon juice, the sugar, ¼ tsp salt, and several grinds of pepper until the sugar dissolves. Slowly whisk in the remaining oil until well blended.

In a large bowl, toss together the fennel, lettuce, remaining dill, ¼ tsp salt, and several grinds of pepper. Whisk the dressing and then drizzle over the lettuce mixture and toss well. Arrange on plates, top with the chickpea mixture and the mozzarella, and serve.

13

STIR-FRIED BOK CHOY
WITH SHIITAKE MUSHROOMS

serves 4–6

¼ cup (2 fl oz/60 ml) chicken broth

1 Tbsp Chinese rice wine

1 Tbsp oyster sauce

1 Tbsp ginger juice

1 tsp Asian sesame oil

½ tsp sugar

½ tsp cornstarch

1 lb (500 g) bok choy

8 shiitake mushrooms

4 Tbsp (2 fl oz/60 ml) canola oil

4 cloves garlic

Crisply cooked vegetables are characteristic of the Chinese table. Here, bok choy and meaty fresh shiitake mushrooms are briefly stir-fried and then flavored with a trio of seasonings from the Asian pantry: rice wine, oyster sauce, and ginger juice. To make the ginger juice, peel and grate fresh ginger, then wrap the grated ginger in cheesecloth and squeeze to release the juice. Look for small heads of bok choy for this dish.

In a small bowl, whisk together the broth, rice wine, oyster sauce, ginger juice, sesame oil, sugar, and cornstarch to make a stir-fry sauce. Just before using, stir briefly to recombine.

Trim the stem ends from the bok choy, then quarter each head lengthwise. Remove the stems from the mushrooms and halve the caps.

In a wok or large frying pan, heat 1 Tbsp of the canola oil over high heat. Add 2 of the garlic cloves and stir-fry until golden brown, about 20 seconds. Discard the garlic. Quickly add half of the bok choy to the hot pan and stir-fry until just wilted, 3–4 minutes. Transfer to a colander. Add 1 Tbsp of the oil to the pan and stir-fry the remaining garlic and bok choy in the same manner. Set the bok choy aside in the colander to drain.

In the same pan, heat the remaining 2 Tbsp oil over high heat. Add the mushrooms and stir-fry until they release their juices, 4–5 minutes. Return the bok choy to the pan, add the sauce, and stir-fry until the bok choy is hot and the sauce has thickened slightly, 1–2 minutes longer. Transfer to a platter and serve.

14

ROASTED SWEET POTATO
SALAD WITH MAPLE & PECANS

serves 4–6

3 lb (1.5 kg) sweet potatoes, peeled and cut into 1-inch (2.5-cm) chunks

2 Tbsp olive oil

Salt and freshly ground pepper

⅓ cup (3 fl oz/80 ml) fresh lime juice

3 Tbsp maple syrup

½ cup (2 oz/60 g) pecans, toasted

½ cup (3 oz/90 g) minced green onions, white and tender green parts

¼ cup (⅓ oz/10 g) chopped fresh cilantro

This colorful roasted vegetable salad is delicious alongside thick steaks. Use any variety of sweet potato you like, including the ones sometimes labeled "garnet yams," which have a pale salmon skin and bright orange, moist, sweet flesh.

Preheat the oven to 400°F (200°C).

Put the sweet potato chunks in a large baking pan, drizzle with 1½ Tbsp of the oil, sprinkle with ½ tsp salt, and stir to coat. Spread the potatoes in a single layer and roast, stirring occasionally, until tender when pierced with a knife, 25–30 minutes.

Meanwhile, in a large bowl, stir together the lime juice, maple syrup, and the remaining 1½ tsp oil. Add the roasted potatoes along with the pecans, green onions, and cilantro. Mix well, season with salt and pepper, and serve.

15

MUSHROOM & POTATO GRATIN WITH THYME & PARMESAN

serves 4–6

Using a combination of wild and cultivated mushrooms, such as chanterelle, cremini, and button, gives this gratin a deep earthiness that enhances the buttery Yukon gold potatoes. Savory garlic, luxurious cream, fragrant thyme, and salty Parmesan bring increased dimension to the dish. Other yellow-fleshed potatoes, such as Yellow Finn or Russian Banana, can be substituted for the Yukon gold.

1½ cups (12 fl oz/375 ml) heavy cream

1 clove garlic, thinly sliced

3 fresh thyme sprigs, plus 1½ tsp minced thyme leaves

Salt and freshly ground pepper

2 lb (1 kg) Yukon gold potatoes, peeled and cut into slices about ⅛ inch (3 mm) thick

1 Tbsp unsalted butter

1 Tbsp olive oil

1 lb (500 g) mixed wild and cultivated mushrooms, tough stems removed and medium and large caps sliced

4 Tbsp (2 oz/60 g) grated Parmesan cheese

Preheat the oven to 375°F (190°C). Butter an 8-inch (20-cm) baking dish.

In a saucepan, combine the cream, garlic, thyme sprigs, and a pinch each of salt and pepper. Bring to a low boil over medium heat, and then remove from the heat. Gently stir the potato slices into the cream mixture, cover, and let stand while you cook the mushrooms.

In a frying pan, melt the butter with the oil over medium heat. Add the mushrooms and a pinch of salt and sauté until the liquid released by the mushrooms evaporates, 7–9 minutes. Add the minced thyme, season with pepper, and cook for 1 minute.

Using a slotted spoon, remove the potatoes from the cream. Arrange one-third of the potato slices, slightly overlapping, on the bottom of the prepared dish. Season lightly with salt and pepper and sprinkle with 1 Tbsp of the Parmesan. Spread half of the mushrooms over the potatoes and sprinkle with another 1 Tbsp of the Parmesan. Repeat the layers, using half of the remaining potatoes and all of the remaining mushrooms, and sprinkling with salt, pepper, and 1 Tbsp Parmesan between the layers of vegetables. Top with the remaining potatoes and season with salt and pepper. Using a spatula, gently press on the vegetables to compact them. Pour the cream mixture through a strainer into the dish and sprinkle with the remaining 1 Tbsp Parmesan. ⇥

Cover the dish with foil and bake until the potatoes are tender when pierced with a knife, about 45 minutes. Remove the foil and bake until the gratin is golden brown and bubbly, about 20 minutes. Let stand for about 10 minutes before serving.

16

BALSAMIC-ROASTED KABOCHA SQUASH

serves 4

This is a simple preparation for kabocha squash, a dense-fleshed, sweet winter squash. Also known as Japanese pumpkin, kabocha is a general term for a family of Japanese squashes that vary in color and shape. Use a top-quality balsamic vinegar for the right balance of sweetness. Line your baking pan with aluminum foil to speed cleanup.

1 kabocha squash, about 2½ lb (1.25 kg)

2 Tbsp olive oil

Salt and freshly ground pepper

2 Tbsp balsamic vinegar

Preheat the oven to 400°F (200°C).

Cut the squash in half lengthwise. Scoop out and discard the seeds. Cut the flesh crosswise into wedges ½–¾ inch (12 mm–2 cm) thick. Peel each wedge.

Put the squash wedges on a baking sheet, drizzle with the oil, and toss to coat. Arrange in a single layer. Season with ¼ tsp salt and a few grinds of pepper. Roast, stirring twice, until the squash is browned and tender when pierced with a knife, 15–18 minutes.

Drizzle the squash with the vinegar, return to the oven, and continue roasting until the vinegar evaporates, about 3 minutes. Let the squash cool slightly before serving.

17

GRILLED PUMPKIN WITH PUMPKIN SEED DRESSING

serves 4–6

¼ cup (1 oz/30 g) pumpkin seeds

½ cup (4 fl oz/125 ml) fresh orange juice

1 Tbsp grape seed oil

1 small red chile, seeded and minced

Salt and freshly ground pepper

1 Sugar Pie pumpkin, ¾–1 lb (375–500 g)

2 Tbsp olive oil

2 green onions, tender white and green parts, thinly sliced

2 Tbsp chopped fresh cilantro (optional)

If October brings some sunny afternoons, roll out the grill and put some wedges of Sugar Pie pumpkin over the flame. Or, if the weather has turned, use a stove-top grill pan, or pop the wedges under the broiler. Either way, the roughly textured pumpkin seed dressing is an unexpected topping.

Prepare a charcoal or gas grill for direct-heat grilling over medium-low heat. Oil the grill rack.

Place the pumpkin seeds in a small, dry frying pan over medium heat and toast, stirring occasionally, until golden, 3–4 minutes. In a blender or food processor, combine the pumpkin seeds, orange juice, grape seed oil, and chile. Season with ½ tsp salt and several grinds of pepper. Process to make a dressing that is almost smooth but retains some texture.

Cut the pumpkin in half lengthwise and remove and discard the seeds. Cut the halves lengthwise into wedges about 3 inch (7.5 cm) thick, and then cut each wedge crosswise into slices about ¼ inch (6 mm) thick. Transfer to a bowl, add the oil, season with salt and pepper, and turn to coat the pumpkin.

Arrange the pumpkin wedges on the grill and cook, turning often, until lightly browned and nearly fork-tender, 8–10 minutes. Transfer to a cutting board and let cool.

Place the squash wedges in a bowl, pour in the dressing, and toss gently to combine. Sprinkle with the green onions and the cilantro, if using, and serve.

18

POMMES FRITES

serves 4

4 or 5 russet baking potatoes

Canola oil for deep-frying

Salt

The secret to great French fries—a creamy interior and a crunchy exterior—is to fry them twice. The first frying cooks the potatoes, and the second frying browns and crisps them. Once you have mastered the cooking technique, you can dress up your fries with sautéed minced garlic, or chopped parsley.

Have ready a bowl of cold water. Peel the potatoes and cut them lengthwise into slices ¼ inch (6 mm) thick. Stack the slices and cut them again lengthwise to form sticks ¼ inch (6 mm) wide. As the potatoes are cut, slip them into the cold water. When all the potatoes have been cut, let them stand in the water for 30–60 minutes.

Just before cooking, drain the potatoes and pat dry thoroughly. Line a large plate with paper towels. Pour oil to a depth of 4 inches (10 cm) into a deep, heavy frying pan and heat to 350°F (180°C) on a deep-frying thermometer. Carefully add about one-fourth of the potatoes to the hot oil and fry until they form a white crust but do not brown, about 2 minutes. Using a slotted spoon, transfer the potatoes to the paper towels to drain. Repeat with the remaining potatoes, allowing the oil to return to 350°F before adding the next batch.

Let the potatoes rest for at least 5 minutes or up to 4 hours before frying a second time. Working in batches, repeat the process, but fry the potatoes until they form a golden crust, about 3 minutes. Transfer to fresh paper towels to drain.

Sprinkle each batch with salt and serve.

19

The addition of raisins and a scattering of pine nuts intensifies the natural sweetness of chard in this Spanish-inspired dish. The dry-cured serrano ham adds a savory edge; look for it at specialty food stores.

CHARD WITH RAISINS & PINE NUTS

serves 4

¼ cup (1½ oz/45 g) raisins, preferably golden

3 Tbsp olive oil

3 Tbsp pine nuts

1¾ lb (875 g) chard

2 cloves garlic, cut lengthwise into 4 slices

1 thick slice serrano ham or prosciutto, about 2 oz (60 g), finely chopped

Salt and freshly ground pepper

In a small bowl, combine the raisins with warm water to cover. Let stand until plump, about 15 minutes, and then drain.

In a frying pan, warm 1 Tbsp of the oil over medium heat. Add the pine nuts and cook, tossing often, until the nuts are just golden, about 2 minutes. Pour onto a plate and let cool.

Trim off the chard stems. Select the most slender stems and cut into ½-inch (12-mm) pieces. Remove the tough center vein from the leaves by cutting along either side and lifting it out. Cut the leaves crosswise into strips 1 inch (2.5 cm) wide.

In a frying pan, heat the remaining 2 Tbsp oil over medium-high heat. Add the garlic and cook, stirring occasionally, until golden on both sides, 2–3 minutes. Discard the garlic. Add the chard stems and ham and cook, stirring, until the ham is golden, about 1 minute. Mix in the chard leaves, cover the pan, and cook for 1 minute. Using tongs, turn the chard so the unwilted leaves are moved to the bottom of the pan. Cover and cook for 1 minute. Repeat once or twice until all the leaves are wilted. Add the raisins and cook uncovered, stirring frequently, until most of the liquid evaporates and the chard is tender, 3–5 minutes. Season with salt and pepper.

Transfer to a bowl, sprinkle with the pine nuts, and serve.

20

This recipe takes advantage of every part of the fennel bulb: the seeds are toasted in a dry pan, the bulbs are cut into wedges and roasted in the oven with the toasted seeds, and the chopped fronds are used as a garnish. Serve alongside poultry or seafood, such as meaty chicken thighs or firm halibut or other whitefish fillets.

ROASTED FENNEL WITH FENNEL SEED

serves 4

1 tsp fennel seeds

3 fennel bulbs, with stems and fronds

2 Tbsp olive oil

½ cup (4 fl oz/125 ml) dry white wine

Salt

¼ cup (2 fl oz/60 ml) vegetable broth, chicken broth, or water

Preheat the oven to 400°F (200°C). Place the fennel seeds in a small frying pan and toast over low heat, shaking the pan frequently, until fragrant, 2–3 minutes. Transfer the seeds to a mortar and crush and grind the seeds with a pestle.

Cut the stalks from the fennel bulbs, reserving a handful of green fronds. Lightly chop enough fronds to measure about ¼ cup (⅓ oz/10 g). Remove any bruised outer leaves from the fennel bulbs and cut the bulbs into wedges about 1½ inch (4 cm) thick. Arrange in a small baking dish. Drizzle with the oil and wine, season with salt, and sprinkle with the crushed fennel seeds. Add the broth and sprinkle with the chopped fennel fronds. Toss to coat evenly.

Cover the dish with foil. Roast in the oven for 30 minutes. Remove the foil and continue roasting until the fennel is golden and tender when pierced with a knife, 15–20 minutes. Remove from the oven and serve warm.

21

SPICED CARROT & PARSNIP SALAD

serves 6

¼ tsp ground cinnamon

¼ tsp ground cumin

¼ tsp ground coriander

⅛ tsp ground ginger

3 large carrots, about ¾ lb (375 g) total

3 large parsnips, about ¾ lb (375 g) total

¼ cup (2 fl oz/60 ml) fresh lemon juice

1 Tbsp honey

¾ tsp prepared harissa

Salt and freshly ground pepper

6 Tbsp (3 fl oz/90 ml) extra-virgin olive oil

½ cup (2 oz/60 g) pistachios, toasted and coarsely chopped

⅔ cup (4 oz/125 g) raisins

¼ cup (⅓ oz/10 g) coarsely chopped fresh cilantro

Harissa, a North African chile-and-spice paste, adds a suggestion of heat to this salad, a flavorful tangle of earthy and sweet ingredients. If you are pressed for time and have a coarse shredding disk for your food processor, use it to shred the carrots and parsnips.

In a small, heavy frying pan, toast the cinnamon, cumin, coriander, and ginger over medium-low heat, stirring constantly, until fragrant, about 2 minutes. Let cool to room temperature.

Peel the carrots and parsnips and shred them on the large holes of a grater-shredder.

In a small bowl, whisk together the toasted spices, lemon juice, honey, and harissa. Season with ½ tsp salt. Slowly whisk in the oil until well blended.

In a bowl, stir together the pistachios and a pinch of salt. Add the carrots and parsnips, raisins, ½ tsp salt, and several grinds of pepper. Pour in the dressing and toss well. Sprinkle with the cilantro and serve.

22

BAKED ACORN SQUASH WITH LEMON & BROWN SUGAR

serves 4–6

2 acorn squashes, about 1½ lb (750 g) each

2 Tbsp olive oil

Salt and freshly ground pepper

4 Tbsp (2 oz/60 g) firmly packed golden brown sugar

1½ Tbsp fresh lemon juice

Winter squashes, such as acorn, butternut, kabocha, and pumpkin, have hard skins and dense, sweet flesh that is rich in vitamins. An acorn squash creates two perfect servings when you cut one in half, scoop out the seeds, and bake until tender. Brush the cavities with brown sugar for a hit of comfort.

Preheat the oven to 425°F (220°C).

Cut each squash in half lengthwise and scoop out the seeds. Place the halves, cut sides up, on a rimmed baking sheet. Pour water to a depth of ¼ inch (6 mm) into the baking sheet. Brush the cut side of each squash half with 1½ tsp oil, and sprinkle the halves with salt and pepper. Sprinkle 1 Tbsp of the brown sugar into each half.

Bake until the squash halves are tender and the sugar melts and caramelizes, about 45 minutes. Transfer the squash halves to a platter and drizzle evenly with the lemon juice. Serve warm or at room temperature.

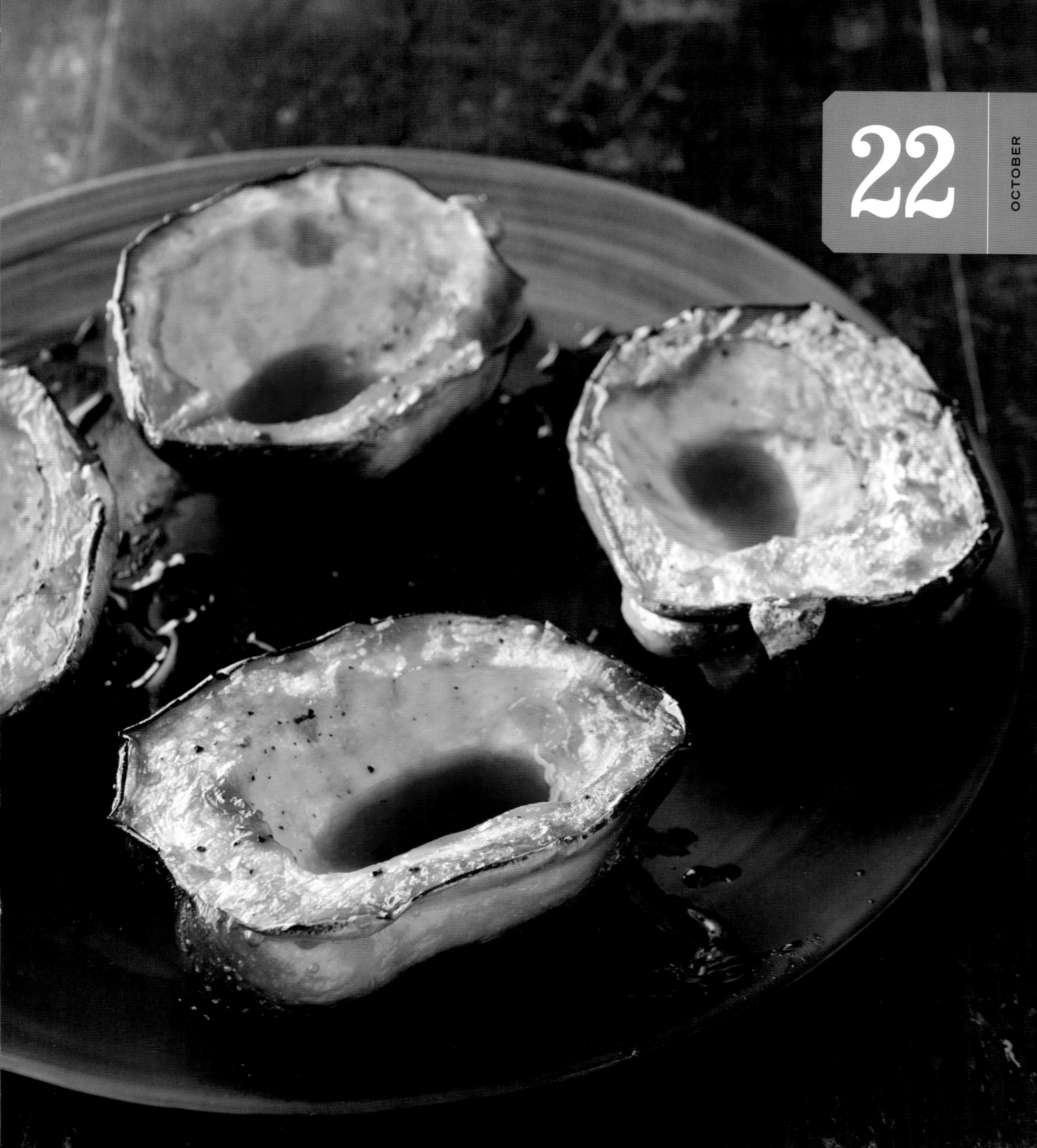

23

SPICY CORN CAKES WITH BLACK BEANS

serves 4

1 can (15 oz/470 g) black beans, drained and rinsed

1 tsp chopped fresh oregano, plus more for garnish

2 tsp chili powder

2/3 cup (3 oz/90 g) stone-ground yellow cornmeal

2 Tbsp all-purpose flour

1/4 tsp baking soda

Salt and freshly ground pepper

3 Tbsp unsalted butter, melted

1 cup (8 fl oz/250 ml) buttermilk

1 egg

1/2 cup (3 oz/90 g) fresh corn kernels, cut from 1 ear of corn

2 tsp canola oil, or as needed

Black beans and stone-ground cornmeal get a kick from chili powder in these substantial cakes. For even more flavor, top corn cakes with sour cream, purchased or homemade salsa, and chopped cilantro. To make a quick homemade salsa combine 1 tomato, seeded and chopped; 1/2 onion, chopped; 2 tablespoons chopped fresh cilantro; and fresh lime juice to taste.

In a large saucepan, stir together the beans, oregano, and 1 tsp of the chili powder. Cook over medium heat, stirring occasionally, until the beans are heated through. Remove from the heat and cover to keep warm.

In a bowl, whisk together the cornmeal, flour, baking soda, remaining 1 tsp chili powder, 1/2 tsp salt, and 1/8 tsp pepper. In another bowl, whisk together the butter, buttermilk, and egg until well combined. Working quickly, mix the wet ingredients into the dry ingredients until just blended, leaving small lumps. Fold in the corn.

Heat a large cast-iron frying pan over medium-high heat. Brush with 1 tsp of the oil. Working in batches, add the batter, using 1/4 cup (2 fl oz/60 ml) for each pancake. Cook the pancakes, turning once, until browned and puffy, about 4 minutes total. Transfer to a plate and cover loosely with foil. Stir the batter and brush the pan with more oil as needed between batches.

Arrange the pancakes on a platter or plates, top with the beans, sprinkle lightly with oregano, and serve.

24

AUTUMN MUSHROOM RAGOUT

serves 4

2 lb (1 kg) mixed fresh mushrooms such as chanterelle, oyster, black trumpet, shiitake, cremini, and white button

2 Tbsp unsalted butter

1 red onion, finely chopped

Salt and freshly ground pepper

1/2 cup (4 fl oz/125 ml) dry white wine

1 cup (8 fl oz/250 ml) vegetable or chicken broth

1/2 oz (15 g) dried porcini mushrooms, broken into small pieces

1/2 cup (4 fl oz/125 ml) heavy cream, or as needed

Small pinch of freshly grated nutmeg

1 Tbsp chopped fresh chives or chervil

Gather together a bounty of wild mushrooms to make this autumn classic. Don't dunk them in water to wash them, rather gently brush them with a soft brush or a damp kitchen towel to loosen and remove any dirt or grit. Dried porcini mushrooms add depth to the broth, and a splash of cream contributes richness. Spoon the ragout over buttered egg noodles or creamy polenta.

Cut the mushrooms coarsely but evenly. In a large frying pan, melt the butter over medium heat. Add the onion and sauté until softened, about 3 minutes. Add the mushrooms, raise the heat to medium-high, and sauté until lightly browned in places, 3–5 minutes.

Season with salt and pepper and add the wine. Raise the heat to high and cook until the wine is nearly evaporated, about 3 minutes. Add the broth and the dried mushrooms, reduce the heat to medium, and cook until the fresh mushrooms are tender and the dried mushrooms are rehydrated, about 10 minutes.

Stir in the 1/2 cup cream and the nutmeg. Adjust the seasoning if necessary. Add more cream as desired to create a creamy but light sauce. Transfer to a bowl, sprinkle with the chives, and serve.

25

These delicate savory custards make an unusual and appealing side dish alongside roasted meat. Or, for an attractive first course, add a swirl of tomato sauce to the top of each timbale. You can substitute chard or kale for the spinach; increase the cooking time for the greens to about 10 minutes.

SPINACH & CHEESE TIMBALES

serves 8

1 bunch spinach, about ¾ lb (375 g), stems removed

4 eggs

1½ cups (12 fl oz/375 ml) whole milk, warmed

⅓ cup (¾ oz/20 g) fresh bread crumbs

½ cup (2 oz/60 g) shredded Cheddar cheese

1 tsp minced yellow onion

Salt and freshly ground pepper

Preheat the oven to 325°F (165°C). Butter eight ½–¾ cup (4–6 fl oz/125–180 ml) custard cups or similar ovenproof dishes, or butter a 9-inch (23-cm) gratin dish.

In a large saucepan, combine the spinach with water to cover by 2 inches (5 cm). Place over high heat and cook until the spinach is tender but still bright green, about 5 minutes. Drain and rinse under running cold water. Squeeze dry, then mince. Squeeze dry again and set aside. You should have about ½ cup (3½ oz/105 g).

In a large bowl, whisk the eggs until blended, then whisk in the milk, bread crumbs, cheese, spinach, and onion. Season with ½ tsp salt and ¼ tsp pepper. Divide the mixture evenly among the prepared cups or pour into the dish. Place the cups or dish in a baking pan. Pour hot water into the pan to reach halfway up the sides of the cups or dish.

Bake until a toothpick inserted into the middle comes out clean and the surface is lightly golden, 40–50 minutes. To serve the cups, remove from the water bath and let cool for about 10 minutes. Run a thin-bladed knife around the inside edge of a cup, invert a serving plate over the cup, invert the plate and cup together, and lift off the cup. To serve the gratin dish, unmold the same way onto a platter, then cut into slices. Serve warm.

26

This fragrant Moroccan stew combines winter squash, sweet potato, onion, and carrot with an aromatic blend of spices and the sweetness of dried currants and honey. It is traditionally cooked in a conical earthenware pot known as a tagine, but a Dutch oven or other heavy pot can be substituted. Butternut squash is the ideal for this dish, as it contains less water than many other types.

SPICED BUTTERNUT SQUASH TAGINE

serves 6

6–8 saffron threads

2 Tbsp olive oil

1 large yellow onion, finely chopped

1 tsp ground ginger

½ tsp ground cinnamon

½ tsp ground turmeric

1 butternut squash, about ¼ lb (625 g), halved, seeded, peeled, and cut into 1-inch (2.5-cm) cubes

1 large carrot, cut on the diagonal into slices ½ inch (12 mm) thick

2 plum tomatoes, halved, seeded, and chopped

3 Tbsp dried currants

1 Tbsp honey

Salt and freshly ground pepper

1 large sweet potato, about ½ lb (250 g), peeled, halved lengthwise, and then each half cut crosswise into slices ¾ inch (2 cm) thick

In a small bowl, combine the saffron with 1 Tbsp warm water and let soak for 10 minutes.

In a large, heavy pot, heat the oil over medium-high heat. Add the onion and cook, stirring frequently, until softened, about 5 minutes. Stir in the ginger, cinnamon, and turmeric and cook, stirring, until the spices are fragrant, about 30 seconds. Add the squash, carrot, tomato, currants, honey, and saffron with its soaking liquid. Pour in ¾ cup (6 fl oz/180 ml) water. Season with salt and pepper. Bring to a boil, reduce the heat to medium, cover, and simmer for 10 minutes.

Add the sweet potato to the pot and cook, covered, until the vegetables are tender but still hold their shape, about 25 minutes. Ladle into bowls and serve hot.

27

CAULIFLOWER SOUP
WITH CHERVIL

serves 6

**1 small head cauliflower,
about ¾ lb (375 g)**

**1 waxy potato, about ½ lb (250 g),
peeled and chopped**

**3¼–3½ cups (26–28 fl oz/810–875 ml)
whole milk**

Salt and freshly ground white pepper

2 Tbsp unsalted butter

⅛ tsp freshly grated nutmeg

¼ cup (⅓ oz/10 g) fresh chervil leaves

*This is one of
the many creamy
vegetable soups
typical of French
home cooking.
A vegetable, in this
case cauliflower, is
cooked with milk or
a mixture of cream
and milk, seasoned
and puréed, and
then garnished
with fresh herbs.
Sometimes a little
potato is added to
thicken the soup,
as is done here.*

Coarsely chop the cauliflower, including
the core. Bring a large saucepan of water to
a boil. Add the cauliflower and potato, reduce
the heat to medium, and cook until the
vegetables soften slightly, about 5 minutes.
Drain well and return to the pan.

Add 2½ cups (20 fl oz/625 ml) of the
milk and ½ tsp salt and bring to a boil
over medium-high heat. Reduce the heat
to medium, cover, and cook until the
cauliflower and potato are easily pierced
with a fork, 15–20 minutes.

Working in batches, purée the soup in
a blender or food processor until smooth,
adding the remaining milk as needed
to reach the desired creamy consistency.

Transfer the soup to a clean saucepan and
bring to a simmer over medium heat. Stir
in the butter, nutmeg, and ¼ tsp pepper.
Ladle into bowls, garnish with the chervil,
and serve.

28

SMASHED TURBAN SQUASH
WITH HONEY BUTTER

serves 4

1 turban squash, about 2½ lb (1.25 kg)

2 Tbsp unsalted butter

**3 Tbsp mild honey such as wildflower
or orange blossom**

Salt and freshly ground pepper

*Turban squash are
brightly colored and
uniquely shaped,
with a bulblike
cap on a flat base.
Drizzle the squash
with a simple sauce
of melted butter and
honey to enhance its
natural sweetness.*

Preheat the oven to 375°F (190°C). Place the
squash on a baking sheet and roast until the
skin begins to look hard and shiny and pulls
away from the flesh and the squash is easily
pierced with a knife, about 2¼ hours.

Just before the squash is ready, in a small
saucepan, combine the butter and honey.
Cook over medium-high heat, stirring, until
the butter melts and the honey is incorporated,
about 3 minutes. Keep warm.

Transfer the squash to a cutting board
and let cool until it can be handled. Cut the
squash in half and scoop out and discard
the seeds and strings. Scoop out the flesh
and spread in a serving dish, breaking up
any chunks. Season with ½ tsp salt and
½ tsp pepper. Pour the honey butter over
the squash and serve.

29

CIPOLLINE IN AGRODOLCE

serves 6–8

1 lb (500 g) cipollini onions, each
about 1½ inches (4 cm) in diameter

2 cups (16 fl oz/500 ml) white wine vinegar

2 cups (16 fl oz/500 ml) balsamic vinegar

3 Tbsp granulated sugar

3 Tbsp firmly packed golden brown sugar

Salt

Agrodolce—"sweet and sour"—is a popular flavoring in southern Italy, where it is traditionally achieved by mixing vinegar and sugar. For this recipe, use inexpensive balsamic vinegar to make the sauce. Cipolline are small, flat Italian onions; large pearl onions or small boiling onions can be substituted. Serve these piquant onions as part of an antipasto platter that includes cheeses and cured meats, such as prosciutto and coppa.

At least 1 week before you plan to serve the onions, bring a large saucepan of water to a boil. Add the onions and cook for 30 seconds. Drain, rinse under cold running water, and drain again. Trim off the root end of each onion and slip off the skin. Do not cut too deeply into the onions or they will fall apart.

In a nonreactive saucepan, combine the white wine and balsamic vinegars, the granulated and brown sugars, and ¼ tsp salt. Bring to a boil over medium-high heat, stirring to dissolve the sugars. Add the onions and cook until softened when pierced with a knife, 2–3 minutes. Let cool for about 1 hour.

Transfer the onions and liquid to a nonreactive container, making sure that the onions are submerged in the liquid. Cover and let stand for 1 week at room temperature, to allow the onions to mellow and absorb the flavors. The onions will keep for up to 6 months in the refrigerator.

30

PUMPKIN PURÉE WITH TOASTED PUMPKIN SEEDS

serves 4

½ cup (2½ oz/75 g) pepitas

1 Sugar Pie pumpkin, about 2 lb (1 kg)

1 tsp ground cinnamon

½ tsp ground cloves

½ tsp ground nutmeg

Salt

Don't try to use a carving pumpkin here. "Cooking" pumpkins have denser flesh and a sweeter flavor and are not as fibrous. If you cannot find a Sugar Pie pumpkin, Sugar Baby, Autumn Gold, and Long Island Cheese pumpkins are also good choices for baking.

Preheat the oven to 350°F (180°C). In a small, dry frying pan, toast the pumpkin seeds over medium heat, stirring occasionally, until they begin to darken. Transfer to a plate to cool.

Place the pumpkin on a baking sheet and bake until tender, about 1 hour. Remove from the oven, let cool until it can be handled, cut in half, discard the seeds and scoop the flesh into a food processor. Process until smooth, then stir in the spices and salt to taste. Spoon into bowls, sprinkle with the seeds, and serve.

31

SPAGHETTI SQUASH WITH PARMESAN & OREGANO

serves 3 or 4

1 spaghetti squash, about 2 lb (1 kg),
halved lengthwise and seeded

1 Tbsp olive oil

½ tsp minced garlic

Salt and freshly ground pepper

¼ cup (1 oz/30 g) grated Parmesan cheese

1 tsp chopped fresh oregano

The hard exterior of spaghetti squash betrays the delicate flesh within. Bake the halves as you would any other winter squash, and then scrape out the flesh with a fork; it will naturally separate into pasta-like strands.

Preheat the oven to 350°F (180°C).

Place the squash halves, cut side down, in a baking dish and add ⅓ cup (3 fl oz/80 ml) water. Bake until tender, about 1 hour. Transfer to a cutting board and let cool.

Using a fork, scrape out the flesh, forming noodlelike strands, scraping all the way to the skin. Place the squash in a bowl. Add the oil, garlic, ½ tsp salt, and ½ tsp pepper. Stir gently to mix well. Sprinkle with the Parmesan and toss to combine. Sprinkle with the oregano and serve.

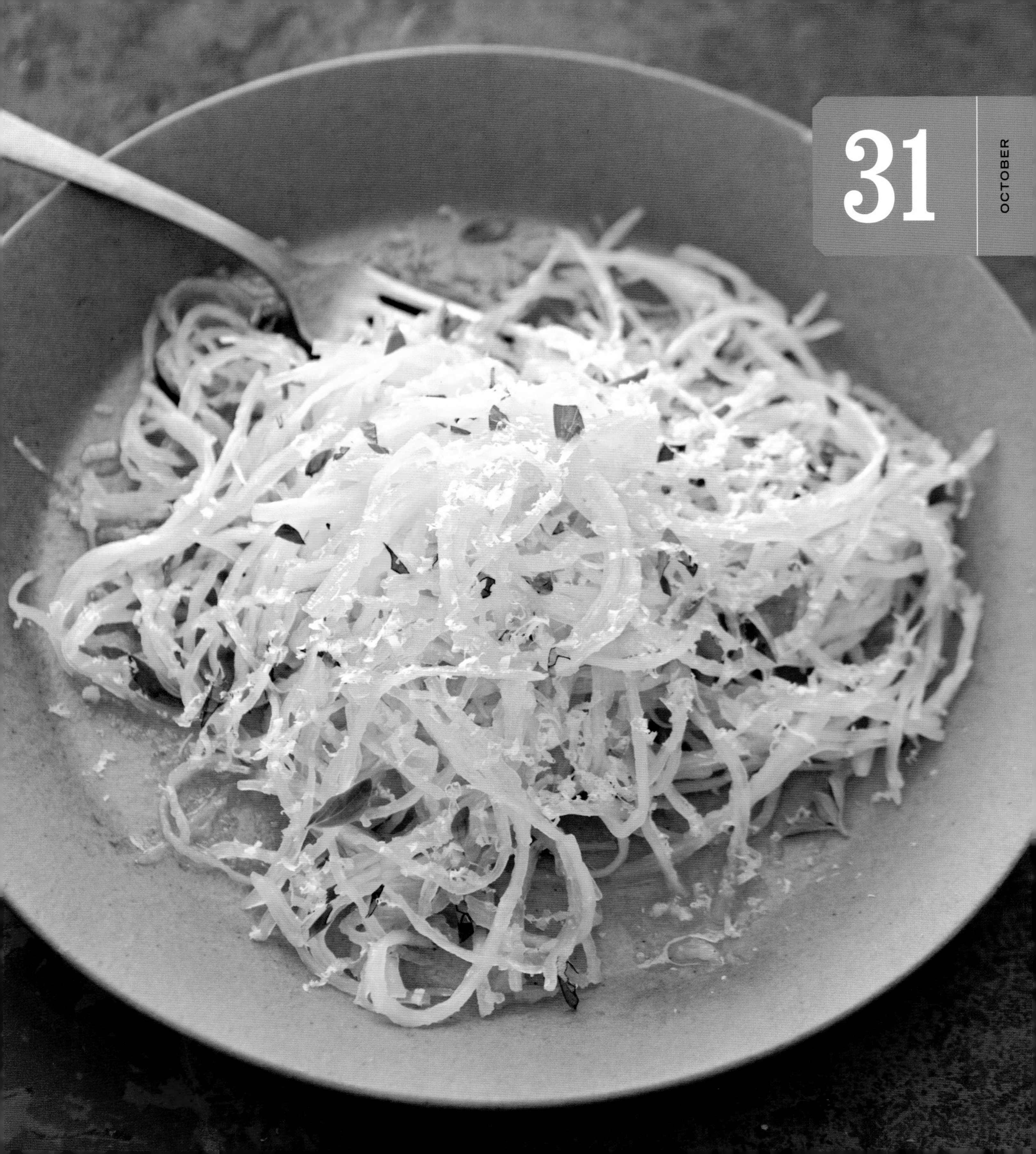

November has cooks pulling out baking dishes and roasting pans, whether for big, festive gatherings or simple dinners with family and friends. Feature vegetables that are time-tested favorites, such as roasted broccoli with pine nuts, green beans in an updated casserole, or pumpkin crowned with golden bread crumbs. Winter squashes and sweet potatoes marry sweetness and spice with holiday-inspired ingredients, like maple syrup, cinnamon, and nutmeg. Try pairing vegetables with autumn fruits, too, such as potatoes and apples in a golden brown galette, or sweet-potato hash studded with cranberries.

4

**BAKED ENDIVE WITH
TOMATOES & PANCETTA**
page 253

5

**SWEET POTATO &
CRANBERRY HASH**
page 254

6

MODERN GREEN BEAN CASSEROLE
page 254

7

SAVOY CABBAGE & TURNIP SAUTÉ
page 255

11

**GRILLED RADICCHIO WITH
BALSAMIC & PARMESAN**
page 258

12

**BAKED PUMPKIN WITH
WHITE BEANS, CARAMELIZED
ONIONS & ROASTED GARLIC**
page 258

13

**MUSHROOM & BROCCOLI
BROWN RICE PILAF**
page 259

14

**ROASTED ACORN SQUASH
WITH CHIPOTLE & CILANTRO**
page 259

18

**WARM SQUASH WITH
SPICED COUSCOUS**
page 262

19

**SPAGHETTI SQUASH
WITH TOMATO SAUCE**
page 263

20

GRATIN DAUPHINOIS
page 263

21

**ROASTED PARSNIPS & SWEET POTATO
WITH HAZELNUTS & BROWN BUTTER**
page 264

25

BUTTERNUT SQUASH LASAGNA
page 267

26

**CABBAGE, ASIAN PEAR
& GINGER SLAW**
page 267

27

**INDIAN-SPICED PUMPKIN
WITH CASHEWS**
page 269

28

**RUTABAGA & GOLDEN BEETS
WITH POMEGRANATE SEEDS**
page 269

november

1

POTATO & APPLE GALETTE

serves 6–8

4 large russet potatoes,
about 2 lb (1 kg) total, peeled

2 Granny Smith, pippin, or Gravenstein
apples, peeled, halved, and cored

1 egg, lightly beaten

½ cup (2½ oz/75 g) all-purpose flour

Salt and freshly ground pepper

2 Tbsp unsalted butter

2 Tbsp olive oil

*This simple but
elegant potato
pancake is flavored
with tart apples and
served in wedges.
Place a wedge on
each dinner plate,
alongside duck or
turkey sauced with
fresh cranberries, so
the galette will soak
up the fruit juices.*

Using the large holes on a grater-shredder,
shred the potatoes into a colander. Press
out any excess liquid, and then transfer the
shredded potatoes to a large bowl. Shred the
apples in the same manner. Stir the apples,
egg, and flour into the bowl until well mixed.
Season with 1 tsp salt and ½ tsp pepper.

In a 12-inch (30-cm) frying pan, melt the
butter with the oil over medium-low heat.
Add the potato mixture and, using a spatula,
spread it evenly and then press down on it
to bind it together. Cook until golden brown
on the underside, about 15 minutes. Slide the
galette onto a flat plate. Invert the pan over
the plate, carefully turn the plate and pan
together, and then lift off the plate. Return
the pan to the heat and continue to cook
until the second side is golden brown,
about 15 minutes.

Remove from the heat and let the galette
rest in the pan for about 4 minutes. Cut into
12 wedges to serve.

2

ROASTED SQUASH WITH CRANBERRIES & THYME

serves 6–8

2–3 small squashes, such as delicata
or acorn, about 1 lb (500g) each

Salt and freshly ground pepper

2 Tbsp unsalted butter

2 Tbsp pure maple syrup

1 Tbsp chopped fresh thyme,
plus sprigs for garnish

2 tsp grated orange zest

3 Tbsp fresh cranberries,
whole or coarsely chopped

*Here, the maple
syrup both
complements the
natural sweetness
of the squash and
lends a smoking
accent. For a lighter
glaze, substitute
honey for the maple
syrup, or use only
butter. You can also
use lemon zest in
place of the orange
zest and fresh
rosemary or sage
as a substitute for
the thyme.*

Preheat the oven to 400°F (200°C).

Oil a baking sheet. Trim the ends from
each squash and cut into slices or quarters.
Scrape out the seeds, reserving some for
roasting. Season the slices generously with
salt and pepper and arrange on the prepared
pan. Roast the squash slices for 10 minutes.

Meanwhile, in a small saucepan, melt the
butter. Stir in the maple syrup, chopped
thyme, and orange zest and remove from
the heat.

When the squash slices have roasted for
10 minutes, remove the pan from the oven
and brush the slices with the butter mixture.
Sprinkle with the cranberries and reserved
seeds. Continue to roast the squash slices
until glazed, browned, and tender when
pierced with a fork, 10–15 minutes.

Transfer the squash slices to a platter.
Garnish with thyme sprigs and serve.

3

BRUSCHETTA WITH SPICY BROCCOLI RABE & TALEGGIO

serves 4–6

8 slices ciabatta bread, each about ½ inch (12 mm) thick

½ cup (4 fl oz/125 ml) olive oil, plus 1 Tbsp and more for brushing

2 cloves garlic

1 lb (500 g) broccoli rabe, trimmed

Salt and freshly ground pepper

⅓ cup (1½ oz/45 g) walnuts, toasted

Grated zest of 1 lemon

⅓ cup (1½ oz/45 g) grated Parmesan cheese

⅛ tsp red pepper flakes

½ lb (250 g) Taleggio cheese, thinly sliced

Broccoli rabe is a versatile and bitter green that is loaded with flavor. This dish gets a double hit from the Taleggio, a pungent cheese from Italy; for a milder option, use brie or burrata. Serve this bruschetta as an appetizer or finger food during the holidays; it's also delicious alongside tomato soup.

Heat a ridged grill pan on the stove top over high heat. Brush both sides of the bread slices with oil. Grill the bread, turning once, until toasted and grill-marked, 2–3 minutes per side. Let cool. Cut a garlic clove in half lengthwise and then rub one side of the bread slices with the cut sides of the garlic halves.

Bring a large pot of salted water to a boil. Add the broccoli rabe and cook until tender, about 3 minutes. Drain, rinse under cold running water, and drain well. Transfer the broccoli rabe to paper towels to drain.

In a food processor or blender, mince the remaining garlic clove with a few pinches of salt. Add half of the broccoli rabe, the walnuts, and lemon zest and pulse until coarsely ground. Add the ½ cup (4 fl oz/125 ml) oil and process until the mixture is finely chopped. Add the Parmesan and pulse just to combine. Season with salt and pepper.

In a frying pan, warm the 1 Tbsp oil over medium-high heat. Add the red pepper flakes and cook, stirring, for about 30 seconds. Add the remaining broccoli rabe and cook, stirring often, until warmed through, about 2 minutes. Season with salt and pepper.

Preheat the broiler. Top the garlic-rubbed side of each bread slice with a spoonful of the puréed broccoli rabe and a few slices of Taleggio. Transfer to a baking sheet and broil just until the cheese melts, about 2 minutes. Transfer to a platter, top each with warmed broccoli rabe, and serve.

4

BAKED ENDIVE WITH TOMATOES & PANCETTA

serves 4

2 Tbsp olive oil

4 heads Belgian endive, red or white, halved lengthwise

1 carrot, finely chopped

1 celery rib, finely chopped

2 oz (60 g) pancetta, minced

1 clove garlic, minced

Salt and freshly ground pepper

¼ cup (2 fl oz/60 ml) dry white wine

1 cup (6 oz/185 g) canned diced tomatoes

½ cup (2 oz/60 g) grated Parmesan cheese

Torpedo-shaped Belgian endive comes in two types, with pale yellow edging on the leaves or with burgundy edging. Either one or a mixture can be used here. Look for endive heads with tightly packed leaves, moist cut ends, and no discoloration. The salty pancetta complements the mild bitterness of the endive. Serve this dish alongside pan-grilled pork or veal chops or roasted chicken.

Preheat the oven to 350°F (180°C). Lightly oil an 8-inch (20-cm) square baking dish.

In a large frying pan, warm the oil over medium heat. Arrange the endive halves, cut side down, in the pan and cook, turning once, until browned on both sides, about 4 minutes per side. Using a slotted spatula, transfer the endive halves to the prepared dish and arrange cut side up.

Add the carrot, celery, pancetta, and garlic to the frying pan and sauté over medium heat until the vegetables begin to soften, about 5 minutes. Add ½ tsp salt, season with pepper, and continue to sauté until the vegetables are soft and the pancetta is starting to crisp, about 5 minutes. Raise the heat to medium-high and pour in the wine. Cook until most of the wine has evaporated, about 1 minute. Stir in the tomatoes and bring to a simmer. Reduce the heat to medium-low and cook until the sauce thickens, about 10 minutes.

Spoon the sauce over the endive halves, cover the dish with foil, and bake for 1 hour. Uncover, sprinkle with the cheese, and continue to bake, uncovered, until the top is golden brown, about 20 minutes. Let cool for 5 minutes before serving.

5

SWEET POTATO & CRANBERRY HASH

serves 6

3 orange-fleshed sweet potatoes, about 2 lb (1 kg) total

3 Tbsp unsalted butter

1 Fuji apple, peeled, cored, and cut into ½-inch (12-mm) cubes

½ cup (1½ oz/45 g) sliced green onion, white and tender green parts

1 cup (4 oz/125 g) fresh cranberries, coarsely chopped

¼ tsp ground cinnamon

Pinch of ground allspice

Salt and freshly ground pepper

Orange-hued sweet potatoes are surprisingly versatile and well suited to much more than a candied side dish or southern-style dessert pie. Here, they are baked until their creamy flesh is still slightly firm, and then diced and combined with green onions, cranberries, and warm spices to make a savory-sweet hash that is delicious served alongside poultry, pork, or game.

Preheat the oven to 350°F (180°C).

Prick the sweet potatoes in several places with a fork. Set the sweet potatoes directly on the oven rack and bake until they feel only slightly firm when pressed, 50–55 minutes. Let cool to room temperature. Place the potatoes on a plate, cover loosely, and refrigerate for 4 hours or up to overnight. (Chilling them firms the flesh, making it hold together better when cut.) Peel the potatoes and cut into 1-inch (2.5-cm) pieces.

In a frying pan, melt 2 Tbsp of the butter over medium-high heat. Add the apple cubes and sauté until the butter browns and the apple cubes start to caramelize and brown around the edges, about 5 minutes. Add the remaining 1 Tbsp butter. When it melts, stir in the green onion and cranberries and cook until the onion wilts, about 1 minute.

Stir in the cinnamon and allspice, add the potatoes, and cook, stirring frequently, until the potatoes are heated through, about 4 minutes. They will break up somewhat, but try to smash them as little as possible. Season with ¼ tsp salt and several grinds of pepper. Serve hot, warm, or at room temperature.

6

MODERN GREEN BEAN CASSEROLE

serves 6–8

1¼ lb (625 g) green beans, trimmed and halved crosswise

2 Tbsp unsalted butter

10 oz (315 g) button mushrooms, sliced

3 large shallots, plus 3 Tbsp minced

⅓ cup (2 oz/60 g) all-purpose flour, plus 3 Tbsp

1 cup (8 fl oz/250 ml) half-and-half

1 cup (8 fl oz/250 ml) chicken broth

1 tsp soy sauce, preferably mushroom soy

Salt and freshly ground pepper

Canola oil for deep-frying

The traditional version of this holiday casserole is made with mushroom soup and French-fried onion rings, both canned. This updated recipe, made with fresh ingredients, is guaranteed to become the new favorite. For a variation, substitute about 1½ pounds (750 g) broccoli, cut into florets, for the green beans. If you don't feel like frying the shallots, top the casserole with ½ cup (2 oz/60 g) sliced almonds, toasted.

Preheat the oven to 350°F (180°C). Lightly butter a deep 2½-qt (2.5-l) baking dish.

Bring a saucepan of water to a boil. Add the green beans and cook until tender-crisp, about 4 minutes. Drain, rinse under cold running water, and pat dry.

In a saucepan, melt the butter over medium heat. Add the mushrooms and cook, stirring, until they release their juices and are browned, 6–7 minutes. Stir in the 3 Tbsp minced shallots and cook until softened, 2–3 minutes. Sprinkle with the 3 Tbsp flour and stir well. Slowly stir in the half-and-half, broth, and soy sauce and then bring to a boil, stirring often. Reduce the heat to low and simmer, stirring, until thickened, 4–5 minutes. Stir in the green beans and season with salt and pepper. Transfer the mixture to the prepared dish. Bake until the liquid is bubbling, about 20 minutes.

Meanwhile, pour oil to a depth of 2 inches (5 cm) into a small, heavy saucepan and heat over high heat to 350°F (180°C) on a deep-frying thermometer. Line a baking sheet with paper towels. Cut the remaining 3 shallots crosswise into slices ⅛ inch (3 mm) thick and separate into rings. Place the ⅓ cup (2 oz/60 g) flour in a small bowl. Toss the shallot rings in the flour to coat evenly, shaking off the excess. Add the shallots to the hot oil and fry until golden brown, about 30 seconds. Using a slotted spoon, transfer to the towel-lined pan to drain.

Remove the beans from the oven, sprinkle with the fried shallots, and serve.

7

SAVOY CABBAGE & TURNIP SAUTÉ

serves 6

2 Tbsp unsalted butter

1 turnip, peeled and cut into
¼-inch (6-mm) cubes

1 carrot, cut into ¼-inch (6-mm) cubes

1 head Savoy cabbage, about 2 lb (1 kg),
cut into quarters, cored, and cut crosswise
into strips ¼ inch (6 mm) wide

¾ cup (6 fl oz/180 ml) chicken broth

Salt and freshly ground pepper

1 Tbsp chopped fresh flat-leaf parsley

*Curly leaves of
Savoy cabbage and
cubes of turnip and
carrot come together
in this simple
sauté of seasonal
vegetables. The
combination makes
an ideal bed for
seared duck breast
or poached or
panfried fish.*

In a large saucepan, melt the butter over
medium-high heat. Add the turnip and
carrot and sauté until lightly browned, about
7 minutes. Add the cabbage and sauté until
wilted, about 2 minutes. Stir in the broth,
reduce the heat to medium-low, and cook,
uncovered, until the cabbage is tender and
most of the cooking liquid evaporates,
about 10 minutes.

Season with salt and pepper, stir in the
parsley, and serve.

8

CAULIFLOWER, POTATO & STILTON GRATIN

serves 6–8

1 lb (500 g) Yukon gold potatoes,
cut into ½-inch (12-mm) pieces

Salt and freshly ground pepper

1 small head cauliflower, cut into
1-inch (2.5-cm) florets

4 Tbsp (2 oz/60 g) unsalted butter

3 Tbsp all-purpose flour

2 cups (16 fl oz/500 ml) whole milk, warmed

6 oz (185 g) Stilton cheese, crumbled

6 Tbsp (1½ oz/45 g) grated Parmesan cheese

¼ cup (⅓ oz/10 g) minced fresh
flat-leaf parsley

1 cup (2 oz/60 g) fresh bread crumbs

*Stilton, an English
blue cheese known
for its strong taste
and pungent smell,
gives this gratin
a flavorful punch.
If it is unavailable,
Gorgonzola or
another sharp-
flavored blue can
be substituted. You
can assemble this
gratin a day or two
ahead of time and
then bake it just
before serving,
making it ideal for
holiday entertaining.
Serve it with a roast
leg of lamb and a
Pinot Noir.*

In a large saucepan, combine the potatoes,
1 tsp salt, and water to cover by 1 inch
(2.5 cm). Bring to a boil over medium-high
heat, reduce the heat to medium-low, and
cook, uncovered, until the potatoes are
tender but still hold their shape, about
10 minutes. Drain the potatoes and transfer
to a bowl.

Bring a large pot of salted water to a boil.
Add the cauliflower and cook until tender
but still firm, 7–10 minutes. Drain and add
to the bowl with the potatoes.

Preheat the oven to 375°F (190°C).

In a saucepan, melt the butter over medium-
high heat. Add the flour and cook, whisking
constantly, for 2 minutes. Continuing to whisk,
slowly add the milk, and continue to cook,
stirring frequently, until the mixture thickens,
about 2 minutes. Remove from the heat and
stir in the Stilton and 4 Tbsp (1 oz/30 g) of
the Parmesan. Season with salt and pepper
and add to the bowl with the vegetables.
Add the parsley and stir to combine.

Transfer to a 9-by-13 (23-by-33-cm) baking
dish and spread evenly. Sprinkle evenly with
the bread crumbs and the remaining 2 Tbsp
Parmesan. Bake until the gratin is bubbly
and the bread crumbs are golden brown,
20–25 minutes. Serve hot.

ACORN SQUASH GLAZED WITH MAPLE & SOY

serves 4

2 acorn squashes, about 1½ lb (750 g) each

¼ cup (2 fl oz/60 ml) pure maple syrup

1 Tbsp soy sauce

½ tsp peeled and grated fresh ginger

Salt and freshly ground pepper

Here, a mixture of sweet maple syrup and salty soy sauce brightens the flavor of acorn squash, a ubiquitous offering at autumn farmers' markets. Look for grade B maple syrup, which has a more intense, more caramel-like flavor and darker color than grade A and is best for cooking. It also costs less.

Preheat the oven to 425°F (220°C). Line a baking sheet with foil. Lightly oil the foil.

Cut off both ends of each squash. Halve each squash lengthwise and scoop out and discard the seeds. Cut each half crosswise into 4 or 5 slices each about ½ inch (12 mm) thick. Arrange the slices in a single layer on the prepared sheet. Cover tightly with foil. Bake the slices for about 15 minutes. Meanwhile, in a small bowl, whisk together the maple syrup, soy sauce, and ginger.

Remove the baking sheet from the oven and remove the foil. Brush half of the maple syrup mixture on the squash slices. Sprinkle with ¼ tsp salt and a few grinds of pepper. Continue to bake the squash, uncovered, for 10 minutes. Remove the baking sheet from the oven and turn the slices. Brush with the remaining maple syrup mixture. Continue to bake until the squash slices are browned and tender when pierced with a knife, 5–10 minutes. Remove from the oven and serve.

WHEAT BERRIES WITH ROASTED PARSNIPS, BUTTERNUT SQUASH & DRIED CRANBERRIES

serves 4–6

1 cup (6 oz/185 g) wheat berries, rinsed

Salt and freshly ground pepper

3 parsnips, cut into ½-inch (12-mm) pieces

1 small butternut squash, halved, seeded, peeled and cut into ½-inch (12-mm) pieces

1 large red onion, cut into ½-inch (12-mm) pieces

5 cloves garlic, unpeeled

¼ cup (2 fl oz/60 ml) olive oil, plus more as needed

2 Tbsp balsamic vinegar

½ cup (¾ oz/20 g) chopped fresh flat-leaf parsley

½ cup (2 oz/60 g) dried cranberries

2 green onions, dark and light green parts, chopped

Just about everyone knows that eating whole grains is a healthful choice, and this appealing recipe, which marries wheat berries—whole wheat kernels— and roasted root vegetables makes that choice easy.

In a pot, combine 3½ cups (28 fl oz/875 ml) water, the wheat berries, and ½ tsp salt and bring to a boil. Reduce the heat to low, cover, and cook until tender, about 1 hour. Drain and place in a large bowl.

Meanwhile, preheat the oven to 450°F (220°C). Line a baking sheet with parchment paper. Put the parsnips, squash, red onion, and garlic on the prepared sheet. Drizzle with the ¼ cup (2 fl oz/60 ml) oil and the vinegar and season generously with salt and pepper. Roast, stirring once, until the vegetables are caramelized and fork-tender, about 25 minutes. Peel the roasted garlic, break into small pieces, and return to the sheet.

Add the roasted vegetables to the bowl with the wheat berries and stir to combine. Add the parsley, cranberries, and green onions and mix well. Drizzle with additional oil if the mixture needs more moisture. Season with salt and pepper and serve.

11

GRILLED RADICCHIO WITH BALSAMIC & PARMESAN

serves 4–6

4 Tbsp (2 fl oz/60 ml) olive oil

1 Tbsp fresh lemon juice

1 tsp sugar

Salt and freshly ground pepper

2 firm heads radicchio, cut into wedges 1 inch (2.5 cm) thick with core intact

½ cup (4 fl oz/125 ml) balsamic vinegar

2 oz (60 g) Parmesan cheese, grated or shaved

Pleasantly bitter winter chicories are delicious raw in salads, especially with bold vinaigrettes, crumbled blue cheese, and toasted nuts. Some of them, such as radicchio, are also good grilled, which softens the leaves and tempers the flavor. Here, a finishing drizzle of syrupy balsamic vinegar balances the bitter edge of the greens.

In a bowl, stir together 2 Tbsp of the oil, the lemon juice, sugar, and a pinch each of salt and pepper. Add the radicchio and turn to coat. Let stand for up to 4 hours.

In a small saucepan, bring the vinegar to a boil over medium heat. Reduce the heat to medium-low and simmer until the vinegar is reduced by half and has the consistency of thick syrup, 10 minutes. Remove from heat.

Heat a ridged grill pan on the stove top over medium heat. Arrange the radicchio in a single layer and cook, turning often, until the wedges are softened and the edges of the leaves are lightly browned, 2–3 minutes per side. Transfer to a platter. Pour the balsamic glaze over the radicchio. Sprinkle with the Parmesan, drizzle with the remaining 2 Tbsp oil, and serve.

12

BAKED PUMPKIN WITH WHITE BEANS, CARAMELIZED ONIONS & ROASTED GARLIC

serves 6–8

2 heads garlic, halved crosswise

3 Tbsp olive oil

2 yellow onions, halved and thinly sliced

4 cans (15 oz/470 g each) cannellini beans, drained and rinsed

1 Sugar Pie pumpkin, about 2 lb (1 kg), peeled, seeded, and cut into ½-inch (12-mm) cubes

1 cup (8 fl oz/250 ml) vegetable broth

½ tsp dried thyme

Salt and freshly ground pepper

1 cup (2 oz/60 g) fresh bread crumbs

¼ cup (1 oz/30 g) grated Parmesan cheese

Pumpkin cubes, white beans, roasted garlic, and savory onions bake under a crisp topping of Parmesan-flavored bread crumbs in this vegetarian main dish. You can roast the garlic, caramelize the onions, and even assemble the dish the day before you plan to serve it. Feel free to substitute kabocha, butternut, or other orange-fleshed squash for the pumpkin.

Preheat the oven to 375°F (190°C). Wrap the garlic halves together in foil. Bake until the cloves are soft, about 45 minutes. Let cool, and then squeeze the cloves from the cut halves into a bowl, discarding the papery skins.

In a large, heavy ovenproof sauté pan, heat 2 Tbsp of the oil over medium-high heat. Add the onions and sauté until softened. Reduce the heat to medium-low and continue to cook, stirring frequently, until the onions are very soft and browned, 25–30 minutes. Reduce the heat to low and stir in 1 Tbsp of water if necessary to keep onions from sticking. Stir in the beans, pumpkin, broth, thyme, and reserved garlic. Season with ¼ tsp salt and ⅛ tsp pepper.

Cover and bake until the pumpkin is tender, about 1 hour. In a small bowl, stir together the bread crumbs, Parmesan, and the remaining 1 Tbsp oil. Uncover the pot and sprinkle the crumb mixture over the top. Continue to bake, uncovered, until the crumbs are browned, 10–15 minutes. Remove from the oven and serve.

13

MUSHROOM & BROCCOLI BROWN RICE PILAF

serves 4

Flavorful rice pilafs are the perfect counterpoint to rich roasts and saucy braises. This healthful combination of brown rice and vegetables gets some extra flavor and heft from the addition of chickpeas and cashews. Leftovers can be packed up and toted to the office the next day for a satisfying lunch.

FOR THE MUSHROOM STOCK

1 Tbsp olive oil

1 yellow onion, chopped

½ lb (250 g) button mushrooms, sliced

¼ oz (7 g) dried shiitake or porcini mushrooms

2 celery ribs celery, chopped

½ tsp peppercorns

2 Tbsp dry sherry

2 Tbsp unsalted butter

1 yellow onion, finely chopped

1 cup (7 oz/220 g) brown basmati rice

1 Tbsp fresh thyme leaves

Salt and freshly ground pepper

1 small head broccoli, cut into 1-inch (2.5-cm) florets

1 cup (7 oz/220 g) canned chickpeas, rinsed and drained

½ cup (2 oz/60 g) salted roasted cashews, coarsely chopped

Pinch of red pepper flakes

To make the mushroom stock, in a large saucepan, warm the oil over medium-high heat. Add the onion and sauté until lightly browned, about 15 minutes. Add the fresh and dried mushrooms, celery, and peppercorns along with 4 cups (32 fl oz/1 l) water. Bring to a boil, reduce the heat to medium-low, and simmer, uncovered, for 40 minutes. Remove from the heat and let stand for 1 hour. Strain into a bowl, pressing lightly on the solids to extract as much liquid possible, and discard the solids.

Preheat the oven to 350°F (180°C).

Pour 2½ cups (20 fl oz/625 ml) of the mushroom stock into an ovenproof saucepan (reserve the remainder for another use). Add the sherry and warm over medium heat until steaming, 8–10 minutes. In a large, heavy ovenproof pot, melt the butter over medium-high heat. Add the onion and sauté until translucent, 4–5 minutes. Add the rice and stir until well coated with the butter, about 1 minute. Pour in the hot stock. Add the ↠

thyme, ½ tsp salt, and a few grinds of pepper. Bring to a boil, cover, and bake for 35 minutes.

Remove the rice from the oven and stir in the broccoli and chickpeas. Cover and bake until the broccoli is tender, 10–15 minutes. Let stand, covered, for 5 minutes.

Uncover and fluff the pilaf. Sprinkle with the cashews and red pepper flakes and serve.

14

ROASTED ACORN SQUASH WITH CHIPOTLE & CILANTRO

serves 4

Here, fragrant cilantro, tart lime juice, and spicy, smoky chipotles deliver an enticing contrast to the sweet flesh of acorn squash. Serve this dish with panfried or broiled lamb or pork chops or with roasted chicken.

2 acorn squashes, about 1½ lb (750 g) each

2 limes

3 Tbsp olive oil

1 chipotle chile in adobo sauce, plus 1 tsp adobo sauce

½ tsp sugar

Salt and freshly ground pepper

2 Tbsp coarsely chopped fresh cilantro

Preheat the oven to 425°F (220°C).

Cut each squash in half, and then scoop out and discard the seeds. Cut each half into wedges about ¾ inch (2 cm) thick.

Halve 1 of the limes and squeeze the juice into a large bowl. Add the oil, adobo sauce, sugar, and a pinch each of salt and pepper, and stir well. Add the squash wedges and toss well to coat. Pour the wedges and their juices onto 1 or 2 baking sheets and arrange them in a single layer. Roast, turning once, until the squash is golden brown and tender when pierced with a knife, about 25 minutes.

Meanwhile, remove the seeds from the chipotle chile, and then mince. Cut the remaining lime into wedges.

Transfer the squash wedges to a large bowl. Add the minced chile and cilantro and toss well to coat. Arrange the squash on a platter, garnish with the lime wedges, and serve.

SPICY FRIED CHICKPEAS

serves 4–6

1 can (15 oz/470 g) chickpeas

Olive or canola oil for frying

3 cloves garlic, unpeeled

6 fresh sage leaves

Sea salt

Cayenne pepper

This quick and easy antipasto is made from just a few ingredients. Crispy, spicy, and savory, the chickpeas are also fantastic for parties. Serve them with a glass of sparkling Prosecco or with a fruity white wine.

Drain the chickpeas, rinse under cold running water, and then transfer to paper towels and dry thoroughly.

Pour oil to a depth of 1 inch (2.5 cm) into a deep, heavy frying pan and heat to 375°F (190°C) on a deep-frying thermometer. Line a platter with paper towels.

Add the garlic cloves to the hot oil and fry until they begin to turn golden, about 1 minute. Add about one-third of the chickpeas and one-third of sage and fry until crisp and browned, 4–5 minutes. Using a slotted spoon, transfer the chickpeas, garlic, and sage to the towel-lined platter to drain. Cook the remaining chickpeas in batches if necessary, allowing the oil to return to 375°F before adding the next batch.

Season the chickpeas with salt and cayenne, transfer to a bowl, and serve.

ROASTED WINTER SQUASH PURÉE WITH BLUE CHEESE

serves 4–6

1 winter squash such as butternut or acorn, about 2 lb (1 kg)

2 Tbsp olive oil

1 Tbsp heavy cream, plus more if needed

1 Tbsp unsalted butter, at room temperature

Salt and freshly ground pepper

3 oz (90 g) mild, soft blue cheese, plus crumbled cheese for garnish

During the height of its season, pair winter squash with a variety of seasonings and ingredients, both sweet and savory. For this dish, roast your favorite squash variety to bring out its earthy sweetness, then mix the flesh with blue cheese and a little cream until smooth and fluffy. Any mild blue cheese, such as Danish Blue, Cambozola, or Gorgonzola, can be used.

Preheat the oven to 350°F (180°C).

Cut the squash in half and scoop out and discard the seeds. Place the halves on a baking sheet and drizzle with 1 Tbsp of the oil. Turn and drizzle with the remaining 1 Tbsp oil. Cover tightly with foil and bake until the flesh is easily pierced with a fork, about 1 hour. Let cool.

Scoop the flesh from the squash halves into a bowl. Add the 1 Tbsp cream, butter, ¼ tsp salt, ½ tsp pepper, and the 3 oz (90 g) blue cheese. Using an electric mixer, purée the squash until fluffy. Add more cream if necessary for a smooth consistency. Adjust the seasoning if necessary.

Just before serving, return the purée to a saucepan and heat over medium heat, stirring, until hot, 3–4 minutes. Spoon into a bowl, garnish with the crumbled blue cheese, sprinkle with pepper, and serve.

17

SMOKY EGGPLANT DIP WITH CUMIN-CRUSTED PITA CHIPS

serves 8

Extra-virgin olive oil for brushing and drizzling

2 eggplants, about 1 lb (500 g) each, halved lengthwise

6 cloves garlic, unpeeled

2 Tbsp fresh lemon juice

¼ cup (2 oz/60 g) tahini

Sea salt

¼ tsp smoked sweet or hot paprika

FOR THE PITA CHIPS

1 tsp cumin seeds

Kosher salt

3 pita breads, 7 inches (18 cm) in diameter

1½ Tbsp olive oil

Charring the eggplant skin in the broiler introduces smoky, earthy flavors to this creamy dip, while the mellow sweetness of the roasted garlic, the tartness of the lemon juice, and the nutty richness of the tahini deliver a satisfying complexity. The pita chips can be served warm or at room temperature. You can bake them alongside the roasting garlic, or you can make them a day ahead and store them in an airtight container at room temperature until serving.

Preheat the broiler. Line a broiler pan with foil and brush the foil with oil. Place the eggplant halves, cut sides down, on the prepared pan and slip the pan in the broiler about 4 inches (10 cm) from the heat source. Broil until the eggplant skins char and the flesh is tender, about 20 minutes. Transfer the eggplants to a colander and set it in the sink to drain and to cool slightly.

Turn the oven temperature to 400°F (200°C). Trim off the stem end of each garlic clove. Place the cloves on a small square of foil, drizzle with 1 tsp oil, and wrap the cloves securely in the foil. Bake the garlic until it is soft when tested with a small knife, about 15 minutes. Unwrap the garlic and let stand until cool enough to handle. Leave the oven on.

Using a spoon, scrape the eggplant flesh out of the skins into a blender; discard the skins. Squeeze the garlic from its peels and add to the blender along with the lemon juice, tahini, and a scant ¼ tsp salt. Blend the ingredients until smooth. Season with salt and then transfer to a serving bowl. Let stand for several minutes to allow the flavors to blend.

Meanwhile, make the pita chips. In a small, dry frying pan, toast the cumin seeds over medium heat until fragrant, about 2 minutes. Pour onto a plate to cool, then transfer to a spice grinder or mortar. Add ¾ tsp salt ⟶

and grind or crush until the mixture is finely ground.

Line a second baking sheet with foil. Brush the pita breads on both sides with the oil. Cut each pita round into 8 wedges, and arrange the wedges on the prepared pan. Sprinkle the tops evenly with the cumin-salt mixture. Bake the wedges, turning them once about halfway through baking, until light golden brown and crisp, 10–15 minutes.

To serve, transfer the dip to a serving dish and garnish with the paprika. Arrange the pita chips alongside and serve.

18

WINTER SQUASH WITH SPICED COUSCOUS

serves 4

2 acorn squashes, 1¼ lb (750 g) each, halved and seeds removed

2 tsp olive oil

Salt and freshly ground pepper

1 cup (8 fl oz/250 ml) vegetable broth

1 cup (6 oz/185 g) instant couscous

½ tsp ground cinnamon

¼ tsp ground ginger

3 Tbsp sliced almonds, toasted

2 Tbsp dried currants

2 green onions, white and tender green parts, finely chopped

½ Golden Delicious apple, cored and chopped

Kick off the New Year with this healthful dish of roasted squash stuffed with cinnamon-scented couscous. Toasty nuts and dried fruits add appealing texture. The sweet, deep-orange flesh of butternut squash also works well here. For an alternative method, peel and seed the squashes, cut the flesh into small cubes, and roast as directed, decreasing the cooking time by about 10 minutes. Stir the cubes into the couscous.

Preheat the oven to 400°F (200°C).

Brush the squash halves with the oil and season with salt and pepper. Place the halves, cut side down, on a baking sheet. Roast until a knife easily pierces the squash, about 20 minutes.

Meanwhile, in a saucepan, bring the broth to a boil. Stir in the couscous, cinnamon, and ginger. Season with salt and pepper. Remove from the heat, cover, and set aside according to the package directions.

Stir the almonds, currants, onions, and apple into the couscous. Spoon the filling into the roasted squash halves, mounding it generously, and serve.

19

Don't let your guests know that you have dressed the noodlelike strands of spaghetti squash with a classic tomato sauce for pasta, and they will likely be surprised when they take their first bite. Round out the menu with a green salad, crusty bread, and a light red wine.

SPAGHETTI SQUASH WITH TOMATO SAUCE

serves 4

FOR THE TOMATO SAUCE

1 Tbsp olive oil

2 cloves garlic, minced

½ cup (2 oz/60 g) chopped yellow onion

¼ cup (1½ oz/45 g) thinly sliced carrot

2 fresh thyme sprigs

1 can (14 oz/440 g) plum tomatoes, with juice

Salt and freshly ground pepper

1 spaghetti squash, about 2 lb (1 kg), halved lengthwise and seeded

1 Tbsp olive oil, plus more for drizzling

Salt and freshly ground pepper

To make the tomato sauce, in a saucepan, warm the oil over medium heat. Add the garlic and onion and sauté until soft and beginning to color, 10–12 minutes. Add the carrot and thyme and sauté until the carrot is soft, about 5 minutes. Add the tomatoes and their juice and crush with a fork. Season with 1 tsp salt and ½ tsp pepper. Bring the sauce to a boil. Reduce to low, cover, and simmer for 1 hour. Let the sauce cool for about 15 minutes, then purée in batches in a blender. Adjust the seasoning if necessary.

Preheat the oven to 400°F (200°C).

Cut the squash in half lengthwise and scoop out the seeds. Brush the flesh with the 1 Tbsp oil and sprinkle with 2 tsp salt and ½ tsp pepper. Place the squash halves, cut side down, on a baking sheet.

Roast until tender and easily pierced with a fork, 45–60 minutes. Remove from the oven and let stand until cool enough to handle. Reheat the tomato sauce over low heat.

Using a fork, scrape out the flesh, forming noodlelike strands, scraping all the way to the skin. Pour half of the warm sauce into a large bowl. Add the squash and toss gently to coat. Drizzle with a little oil, season with salt and pepper, and serve, passing the remaining sauce at the table.

20

This rich potato dish is a specialty of France, though it is enjoyed all over the world for its golden crown of melted cheese covering layers of creamy potatoes. Splurge on a cave-aged Gruyère for the best results. Serve this dish with hearty fare, such as a pork or veal roast or chops.

GRATIN DAUPHINOIS

serves 6

1 clove garlic, crushed

3 Tbsp unsalted butter

2 lb (1 kg) russet potatoes, peeled and cut into slices ⅛ inch (3 mm) thick

Salt and freshly ground pepper

2 tsp minced fresh thyme or 1 tsp dried thyme

4 oz (125 g) Gruyère cheese, shredded

1 cup (8 fl oz/250 ml) whole milk

Preheat the oven to 425°F (220°C). Rub a flameproof baking dish with the garlic, and then coat it with 1 Tbsp of the butter.

Arrange half of the potato slices in a single layer in the prepared dish, overlapping them slightly. Sprinkle evenly with ½ tsp salt, ½ tsp pepper, 1 tsp of the thyme, and half of the cheese. Cut the remaining 2 Tbsp butter into small pieces and scatter half of the pieces over the cheese. Arrange the remaining potato slices on top, and sprinkle with ½ tsp salt, ½ tsp pepper, and the remaining 1 tsp thyme. Sprinkle with the remaining cheese and butter pieces.

In a small saucepan, bring the milk to a boil over medium-high heat. Remove from the heat and pour over the potato slices. Place the dish over medium-low heat and cook until the milk begins to simmer. Immediately transfer to the oven and bake until the potatoes are easily pierced with a fork, the milk has been absorbed, and the top is slightly golden, 35–45 minutes.

Let stand for 5 minutes before serving.

21

Here, mildly nutty hazelnuts are married with deep, rich browned butter. Both ingredients pair well with earthy root vegetables, whose natural sugars caramelize in the heat of the oven. Fragrant thyme leaves impart a fresh taste to this easy cold-weather side dish.

ROASTED PARSNIPS & SWEET POTATO WITH HAZELNUTS & BROWN BUTTER

serves 4

3 Tbsp hazelnuts, coarsely chopped

3 Tbsp canola oil

2 parsnips, about 1 lb (500 g) total

1 sweet potato, about 1 lb (500 g)

Salt and freshly ground pepper

2 Tbsp unsalted butter

1 tsp minced fresh thyme

In a small, dry frying pan, toast the hazelnuts over medium-low heat until they turn deep brown and are fragrant, 3–5 minutes. Pour onto a plate.

Preheat the oven to 425°F (220°C). Drizzle 1½ Tbsp of the oil onto each of 2 rimmed baking sheets. Place the sheets in the oven to preheat.

Peel the parsnips and sweet potato, and then cut into pieces about ½ inch (12 mm) thick and 2–3 inches (5–7.5 cm) long. Remove the baking sheets from the oven and divide the vegetables evenly between them. Season lightly with salt and pepper, toss the vegetables to coat with the warm oil, and spread out in a single layer. Roast until the undersides are nicely browned and crisp, 10–12 minutes. Turn each vegetable piece once or twice and roast until the vegetables are browned on all sides, 8–10 minutes.

In a small frying pan, warm the butter over medium heat, stirring occasionally, until it begins to turn brown and smell nutty, about 1 minute. Remove the pan from the heat and stir in the hazelnuts and thyme.

Transfer the roasted vegetables to a large bowl, drizzle with the browned butter, and toss gently to coat. Adjust the seasoning if necessary and serve.

22

This stuffed cabbage is packed with Asian flavors like fresh ginger, cilantro, and shiitake mushrooms. It bakes with a hoisin and rice wine vinegar glaze, which keeps the bundles moist. You can adjust the spiciness by adding more or less red pepper flakes. Serve this dish with a cold soba noodle salad.

ASIAN-STYLE CABBAGE ROLLS

serves 4–6

2 Tbsp canola oil

1 tsp Asian sesame oil

2-inch (5-cm) piece fresh ginger, peeled and minced

3 cloves garlic, minced

4 oz (125 g) shiitake mushrooms, stems removed and caps thinly sliced

1 lb (500 g) ground pork

¾ cup (4 oz/125 g) cooked brown rice

1 carrot, shredded

2 green onions, white and tender green parts, sliced

¼ cup (⅓ oz/10 g) fresh cilantro leaves, minced

½ tsp red pepper flakes

1 Tbsp soy sauce

3 tsp rice vinegar

1 head napa cabbage, cored and leaves separated

¼ cup (2 fl oz/60 ml) hoisin sauce

In a frying pan, heat the canola and sesame oils over medium-high heat. Add the ginger, garlic, and mushrooms and sauté until the mushrooms begin to caramelize, about 5 minutes. Let cool slightly and transfer to a bowl.

Add the pork, rice, carrot, green onions, cilantro, pepper flakes, and soy sauce to the bowl. Sprinkle with 1 tsp of the vinegar. Using your hands, mix until well combined.

Lay a cabbage leaf on a work surface with the stem end closest to you. Put a heaping ¼ cup (2 oz/60 g) of the pork mixture near the stem end, fold the stem end over the filling, fold both sides toward the middle, and roll up the leaf tightly around the filling. Place the roll, seam side down, in a 9-by-9-inch (22-by-22-cm) baking dish. Repeat rolling cabbage leaves until all the filling is used (reserve any extra leaves for another use).

In a small bowl, stir together the hoisin sauce and the remaining 2 tsp vinegar. Brush the sauce over the rolls. Bake until the pork is cooked through, about 30 minutes. To test for doneness, carefully unwrap a bundle and check that the pork is cooked through. Remove from the oven and serve.

23

GOLDEN POTATO & CAULIFLOWER CURRY

serves 4

2 Tbsp olive oil

½ tsp fennel seeds

1 yellow onion, halved and thinly sliced

Salt

2 cloves garlic, minced

1–2 serrano chiles, seeded and minced

2 Tbsp Madras curry powder

1 tsp ground cumin

1¼ lb (625 g) Yukon gold potatoes, cut into ¾-inch (2-cm) chunks

1 small head cauliflower, cored and cut into ¾-inch (2-cm) florets

¼ cup (⅓ oz/10 g) chopped fresh flat-leaf parsley (optional)

This is a loose adaptation of aloo gobi, a mildly seasoned classic of Indian cooking that combines potatoes and cauliflower with spices that give it a yellowish cast. Make a raita to spoon alongside: mix 1 cup (8 oz/250 g) low-fat or nonfat plain yogurt with ½ cup (2 oz/60 g) grated cucumber, then season to taste with fresh lemon juice, paprika, and salt.

In a large frying pan, warm the oil over medium heat. Add the fennel seeds and cook, stirring, until fragrant, about 30 seconds. Add the onion and ¾ tsp salt and cook, stirring frequently and reducing the heat as necessary to prevent scorching, until the onion is soft and starting to brown, 7–10 minutes. Stir in the garlic and chiles and cook for 1 minute. Stir in the curry powder and cumin and cook for 1 minute.

Add the potatoes, cauliflower, and 1½ cups (12 fl oz/375 ml) water to the pan and bring to a boil. Reduce the heat to medium-low, cover, and simmer, stirring occasionally, until the vegetables are tender when pierced with a knife, 15–20 minutes. Increase the heat to medium and cook, uncovered, until any remaining liquid evaporates. Stir in the parsley, if using, and serve.

24

GLAZED CARROTS WITH CORIANDER

serves 4

2 lb (1 kg) carrots, preferably a mixture of colors

1 tsp coriander seeds

4 Tbsp (2 oz/60 g) unsalted butter

½ lemon

3 Tbsp honey

Salt and freshly ground pepper

2 Tbsp coarsely chopped fresh cilantro

Lightly toasted coriander seeds deliver citrusy, nutty notes to this simple-to-assemble side dish. Cilantro, the fresh leaves of the same plant, complements the honey-lemon glaze that coats the naturally sweet carrots. Serve alongside a pork roast or a platter of pan-fried bratwurst or other pork sausages.

Peel the carrots, and then cut them on the diagonal into slices ¼ inch (6 mm) thick.

In a small, dry frying pan, toast the coriander seeds over medium heat, shaking the pan occasionally, until the seeds are a shade or two darker and fragrant, about 1 minute. Let cool slightly, then transfer the seeds to a spice grinder or a mortar and grind to a fine powder.

In a frying pan, melt the butter over medium heat. Add the ground coriander and cook, stirring occasionally, until fragrant, about 1 minute. Squeeze the juice from the lemon half into the pan, add the honey and ⅔ cup (5 fl oz/160 ml) water, and sauté for 1 minute. Add the carrots and a pinch each of salt and pepper, and stir well. Raise the heat to medium-high and cook, stirring occasionally, until the carrots are just tender and the liquid is reduced to a glaze, 12–15 minutes. If the carrots are still not tender after the liquid has reduced, add a bit more water to the pan and continue to cook.

Stir the cilantro into the carrots, adjust the seasoning if necessary, and serve.

25

BUTTERNUT SQUASH LASAGNA

serves 6

1 butternut squash, about 2½ lb (1.25 kg), halved, seeded, peeled, and cut into ½-inch (12-mm) cubes

3 Tbsp olive oil

Salt and freshly ground pepper

1 Tbsp unsalted butter

2 cloves garlic, minced

1 yelllow onion, chopped

1 Tbsp chopped fresh rosemary

2 cups (1 lb/500 g) ricotta cheese

1 egg, beaten

½ cup (4 fl oz/125 ml) heavy cream

½ lb (250 g) mozzarella cheese, shredded

¼ cup (1 oz/30 g) grated Parmesan cheese, plus 2 Tbsp

Pinch of freshly grated nutmeg

1 can (14½ oz/455 g) diced tomatoes

6 oz (186 g) lasagna noodles, cooked according to package directions

Lasagna is both a quintessential comfort food and a great party food: it can be assembled ahead and then baked just before serving. This vegetarian version relies on butternut squash, tomatoes, and a trio of cheeses for its rich, satisfying flavor. Serve it with a green salad and coarse country bread and pour a Pinot Noir.

Preheat the oven to 450°F (230°C). Oil a 9-by-13-inch (23-by-33-cm) baking dish.

Line a baking sheet with parchment paper. Place the squash on the prepared baking sheet, drizzle with 2 Tbsp of the oil, season with salt and pepper, and toss to coat. Spread the squash out evenly. Roast, stirring once, until the squash is tender and caramelized, about 25 minutes. Remove from the oven and reduce the oven temperature to 375°F (190°C).

In a large frying pan, melt the butter with the remaining 1 Tbsp oil over medium-high heat. Add the garlic, onion, and rosemary and cook, stirring, until the onion is translucent, about 6 minutes. Turn off the heat, add the squash, and stir to combine, then gently mash about half of the squash.

In a bowl, combine the ricotta, egg, cream, mozzarella, and ¼ cup (1 oz/30 g) Parmesan. Season with the nutmeg and with salt and pepper, and stir to combine.

Spread one-third of the ricotta mixture on the bottom of the prepared baking dish. Top with half of the squash and half of the tomatoes and their juice, and cover with a single layer of lasagna noodles. Spread half of the remaining ricotta mixture on top »→

of the noodles and cover with the remaining squash and the remaining tomatoes and their juice. Top with a single layer of the lasagna noodles. Finish with the remaining ricotta mixture and sprinkle with the 2 Tbsp Parmesan.

Bake until the cheese turns golden brown and the lasagna is bubbling around the edges, 25–30 minutes. Let cool slightly before serving.

CABBAGE, ASIAN PEAR & GINGER SLAW

serves 4

¼ cup (2 fl oz/60 ml) seasoned rice vinegar

1 Tbsp Asian sesame oil

1 tsp peeled and grated fresh ginger

1 tsp firmly packed golden brown sugar

1 tsp soy sauce

1 firm mango, peeled

½ head napa cabbage

1 Asian pear, halved and cored

1 red serrano chile

Salt and freshly ground pepper

Sweet and savory, this wintry slaw combines peppery cabbage with two favorite seasonal fruits: Asian pear and mango. Toss everything together with a gingery dressing, and slip in some chile for a touch of bright heat.

In a small bowl, whisk together the vinegar, sesame oil, ginger, sugar, and soy sauce.

Stand the mango on a narrow edge with the stem end facing you. Using a sharp knife, cut down about ¾ inch (2 cm) to one side of the stem. Cut the other side of the fruit in the same way. Using a mandoline or the sharp knife, shave the mango halves into thin slices. Repeat to make thin slices of cabbage and Asian pear. Transfer the mango, cabbage, and pear to a bowl. Cut the chile crosswise into thin rings, and then remove the seeds. Add the chile to the bowl.

Drizzle the dressing over the cabbage and fruit, and toss to combine. Season with salt and pepper, and serve.

28

27

INDIAN-SPICED PUMPKIN WITH CASHEWS

serves 6

Sweet squash, coconut, and, rich cashews make a delicious trio in this flavorful dish. To make peeling the squash easier, microwave it for 1 minute to soften the skin.

½ tsp ground cumin

½ tsp sweet paprika

¼ tsp ground turmeric

Pinch of cayenne pepper

Salt

¾ lb (375 g) Sugar Pie pumpkin, halved, seeded, peeled, and cut into slices ¼ inch (6 mm) thick

1 Tbsp olive oil

2 Tbsp unsweetened shredded dried coconut

2 Tbsp roasted cashews, coarsely chopped

In a small bowl, combine the cumin, paprika, turmeric, cayenne, and ½ tsp salt. Arrange the pumpkin slices on a plate and sprinkle with the spice mixture, coating the slices on both sides. Let stand for 30 minutes.

In a large frying pan, warm the oil over medium-high heat. Add the pumpkin slices in a single layer and cook, turning once, until fork-tender, about 6 minutes. Using tongs, transfer the pumpkin to a platter. Wipe out the pan with paper towels.

Return the pan to medium-high heat and add the coconut and cashews. Toast, stirring, until the coconut is golden and the nuts are warm, 1–2 minutes. Sprinkle the toasted coconut and nuts over the squash, season with ½ tsp salt, and serve.

28

RUTABAGA & GOLDEN BEETS WITH POMEGRANATE SEEDS

serves 4–6

Frost helps to sweeten all kinds of root vegetables, including the infrequently encountered rutabaga and the popular beet. Here, these two roots are cut into wedges and quickly cooked in a gentle braise. Tart pomegranate seeds are the perfect seasonal garnish.

1 rutabaga, ¾ lb (375 g), peeled and 1 Tbsp olive oil

halved lengthwise

2 large golden beets, 1 lb (500 g) total, peeled and cut into wedges

2 large red beets, 1 lb (500 g) total, peeled and cut into wedges

1 tsp sugar

¾ cup (6 fl oz/180 ml) chicken or vegetable broth

½ cup (4 oz/125 g) pomegranate seeds

Salt and freshly ground pepper

In a frying pan, warm the oil over medium-high heat. Add the rutabaga and sauté for about 5 minutes. Add the beets and sauté until all the vegetables begin to soften, about 5 minutes longer. Add the sugar and broth, lower the heat to medium-low, and cover. Cook until the vegetables are fork-tender, about 15 minutes.

Using a slotted spoon, transfer the vegetables to a bowl. Sprinkle with the pomegranate seeds, season with salt and pepper, toss, and serve.

29

WARM BORLOTTI BEAN & RADICCHIO SALAD

serves 4

¾ cup (5 oz/155 g) dried borlotti or cranberry beans, picked over and rinsed, then soaked overnight in water to cover

2 oz (60 g) pancetta, chopped

3 Tbsp extra-virgin olive oil

1 clove garlic, lightly crushed

2-inch (5-cm) fresh rosemary sprig

Salt and freshly ground pepper

1 small head radicchio, about 4 oz (125 g), halved and cut crosswise into narrow strips

1 Tbsp fresh lemon juice

2 Tbsp chopped fresh flat-leaf parsley

This Italian-style bean salad is a study in contrasts: warm, creamy, sweet-tasting beans against crisp, cool, lightly bitter radicchio and salty, crisp pancetta. Cannellini or other white kidney beans can be substituted for the borlotti beans. Serve as an accompaniment to grilled fish.

Drain the beans, place in a saucepan with water to cover by about 4 inches (10 cm), and bring to a boil, skimming off the foam that rises to the surface. Reduce the heat to low, cover partially, and simmer until the beans are tender, 1½–2 hours. Remove from the heat, drain, and keep warm.

In a saucepan large enough to hold the beans, cook the pancetta over medium heat, stirring often, until crisp, about 5 minutes. Using a slotted spoon, transfer the pancetta to paper towels to drain.

Add 1 Tbsp of the oil to the fat in the pan and warm over medium heat. Add the garlic and rosemary and sauté until the garlic is lightly golden, about 2 minutes. Stir in the beans and season with salt and pepper. Reduce the heat to medium-low, cover, and simmer, stirring occasionally, for 5 minutes to blend the flavors.

Remove the beans from the heat and remove and discard the rosemary and garlic. In a bowl, toss together the beans, radicchio, and reserved pancetta. Add the remaining 2 Tbsp oil and the lemon juice and toss again.

Season with salt and pepper, sprinkle with the parsley, and serve.

30

VEGETABLE CRISPS

serves 6

1 large parsnip, peeled

1 russet potato, peeled

1 small celery root, peeled and halved lengthwise

1 large red beet, peeled

Sunflower oil for deep-frying

Fine sea salt

Salty snacks such as these root-vegetable crisps are often good cocktail-party fare. Here, the crisps are seasoned with sea salt, but they can also be flavored with a dusting of chili powder, minced fresh thyme, or curry powder or other spice blend. Be sure not to skip the soaking step, as it helps to remove the excess surface starch that can cause the crisps to stick to one another in the hot oil.

Have ready 4 bowls of water. Using a mandoline or sharp knife, cut the parsnip lengthwise into slices slightly thinner than a coin. As you cut the slices, place them in 1 of the bowls of water. Repeat with the potato, celery root, and beet, placing the slices of each vegetable into a separate bowl of water. Set aside to soak for 20 minutes.

Pour oil to a depth of 4 inches (10 cm) into a large, deep heavy frying pan or heavy, wide saucepan and heat to 375°F (190°C) on a deep-frying thermometer. Place a wire rack on a baking sheet, line the rack with paper towels, and place the baking sheet near the stove.

Drain the vegetable slices and pat thoroughly dry with a clean kitchen towel. Carefully place a handful of parsnip slices in the hot oil and fry until golden and crisp, about 3 minutes. Using a slotted spoon, transfer the chips to the lined wire rack to drain. Cook the remaining parsnip slices and the potato slices, then the celery root slices, and finally the beet slices in the same way, always letting the oil return to 375°F (190°C) before adding each batch to the pan. The potato slices will cook in about 3 minutes; the celery root and beet slices will cook in about 4 minutes, will crinkle slightly, and will become crisp only after they begin to cool.

Place the crisps in a bowl, season with salt, and serve.

Cocktail parties and winter feasts fill the December calendar. Guests will quickly whisk crispy sweet potato pancakes or cheese-stuffed jalapeños off of passing trays. Put holiday favorites like creamy scalloped potatoes and root vegetable gratins next to big burnished roasts, whether turkey or prime rib. Splurge on special-occasion ingredients to elevate humble winter vegetables, such as Brussels sprouts with chestnuts and walnut oil, braised fennel perfumed with saffron, or mustard greens infused with rich, salty pancetta.

1
WINTER SQUASH & PECORINO TART
page 274

2
ROASTED BROCCOLI WITH ORANGE ZEST & ALMONDS
page 274

3
BAKED CURRIED ROOT VEGETABLES
page 277

8
PICKLED BRUSSELS SPROUTS
page 279

9
ENDIVE & RADICCHIO GRATIN
page 280

10
BREAD PUDDING WITH CHARD, SUN-DRIED TOMATOES & FONTINA
page 280

15
WINTER SALAD OF RED CABBAGE & DRIED FRUITS
page 285

16
BRAISED DINOSAUR KALE WITH WHITE BEANS & SMOKED HAM
page 285

17
RICH SCALLOPED POTATOES
page 286

22
ROASTED TOMATO SOUP
page 289

23
HERB-ROASTED CARROTS, FENNEL & FINGERLING POTATOES
page 291

24
BABY BEETS WITH ORANGE VINAIGRETTE & GOAT CHEESE
page 291

29
BRUSSELS SPROUTS, PANCETTA & CARAMELIZED ONIONS
page 294

30
BUTTERNUT SQUASH & PEAR WITH ROSEMARY
page 294

31
BOK CHOY WITH SOY & LEMON
page 294

december

1

WINTER SQUASH & PECORINO TART
serves 6–8

So many winter squash varieties are available nowadays that you do not have to be limited to the two suggested here. Others, such as Banana, Buttercup, Golden Nugget, or Table Queen, would be equally good in this savory tart. Most pecorinos you see are aged, but a quality cheese counter will carry a pecorino fresco, or "young pecorino."

FOR THE PASTRY

1⅓ cups (7 oz/220 g) all-purpose flour

¼ tsp sugar

Salt

½ cup (4 oz/125 g) cold unsalted butter, cut into 1/2-inch (12-mm) pieces

¼ cup (2 fl oz/60 ml) ice water

1 butternut or kabocha squash, about 2 lb (1 kg)

4 Tbsp (2 fl oz/60 ml) olive oil

1 red onion, finely chopped

1 tsp minced fresh thyme

2 eggs

1 cup (8 fl oz/250 ml) heavy cream

Salt and freshly ground pepper

½ cup (2 oz/60 g) grated pecorino fresco or other mild, semifirm sheep's milk cheese

½ cup (2 oz/60 g) grated Parmesan cheese

To make the dough, in a food processor, combine the flour, sugar, and ¼ tsp salt and pulse to blend. Add the butter and pulse until the mixture resembles coarse crumbs. With the motor running, drizzle in the ice water and process just until a ball of dough begins to form. Turn the dough out onto a lightly floured work surface and pat it into a disk. Wrap in plastic wrap and refrigerate for at least 1 hour or up to overnight. Remove the dough from the refrigerator about 20 minutes before rolling it out.

Preheat the oven to 425°F (220°C).

Cut the squash in half lengthwise and remove the seeds and strings. Rub 1 Tbsp of the oil over the flesh and place the halves, cut side down, on a baking sheet. Bake until the skin is browned and the flesh is soft, about 40 minutes. Let cool for 15 minutes. Scoop the flesh into a bowl and mash with a fork until smooth.

In a frying pan, heat the remaining 3 Tbsp oil over medium-low heat. Add the onion and thyme and sauté until the onion is softened, 7–8 minutes. Reduce the heat to low and cook, stirring occasionally, until the onion is very soft, about 30 minutes. ↠

In a large bowl, whisk together the eggs, cream, ¾ tsp salt, and a grind of pepper. Add the mashed squash and stir until smooth.

On a lightly floured work surface, roll out the dough into an 11-inch (28-cm) circle. Transfer the dough to a 9-inch (23-cm) tart pan with a removable bottom. Trim the overhanging dough flush with the top of the pan sides. Place the pan on a baking sheet. Spoon the onion into the dough-lined pan and sprinkle with the cheeses. Pour the squash mixture over the cheese. Bake for 10 minutes. Reduce the oven temperature to 400°F (200°C) and bake until the filling is puffed up and set, about 20 minutes.

Transfer the tart to a wire rack and let cool for 10 minutes. Remove from the pan and transfer to a plate. Serve warm or at room temperature.

2

ROASTED BROCCOLI WITH ORANGE ZEST & ALMONDS
serves 8

Everyday broccoli takes on a whole new profile when roasted until the florets turn crispy and golden at the edges. This easy, five-ingredient recipe includes a double dose of orange—zest and juice—and a handful of toasted almonds that yield a flavor-rich dish.

3 lb (1.5 kg) broccoli

4 Tbsp (2 fl oz/60 ml) olive oil

Salt and freshly ground pepper

2 Tbsp fresh orange juice

2 tsp freshly shredded orange zest

¼ cup (2 oz/60 g) almonds, toasted and coarsely chopped

Preheat the oven to 425°F (220°C).

Trim the broccoli and cut it into florets. In a large bowl, toss the broccoli with 3 Tbsp of the oil. Transfer to a rimmed baking sheet and season with salt and pepper. Roast until the broccoli is just tender and begins to brown, about 25 minutes.

Transfer the roasted broccoli to a serving dish and drizzle with the remaining 1 Tbsp oil and the orange juice. Sprinkle with the orange zest and almonds and serve.

3

BAKED CURRIED ROOT VEGETABLES

serves 4–6

3 Tbsp unsalted butter

½ cup (2 oz/60 g) chopped yellow onion

2 carrots, cut into slices ½ inch (12 mm) thick

1 parsnip, peeled and cut into 1-inch (2.5-cm) cubes

1 large yellow-fleshed sweet potato, peeled, halved lengthwise, and then cut crosswise into slices 1 inch (2.5 cm) thick

½ head cauliflower, cut into florets

1½ Tbsp all-purpose flour

1½ tsp coriander seeds, crushed

1½ tsp fennel seeds, crushed

1½ tsp ground turmeric

1½ tsp pure chile powder

1 tsp ground cumin

Salt and freshly ground pepper

¼ cup (2 fl oz/60 ml) chicken broth

1 can (14 fl oz/430 ml) coconut milk

Steamed brown or white rice for serving (optional)

Chopped fresh cilantro for garnish

This one-pot meal combines parsnips, sweet potatoes, and cauliflower for a satisfying meatless main course. An Indian-inspired blend of spices brings complexity, while coconut milk imparts smooth richness. Add a pinch of cayenne pepper for extra heat.

Preheat the oven to 400°F (200°C).

In a large, heavy ovenproof pot, melt the butter over medium-high heat. Add the onion and sauté until translucent, about 2 minutes. Add the carrots, parsnip, sweet potato, and cauliflower and sauté until the vegetables begin to soften, about 10 minutes.

In a small bowl, combine the flour, coriander and fennel seeds, turmeric, chile powder, and cumin. Add 1 tsp salt and 1 tsp pepper and stir to blend. Sprinkle the flour mixture over the vegetables and continue to cook, stirring occasionally, until the flour mixture begins to stick to the bottom of the pot and browns, 3–4 minutes.

Add the broth and stir to scrape up any browned bits from the bottom of the pot. Stir in the coconut milk, raise the heat to high, and bring to a boil, stirring occasionally. Cover, place in oven, and bake until the vegetables are tender, about 25 minutes.

Serve the stew spooned over rice, if desired, garnished with cilantro and pepper.

4

PAN-GRILLED RADICCHIO WITH SALSA VERDE

serves 4

4 heads Treviso radicchio

8 Tbsp (4 fl oz/125 ml) olive oil, plus more for drizzling

Salt and freshly ground pepper

1 lemon

2 cloves garlic, smashed

1 tsp prepared horseradish

2 Tbsp capers, drained

2 olive oil–packed anchovy fillets

Leaves from 1 bunch fresh flat-leaf parsley

Leaves from ½ bunch fresh mint

Purple-red radicchio is delightfully bitter, and grilling thick wedges of it chars and sweetens the outer leaves. The salsa verde adds a contrasting color and a dose of piquancy that brighten the winter chicory. Serve this bold-flavored side as an accompaniment to fennel-scented pork sausages, veal chops, or seared sea scallops.

Remove any blemished or discolored leaves from the radicchio. Cut each head lengthwise into quarters. Arrange the quarters on a baking sheet, drizzle lightly with oil, sprinkle lightly with salt and pepper, and toss to coat.

Grate the zest from the lemon. Halve the fruit and squeeze the juice from 1 lemon half into a small bowl. Reserve the remaining half.

In a food processor, combine the lemon zest, garlic, horseradish, capers, and anchovies. Process until well chopped. Add the parsley and mint leaves, lemon juice, and 2 Tbsp of the oil. Pulse until the mixture forms a coarse purée. With the motor running, slowly pour in the remaining 6 Tbsp (3 fl oz/90 ml) oil and process until smooth; the salsa should have the consistency of pesto. Transfer to a bowl. If desired, add a bit more lemon juice.

Heat a ridged grill pan on the stove top over medium heat. Add the radicchio quarters in a single layer and cook, turning as needed, until they just begin to wilt and caramelize, 2–3 minutes per side. Transfer to a plate and top with the salsa. Serve warm or at room temperature.

5

STUFFED GRAPE LEAVES WITH FENNEL & DRIED CRANBERRIES

serves 6–8

This seasonal version of classic stuffed grape leaves calls for sweet-tart dried cranberries and crisp fennel, and makes fantastic holiday party fare. Look for jarred grape leaves in well-stocked markets. The sturdy leaves come rolled and stored in brine, so be sure to rinse them.

1 small fennel bulb

3 Tbsp olive oil

1 yellow onion, chopped

1 cup (7 oz/220 g) long-grain white rice

2 cups (16 fl oz/500 ml) chicken or vegetable broth

1/3 cup (1 1/2 oz/45 g) dried cranberries

1/2 cup (3/4 oz/20 g) chopped fresh flat-leaf parsley

2 Tbsp chopped fresh dill

Salt and freshly ground pepper

1 jar (8 oz/250 g) grape leaves, drained and rinsed

Cut any stalks and feathery leaves from the fennel bulb; discard or reserve for another use. Chop the bulb, trimming the core if it seems very tough.

In a frying pan, warm 2 Tbsp of the oil over medium-high heat. Add the onion and fennel and sauté until softened, about 8 minutes. Add the rice and cook, stirring frequently, until toasted, about 2 minutes. Add 3/4 cup (6 fl oz/180 ml) of the broth and bring to a boil. Reduce the heat to low and cook, stirring occasionally, for 10 minutes. The rice will not be completely cooked. Let cool and transfer to a bowl. Add the cranberries, parsley, and dill to the rice and stir to combine. Season with salt and pepper.

Lay a grape leaf, vein side up, on a work surface. Place about 2 Tbsp of the rice filling near the stem end of the leaf. Fold the stem end over the filling and then bring both sides of the leaf into the middle. Finally, roll up the leaf neatly and tightly. Place, seam side down, in a large, heavy-bottomed saucepan. Repeat to fill and roll the remaining leaves.

Pour the remaining broth into the pan to reach halfway up the sides of the stuffed grape leaves. Use water if additional liquid is needed. Drizzle the remaining 1 Tbsp oil over the top. Simmer over medium heat until the cabbage and filling are fork-tender, about 30 minutes. Serve warm, cold, or at room temperature.

6

BRAISED MUSTARD GREENS WITH PANCETTA & LEMON

serves 4

Here, peppery, deep green mustard greens are braised in broth and then finished with crisp, rich, salty pancetta and tart lemon juice. Serve alongside panfried pork chops or sweet or hot pork sausages.

2 oz (60 g) pancetta, diced

1 Tbsp unsalted butter

1 clove garlic, minced

2 bunches mustard greens, about 3 lb (1.5 kg) total, tough stems removed, leaves coarsely chopped

Salt and freshly ground pepper

1 cup (8 fl oz/250 ml) chicken broth

1/2 lemon

In a frying pan, sauté the pancetta over medium-high heat until lightly browned and crisp, 4–5 minutes. Transfer to paper towels to drain.

Pour out all but 1 Tbsp of the fat from the pan and reduce the heat to medium-low. Add the butter. When it has melted, add the garlic and sauté until fragrant, about 1 minute. Add the mustard greens and a generous pinch each of salt and pepper, and cook, stirring occasionally, until the greens begin to wilt, 3–4 minutes. Add the broth and cook, stirring occasionally, until the greens are tender but still bright green and the liquid reduces to a glaze, 8–10 minutes.

Transfer the greens to a bowl and keep warm. Simmer any cooking liquid left in the pan until it is syrupy and reduces to about 1 Tbsp. Pour the liquid over the greens and toss to combine. Adjust the seasonings and squeeze the juice from the lemon half over the greens. Top with the crisp pancetta and serve.

POMMES ANNA

serves 6

5 Tbsp (2½ oz/75 g) unsalted butter

1½ lb (750 g) russet potatoes

Salt and freshly ground pepper

This famed French dish calls for just two ingredients, thinly sliced russet potatoes and high-quality butter. Traditionally, the layered potatoes are cooked until tender and then the "cake" is flipped a few times until crisp and golden on both the top and bottom. In this simplified version, the potatoes are baked until golden on top and then carefully turned out of the pan onto a serving plate.

Preheat the oven to 375°F (190°C). Coat a 9-inch (23-cm) metal pie pan with 1 Tbsp of the butter.

Peel the potatoes, and then rinse and pat dry. Using a mandoline or a very sharp chef's knife, cut the potatoes into slices ⅛ inch (3 mm) thick.

In a small saucepan, melt the remaining 4 Tbsp (2 oz/60 g) butter over medium heat.

Arrange some of the potato slices in a single layer in the prepared pie pan, overlapping them slightly. Lightly sprinkle with salt and pepper and drizzle with some of the melted butter. Repeat the layering until all of the potato slices have been used.

Bake until the potatoes are tender when pierced with a fork and the top is crisp and golden in color, 45–60 minutes. Transfer to a wire rack and let stand for 5 minutes.

Run a table knife around the inside edge of the pan to loosen the potatoes. To unmold, invert a plate over the top, invert the pan and plate together, and then lift off the pan. Cut into wedges and serve.

PICKLED BRUSSELS SPROUTS

makes 6 one-pint (16–fl oz/500-ml) jars

Ice water

3½ lb (1.75 kg) Brussels sprouts

3 cups (24 fl oz/750 ml) white wine vinegar

Kosher salt

2 shallots, finely chopped

18 fresh tarragon sprigs

Here, the assertive flavor of Brussels sprouts is balanced by the addition of aromatic tarragon and pleasantly sharp-tasting shallots. For spicy sprouts, add 1 or 2 habanero slices, each ¼ inch (6 mm) thick, to each jar. The pickled sprouts make a wonderful snack or gift. Put out a bowl of them at cocktail hour.

Have ready six 1-pt (16–fl oz/500-ml) hot, sterilized jars and their lids.

Have ready a large bowl of ice water. Bring a large saucepan of water to a boil over high heat. Trim ¼ inch (6 mm) from the stem end of each Brussels sprout, then remove and discard the outer leaves. Add the Brussels sprouts to the boiling water and blanch for 1 minute. Drain the Brussels sprouts and plunge them into the ice water. Let stand until cool to the touch. Drain well.

In a large nonreactive saucepan, combine the vinegar and 2 Tbsp plus 1 tsp salt. Add 3 cups (24 fl oz/750 ml) water and bring to a boil over medium-high heat, stirring to dissolve the salt.

Meanwhile, divide the shallots evenly among the jars, and place 3 tarragon sprigs in each jar. Pack the jars tightly with the Brussels sprouts, filling them to within 1 inch (2.5 cm) of the rims.

Ladle the hot brine into the jars, leaving ½ inch (12 mm) of headspace. Remove any air bubbles and adjust the headspace, if necessary. Wipe the rims clean and seal tightly with the lids.

Process the jars for 10 minutes in a boiling-water bath. Let the jars stand undisturbed for 12 hours and then set them aside for 2 weeks for the flavors to develop. The sealed jars can be stored in a cool, dark place for up to 1 year. If a seal has failed, store the jar in the refrigerator for up to 1 week.

9

ENDIVE & RADICCHIO GRATIN

serves 4

4 large heads Belgian endive, halved lengthwise and cut into wide ribbons

2 small heads radicchio, halved lengthwise and cut into wide ribbons

1½ cups (12 fl oz/375 ml) whole milk

3 Tbsp unsalted butter

2 Tbsp all-purpose flour

1 cup (4 oz/125 g) shredded Gruyère or Comté cheese

Salt and freshly ground pepper

¼ cup (1 oz/30 g) grated Parmesan cheese

Wide ribbons of bittersweet endive and radicchio, in pale green and garnet red, make for an elegant gratin. When making the béchamel, or white, sauce, be careful not to let the flour burn. For the best results, stir the butter and flour together over medium-low heat just until the raw taste of the flour has cooked away, then begin adding the milk. The butter and flour mixture should not brown or the béchamel will not be a beautiful white.

Preheat the oven to 400°F (200°C). Butter a shallow 2-qt (2-l) gratin or baking dish. Add the endive and radicchio to the prepared dish and toss to combine.

In a small saucepan, warm the milk over medium heat until small bubbles begin to appear around the edge of the pan. Remove from the heat. In a saucepan, melt 2 Tbsp of the butter over low heat. Add the flour and whisk to incorporate. Raise the heat to medium-low and cook, stirring often, for 2 minutes. Gradually whisk in the hot milk. Cook, stirring frequently, until the sauce is thick enough to coat the back of a spoon, 3–4 minutes. Add ¾ cup (3 oz/90 g) of the Gruyère and stir until it melts. Season with salt and pepper.

Spoon the sauce over the vegetables and dot with the remaining 1 Tbsp butter. Sprinkle with the Parmesan and the remaining Gruyère. Bake until the vegetables are tender and the top of the gratin is golden, about 30 minutes. Remove from the oven and serve.

10

BREAD PUDDING WITH CHARD, SUN-DRIED TOMATOES & FONTINA

serves 4–6

2 cups (16 fl oz/500 ml) milk

4 eggs

Salt and freshly ground pepper

8 slices coarse country bread, cut into 1-inch (2.5-cm) cubes

2 Tbsp unsalted butter

1 small yellow onion, chopped

2 cloves garlic, minced

1 bunch chard, tough stems removed, leaves chopped

¼ cup (2 fl oz/60 ml) chicken or vegetable broth

⅓ cup (3 oz/90 g) oil-packed sun-dried tomatoes, chopped

½ cup (½ oz/15 g) packed fresh basil leaves

3 oz (90 g) fontina cheese, shredded

Look for a crusty country loaf for this recipe to ensure good texture in the finished dish, and if your budget allows, buy an authentic creamy, nutty fontina from Italy's Aosta Valley for the best flavor. Accompany the dish with a salad of butter lettuce, sliced pears, and toasted walnuts and pour a crisp Sauvignon Blanc at the table.

Preheat the oven to 350°F (180°C). Butter a 2-qt (1-l) baking dish.

In a large bowl, whisk together the milk, eggs, 1 tsp salt, and ½ tsp pepper. Add the bread cubes and stir to combine. Let stand for 15 minutes. Occasionally press down on the bread cubes with a spatula to immerse them in the liquid.

In a frying pan, melt the butter over medium-high heat. Add the onion and garlic and cook, stirring occasionally, until the onion is translucent, about 5 minutes. Add the chard and season with salt and pepper. Cook, stirring, until it begins to wilt, about 2 minutes. Add the broth and cook until most of the liquid is absorbed, about 5 minutes.

Add the chard mixture, sun-dried tomatoes, basil, and fontina to the bowl with the bread and toss to combine. Season with salt and pepper. Transfer the mixture to the prepared dish. Bake the pudding until browned on top, about 55 minutes. Remove from the oven and serve.

STUFFED JALAPEÑOS

serves 6

2 thick slices applewood-smoked bacon, finely chopped

12 small jalapeño chiles

4 oz (125 g) cream cheese, at room temperature

½ cup (2 oz/60 g) finely shredded sharp Cheddar cheese

½ cup (2 oz/60 g) finely shredded Monterey jack cheese

1 tsp hot-pepper sauce

Salt and freshly ground pepper

2 eggs

1 Tbsp whole milk

1 cup (4 oz/125 g) fine dried bread crumbs or panko

Canola oil for deep-frying

If you are pressed for time, stuff the chiles with a simple combination of Cheddar and Monterey jack cheeses, omitting the cream cheese and bacon. For an extra kick, set out Thai sweet chile sauce for dipping.

In a frying pan, cook the bacon over medium heat, stirring occasionally, until crisp and browned, about 5 minutes. Transfer to paper towels to drain.

Using a sharp paring knife, slit each chile on one side from the stem to the tip, then make a partial cut at the base of the stem, leaving the stem end intact. Gently open the chile and remove the seeds.

In a bowl, mix together the bacon, cream cheese, Cheddar and Monterey jack cheeses, and hot-pepper sauce until well blended. Season with salt and pepper. Using a small spoon, fill the chiles with the cheese mixture. Close the filled chiles, pressing firmly on the seams so they retain their shape.

In a shallow bowl, whisk together the eggs and milk. In a second shallow bowl, stir together the bread crumbs and a pinch each of salt and pepper. One at a time, dip the filled chiles into the egg mixture, allow the excess to drip back into the bowl. Then dip into the bread crumbs, patting gently to help them adhere. Transfer to a baking sheet. Let dry for about 10 minutes. Repeat, dipping the chiles first in the egg mixture and then in the crumbs to form a second coating.

Pour oil to a depth of at least 3 inches (7.5 cm) into a deep, heavy saucepan and heat over medium-high heat to 325°F (165°C) on a ⟶

deep-frying thermometer. Preheat the oven to 200°F (95°C). Line a baking sheet with paper towels.

Working in batches, add the chiles to the hot oil and cook, stirring occasionally with a wire skimmer, until golden brown, about 6 minutes. Using the skimmer, transfer to the towel-lined sheet to drain. Keep warm in the oven while you fry the remaining chiles, allowing the oil to return to 325°F between batches. Serve the stuffed jalapeños warm.

BRUSSELS SPROUTS WITH TOASTED HAZELNUTS

serves 4–6

1½ lb (750 g) Brussels sprouts, trimmed and halved lengthwise

5 Tbsp (3 fl oz/80 ml) olive oil

Salt and freshly ground pepper

1½ Tbsp Champagne or white wine vinegar

1 Tbsp hazelnut oil (optional)

½ cup (2 oz/60 g) hazelnuts, toasted and coarsely chopped

People who say they don't like Brussels sprouts have probably only had them one way: overcooked. Treat these little cabbages right, with a quick blast in a hot oven to singe their leaves and bring out their inherent nuttiness, followed by a light dressing of oil and vinegar. A scattering of crisp hazelnuts completes the dish.

Preheat the oven to 400°F (200°C).

Place the Brussels sprouts in a large bowl. Drizzle with 3 Tbsp of the olive oil, season generously with salt and pepper, and toss to coat the sprouts evenly. Transfer the Brussels sprouts to a rimmed baking sheet and spread out evenly.

Roast the Brussels sprouts, stirring once or twice, until they are browned in spots and just tender when pierced with a knife, 30–35 minutes.

Transfer the Brussels sprouts to a bowl. Sprinkle with the vinegar, the remaining 2 Tbsp olive oil, and the hazelnut oil, if using. Toss well, add the toasted hazelnuts, and toss again. Season with salt and serve.

13

Saffron is a special-occasion ingredient that lends subtle spice and vibrant color to any dish that it joins. Here, it bathes the fennel in a rich golden hue. Sweet raisins become juicy and plump in the braising liquid.

BRAISED FENNEL WITH RAISINS & SAFFRON

serves 6

4 medium or 6 small fennel bulbs, 3–4 lb (1.5–2 kg) total

¼ tsp saffron threads

½ cup (4 fl oz/125 ml) chicken broth or water, heated

2 Tbsp olive oil

1 clove garlic, minced

Salt and freshly ground pepper

¼ cup (1½ oz/45 g) raisins

Cut any stalks and feathery leaves from each fennel bulb; discard or reserve for another use. Peel away the tough outer layer of the bulb and then cut the bulb lengthwise into quarters. If the core seems very tough, trim it, but do not cut it away fully or the quarters will fall apart.

Place the saffron in a heatproof bowl and cover with the hot broth.

In a frying pan, heat the oil over medium-high heat. Add the garlic and fennel, one cut side down, and season with salt and pepper. Reduce the heat to medium and cook the fennel, turning occasionally, until lightly browned, about 10 minutes. Gradually pour in the saffron-broth mixture, stirring to scrape up any browned bits on the bottom of the pan. Raise the heat to high and bring to a boil. Reduce the heat to low, add the raisins, cover, and simmer until the fennel is easily pierced with a fork, 30–40 minutes.

Transfer the fennel to a platter and serve hot or at room temperature.

14

Cooking cauliflower in a little butter and oil until well browned accentuates its natural sweetness. This caramel-like flavor is then heightened by the addition of a honey glaze and brightened by smoked paprika, red pepper flakes, and a touch of citrus.

CARAMELIZED CAULIFLOWER WITH HONEY & SMOKED PAPRIKA

serves 4

1 large head cauliflower, about 3 lb (1.5 kg)

2 Tbsp unsalted butter

3 Tbsp olive oil

Salt and freshly ground pepper

1 shallot, minced

¼ tsp red pepper flakes

½ tsp sweet Spanish smoked paprika

2 Tbsp honey

½ lemon

Trim the cauliflower and cut it into 1-inch (2.5-cm) florets.

In a large frying pan, melt the butter with 2 Tbsp of the oil over medium heat. Add the cauliflower florets, sprinkle with a generous pinch of salt, and toss gently to coat the florets. Spread the florets in a single layer and cook, without stirring, until the undersides are lightly browned, 3–4 minutes. Turn the florets and continue cooking, undisturbed, until evenly browned, 3–4 minutes. Repeat until all sides are evenly browned, 3–5 minutes.

Add the remaining 1 Tbsp oil, the shallot, red pepper flakes, and paprika to the pan. Cook, stirring occasionally, until the shallot is softened, 2–3 minutes. Add the honey and 2 Tbsp water and sauté until the liquid reduces to a glaze, 2–3 minutes. Squeeze the juice from the lemon half over the cauliflower, stir to combine, and cook for 30 seconds. Remove from the heat, and adjust the seasoning if necessary.

Transfer the cauliflower to a bowl and serve.

15

WINTER SALAD OF RED CABBAGE & DRIED FRUITS

serves 4

½ head red cabbage, about 1 lb (500 g), cored and shredded or thinly sliced

Salt and freshly ground pepper

Red wine vinegar or cider vinegar

5 dried apricots, chopped

5 dried golden figs such as Calimyrna, chopped

5 dried pears, chopped

5 prunes, pitted and chopped

1 tart apple such as Granny Smith, cored and cut into matchsticks

1–2 Tbsp canola oil

Several pinches of ground cumin

½ tsp sugar, or to taste

2–3 Tbsp walnut pieces (optional)

Tame cabbage with vinegar and seasonings, letting it sit and then draining it before proceeding. This will transform it from rough textured to silky and from strong flavored to mellow. The vinegar also turns the natural blue tinge of red cabbage a bright shade of scarlet.

In a bowl, combine the cabbage along with salt, pepper, and vinegar to taste, and toss well. Cover and let stand for at least 2 hours at room temperature or, preferably, overnight in the refrigerator. Drain off all but 1 Tbsp of the liquid.

Add the apricots, figs, pears, prunes, and apple to the cabbage and toss well. Drizzle with 1 Tbsp of the oil and add the cumin and sugar. Season with salt and pepper and toss well. Adjust the seasoning with additional vinegar, cumin, sugar, salt, and pepper, if desired. Stir in additional oil if you feel it needs more moisture.

Add the walnuts, if using, toss to mix well, and serve.

16

BRAISED DINOSAUR KALE WITH WHITE BEANS & SMOKED HAM

serves 4

2 bunches dinosaur kale, about 1 lb (500 g) total

2 tsp olive oil

2 cloves garlic, thinly sliced

4 oz (125 g) smoked ham such as Black Forest, diced

½ cup (4 fl oz/125 ml) chicken broth

Salt and freshly ground pepper

1 can (15 oz/470 g) cannellini beans, rinsed and drained

½ tsp minced fresh rosemary

High-quality ham contributes a smoky, meaty flavor that mimics long cooking in this quick braise of peppery kale. Creamy white beans and woodsy rosemary combine to create a hearty dish that can be served as a main course with just salad, bread, and perhaps a cheese plate on the side.

Strip the stalks and ribs from the kale leaves, and then tear the leaves into 2-inch (5-cm) pieces.

In a frying pan, warm the oil over medium-low heat. Add the garlic and sauté until lightly browned, about 1 minute. Add the ham and sauté for 1 minute. Add the kale, cover, and cook, turning occasionally, until the kale leaves just begin to wilt, 2–3 minutes. Add the broth and a pinch each of salt and pepper and cook until the leaves are just tender and the liquid has almost evaporated, 4–5 minutes.

Add the beans and rosemary to the pan and raise the heat to medium-high. Cook, tossing gently, until the beans are heated through, 2–3 minutes. Adjust the seasoning if necessary and serve.

17

RICH SCALLOPED POTATOES

serves 8

2 Tbsp unsalted butter

3 cups (12 oz/375 g) chopped leeks, white and pale green parts

Salt and freshly ground pepper

3¾ lb (1.85 kg) russet potatoes, peeled and thinly sliced

2 cups (8 oz/250 g) shredded Gruyère cheese

3 cups (24 fl oz/750 ml) heavy cream

Most recipes for scalloped potatoes call for Cheddar cheese and milk, thickened with a sprinkling of flour, but this version relies on rich cream, nutty Gruyère cheese, and tender leeks. For the classic all-American version, omit the leeks and substitute sharp white Cheddar for the Gruyère and whole milk for the cream. As you add the potatoes, sprinkle each layer with 1 Tbsp all-purpose flour.

Preheat the oven to 350°F (180°C). Generously butter a 9-by-13-inch (23-by-33-cm) baking dish.

In a large frying pan, melt the butter over medium heat. Add the leeks and cook, stirring occasionally, until tender, about 7 minutes. Remove from the heat.

In a small bowl, mix together 2 tsp salt and ½ tsp pepper. Spread one-third of the potatoes in an even layer in the prepared dish and season with about one-fourth of the salt mixture. Top with one-third of the Gruyère and half of the leeks and season with about one-third of the remaining salt mixture. Top with half of the remaining potato slices, half of the remaining Gruyère, and the rest of the leeks, seasoning with half of the remaining salt mixture. Finish with the remaining potatoes and Gruyère and season with the remaining salt mixture.

In a small saucepan, bring the cream to a simmer over medium-high heat. Pour the hot cream over the potatoes. Cover the dish tightly with foil and place on a baking sheet. Bake for 1 hour.

Remove the foil and continue baking until the potatoes are tender, coated with a creamy sauce, and golden brown on top, about 30 minutes. Let stand for about 5 minutes before serving.

18

SHREDDED ENDIVE SALAD WITH PEAR & POMEGRANATE

serves 4–6

FOR THE DRESSING

¼ cup (2 fl oz/60 ml) buttermilk

¼ cup (2 fl oz/60 ml) mayonnaise

¼ cup (2 oz/60 g) sour cream

1 clove garlic, minced

1 Tbsp minced shallot

Juice of 1 lemon

Salt and freshly ground pepper

4 large heads Belgian endive, trimmed and thinly sliced

1 pear, quartered, cored, and thinly sliced

½ cup (2 oz/60 g) pomegranate seeds

½ cup (2 oz/60 g) pistachios (optional)

2 Tbsp snipped chives

The dressing can be made up to a week in advance but don't cut the endive in advance as it will brown quickly. Just before serving, first toss the endive with the dressing and then scatter the remaining elements so you can see all the colorful ingredients. The optional addition of pistachios adds a delightful crunch.

To make the dressing, in a small bowl, whisk together the buttermilk, mayonnaise, sour cream, garlic, shallot, and lemon juice. Season with salt and pepper.

Put the endive in a large bowl, add all but 2 Tbsp of the dressing, and toss to coat. Transfer to a platter. Scatter the pear, pomegranate seeds, and pistachios, if using, over the salad. Drizzle with the reserved dressing and the snipped chives and serve.

19

This vegetarian adaptation of the Greek national dish uses mushrooms in place of the traditional lamb, adds a layer of cubed potatoes, and favors Parmesan over the usual feta. Accompany with a simple lettuce or spinach salad and uncork a bottle of retsina for the table.

VEGETARIAN MOUSSAKA

serves 8

2 small eggplants, cut into slices ½ inch (12 mm) thick

Salt and freshly ground black pepper

6 Tbsp (3 fl oz/90 ml) olive oil

2 russet potatoes, peeled and cut into ½-inch (2.5-cm) cubes

1 yellow onion, chopped

2 portobello mushrooms, stems trimmed, caps cut into ½-inch (2.5-cm) cubes

1 tsp dried oregano

½ tsp ground cinnamon

1 can (28 oz/875 g) crushed tomatoes

½ cup (4 oz/125 g) unsalted butter

7 Tbsp (2½ oz/75 g) all-purpose flour

4 cups (32 fl oz/1 l) whole milk, heated

½ cup (2 oz/60 g) grated Parmesan cheese, plus 3 Tbsp

¼ tsp freshly grated nutmeg

4 egg yolks

Freshly ground white pepper

Lay the eggplant slices on a baking sheet and sprinkle with salt. Let stand for 30 minutes and then pat dry with paper towels.

Preheat the oven to 450°F (230°C). Line a baking sheet with parchment paper.

Brush both sides of the eggplant slices with 2 Tbsp of the oil and season with salt and black pepper. In a bowl, toss the potato cubes with 2 Tbsp of the oil and season with salt and black pepper. Transfer to the prepared sheet. Roast the eggplants and potatoes until tender but not fully cooked, about 20 minutes. Remove from the oven. Reduce the oven temperature to 350°F (180°C).

In a frying pan, heat the remaining 2 Tbsp oil over medium-high heat. Add the onion and cook until translucent, about 5 minutes. Add the mushrooms, oregano, and cinnamon and sauté until the mushrooms are tender, about 8 minutes. Add the tomatoes, stir to combine, and remove from the heat. Season with salt and black pepper.

In a saucepan, melt the butter over medium-high heat. Whisk in the flour and cook for about 2 minutes. Slowly whisk in the milk ⟫

and continue cooking until the sauce begins to thicken, about 5 minutes. Stir in the ½ cup Parmesan and the nutmeg.

In a large bowl, beat the egg yolks. Stir in 2 Tbsp of the milk mixture and then slowly stir in the remainder. Season with white pepper.

Spoon a small amount of the tomato sauce onto the bottom of a 9-by-13-inch (23-by-33-cm) baking dish. Cover the bottom with half of the eggplant slices in a single layer. Top with all of the potatoes and half of the tomato sauce. Drizzle 1 cup (8 fl oz/250 ml) of the cream sauce over the top and cover with the remaining eggplant. Spread the remaining tomato sauce on the eggplant and finish with the remaining cream sauce. Sprinkle with the 3 Tbsp Parmesan.

Bake until the top is golden brown, about 45 minutes. Remove from the oven and serve.

20

Here, broccoli rabe is boiled just until tender and then briefly tossed in a hot frying pan with a trio of seasonings. Boiling it first removes some of the natural bitterness of the green and also ensures that it is evenly tender when it is served.

SPICY BROCCOLI RABE WITH LEMON & GARLIC

serves 4–6

1 lb (500 g) broccoli rabe, trimmed

1 Tbsp olive oil

3 cloves garlic, thinly sliced

¼ tsp red pepper flakes

Salt

1 Tbsp fresh lemon juice

Bring a large pot of salted water to a boil. Add the broccoli rabe and cook until just tender, about 4 minutes. Drain well.

In a large frying pan, warm the oil over medium-high heat. Add the garlic and red pepper flakes and cook until the garlic is fragrant but not browned, about 30 seconds. Add the broccoli rabe and ½ tsp salt. Stir to coat and heat through, 1–2 minutes. Remove from the heat and stir in the lemon juice. Transfer to a platter and serve.

BRAISED WINTER VEGETABLES WITH COCONUT & RED CURRY

serves 4

2 tsp canola oil

1 clove garlic, minced

¼-inch (6-mm) slice fresh ginger, peeled and grated

2 tsp Thai red curry paste

1 tsp Thai fish sauce

1 sweet potato, about ½ lb (250 g), peeled and cut into ½-inch (12-mm) chunks

1 celery root, about ½ lb (250 g), peeled and cut into ½-inch (12-mm) chunks

3 cups (24 fl oz/750 ml) coconut milk

1 delicata squash, about ½ lb (250 g)

2 limes

8 fresh cilantro sprigs

Coconut milk lends richness and an exotic flavor to this seasonal mixture of sweet potato, celery root, and winter squash. At the same time, it helps to offset the spiciness of the red curry paste and pungency of the fish sauce that spike the broth. Accompany with steamed white or brown rice and serve fresh fruit for dessert.

In a large saucepan, warm the oil over medium heat. Add the garlic and ginger and sauté until fragrant but not browned, about 1 minute. Add the curry paste and cook, stirring, for 1 minute. Add the fish sauce, sweet potato, and celery root and stir to combine. Reduce the heat to medium-low, pour in the coconut milk, and cook, stirring occasionally, for 10 minutes. Add the squash and cook until the vegetables are just tender when pierced with a knife but are not falling apart, 12–15 minutes.

Meanwhile, finely grate the zest from 1 of the limes and reserve the fruit for another use. Stir the lime zest into the vegetables.

Spoon the vegetables and braising liquid into bowls. Garnish each serving with the cilantro. Cut the second lime into wedges and serve the lime wedges on the side of the curry for squeezing.

ROASTED TOMATO SOUP

serves 4–6

2 cans (28 oz/875 g each) plum tomatoes, drained, juice reserved

¼ cup (2 oz/60 g) firmly packed golden brown sugar

4 Tbsp (2 oz/60 g) unsalted butter

3 shallots, finely chopped

1 Tbsp tomato paste

1 Tbsp all-purpose flour

4 cups (32 fl oz/1 l) vegetable broth

½ cup (4 fl oz/125 ml) heavy cream

Salt and freshly ground pepper

Taking the time to roast the tomatoes before combining them with the other ingredients will yield a particularly flavorful, deeply colored soup. If you prefer a lighter, lower-calorie dish, omit the cream. This soup also freezes well; store it in an airtight container in the freezer for up to 2 months.

Preheat the oven to 400°F (200°C). Line a rimmed baking sheet with parchment paper.

Spread the tomatoes in a single layer on the prepared sheet and sprinkle evenly with the brown sugar. Roast until the juices have evaporated and the tomatoes begin to caramelize, about 20 minutes. Let cool.

In a large saucepan, melt the butter over medium-low heat. Add the shallots and tomato paste and cook, stirring occasionally, until the shallots are softened, about 5 minutes. Sprinkle in the flour and stir to incorporate. Cook, stirring, until thickened, about 2 minutes. Whisking constantly, slowly pour in the broth and the reserved tomato juice.

Add the roasted tomatoes to the saucepan, raise the heat to medium-high, and bring to a boil. Reduce the heat to medium-low and simmer until the tomatoes are tender and breaking apart, 10–15 minutes. Let cool slightly.

Working in batches, purée the soup in a blender or food processor until smooth. Return to the saucepan, place over low heat, and stir in the cream, 1 tsp salt, and ½ tsp pepper. Ladle into bowls and serve.

23

HERB-ROASTED CARROTS, FENNEL & FINGERLING POTATOES

serves 6

Here, the two-step roasting method results in tender, caramelized vegetables with richly blended flavors. You can also substitute other herbs, such as sage or marjoram. The addition of white balsamic vinegar at the end brightens the sweetness of the vegetables.

2 small fennel bulbs

8 baby carrots, peeled and halved lengthwise

1 lb (500 g) fingerling potatoes, halved lengthwise

1 whole head garlic

¼ cup (2 fl oz/60 ml) olive oil

1 Tbsp chopped fresh thyme

1 Tbsp chopped fresh rosemary

Salt and freshly ground pepper

1 Tbsp white balsamic vinegar

Preheat the oven to 400°F (200°C).

Cut any stalks and feathery leaves from the fennel bulb; discard or reserve for another use and trim off the base of the bulbs. If the outer layer is tough or discolored, discard it. Cut the bulb lengthwise into slices. Cut off the top of the head of garlic just to expose the tops of the cloves. Combine all the vegetables and the garlic in a large roasting pan or on a rimmed baking sheet. Drizzle with the oil, thyme, and rosemary. Season generously with salt and pepper. Toss to coat the vegetables with the seasonings then spread in a single layer.

Roast the vegetables for about 15 minutes. Reduce the oven temperature to 350°F (180°C) and continue to roast them, stirring once or twice, until golden, caramelized, and tender when pierced with a fork, 35–40 minutes. Using a large spatula, transfer the vegetables to a bowl. Reserve the pan juices.

Pour the pan juices into a small bowl and whisk in the vinegar. Drizzle over the vegetables, toss, and serve.

24

BABY BEETS WITH ORANGE VINAIGRETTE & GOAT CHEESE

serves 4

Seek out baby beets, which roast more quickly than their larger kin. Showcase color in this pretty salad by combining various varieties: golden, white, red, and striped. You can use crumbled blue cheese in place of the goat cheese and two clementines in place of the orange; add a handful of toasted walnuts or pine nuts for crunch.

1 lb (500 g) baby beets in various colors, each 1–2 inches (2.5–5 cm) in diameter

Salt and freshly ground pepper

4 Tbsp (2 fl oz/60 ml) olive oil

1 navel orange, peeled and cut into 1-inch (2.5-inch) chunks

2 Tbsp red wine vinegar

2 Tbsp fresh orange juice

1 bunch watercress or arugula, stems removed

⅓ cup (1½ oz/45 g) crumbled fresh goat cheese

If the greens are still attached to the beets, remove them, leaving 1 inch (2.5 cm) of the stem intact. Place the beets in a shallow baking dish just large enough to hold them in a single layer and season generously with salt and pepper. Drizzle with 1½ Tbsp of the oil and toss to coat evenly, then spread the beets out evenly.

Roast the beets, stirring once or twice, until nearly tender, about 25 minutes. Remove from the oven, add the orange chunks, drizzle with 1½ tsp of the oil, and toss to coat. Continue to roast until the orange chunks are softened and tinged with gold and the beets are tender when pierced with a knife, about 10 minutes. Let the beets cool. Remove the skins from the beets and return them to the dish.

In a small bowl, whisk together the remaining 2 Tbsp oil, the vinegar, and the orange juice. Drizzle over the beets and orange chunks. Season with salt and pepper, and toss well.

Arrange the watercress on salad plates. Top with the beets and orange chunks. Sprinkle with the goat cheese and serve.

25

Fontina Val d'Aosta, a cow's milk cheese with a mild nuttiness, develops a subtle earthy, woodsy bouquet when melted, a quality that pairs well with the potent flavor of truffle. Here, the cheese is combined with cream, butter, and eggs and dressed with truffle oil to create an indulgent companion for seasonal vegetables.

ROASTED WINTER VEGETABLES WITH TRUFFLED FONDUTA

serves 4

½ lb (250 g) fontina cheese, shredded

1 cup (8 fl oz/250 ml) heavy cream

1 cup (2 oz/60 g) bite-sized broccoli florets

1 cup (2 oz/60 g) bite-sized cauliflower florets

¾ lb (375 g) fingerling potatoes, halved lengthwise

4 Tbsp (2 oz/60 g) unsalted butter

2 egg yolks

1–2 tsp white truffle oil

1 baguette, cut into ½-inch (12-mm) cubes

Put the cheese and cream in a small bowl and let stand at room temperature for 2 hours.

In a large pot fitted with a steamer basket, bring 1–2 inches (2.5–5 cm) of water to a boil. Arrange the broccoli, cauliflower, and potatoes in the steamer basket, cover, reduce the heat to medium, and steam until the broccoli and cauliflower are tender-crisp and the potatoes are cooked through, about 10 minutes. Set aside at room temperature.

Pour water to a depth of 1 inch (2.5 cm) in another saucepan and bring to a simmer over low heat. Put the butter in a heatproof bowl and place over (not touching) the water. Heat just until the butter softens and begins to melt. Increase the heat to medium and gently whisk in the cheese mixture, 1 Tbsp at a time. When all of the cheese mixture has been added and the cheese has melted, remove the bowl from the pan, place on a work surface, and whisk in the egg yolks, one at time. Transfer the mixture to a blender and process until the mixture is thick and well blended.

Immediately divide the mixture evenly among individual ramekins and drizzle a little truffle oil on top of each portion. Divide the vegetables and bread cubes among individual plates and place a ramekin of the cheese mixture on each plate, then serve. Or, spoon the cheese mixture over the vegetables and bread cubes, dividing it evenly, and drizzle with the truffle oil, then serve.

26

Pomegranate seeds lend a tart-sweet quality and an appealing crunch to this easy-to-assemble dip, a modern twist on hummus. The flavor of cumin seeds is released when they are toasted, delivering a pleasant smokiness to the mixture. The cumin-crusted pita chips on page 262 are a good alternative to the baguette slices.

CHICKPEA DIP WITH ROASTED CUMIN & POMEGRANATE

serves 8–10

1 tsp cumin

2 cloves garlic

Salt

2 lemons

1 pomegranate

2 cans (15 oz/470 g each) chickpeas, drained and rinsed

¼ cup (2 fl oz/60 ml) extra-virgin olive oil, plus more for drizzling

Baguette slices for serving

In a small, dry frying pan, toast the cumin seeds over medium heat until fragrant, about 2 minutes. Pour onto a plate to cool.

In a mortar, combine the garlic and a pinch of salt and crush to a paste with a pestle. Add the cumin seeds and grind them together with the garlic. Grate zest from 1 lemon to measure ½ tsp, and then halve and juice both lemons.

Score the pomegranate into quarters with a sharp knife, and pull the fruit apart into sections. Place the sections in a bowl and add water to cover. Using your fingers, pry the seeds away from the membranes; the seeds will sink to the bottom of the bowl and the membrane and skin will float to the top. Scoop out and discard the membrane and skin, and then drain the seeds and set aside.

In a food processor or blender, combine the chickpeas, the garlic-cumin mixture, the lemon zest, ¼ cup (2 fl oz/60 ml) of the lemon juice, the ¼ cup oil, and ¼ cup water. Process the mixture until very creamy, adding more water if needed to achieve the desired consistency. Season with salt and more lemon juice.

Scrape the dip onto a large plate. Drizzle with oil and sprinkle with about ½ cup (3 oz/90 g) pomegranate seeds (reserve any remaining seeds for another use or for snacking). Serve with the baguette slices.

27

SWEET POTATO CAKES WITH SMOKED TROUT & HERBED CRÈME FRAÎCHE

serves 4

These colorful 2-inch (5-cm) pancakes become wonderfully crispy in a hot pan. The slight sugariness of the root vegetable contributes a pleasing contrast to the smokiness of the trout and the tangy topping of herb-spiked crème fraîche. Serve them for dinner with a tossed green salad alongside, or make pancakes half the size and serve as a savory hors d'oeuvre.

1 lemon

½ cup (4 oz/125 g) crème fraîche

1½ tsp minced fresh dill

1 tsp minced fresh chives

1 sweet potato, about ½ lb (250 g)

1 russet potato, about ½ lb (250 g)

Sea salt and freshly ground pepper

2 eggs

⅓ cup (2 oz/60 g) all-purpose flour

½ cup (4 fl oz/125 ml) rice bran oil or canola oil

4 oz (125 g) hot-smoked trout fillet

Grate the zest from the lemon, then halve and juice the fruit. In a bowl, combine the crème fraîche, dill, chives, and the lemon zest and juice and mix well. Cover and refrigerate until serving.

Peel the sweet potato and russet potato. Shred the potatoes on the large holes of a grater-shredder into a bowl. Add 1 tsp salt and toss well. Let stand for 10 minutes, then transfer to a sieve, rinse under cold running water, and drain well. Return the potatoes to the bowl.

In a small bowl, whisk the eggs until blended. Add to the potatoes along with the flour, ½ tsp salt, and a pinch of pepper and mix well.

Preheat the oven to 200°F (95°C). Set a wire rack on a large baking sheet and place near the stove. Pour the oil into a deep, heavy 12-inch (30-cm) frying pan and heat over medium-high heat until hot but not smoking. Spoon a heaping 1 Tbsp of the potato mixture into the hot oil and, using a slotted spatula, flatten it into a cake about 3 inches (7.5 cm) in diameter. Repeat to form 4 more cakes, spacing them well apart. Fry, turning once, until golden on both sides, about 3 minutes total. Using the spatula, transfer the pancakes to the wire rack to drain and keep warm in the oven. Repeat with the remaining potato mixture in 2 batches. ⟩⟩

To serve, use your fingers to break the trout into large flakes. Arrange the pancakes on a large platter. Top each pancake with a piece of trout and a dollop of the herbed crème fraîche, then serve.

28

BEET GRATIN WITH FONTINA & WALNUTS

serves 6

Be inspired by cooks in northern Italy, who use beets in a variety of ways: stirred into risotto, puréed and mixed into pasta dough, in salads, or baked, as in this scarlet gratin enriched with fontina cheese and walnuts.

6 beets, peeled and thinly sliced

2–3 Tbsp olive oil

6 oz (185 g) fontina cheese, shredded

2 tsp minced fresh thyme

Salt and freshly ground pepper

3 Tbsp heavy cream

3 Tbsp coarsely chopped walnuts

Preheat the oven to 375°F (190°C). Butter an 8-inch (20-cm) square baking dish.

In a large bowl, combine the beets and oil and toss gently to coat. In a small bowl, stir together the cheese and thyme. Arrange about one-fourth of the beets in the bottom of the prepared dish, overlapping them slightly. Sprinkle about one-fourth of the cheese mixture over the beets and season lightly with salt and pepper. Repeat to make 3 more layers, sprinkling the last layer of the herbed cheese with a little more salt and pepper. Drizzle the cream over the surface and sprinkle the walnuts on top.

Bake until the beets are tender and the walnuts are nicely browned, about 45 minutes. Remove from the oven and let rest for 5 minutes before serving.

29

Pairing roasted Brussels sprouts with caramelized onions and balsamic vinegar brings out the sprouts' natural sweetness, which is then balanced by the saltiness of the pancetta. Serve alongside a roasted turkey breast or a platter of pork chops.

BRUSSELS SPROUTS, PANCETTA & CARAMELIZED ONIONS

serves 6–8

½ lb (250 g) yellow onions

½ lb (250 g) thinly sliced pancetta, cut into ½-inch (12-mm) pieces

2 Tbsp unsalted butter

2½ Tbsp olive oil

2 lb (1 kg) Brussels sprouts, trimmed and halved lengthwise

2 tsp balsamic vinegar

Salt and freshly ground pepper

Preheat the oven to 450°F (230°C).

Cut the onions in half and then into very thin slices. In a frying pan, cook the pancetta over medium-high heat, stirring occasionally, until it is crisp and its fat has rendered, 8–10 minutes. Using a slotted spoon, transfer the cooked pancetta to paper towels to drain.

Add the butter and 1 Tbsp of the oil to the fat in the pan. Add the onions, reduce the heat to low, and cook uncovered, stirring occasionally, until deep golden brown, about 20 minutes. Remove from the heat.

Meanwhile, place the Brussels sprouts in a bowl and add the remaining 1½ Tbsp oil and 1 tsp of the vinegar. Stir well to coat. Season with the salt and pepper. Transfer the sprouts to a rimmed baking sheet and spread in a single layer. Roast until the sprouts are tender when pierced with a fork and the edges are lightly browned, about 20 minutes.

Add the roasted sprouts to the pan with the onions along with the pancetta and remaining 1 tsp balsamic vinegar. Cook over medium heat, turning to mix well, until the flavors are blended, 4–5 minutes. Transfer to a platter and serve.

30

The sweetness of butternut squash makes it a natural partner for cool-weather fruit. Here, thin pear and squash slices are cooked with apple juice and seasonings to create a side that will complement a pork roast flavored with rosemary and garlic or a whole chicken with herbed butter slipped under its skin before roasting.

BUTTERNUT SQUASH & PEAR WITH ROSEMARY

serves 4

1 small butternut squash, ¾ lb (375 g)

1 Tbsp grape seed or canola oil

Salt

1 Bosc pear, halved, cored, and thinly sliced

1 Tbsp finely chopped fresh rosemary

Pinch of cayenne pepper

½ cup (4 fl oz/125 ml) apple juice

Cut the squash in half lengthwise and remove and discard the seeds. Peel the halves and thinly slice lengthwise.

In a frying pan, heat the oil over medium-high heat. Add the squash and season with 1 tsp salt. Sauté until the squash begins to soften, about 5 minutes, reducing the heat if needed so the squash does not color. Add the pear, rosemary, cayenne, and apple juice and cook until the liquid evaporates and the squash is tender, 6–8 minutes. Serve hot, warm, or at room temperature.

31

For many people, bok choy, with its crunchy stems and pleasantly mild, leafy green tops, is the introduction to Asian cuisine. Here it is tossed with soy sauce for a bright and simple dish. This same cooking method and sauce can used for other dark greens, such as kale or chard.

BOK CHOY WITH SOY & LEMON

serves 4–6

2 lb (1 kg) baby bok choy

¼ cup (2 fl oz/60 ml) Asian sesame oil

⅓ cup (3 fl oz/80 ml) soy sauce

Juice of 1 lemon

Trim the base of each head of bok choy. Cut each head in half lengthwise, or into quarters if large.

In a large frying pan, warm the sesame oil over medium-high heat until it ripples but is not smoking. Add the bok choy and sear until the leaves have wilted slightly and the stems are tender, 3–4 minutes.

Pour the soy sauce and lemon juice around the pan, and toss and stir just until the bok choy is lightly glazed with the sauce, about 1 minute. Transfer to a platter and serve.

VEGETABLE RECIPES BY TYPE

weldonowen

415 Jackson Street, Suite 200, San Francisco, CA 94111
www.weldonowen.com

VEGETABLE OF THE DAY

Conceived and produced by Weldon Owen, Inc.
In collaboration with Williams-Sonoma, Inc.
3250 Van Ness Avenue, San Francisco, CA 94109

A WELDON OWEN PRODUCTION

Printed and bound in China by Toppan-Leefung Printing Limited

First printed in 2012
10 9 8 7 6 5 4 3 2

Library of Congress Control Number: 2012952913

ISBN 13: 978-1-61628-495-4
ISBN 10: 1-61628-495-1

Weldon Owen is a division of
BONNIER

WILLIAMS-SONOMA, INC.

Founder and Vice-Chairman Chuck Williams

WELDON OWEN, INC.

CEO and President Terry Newell
VP, Sales and Marketing Amy Kaneko
Director of Finance Mark Perrigo

VP and Publisher Hannah Rahill
Associate Publisher Amy Marr

Creative Director Emma Boys
Senior Designer Lauren Charles

Production Director Chris Hemesath
Production Manager Michelle Duggan

Photographer Erin Kunkel
Food Stylist Robyn Valarik
Prop Stylist Leigh Noe

ACKNOWLEDGMENTS

Weldon Owen wishes to thank the following people for their generous support in producing
this book: David Bornfriend, Carolyn Cuykendall, Becky Duffett, Judith Dunham, Alexa Hyman,
Kim Laidlaw, Jennifer Newens, Elizabeth Parson, Katie Schlossberg, Sharon Silva, and Jason Wheeler